C000143157

Liquidity Risk Measurement and Management

A practitioner's guide to global best practices

Liquidity Risk Measurement and Management

A practitioner's guide to global best practices

Edited by

Leonard Matz
and
Peter Neu

BICENTENNIAL
1807
WILEY
2007
BICENTENNIAL

John Wiley & Sons (Asia) Pte Ltd

Copyright © 2007 by John Wiley & Sons (Asia) Pte Ltd

Published in 2007 by John Wiley & Sons (Asia) Pte Ltd
2 Clementi Loop, #02-01, Singapore 129809

All rights reserved.

No part of this publication may be reproduced, stored in a retrieval system, or transmitted in any form or by any means, electronic, mechanical, photocopying, recording, scanning, or otherwise, except as expressly permitted by law, without either the prior written permission of the Publisher, or authorization through payment of the appropriate photocopy fee to the Copyright Clearance Center. Requests for permission should be addressed to the Publisher, John Wiley & Sons (Asia) Pte Ltd, 2 Clementi Loop, #02-01, Singapore 129809, tel: 65-64632400, fax: 65-64646912, e-mail: enquiry@wiley.com.sg.

This publication is designed to provide accurate and authoritative information in regard to the subject matter covered. It is sold with the understanding that the publisher is not engaged in rendering professional services. If professional advice or other expert assistance is required, the services of a competent professional person should be sought.

Other Wiley Editorial Offices

John Wiley & Sons, 111 River Street, Hoboken, NJ 07030, USA
John Wiley & Sons, The Atrium Southern Gate, Chichester P019 8SQ, England
John Wiley & Sons (Canada) Ltd, 5353 Dundas Street West, Suite 400, Toronto, Ontario M9B 6HB. Canada
John Wiley & Sons Australia Ltd, 42 McDougall Street, Milton, Queensland 4064, Australia
Wiley-VCH, Boschstrasse 12, D-69469 Weinheim, Germany

Library of Congress Cataloging-in-Publication Data

ISBN-13   978-0-470-82182-4
ISBN-10   0-470-82182-5

Typeset in 10.5/13pt Palatino by Laserwords Private Limited, Chennai, India.
Printed in Singapore by Markono Print Media Pte Ltd.

10 9 8 7 6 5 4 3 2 1

Leonard
To Cate and Kylee

Peter
To my wife Maria

Contents

Acknowledgments

We would like to thank each of the contributing authors for taking the time to write their chapters. No attempt to describe global best practices can be complete without reflecting the depth and breadth of contemporary practice. This book is far richer because these bankers shared their ideas. Thank you to Martin M. Bardenhewer, Dierk Brandenburg, Karl Frauendorfer, Robert A. Jarrow, Martin Knippschild, Armin Leistenschneider, Bruce W. Mason, Louis D. Raffis, Michael Schürle and Bernhard Wondrak.

We also wish to acknowledge that the concepts and practices described in the chapters written by them owe a great deal to information shared by other experts in articles published in industry magazines, in presentations at industry conferences, and in private conversations. Particularly, thanks to Johannes Boller, Dr. Robert Fiedler, Bruce Mclean Forrest, Dr Kai Franzmeyer, Kurt Marosz, Michael Reuther, William Schomburg and Armin Widjojoatomodjo.

Leonard Matz
Peter Neu
September 2006

About the Contributors

Martin M. Bardenhewer is currently a director of the risk control group at ZKB in Zurich, where he is responsible for market risk controlling and for bank-wide risk reporting. Prior to that he was head of modeling and worked on risk and valuation models for asset liability management and on benchmarking schemes. Before joining ZKB he was with KPMG. Martin holds a Ph.D. in Economics from the University of Mannheim and a Master in Economics from University Bonn, Germany. He is a visiting lecturer for Risk Management at the University of Cologne.

Dierk Brandenburg is director of research for Structured Products at Fidelity Investments International in London. He joined Fidelity from Deutsche Bank AG in 2003 as a credit analyst focusing on European banks and insurance companies, as well as structured finance. At Deutsche Bank AG in London, he was a vice president of Global Portfolio Management and Securities Lending. Prior to the move to London, he spent eight years with the Bank for International Settlements in Switzerland, where he was deputy head of Credit Risk Control until 2001. Dierk studied Economics in Freiburg, Germany, and at the London School of Economics and received his Ph.D. from Freiburg in 1993.

Dr. Robert Fiedler is a member of the board of FERNBACH-Software S.A., Luxembourg, involved in an Enterprise-wide Value & Risk Management solution. After he obtained his doctorate in mathematics (differential geometry) at the University of Darmstadt where he also worked as a scientist and lecturer, he joined Banque Nationale de Paris in Frankfurt as a money market/interest rate derivatives trader, later heading up asset liability management. In 1997, he joined Deutsche Bank in Frankfurt, where he headed the team in Group Risk Management dealing with treasury and liquidity risk issues. After developing a new methodological framework for funding liquidity risk, he implemented this approach as a firm-wide liquidity risk IT solution.

Karl Frauendorfer is full professor for Operations Research at the University of St. Gallen, Switzerland, and director of the Institute for Operations Research and Computational Finance. His area of research is stochastic optimization with an emphasis on applications for the finance industry and the energy sector. In 1995, he received the Latis Prize for his research work on the solution of stochastic optimization problems. Within the context of several research and application projects, Karl Frauendorfer also works as a consultant for banks, insurance companies and energy supply companies.

Robert A. Jarrow is a professor at the Johnson Graduate School of Management at Cornell University and managing director of Kamakura Corporation. He was the 1997 IAFE Financial Engineer of the Year. His publications include four books as well as more than 100 articles in finance and economic journals. He is renowned for his work on the Heath-Jarrow-Morton model and the Jarrow-Turnbull reduced form credit risk model. He is also the originator of the forward price measure, and one of the first to characterize forward and futures prices under stochastic interest rates. He is an advisory editor and an associate editor for various journals.

Martin Knippschild studied economics at the University of Münster. After receiving a doctor's degree, he joined Controlling/Risk Controlling of Deutsche Bank AG in 1991 where he was Head of Market Risk Control and deputy head of Risk Control. Since July 1996, he works at the Dresdner Bank as a director in Group Risk Control and head of Strategic Risk and Treasury Control, responsible for Treasury Controlling (controlling interest rate risk within the banking book and controlling liquidity risk) in regulatory issues and internal capital allocation. He is a member of the ALM and the Liquidity Management Committees. Since 2005, he is also the deputy head of Risk Governance and Controlling. He frequently speaks at industry conferences and training courses and has published articles on capital allocation, Basel II and Treasury Management.

Armin Leistenschneider is a banker living with his wife and daughter near Frankfurt, Germany. He completed his Ph.D. in Physics on the "Structure of Exotic Oxygen Nuclei" working as a scientist at the Gesellschaft für Schwerionenforschung (GSI) in Darmstadt. In 2001 Armin joined Dresdner Bank AG, Group Risk Control to work for the Liquidity Risk Control department, where he took over responsibility for Methods and Analytics. In 2006 he changed to the Treasury Control department and is now responsible for the ALM Risk Control team. He speaks frequently at conferences and training courses and holds a lectureship in mathematics and statistics at a private university.

Bruce W. Mason is the chief economist, asset liability manager, information security officer and is the assistant to the chairman of the Board at Union State Bank in Orangeburg, N.Y. He has been in banking for 30 years. Mr. Mason is a member of the bank's ALCO and Investment Committees and is involved with budgeting, forecasting and computer automation areas of the bank. He earned a Bachelor in Economics from Colgate University, completed his MBA in Finance from Fairleigh Dickinson University and holds a graduate degree in Banking from the Stonier Graduate School of Banking at the University of Delaware.

Leonard Matz is an author, consultant and bank trainer. He is a 1973 graduate of Case Western Reserve University in Cleveland, Ohio. After spending five years with the Federal Reserve as a bank examiner, he spent 14 years in various bank management positions. Mr. Matz is the author of numerous books as well as magazine and journal articles. His other books include *Interest Rate Risk Management* and the *Self Paced Guide to Asset/Liability Management Training*. He is a frequent speaker at industry conferences and training programs, and has been a member of the National Asset/Liability Management Association since 1989. Mr. Matz has four children and two granddaughters. He currently resides in western Pennsylvania with his wife.

Bruce McLean Forrest is a banker with UBS. After majoring in Mathematical Physics in 1985 and receiving a Ph.D. in Physics in 1988 from the University of Edinburgh, he subsequently conducted research in Germany, Spain and Switzerland, specializing in stochastic simulations of physical and chemical systems. He joined the ALM group of Swiss Bank Corporation in 1995, focusing on non-trading interest rates. Since 1998, McLean Forrest has been in UBS Group Treasury in Zurich and was responsible for Group Liquidity for three years, implementing UBS's liquidity stress simulations and establishing and monitoring liquidity exposure limits. Since 2006, he has been responsible for Balance Sheet Analysis and Reporting within Group Treasury.

Peter Neu is an author, consultant and former banker living with his wife in Frankfurt, Germany. He is a 1994 Ph.D. graduate of the University of Heidelberg in Theoretical Physics. After completing a post-doctoral position at MIT in Cambridge, Massachusetts, Peter joined Group Risk Control at Dresdner Bank AG in 1997. As a member of Group Strategic Risk & Treasury Control he worked on various market and credit risk projects and was involved in building Dresdner's economic capital model before taking over the responsibility for liquidity risk control. In 2005, he joined the Boston Consulting Group as European head of a risk expert team. In this function he conducts client projects on capital management, risk organization and PMIs, risk-based pricing, and treasury optimization. He frequently speaks at industry conferences and training courses and has published articles on credit risk and operational risk measurement.

Louis D. Raffis is a senior vice president at KeyCorp, a super-regional financial institution headquartered in Cleveland, Ohio. He has more than 20 years of banking experience in Treasury management at KeyCorp and its predecessor organization – Society Corporation. His primary responsibilities includes management of the bank's capital position, target capital structure, cost of capital, dividend policy and capital raising activities.

He is also responsible for holding company funding and liquidity management. Mr. Raffis has a BBA in Finance (*summa cum laude*) from Kent State University and an MBA from Harvard Business School. He currently resides in Cleveland Heights, Ohio.

Michael Schürle is a research associate and vice director at the Institute for Operations Research and Computational Finance at the University of St. Gallen, Switzerland, where he also acts as lecturer. After he obtained a doctorate for a thesis on stochastic optimization models for non-maturing accounts, he worked in a consultancy and was responsible for projects in the field of ALM and risk management with major banks. The emphasis of his research is on applications of optimization methods in the finance industry and interest rate risk management.

Bernhard Wondrak is a banker living with his wife near Frankfurt, Germany. He studied economy and finance in Frankfurt. After completing a post-doctoral position at the University of Frankfurt, he joined the Controlling department of Deutsche Bank AG in 1987. At Deutsche Bank, he worked on implementation of transfer price models and interest income simulations. After two years, he changed to the Treasury department where he took over responsibility for Methods, Analytics and Reporting. In 1997, Bernhard joined Dresdner Bank AG Group Risk Control to set up the Treasury Control Department. He is now responsible for market risk analyses and reporting for banking books in the Dresdner Bank Group. He frequently speaks at conferences and training courses and has published a book about interest rate risk management under IAS regime in 2004.

CHAPTER 1

Introduction

Peter Neu and Leonard Matz

A PANORAMA

Risk management in general, and liquidity risk management in particular, are rapidly evolving. Both have become key focuses for management and regulatory attention. Emphasis on liquidity risk management has also spread. Over the last 15 years risk management has become a key topic in banking and, recently, in other areas of the financial services industry. Starting with statistical approaches to measure market risks in the early 1990s, the value of internal risk models has found recognition both by senior bank managers and regulators. Advances in risk management occurred both in qualitative and quantitative aspects. The latter mainly addressed minimum standards for risk management and control such as 1) the necessity for an independent risk monitoring and controlling function, 2) regular risk reporting, 3) comprehensive limit systems, and so on. This revolution in bank risk management migrated through different risk categories, starting first with that risk which can most easily be quantified – market risk in trading books. Regarding the quantification of non-trading book risks like credit risk and interest rate risk, the New Basel Accord has contributed major advances.

Prior to the promulgation of the Basel II risk-based capital proposals, regulators first addressed the quantification of risks impacting the bank as a whole and not just specific books or balance sheet segments. These risks are operational risk and liquidity risk. Although liquidity risk is not a major focus of Basel II it is still an integral part of the Pillar II requirements. The publication, "Sound Practices for Managing Liquidity Risk"[1], by the Bank for International Settlements (BIS) of February 2000 not only predated publication of the new capital rules, but effectively defined the requirements for Pillar II compliance for liquidity risk management. Since then liquidity risk has attracted more and more attention by regulators and senior management in banks. From the regulatory viewpoint this is not surprising, since regulators' intention is to protect the stability of the entire financial system, for which liquidity is the key ingredient. Also, most bank failures are – as practice has shown – eventually caused or contributed to by a sector or systemic liquidity squeeze. As a consequence, early indicators and stress analyses for liquidity risk should be an area of focus for regulators.

For senior bank management the view on liquidity risk has been slightly different. The common wisdom has been that liquidity risk will not appear in the first place, if care is taken properly on all other risk categories like market and credit risk. Bank managers used to rely on high-grade ratings (AAA-AA) and stable deposit bases. Although this viewpoint is not totally wrong it misses the interdependencies between risk categories that often cumulate in a loss of investors' confidence and a liquidity crisis. It also misses failure to monitor the vulnerability of a bank with regard to such events; for example, if a bank heavily relies on maturity transformation (funding long-term assets excessively by short-term volatile money markets funding) or if a bank has exposed itself heavily on contingent liquidity risk by granting large committed credit lines in order to increase its fee income.

Liquidity risks are clearly evident in historical events like the Asian and Russian crises, the downfall of the large hedge fund, Long-term Capital Management (LTCM), and the major defaults of Enron and Worldcom. In particular, the first two events have proven that banks hold significant hidden liquidity risk in their balance sheets. Assets that are liquid under normal market conditions can quickly become illiquid if markets deteriorate for broad asset classes.

The case of LTCM is very illustrative in this regard. In a nutshell, the hedge fund's trading strategy was characterized by relative value trades in which the fund was long on less liquid (high credit spread) assets and short on liquid (low credit spread) assets. Examples were long off-the-run Treasuries and short on-the-run Treasuries, or long Italian Treasuries and short Bunds. To make sufficient profit and loss (P&L) out of these strategies required a high leverage that had been achieved via lending and repo transactions. Although each asset class was sufficiently liquid in the market and could have been sold or repo'd on short notice, the trading strategy was not. It required a long-term investment horizon to make the convergence deal between the asset classes pay off in P&L. Clearly, the LTCM management had underestimated this aspect when it came to the Russian default on short-term debt in August 1998. It had failed to reserve parts of the fund's P&L for increasing the stock of unencumbered liquid securities to be used as collateral when margin calls on the leveraged position came in during the crisis. Investors learnt quickly from these crises and asked for an explicit liquidity spread above Libor on long-term senior unsecured bank debt.

Bank managers also started to think about liquidity risk differently, realizing that:

- Going concern analyses are useless. Scenario-based stress analyses are mandatory.

- Retrospective and concurrent measures of liquidity have little value. Prospective views are critical.
- Liquidity risk cannot easily be hedged (like interest rate risk in the banking book). Consequently, rigorous monitoring and control must be imposed.
- Appropriately, internal pricing incentives are required to appropriate value and to "incent" management of liquid and illiquid assets and stable and volatile funding.

Of course, the four realizations just listed describe only the tip of the iceberg. Many other aspects and key concepts that came up as a consequence will be laid out in this book.

In a sense, managers realized that running a funding desk is a lot like flying a big jet. A perfect landing isn't much different from an average landing. But a bad landing is a lot worse than an average landing. Every day, managers make a variety of funding decisions. These decisions can be said to be responses to extremely low severity but high-probability liquidity risks. Major liquidity problems are, thankfully, quite rare. Yet, it is the very low probability but very high severity events – the potential bad landings – that keep us awake at night.

Considering the high stakes, it is noteworthy that a confidential 2005 survey of mid-size and large North American banks found that 29% were not satisfied with the accuracy of their liquidity risk measurement. This is a marked improvement from the 54% who reported dissatisfaction in a similar survey conducted in 1997, but it is still a surprisingly large proportion of the respondents.

A liquidity crisis can have a severe impact on a bank's funding costs, its market access – which can be reduced or even impaired due to reputation risk – and short-term funding capabilities. Banks have realized that adequate systems and processes for identifying, measuring, monitoring and controlling liquidity risks help them to maintain a strong liquidity position, which in turn will increase the confidence of investors and rating agencies, and improve funding costs and availability. Furthermore, supervisors also recognized the importance of liquidity for the stability of the financial system and strive to minimize the impact of liquidity failures on the system as a whole.

In the following chapters, we will explore both the requirements for excellent landings and the precautions needed to minimize the severity of potential bad landings.

KEY CONCEPTS

In the broadest sense, liquidity is simply the capacity to obtain cash when it is needed. All types of financial and non-financial enterprises share this objective. Do not confuse this definition with a narrower view of liquidity defined as possession of cash or assets that can be readily converted into cash. Those are merely examples of the most common sources of liquidity.

Liquidity Is a Consequential Risk

Funding crises do not arise in a vacuum – they are triggered by underlying problems. These can be endogenous or exogenous. Endogenous problems are most often credit risk deterioration and, occasionally, operations risk events. Exogenous problems are most often triggered by market disruptions, but they can also result from payment system events, country risk flare-ups, and a variety of other events. Liquidity is a consequential risk.

Liquidity and Liquidation Are Not the Same

It is important to understand the difference between liquidity and liquidation. The fact that all, or almost all, of a bank's assets can, eventually, be converted into cash to pay off all obligations is related to its liquidation value, not its liquidity. Liquidity is the ability to efficiently meet present and anticipated cash flow needs without adversely affecting daily operations. In other words, the goal of liquidity management is not to steer the ship in such a way that no one drowns if the ship sinks. That is a liquidation perspective. Instead, the goal is to steer the ship in such a way that it does not sink.

Bank managers need enough liquidity to keep liquidity risk from causing, or contributing to, a bank failure. This distinction is not really a difference in the quantity of liquidity needed. It is more a difference in the identification of liquidity sources and risks. For example, cash is a liquid asset if the bank must be shut down, but it is a fixed asset if our goal is to keep the bank in business.

Reputation Risk, Credit Risk, and the Perception of Sufficient Liquidity

While liquidity in general is simply the ability to access cash when needed, liquidity risk for a bank is more specific. Liquidity risk is that risk where a financial institution will not be *perceived* as having sufficient cash, at one or more future periods in time, to meet such requirements. The famous nineteenth-century economist and author, Walter Bagehot, observed that: "Every banker knows that if he has to prove that he is worthy of credit, however good may be his arguments, in fact his credit is gone." The point is as valid today as it has ever been.

Banks cannot survive unless funds providers have confidence that they can get their funds back. On a strictly contractual basis, banks always have far more obligations due on demand or within a very short time frame than they have assets due on demand or maturing within a very short time frame. Maturity transformation is, after all, one of the two primary economic functions that banks provide. As discussed later in this chapter, banks operate with this huge mismatch because counterparties as a group almost never exercise their options to remove their funds from the bank. (Various influences on the exercise of these counterparty options are discussed in Chapter 2.) Nothing is more critical to the maintenance of those liabilities than counterparty perceptions of the soundness of the bank. Liquidity risk is therefore highly dependent upon counterparty perceptions of bank soundness.

Best Practice Requires Risk Segmentation

Even after encompassing the perception of solvency, the definition presented above is too general. The level of liquidity risk, as well as the quantity of the available sources of liquidity, varies, depending on the circumstances and upon the duration that these circumstances prevail. In other words, quite separate environments are defined by the nature of the funding need, the available sources of funds to meet that need, and the time or duration that those circumstances prevail. Even the identification of "liquidity assets" depends upon definitional points of view. A single definition of liquidity blurs key distinctions.

Specificity is required for sound understanding, measuring, and managing of liquidity risk. Best practice segments liquidity risk into three categories. Each is best viewed as a separate type of liquidity risk:

- mismatch or structural liquidity risk
- contingency liquidity risk
- market liquidity risk.

Mismatch or structural liquidity risk refers to the liquidity risk in the bank's current balance sheet structure due to maturity transformation in the cash flows of individual positions. As we will discuss in Chapter 2, mismatch risk results from both contractually and behavior-driven cash flows.

Contingency liquidity risk is the risk that future events may require a significantly larger amount of cash than a bank projects it will need. In other words, contingency liquidity risk is the risk of not having sufficient funds to meet sudden and unexpected short-term obligations. Unexpected obligations can arise due to unusual deviations in the timing of cash flows (*term liquidity risk*); for example, non-contractual prolongation of loans, or unexpected draws on committed loan facilities, or deposit withdrawals (*call liquidity risk*).

Market liquidity risk refers to the inability to sell assets at or near the fair value (discounted cash flow). Market liquidity risk may arise when a market disruption impairs the bank's ability to sell large positions or lower quality positions. Market liquidity may also result from impaired access to the respective markets; for example, after loss of reputation.

CURRENT CHALLENGES

Aggressive expansion of bank lending, increased competition for liabilities, and changes in capital markets continue to impact both the level of liquidity risk and the available tactics for managing risk. While the changes from one year to the next are actually fairly minor, the cumulative impact is dramatic in some markets.

Three major trends in particular are reshaping liquidity risk for most banks. One is the relentless growth in off-balance sheet obligations. Exhibit 1.1 compares levels of five selected off-balance sheet obligations in 1997 to the levels for the same five at the end of 2005. For the largest quartile of US banks, these off-balance sheet commitments grew from an amount equivalent to about 82% of total assets to the equivalent of more than 90%.

The second major trend is a shift in the mix of liabilities funding bank assets. This can be seen in Exhibit 1.2. In that chart, we show a pair of stacked bars for each year. The left bar in each pair shows the percentage change in total assets for the year. The right bar in each pair shows the percentage change for only insured deposits and capital. Notice that the pace of asset growth exceeded growth in retail deposits and capital in seven out of the eight years shown for the US banks. In each of those years, the portion of new assets not funded by new retail deposits or capital had to be funded by new wholesale liabilities. As a result, reliance on wholesale funding – either secured or unsecured – is steadily increasing.

The third trend is an increased sensitivity of wholesale term-funding costs for most banks to general and bank-specific market conditions (narrowing and widening spreads of senior unsecured bank bonds). For instance, in Germany, 10-year asset swap levels for bank bonds have

EXHIBIT 1.1   Off-balance sheet commitments of selected US banks (excluding derivatives), 1997–2005

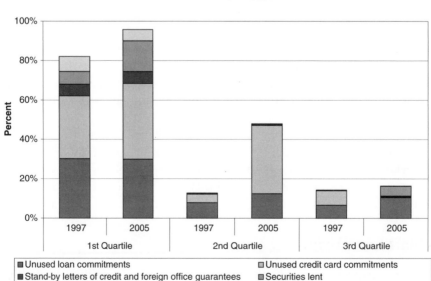

Source: Highline Data

EXHIBIT 1.2   Annual percentage change in selected balance sheet components, 1997–2005

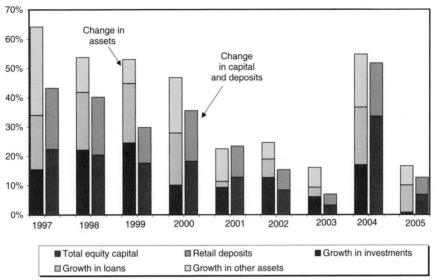

Source: Highline Data

widened from 15–25 basis points (bps) before the Enron and Worldcom crises to 60–100 bps shortly afterwards. In most cases, this spread widening was accompanied by big loan loss provisions and downgrades by Standard & Poor's, Moody's or Fitch.

The first trend is, obviously, an increase in liquidity risk arising from the growth in potential cash requirements. The second is a *potential* increase in liquidity risk resulting from a reduction in the reliability or "stickiness" of bank liabilities.[2] The third trend is a reaction of investors to risks in banks' balance sheets and an increasing deterioration of banks' external ratings. As a result most banks nowadays need to pay a spread above Libor for term funding and see the necessity to pass these term funding costs on to long-term, sticky assets via internal fund transfer pricing.

Together, all three trends have implications for the measurement, management and pricing of liquidity risk.

HOT TOPICS AND BEST PRACTICE

Liquidity risk management is essential for the long-term viability of a bank. A lack of liquidity doesn't cause a bank funding crisis. But liquidity can make the difference between surviving and failing such an event. As a Citicorp CFO once observed: "Liquidity always comes first; without it, a bank doesn't open its doors; with it, a bank may have time to solve its basic problems."[3]

Liquidity risk may possibly be the most challenging financial risk. Challenging, not because risk managers don't understand it, but challenging in the sense that risk managers often take quite different approaches to the subject. Standard tools may be applied or combined differently. In too many cases, liquidity risk managers still rely on old, inadequate tools such as loan-to-deposit ratios. Our goal is to identify, explain and evaluate global best practices.

Today, a common standard on measuring and managing liquidity risk has evolved among the major banks in the United States and Europe. This standard is characterized by:

- cash flow-based liquidity gap analysis, including behavioral adjustments per currency and region
- stress and scenario analysis
- limit system and limit breach escalation processes
- analyses of the diversification on funding resources
- fund transfer pricing
- an independent oversight of liquidity risk management by a liquidity risk control unit that regularly reports on the liquidity status to senior management
- a contingency funding plan
- a liquidity policy that documents methodology, processes and responsibilities.

Clearly, most banks would agree on these steps for a sound liquidity risk management and control system. However, the detailed implementation – for example, the detailed cash flow modulation of individual asset and liability classes – would, and needs to, vary from bank to bank. This fact, which often bothers regulators, who naturally want to standardize risk measurement, arises from the different market accesses and different customer structures of each individual bank. To give an example, independent of the asset quality, a bank that is an active repo-player in the market can more easily turn bonds into cash than a bank that does not frequently use this funding channel. There will just be more counterparty limits available in the market for the first bank.

Another issue to be considered is the ability to communicate certain management approaches within the bank and to receive acceptance at Board level and in sales forces. What is the value of stress and scenario analyses if the consequences and measures to be taken are left unspecified? Will the treasurer really change its funding strategy, if the bank looks bad under a bank-run or a downgrade scenario? Is the payment of term funding cost and collateral costs for revolving credit lines with short-term drawdown really necessary? Can't it be explained to anyone in a sales unit?

As we will see in this book, liquidity risk is apparently less intuitive than market risk. There is no single number like Value-at-Risk (VaR), in which – as some believe – everything can be cumulated. There is also no single statistical measure that is sufficiently comprehensive to measure liquidity risk. Besides the pure cash flow modeling aspect, there is still a thorough understanding of market dynamics and product know-how required, even if liquidity risk is not managed, but only controlled and monitored.

The result of all these points is a certain diversity in the implementation of a liquidity management and control system between banks. There are different levels of sophistication, for example, in a fund transfer price system, in the cash flow modeling (in particular, if behavioral adjustments are concerned), in the number and character of stress scenarios, and in limit systems.

In this book we will explore all the pillars that are necessary to build a liquidity risk management and control system. We will also lay down a best practice standard. But we will also highlight the tightly intertwined fabric of the liquidity tapestry.

OUTLINE AND CONTENTS OF THE BOOK

The book has five parts. In Part 1 we describe best practice in the measurement, monitoring, and controlling of liquidity risk, thereby addressing topics like gap analysis, behavioral-adjusted cash flow mapping for assets and liability classes, stress and scenario analysis, liquidity policies, limit systems, organizational set-up, and controlling functions.

- In Chapter 2, Peter Neu begins with an overview of sources of liquidity risk and liquidity. Then he explains principal measurement methods including balance sheet analysis, ratios for cash capital and cash flow forecasting.
- In Chapter 3, Leonard Matz provides detailed discussions of liquidity scenario analysis and stress testing. This chapter includes a wealth of practical information including a nine-step process for stress testing and 16 exhibits.

In Part 2 we describe best practice in liquidity risk management and transfer pricing, thereby addressing topics such as funding sources and instruments; stand-by liquidity reserve; strategies and tactics to manage liquidity risk; constructing a liquidity term curve; transfer pricing for structural and contingent liquidity risk; and examples of transfer pricing various asset and liability classes.

- In Chapter 4, Leonard Matz focuses on how well-articulated strategies, policies, risk limits, reporting systems and internal controls enable bank managers at all levels to monitor and control liquidity risk. Specific suggestions and examples for best practice are included throughout this chapter.
- A wide range of detailed liquidity management tactics, along with key strategic objectives, is provided in Chapter 5. Specific information in this chapter includes tactics for managing assets, managing

liabilities, diversifying liquidity risk, testing market access and managing intra-day liquidity risk. In addition, the authors provide general liquidity risk management guidance.

- Chapter 6 focuses on the key elements for liquidity contingency risk management and contingency funding plans. Detailed guidance for triggers, remedial actions, crisis communications and other key elements are included.

- In Chapter 7, Peter Neu, Armin Leistenschneider, Bernhard Wondrak, and Martin Knippschild present best practice methods for quantifying and implementing liquidity transfer pricing. Detailed examples, a case study, and 11 exhibits illustrate the key points.

In Part 3 we have invited leading practitioners to contribute their views.

- Robert Fiedler, one of the pioneers of modern best practice, highlights how modern liquidity risk management fits in the context of comprehensive asset liability management. Chapter 8 is bursting with critical details, examples and illustrations.

- In Chapter 9, Louis D. Raffis, Bank One, presents his views on the liquidity impact of derivatives collateral.

- For Chapter 10, Martin Bardenhewer, ZKB, gives us an overview on the vitally important topic of modeling indeterminate maturity accounts. In addition to a most comprehensive discussion of the available methodologies, the text focuses on the particular impact on liquidity risk.

- In Chapter 11, Louis D. Raffis shares how Bank One has integrated the net cash capital tool into its liquidity management system. This chapter is particularly valuable because it illustrates one of the few applications of the net cash capital tool for more than merely complying with a rating agency's point of view.

- In Chapter 12, Bruce W. Mason reports on the unfolding and management of a real funding crisis. While the case study is for a small bank, many insights, useful to banks of all sizes, can be gleaned from the experiences described.

- Bruce McLean Forrest, another of the pioneers of modern best practice for liquidity risk management, describes in Chapter 13 UBS' liquidity risk management system and shares insights from his experience.

- In Chapter 14, Dierk Brandenburg, Fidelity, writes on liquidity risk in structured capital market instruments like CDOs.

For Part 4 we asked three leading academics to present their views on cutting-edge topics for liquidity risk.

- Karl Frauendorfer and Michael Schürle summarize their dynamic modeling approach of indeterminate maturity accounts in Chapter 15.

- In Chapter 16, Robert A. Jarrow presents insights into liquidity risk in the context of classical option pricing theory.

Finally, in Part 5 we wrap up and close this book by commenting on open issues and our views on future developments in liquidity risk.

NOTES

[1] BIS paper: "Sound Practices on Managing Liquidity Risk," BIS, February 2000.

[2] An important note: Just because reliance on capital markets funding sources is growing it does not necessarily mean that liquidity risk is increasing. Some of the liability growth may be secured funding, which is stickier than unsecured, uninsured funding. In addition, some of the capital markets funding may be short-term borrowings that fund longer term, liquid assets, thus reducing liquidity risk for the period of time equal to the difference in maturities.

[3] Donald Howard, quote from 1977 reprinted in "Liquidity Lessons for the 90s," David Cates, *Bank Management*, April 1990, page 20.

Part 1

Measuring and Monitoring Liquidity Risk

CHAPTER 2

Liquidity Risk Measurement

Peter Neu

KEY DIFFERENCES BETWEEN LIQUIDITY RISK, CAPITAL AND OTHER FINANCIAL RISKS

We cannot measure what we don't understand. Any understanding of liquidity risk must start with an understanding of key characteristics. It is important to note that "liquidity" is different from "capital." To see the difference we compare liquidity risk with other financial risks like market, credit or operational risks. We will see that liquidity risk is different in many aspects.

First, liquidity risk is secondary risk in the sense that liquidity risk increases always follow one or more spikes in other financial risks. For this reason, liquidity risk is often called a "consequential risk." Usually, a bank's main function is to provide liquidity to the economy and not to generate a liquidity crisis. It is hard to imagine that a bank can have a liquidity problem without having incurred earlier severe losses due to market, credit or operational risk.

Second, the coverage of liquidity risk is different from the coverage of the other financial risks. We are all used to holding (economic or regulatory) capital against potential losses in net asset value. The adequate amount is determined in a VaR framework; that is, by calculating a loss distribution over a certain time horizon (one day, 10 days, one year) and by deriving the appropriate amount of equity capital held as a buffer against unexpected losses from the tail of this distribution with a certain confidence interval (99%; 99.95%).

This well-known framework does not work for liquidity risk. Here, the risk is to meet the *net cumulative cash outflow* (NCO) within a certain time period, starting with one day and reaching out to one month or longer. Clearly, capital is only of limited usage for this task. Cash inflows need to be generated instead. This can most easily be done by selling liquid, high-quality assets, such as Treasuries, or using them as collateral for a short-term loan in a repurchase agreement (repo) transaction either in the market or with central banks.

Hence, in the context of liquidity risk the capital is replaced by a combination of risk reduction management to reduce NCO and *unencumbered eligible assets to offset NCO*. Liquidity risk is adequately covered if the cash inflow which could be generated from unencumbered eligible assets within a time interval t *exceeds* the net cumulative cash outflow within the same time interval t. It is clear that both the NCO and the cash inflow after selling unencumbered securities strongly depend on the bank's total balance sheet position, the bank's position in the market, and the general capability of the market to absorb these additional assets, when they are offered by the bank. Consequently, liquidity risk must be analyzed under different *bank-specific and market-systemic scenarios*. (Scenario analysis is discussed in Chapter 3.)

Exhibit 2.1 illustrates the concept for liquidity risk management compared to market, credit and operational risk.

Two points need to be considered with great care when calculating the potential liquidity inflow from unencumbered assets. First, the cash equivalent from liquid securities can be rather different for banks that have different market accesses. To illustrate this point, consider two banks both holding US$30 billion of liquid securities that are funded unsecured. Both banks incur a downgrade to non-investment grade so that these securities can no longer be funded unsecured. One bank is a security firm with additional security holdings that are funded in the repo market. The other institution used its security position only as a liquidity reserve and has no further significant security holdings. It is not a player in the repo market. As a result of the different position in the secured funding market, the cash equivalent of the identical security position is very different for both banks. The second bank, which is not a repo player, will have no

EXHIBIT 2.1   Different approaches to market, credit, operational and liquidity risk

	Risk	Coverage	Adequacy
Market, credit, Op-risk	Loss in net asset value and in P&L	Economic or regulatory capital	Capital exceeds potential losses within a risk horizon (10D, 1Y) with a certain confidence (99%, 99.95%)
Liquidity risk	Net cumulative cash outflow (NCO) within a time interval *t*	Unencumbered eligible securities which can be sold, repo'd until time *t*, cash and received backup-lines (BAL)	Cash, BAL & unencumbered securities exceed NCO within a risk horizon (O/N, 8D, 14D, 1M) under different liquidation scenarios

counterparty limits for a repo transaction at other banks. It has to sell most of its security position in the market that has an immediately lasting impact on its P&L and its balance sheet position. The first bank is in a much more comfortable situation because it is already an active repo player and has counterparty limits available in the market. It can switch – although with higher haircuts and cut-down limits – from unsecured to secured funding. By doing this, the first bank wins time to bridge a liquidity crisis. Such a difference in market access must be considered when accounting for cash inflows from unencumbered assets.

The second point refers to committed liquidity lines at other banks. Clearly, in a going concern situation such lines will be at the banks's disposal; for example, to bridge-funding certain assets. In a bank-specific crisis, however, the availability of such a line will be rather different. Although, the line is committed to the bank which is providing liquidity, in this case it will weigh up two possibilities: either taking the credit risk by letting the troubled bank draw, or refusing the drawdown and accepting the legal and reputation risks. The decision only depends on how bad things are at the drawing bank. It might well be that the drawing bank will not live long enough to fight its case in court. The conclusion is that when modeling a crisis situation, potential cash inflows coming from the use of committed lines at other banks should not be counted.

In summary, the ability of a bank to bear liquidity risk is linked to the amount of capital it possesses and the losses it can absorb. However, the assets of a well-capitalized bank may not be sufficiently liquid to be readily sold in a crisis situation. Similarly, a bank may have sufficient liquid assets but be low on economic or regulatory capital at the same time. As such, although a sufficient capitalization is a precondition for a high-investment grade rating, and, therefore, necessary for improving funding costs and availability, capital may not be an appropriate buffer in a liquidity crisis situation.

SOURCES OF LIQUIDITY RISK

Liquidity risk can arise on both sides of the balance sheet, if either the liquidity generated from selling or repo'ing assets or the liquidity available from various funding sources (secured and unsecured) is insufficient to meet obligations as they fall due. In most cases a trigger event meets already existing vulnerability in a bank's balance sheet and causes an adverse liquidity outcome.

There are many examples of trigger events to be found in the market: the crystallization of market, credit or operational losses in the bank, damages of the bank's reputation, or a market-wide liquidity stress. The most common sources of bank vulnerability lie in liquidity mismatches between assets and liabilities (assets being less liquid than liabilities), and significant short options of the bank with respect to counterparties and customers (such as the right of holders of sight deposits to withdraw them at any time, or the right of providers of short-term money markets financing not to roll over that funding at the end of the contract).

An examples of a trigger event is large losses in trading portfolios that can – after becoming known in the market – cause unsecured funding from other banks ceasing to be available. Another example is a decline in the market value of a derivative trading position, which initiates additional posting of collateral to the counterparty or triggers the liquidation of the position under adverse conditions. Similarly, the disclosure of large losses from credit portfolios (for example, large loan loss provision) or large losses due to operational risks (for example, wrong settlement processes) can initiate a downgrade of a bank's external rating, which will probably cause a liquidity crisis for the bank. These risks are often interrelated and their disclosure can impact seriously upon a bank's reputation and, therefore, liquidity situation.

Ultimately, impaired liquidity can cause insolvency and can, depending on the size of the institution becoming insolvent, disrupt the markets and generate systemic risk.

QUANTITATIVE FRAMEWORKS FOR LIQUIDITY RISK MEASUREMENT

To assess liquidity risk quantitatively, banks apply three types of analysis: a balance sheet liquidity analysis, a cash capital analysis and a maturity mismatch analysis. Each is discussed in the following paragraphs.

Whereas a balance sheet liquidity analysis requires only the evaluation of liquidity of different balance sheet items, the maturity mismatch approach uses quite an amount of modeling and behavioral adjustments. Thus the degree of sophistication and, hopefully, the degree of accuracy increase when going from the balance sheet liquidity analysis to the maturity mismatch approach.

Balance Sheet Liquidity Analysis

The balance sheet liquidity approach sets different balance sheet items on the asset side and the liability side into relation, depending on whether assets are liquid or illiquid, and on whether their funding is stable (sticky) or volatile.

To secure an appropriate balance sheet structure with respect to liquidity risk, sticky assets should be funded by stable liabilities, and liquid assets can be funded by volatile liabilities.

Exhibits 2.2 and 2.3 show balance sheet items that are relevant for a liquidity analysis. Not included are intangibles, strategic investments and equity capital, which are not at disposal for liquidation.

To illustrate a balance sheet liquidity analysis, consider the balance sheet structure of the following two banks:

EXHIBIT 2.2   Balance sheet liquidity analysis

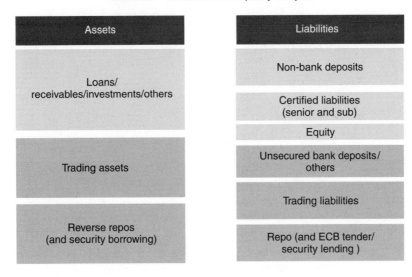

EXHIBIT 2.3   Balance sheet liquidity analysis for two exemplary banks

Liquefiable assets (US$)	Bank A	Bank B
Loans and receivables, investments, and others	50	100
Trading assets	30	10
Reverse repos	30	0

Liquefiable liabilities (US$)	Bank A	Bank B
Non-bank deposits	20	70
Certified liabilities	20	10
Equity	10	10
Unsecured bank deposits/others	20	15
Trading liabilities	30	5
Repos	10	0

Bank A is a typical universal bank like Deutsche Bank, Dresdner Bank or UBS, with a strong security franchise and strong dependence on interbank and capital markets funding. Bank B is a typical savings bank, which holds securities only as stand-by liquidity and relies mainly on deposit funding.

One would imagine that Bank A, working in the volatile business of capital markets, has much more liquidity risk in its balance sheet than Bank B doing classical retail banking. However, from the pure balance sheet structure the analysis reveals a different picture. Bank A has $50 of sticky assets in loans and receivables that perfectly match with $20 of stable funding from non-bank deposits, $20 of stable funding from certified liabilities, and $10 of equity. For Bank B the picture looks worse: there are $100 of sticky assets in loans and receivables that do not match with $70 of stable funding from non-bank deposits, $10 of stable funding from certified liabilities, and $10 of equity. An analysis of liquid assets with volatile funding gives the same result: Bank A's volatile liabilities in $20 of unsecured bank deposits, $30 of trading liabilities, and $10 of repos are covered by $30 of trading assets and $30 of reverse repos. Again Bank B looks worse: There are $15 in unsecured bank deposits and $5 in trading liabilities that are not covered by the stand-by liquidity of $10 in trading assets.

Clearly, such an analysis looks pretty simple. One only needs the annual report of the bank to assess its liquidity risk in its balance sheet structure. Naturally, the evaluation of liquidity risk is not simple, and in particular not related to accounting rules. There are a few problems with this analysis.

- *Missing time dimension*: The balance sheet liquidity analysis characterizes balance sheet positions only as liquid or illiquid. There are no statements about in which time frame positions can be liquidated or become due. In particular, management cannot know from this analysis whether cash outflows becoming due within, say, the next eight days can be met. For instance, a bond issue is generally considered as stable funding. If the time to maturity of this bond is, however, in eight days, it cannot truly be considered as long-term funding.

    Time affects or is affected by liquidity in three different ways. Each of these is summarized below:

    1. Liquidity sources have a clear temporal element. In a severe crisis that is resolved, one way or the other, within days, liquidity risk managers generally only have access to stand-by liquidity held on the balance sheet at the start of the problem. On the other hand, some bank-specific crises in the 1980s and 1990s endured for over a year. In those types of need environments, sources such as the sale of loans may be accessible.

    2. Liquidity also needs to have a temporal element. Most, but not all, liquidity needs are not instantaneous shocks; instead, they develop in stages. Moreover, the stages can unfold very quickly or drag on for a year or more.

    3. Most importantly, holding prudential or stand-by liquidity buys time. A bank that has lots of eligible collateral is more likely to have enough time to resolve whatever underlying problems triggered the crisis in the first place. Since it is ruinous and costly to always have enough liquidity to survive all possible crises, holding enough to buy sufficient time to access contingent sources is a critical requirement.

        Perception plays an integral role in buying time. A bank that is perceived as having lots of liquidity is less likely to lose the confidence of funds providers. Consequently, the seriousness of the crisis isn't as bad. That, in turn, stretches resources out over a longer period of time.

- *Impact of accounting rules*:   Balance sheet figures are shown according to accounting rules, which do not necessarily reflect the economic cash flows of a bank. Examples are securities in the banking book being partly shown at book and not at market value. Furthermore, the individual balance sheet position might be fine-tuned exactly for the reporting day and might look quite different on the following day. Examples are positions in securities, repos/reverse repos and unsecured inter-bank funding.
- *Off-balance sheet commitments*:   There is significant liquidity risk from off-balance sheet items. These activities may not be reflected on the balance sheet, but they still must be thoroughly reviewed because they can expose the bank to contingent liquidity risk. Examples are drawdowns on committed credit lines, collateral agreements in International Swap and Derivatives Association (ISDA) derivative contracts, and commercial paper (CP)-backup lines to special purpose vehicles (SPVs). Furthermore, securities shown under trading assets might already be pledged as collateral or used in a security-lending transaction. Similarly, borrowed securities that are shown off-balance sheet can be used in repo transactions to generate liquidity. To view the unencumbered security position, which is at the bank's disposal to replace unsecured funding with secured funding in case of a crisis, off-balance positions from the security lending and borrowing business must be included in the analysis.
- *Marketability of securities*:   Security positions are shown in the balance sheet according to their current market or book value. For liquidity risk this information is, however, not sufficient. What is really needed is the future collateral value or the cash value when pledging or selling these positions. Thus, haircuts for future market value volatility and liquidation discounts must be considered. These haircuts essentially depend on the credit quality, central bank eligibility, and the market depth of the security to be sold. Those characteristics, in turn, depend upon the economic, market and bank-specific conditions at such a future time. Haircuts also need to be applied in the securities financing business to account for counterparty risk.
- *Commercial papers*:   In some balance sheet liabilities, stable and volatile products are put together. Examples are certified liabilities, which contain stable long-term capital market funding (bonds, private placements), but also short-term commercial papers. Clearly, in the context of liquidity risk, CPs must be treated like unsecured money markets funding.
- *Non-bank deposits*:   Very similar is the situation for non-bank deposits (sight and saving deposits). Significant differences in the

stickiness of insured versus uninsured and secured versus unsecured deposits must be taken into account. Differences in stickiness between non-bank deposits provided by consumers, businesses or brokers can also be material.

Although a core level of the non-bank deposit balance can be considered as stable, long-term funding, a fraction will always be volatile and must rather be treated like unsecured money markets funding under liquidity risk. The differentiation of core and volatile deposits – for example, by applying a statistical analysis or taking only the insured deposits balance – is part of the art of liquidity risk management.

The cash capital concept outlined in the following section remedies some of these shortcomings of the balance sheet analysis.

Cash Capital Position

Moody's originally invented the cash capital concept to analyze the liquidity structure of a bank's balance sheet as part of its external rating process (see Exhibit 2.4). Its intention is to measure the bank's ability to fund its assets on a fully collateralized basis assuming that the access to unsecured funding has been lost. For example, such a scenario can occur after the downgrade of a bank's (short-term) rating.

EXHIBIT 2.4   Cash capital position

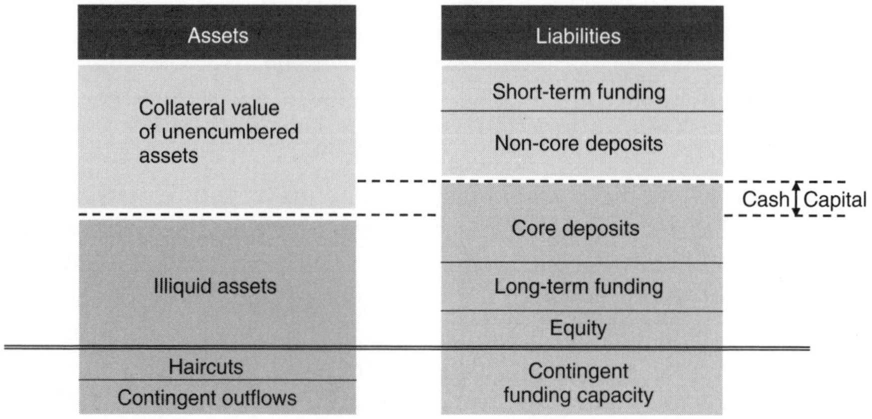

Cash capital is the gap between the collateral value of unencumbered assets, and the volume of short-term inter-bank funding and non-core parts of non-bank deposits. Stated differently, cash capital is defined as the aggregate of long-term debt, core deposits and equity (and contingency funding capacities) minus firm-wide haircuts, contingent outflows and illiquid assets.

Unencumbered assets are defined as assets that are available to be used as collateral. Usually, unencumbered assets are calculated as the market value of the net security position after accounting for bond/equity financing transactions:

$$\text{Unencumbered securities} = \text{long securities}$$

$$./.\ \text{short security position}$$

$$+\ \text{reverse repo'd securities}$$

$$./.\ \text{repo'd securities}$$

$$+\ \text{borrowed securities}$$

$$./.\ \text{lent securities}$$

The collateral value is then determined by subtracting haircuts from the current market value of the unencumbered securities. These haircuts account for the marketability of the securities. Haircuts used by Moody's for the Canadian banking market[1] and haircuts used by a security firm[2] are given in Exhibit 2.5. Additional examples of haircuts, from the ECB and FRB, can be found in Chapter 3.

It is important to note that borrowed securities can be counted as unencumbered securities in the cash capital framework. The reason is that they can be used as collateral; for instance, in a repo transaction. However, in the mismatch framework discussed below, they only provide liquidity for the time window between the borrowing and returning of them. Furthermore, it must be noted that the accounting treatment of the security – being classified as trading assets, available for sale or held-to-maturity – is irrelevant. Even a bond being classified as held-to-maturity can be used as collateral in a repo transaction, although it cannot be sold.

EXHIBIT 2.5   Examples of haircuts for marketability of securities from Moody's and IOSCO

Asset class	Moody's	Security firm
Government bonds	2%	5%
Highly liquid mortgage-backed securities	2%	10%
Prime CPs and bank acceptances	10%	5%
Listed equities	15%	30%
Bank debt	33%	15%
Corporate debt	33%	20%
Money market instruments	2%	5%

Further details on the cash capital approach will be given in Chapter 11.

Maturity Mismatch Approach

In a quantitative approach to measuring liquidity risk, the NCO and the unencumbered assets (to cover the NCO) must be estimated per time period and under different scenarios.

For this purpose liquidation cash flows from all liquefiable balance sheet and off-balance sheet items are mapped to a maturity ladder. There are four categories to be distinguished, depending on whether the amount and the timing of cash flows are deterministic or stochastic (see Exhibit 2.6):[3]

- *Category I: Cash flow amount and cash flow timing are deterministic.* Examples are: Coupon and amortization payments of fixed-rate loans and fixed-rate bonds, cash flows from secured and unsecured money markets funds, and term deposits.
- *Category II: Cash flow amount is stochastic and cash flow timing is deterministic.* Examples are: variation margins from futures, coupon payments from floating rate loans and bonds, future swaps floating leg payments, stock dividend payments, zero-bond repayments with structured yield, and settlement payments of European options.
- *Category III: Cash flow amount deterministic and cash flow timing is stochastic.* Examples are: repayments of callable bonds, repayment of loans with flexible amortization schedule, traveler's checks.
- *Category IV: Cash flow amount and cash flow timing are stochastic.* Examples are: sight (demand) and saving deposits, drawdowns

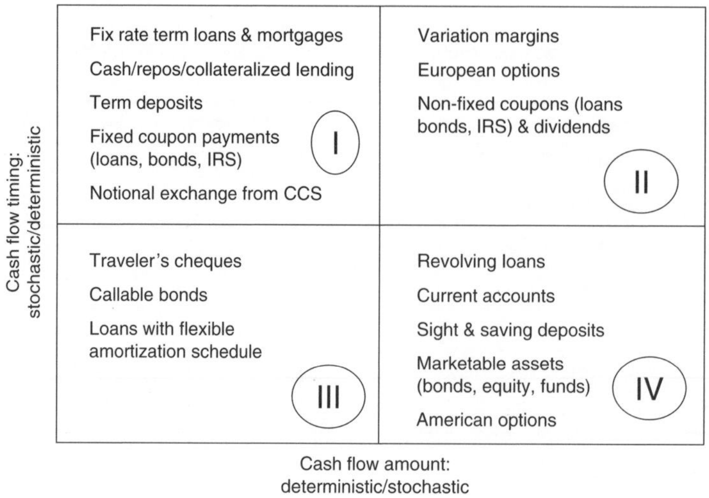

EXHIBIT 2.6   Maturity–volume matrix for liquidity cash flow mapping

on committed credit lines and revolving loans, collateral value of marketable assets (bonds, stock, funds), and settlement payments of US options.

Whereas the cash flow mapping of Category I assets is fairly straight forward – it only requires a proper data infrastructure that provides the correct balance sheet position – Category II–IV assets require additional model assumptions and behavioral adjustments in dependence of the scenario under consideration. The derivation and calibration of these models can be quite elaborate. In most cases there is no clear mathematical way of doing this. Instead, market experience and product knowledge are frequently more important; in particular, when considering cash flows of such assets under different scenarios. Each of these is discussed in a scenario context in Chapter 3.

Exhibit 2.7 shows a liquidity gap profile for a hypothetical balance sheet in a pure run-off mode; that is, no new business and no rollover of funding is assumed.

The net cumulative inflows comprise cash flows from:

- *the cash position* modeled as inflow in the overnight time bucket. Alternatively, one may consider it as working capital and not count it as an inflow at all
- *committed backup lines* at other banks modeled as inflow in the overnight time bucket (As we will discuss in Chapter 3, access to this source of funds is extremely scenario dependent.)
- *unencumbered securities* modeled according to a liquidation scenario depending on the credit quality, central bank and collateral markets eligibility, daily turnover, and market depth of each security. Liquid bonds typically generate short-term liquidity inflow irrespective of their interest rate risk duration or maturity. The maturity of a bond

EXHIBIT 2.7 Gap profile in a maturity mismatch approach

	Balance	Gap profile O/N	8D	14D	1M	3M	1Y	3Y	6Y	>=10Y
Cash	15	15								
Unencumbered securities	50	18	11	10	8	1	2			
Cont. inflow	5	5								
Net inflow		38	11	10	8	1	2	0	0	0
Net cumulative inflow		38	49	59	67	68	70	70	70	70
Loans	50	2	2	5	1	1	4	10	10	15
Retail deposits	−40	−4	−4	−4	−8	−4	−4	−4	−4	−4
MM deposits & CD	−50	−15	−15	−5	−7	−8				
Own funds	−30	0	−1	−2	−1	−1	−4	−7	−7	−7
Cont. outflow	−10	−4	−3	−2	−1					
Net outflow		−21	−21	−8	−16	−12	−4	−1	−1	5
Net cumulative outflow		−21	−42	−50	−66	−78	−82	−83	−84	−79
Net cumulative gap		17	7	9	1	−10	−12	−13	−14	−9

	>1Y	>3Y	>6Y	>=10Y
Assets	41	35	25	15
Funds available	41	33	22	11
Funding ratio	99%	93%	86%	70%

is only relevant in that aspect as the liquidation period cannot be longer than the final maturity of the bond.

The cumulative sum of all inflows comprises the liquidity available to cover liquidity outflows from other balance sheet and off-balance sheet positions. Analogously to capital covering potential losses in net asset value due to market, credit and operational risk, net cumulative inflows covers the liquidity risk in potential net cumulative outflows.

The net cumulative outflow[4] comprises cash inflows and outflows from:

- *loans* (coupon and national) modeled according to the coupon and amortization schedule
- *non-bank (retail) deposits* modeled according to a core level model (see below)
- *deposits from banks, corporations and governments, as well as CDs,* modeled according to residual maturity
- *own capital market funds* (issued bonds and private placements) modeled according to residual maturity
- *off-balance sheet commitment* in revolving loans, committed credit lines, and other off-balance sheet items modeled as short-term outflow.

One should emphasize that including ongoing new loan business also requires a certain assumption on a rollover rate for funding. Although this is certainly valid in a going concern scenario, it will add further assumption on the cash flow modeling side. According to this, most banks only consider a pure run-off gap profile without new loan and rolled over funding transactions.

Not shown in the gap profile are equity capital on the liability side and strategic investments (participations) on the asset side. Both positions are not at the disposal of a Treasurer's daily liquidity management process, but require the strategic decision of the Board. Knowing the investment horizon of participations, equity capital could be modeled congruently in a rolling portfolio approach.

The cumulative sum comprises the net cumulative outflows, which is the liquidity risk measure analogous to VaR being the risk measure for market, credit or operational risks.

Subtracting the net cumulative inflows from the net cumulative outflows provides the net cumulative liquidity gap per time bucket (see Exhibit 2.8).

A positive net cumulative gap indicates that the bank can cover all its outflows by liquidating its unencumbered assets. A negative gap does not necessarily mean that the bank is insolvent. It only indicates that the liquidation of its inventory will not be sufficient to cover its outflows with respect to today's balance sheet positions; that is, without any rollover of

EXHIBIT 2.8   Net cumulative gap profile

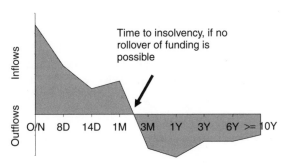

funding and new assets, and with respect to the scenario assumed for the cash flow modeling. Due to the fact that banks are doing liquidity maturity transformation, that is, they are funding parts of their long-term assets at money markets, eventually the net cumulative gap will become negative if a pure run-off gap scenario is applied. Prudent liquidity management requires that this point in time lies between 14 days to one month, even in a crisis situation.

The last box in Exhibit 2.7 shows the long-term assets and the available term funding above one, three, six, and 10 years. The funding ratio is defined as:

$$\text{Funding ratio above n years} = \frac{\text{sum of available funding above n years}}{\text{sum of assets maturing above n years}}.$$

The position in long-term assets usually consists of loans. Long-term funding is composed of issued bonds and core deposits. A funding ratio is a key figure to observe the structural liquidity risk in a bank's balance sheet. In contrast to the interest rate risk positioning of the balance sheet, which can – thanks to a liquid swap market – easily be changed on short notice, deficiencies in the liquidity risk structure in the balance sheet cannot easily be fixed. Management of liquidity risk requires a long-term horizon. The funding ratio is a useful tool to monitor the long-term funding structure.

A liquidity gap analysis is usually done under different scenarios. Besides an operating liquidity scenario, other scenarios refer to a general market disruption, a national macroeconomic disruption, a banking industry-wide disruption, a bank-specific crisis, a downgrade, a loss of a big investor, a bank run, and so on. Such scenarios influence the cash flow modeling of each deal-type differently. For example, in the market disruption scenario, it is unlikely that insured deposits will decline, while in the bank-specific crisis scenario, it is quite likely that even bank-insured deposits will be withdrawn. Similarly, in the market disruption scenario, backup lines of credit may have to be funded, but in the normal operating liquidity scenario, backup lines are unlikely to be drawn upon. Generally, inflows in the liquidity gap profile will be shifted to later time buckets and outflows to earlier time buckets (see Chapter 4).

Some banks also include new assets and/or rollovers of funding in their gap analysis. In this case the net cumulative gap must always be positive. Although such an analysis is more realistic, it requires even more assumptions concerning future cash flows. For other banks this is the reason to stay away from such a setting and to use a pure run-off profile.

Liquidity Ratios

Banks look at a number of ratios or indicators to measure their ability to meet their liquidity needs under going concern and stressed market conditions. These ratios are also the basis of the limit system for liquidity risk.

Examples are:[5]

- (cash + collateral value of unencumbered securities + unsecured revolving lines of committed facilities)/short-term unsecured obligations
- positive net cash capital defined as "long-term debt" > 1 year (including core balance of deposits) + equity./. (haircuts + illiquid assets)
- cash capital used < available cash capital, where "cash capital used" is defined as the extent to which a balance sheet asset is not self-financing in a liquidity crisis, and "available cash capital" is defined as the aggregate of 1) shareholders' equity, 2) borrowing that will not mature in the coming 12 months, 3) the collateral value of assets in the balance sheet, and 4) committed unsecured credit lines
- (cash inflows for the following month + collateral value of marketable securities)/cash outflow for the following month
- liquidity barometer defined as the number of days that the bank could survive, if it would not be able to roll over funding
- maximum cumulative outflow standard (defined as the amount of short-term unsecured funds required to fund cash outflows in a stress event) in order to maintain a funded liquidity cushion.

Most banks target a liquidity ratio well above 100%.

Cash Flow Modeling for Specific Asset and Liability Classes

The gap analysis in the previous section has shown that some deal-types can be modeled with fixed cash flow amounts and fixed cash flow timing. Examples are term loans with a fixed amortization schedule or a short-term money market funding. Most other deal-types require behavioral adjustments and cash flow modeling. In the following pages we will outline how this is done for three specific deal-type groups: securities, revolving loans/committed credit lines, and non-maturing assets and liabilities (current accounts and sight deposits).

Cash Flow Modeling for Securities

Securities typically generate short-term liquidity inflow. The reason is that secondary markets exist where securities can be sold or used as collateral for cash lending (for example, repo markets or collateralized lending markets). Thus, the depth or liquidity of these secondary markets determines the liquidation horizon. Interest rate risk duration or maturities are generally irrelevant. The maturity of a bond is only relevant in that aspect, as the liquidation period cannot be longer than the final maturity of the bond.

To determine an appropriate cash flow model of securities in a liquidity gap profile, one thus has to estimate the liquefiability of a security position under different scenarios. Criteria to do this are, for example, position size, rating (high investment grade, investment grade, non-investment grade), issuer group (government, bank, corporation), country group and country rating (OECD, G7, emerging markets), listing location (for example, major exchange), currency, own position relative to outstanding volume, degree of structuring (plain vanilla versus structured collateralized debt obligations), and so on.

According to these criteria securities should have different liquidation horizons. For example, for highly liquid bonds, such as G7 Treasuries, say, 35% of the position can be liquidated overnight, another 35% within one week, and the final 30% within two weeks. Clearly, such an assignment of a liquidation run-off also depends on the position size relative to the absolute issued amount. More illiquid securities are assigned a respectively longer liquidation horizon. One could also include a haircut, which would be mapped at the final maturity of the security. Such cash flow modeling would also be the basis for assigning term funding costs to securities (see Chapter 7).

Cash Flow Modeling for Revolving Loans and Committed Credit Lines

The current use of a revolving loan facility is characterized by the drawn amount and the tenor of the drawdown. For the bank only, the current usage, the current open line and the current tenor of a drawdown are known. Future drawdowns and repayments under the loan facility must, however, be considered by the Treasurer when managing a gap profile of a portfolio with revolving loan facilities and committed credit lines.

Liquidity risk managers need to pay particular attention to potential liquidity risks in loan commitments, lines of credit, performance guarantees and financial guarantees. Both the amount and timing of potential cash flows from off-balance sheet claims must be estimated by the banks.

Considering cash flows from revolving loan facilities and committed lines in a gap profile cannot be done for each individual transaction, only a portfolio approach with a certain estimation – based on historical experience – can yield a meaningful answer. The portfolio approach, in turn, has two parts. First, the current usage is separated into a core usage, which will remain drawn for the entire lifetime of the facility; and a volatile usage, which fluctuates on short terms. The volatile usage (haircut) is modeled as a short-term inflow, whereas the core usage is assigned to a liquidity inflow in the time bucket at the end of the facility.

Second, portfolios should recognize that distinct types of off-balance sheet requirements must be evaluated differently. Always consider the following three approaches when estimating the cash flow amounts and timing:

1.   Funding under some types of commitments tends to be correlated with changes in macroeconomic conditions. When builders cannot fulfill their contracts, stand-by letters of credit are issued in lieu of construction completion bonds. Some types of lines of credit, used to provide working capital to businesses, are most heavily used when either the borrower's accounts receivables or inventory are accumulating faster than sales and collections of accounts payable. These trends should be tracked by liquidity risk managers, working with the appropriate lending managers.

2.   Funding under some types of commitments is highly correlated with the counterparty's credit quality. Financial stand-by letters of credit are often used to back the counterparty's direct financial obligations, such as CP, tax-exempt securities or the margin requirements of securities exchanges. At some banks, a major portion of off-balance sheet claims is comprised of letters of credit supporting CP. If the bank's customer issues commercial paper supported by a stand-by letter of credit, and the bank's customer is unable to repay the CP at maturity, the holder of the CP will request that the bank makes payment. Liquidity risk managers should work with the appropriate lending manager to 1) monitor the credit grade or default probability of counterparties, and 2) manage the industry diversification of these commitments to reduce the probability that the multiple counterparties will be forced to draw against the bank's commitment at the same time.

3.   Funding under some types of commitments is highly correlated with changes in the bank's credit quality. The fastest growing types of off-balance sheet commitment may be commitments supporting various types of asset-backed securities and asset-backed CP. Securitized assets almost always use some form of credit enhancement. The credit enhancement can take many forms. One of those forms is a stand-by letter of credit or guarantee

issued by a bank. Similarly, many structures employ "special purpose entities" (SPEs) that own the collateral securing asset-backed commercial paper. Bank letters of credit or guarantees often support those SPEs.

As long as the bank's credit quality remains above defined minimums – usually based on ratings from a major rating agency – few or none will fund. As soon as the bank's credit rating fall below the minimum, *all of these commitments may fund at virtually the same time.* For liquidity risk managers, these are unquestionably the off-balance sheet commitments with the most liquidity risk and require the closest attention.

Having separated the current usage into a core and volatile part, the potential future drawdown on the open limit remains to be estimated. The bases for this are usually the bank's historical experiences of customer behavior and contract type. For instance, for a revolving loan the contingent drawdown ratio can be linked to the default or downgrade probability of the customer. This assumes that customers will extensively draw on the line if they come into financial difficulties. Other examples are CP backup lines for a conduit that issues asset-backed commercial paper (ABCP) to fund its assets. In case that the CP cannot be rolled over, the conduit will draw on the CP-backup lines. Here, the drawdown ratio is linked to the likelihood of a systemic market disruption in the ABCP market or the liquidity bank's specific downgrade probability. These probability-weighted drawdowns enter the gap profile as a short-term outflow.

Cash Flow Modeling for Indeterminate Maturity Accounts

The less future cash flows are known the more complicated the modeling of cash flows in a liquidity gap profile. In this case the bank must estimate the amount and the timing of cash flows based on market scenarios and customer behavior. Products where this applies in the most complicated way are demandable indeterminate maturity deposits such as sight, savings and term deposits; and demandable loans such as current accounts (sight loans) and credit card loans.

The cash flow modeling of indeterminate maturity products requires an estimation of the stable and volatile part of the current balance. The stable fraction of the current balance is called "core level." It is modeled as long-term inflow (for example, for sight loans) or long-term outflow (for example, for sight deposits). The volatile fraction is assigned to maturity buckets usually within the first month of the gap profile (see Exhibit 2.9 on page 32).

The clear challenge is to:

- determine the amount of the core level
- identify the maturity of the core level.

EXHIBIT 2.9   Tranching the balance of indeterminate maturity accounts

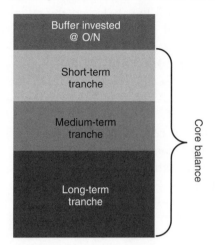

EXHIBIT 2.10   Term structure of liquidity run-off

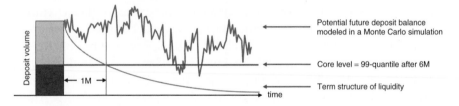

For both tasks no commonly recognized mathematical approach exists. Some banks use pure management judgment, others apply more or less elaborated statistical models in addition to management judgment.

All statistical models consider the historical balance of the indeterminate maturity products; for example, drifts, trends and volatilities. More elaborated models also include regressions to macroeconomic factors like interest rates, default rates, equity markets indices, and so on. Results of such models are the amount and a run-off fiction – the liquidity term structure – for the core-level balance. The liquidity term structure can be determined, for example, from the 99%-quantile line of the balance run-off.

$$\text{Prob(Deposit balance @ 6M} \leq \text{Core balance)} = 1 - 99\%$$

The core level of the balance can be defined as the balance amount that will not run-off within the first month with, for example, a 99%-confidence interval as shown above in Exhibit 2.10.

Usually, the core level is then modeled in rolling tranches with different maturities. Aggregating the amortization cash flows of these tranches within different time buckets, then, provides the run-off cash flows of these products in the liquidity gap profile as shown in Exhibit 2.11.

EXHIBIT 2.11   Rolling tranches reproduce liquidity run-off and cash flows

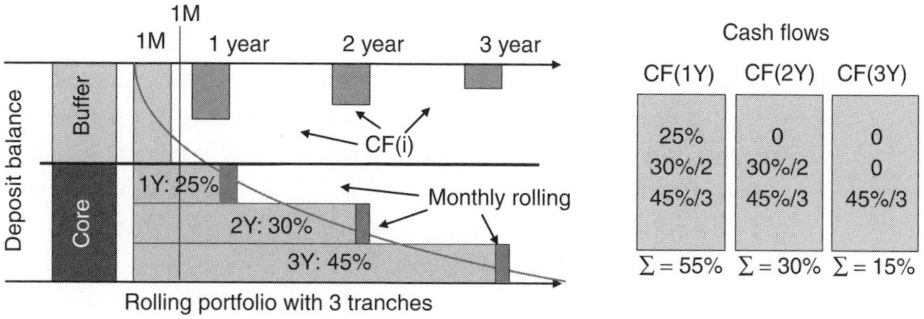

A simple mathematical framework is the following. One models the future balance by a log-normal diffusion:

$$\log V(t) = \alpha + \beta t + \sigma \varepsilon_t$$

with parameters α and β being determined from a linear regression on the historical balance time series. ε_t is a Gaussian noise term (standard normally distributed random number). σ is the volatility of the historical balance time series. It can then easily be shown that the liquidity term structure with respect to the q-confidence is given by:

$$\log V_q(t) = \alpha + \beta t - \sigma \Phi^{-1}(q)\sqrt{t}$$

where $\Phi^{-1}(x)$ is the inverse cumulative normal distribution. Hence, the core-level amount is derived by setting $\alpha = \log V_0$ and $t = 1$ month, where V_0 is the current balance.

Further mathematical models will be explained in the chapters written by Martin Bardenhewer (see Chapter 10) and Frauendorfer and Schürle (Chapter 15).

A QUALITATIVE FRAMEWORK FOR LIQUIDITY RISK MEASUREMENT

As we have seen in the previous section, a quantitative approach to liquidity risk measurement is very much assumption driven. There is generally no clear mathematical way of deriving behavioral adjustments from first principles. Similar to Basel II, where the second and third pillar might eventually turn out to be more important than Pillar I, it may well be that a qualitative assessment of liquidity risk is at least as important as a quantitative measurement based on models.

A quantitative assessment of liquidity risk focuses on the available IT-system infrastructure, on whether management and control processes are in place, and on whether a diversified market access for funding (for example, by products and investors) exists and is used.

Key questions to address are:

- *Are diversified funding sources established, in use and back-tested?* A bank does not only rely on unsecured inter-bank funding, non-bank deposits and long-term own-bond issues. Depending on the size and structure of its balance sheet, a bank should have established alternative funding sources such as a CD/CP-program, secured funding via repos (bi-party and tri-party), and securitization. Its own bond issues should be diversified on maturities, investors, and structure (plain vanilla, equity, interest, and credit linked). In particular, there should be no big reliance on liquidity backup lines from other banks, as such sources will cease to be available in a crisis. It is important that funding sources are not only laid down in some contingency funding plan, but that they exist and are back-tested in the day-to-day business. In case of an emergency there will generally be no way to establish new funding channels.
- *What is the current long-/short-term rating and what is the outlook?* The greatest danger for the short-term solvency of a bank is a downgrade of its short-term rating to a non-prime status. In this case, generally, unsecured funding sources will be significantly reduced and must be replaced by alternative, generally secured, funding sources.
- *Is there a board-approved liquidity policy in place with fixed standards on responsibilities, methodologies, limit system and reporting?* Managing liquidity risk quite often requires actions which go against the bank's P&L. For instance, reducing the maturity transformation by doing a six-month funding ticket instead of an overnight funding ticket usually reduces the P&L of the money markets trader. From this background, Board approval and endorsement is absolutely crucial. Decisions on liquidity cannot be left on some money markets trading desk. It is a central responsibility of the Board. Therefore, group-wide standards must be defined.
- *Has the bank implemented an IT-infrastructure that allows for daily quantitative assessment of liquidity risk; for example, by a gap analysis?* At least for big banks with a strong reliance on inter-bank funding and strong security trading activities, a daily gap analysis is important to secure its short-term liquidity. Both positions can change daily by a significant amount. Furthermore, the existence of such an IT-system helps to improve data quality to high standards, because, before developing a liquidity management system, the bank must be able to collect almost all positions in its balance sheet on a daily basis.
- *Does the bank measure liquidity risk under different environments, including stress levels? Does the bank only consider fixed cash flows or does it model cash flows by taking into account behavioral adjustments?* Scenario analyses, in particular, at stress levels are the key to proper

liquidity management. The impact of various "what-if" scenarios on the liquidity profile must be analyzed to bring the subject to the appropriate attention at senior management level. The impact of various "what-if" scenarios on the liquidity profile must be analyzed. In such scenarios non-fixed cash flows that need to be modeled by behavioral adjustments are affected most. Hence, a pragmatic modeling of such products, like revolving lines of credit, non-maturing on-demand loans and deposits, must be part of the cash flow mapping methodology in the gap analysis. These critical issues are discussed in Chapter 3.

- *Does a liquidity contingency plan exist that addresses responsibilities of each unit and the measures to be taken?* In a crisis situation, management usually does not have much time to react. From this perspective it is inevitable that each unit knows *a priori* what to do. Such a contingency plan will refer to events that trigger its initialization, and to responsibilities, committee meetings, and measures (capital markets, communication).

- *Has the bank established an internal transfer pricing system for liquidity risk?* To secure a proper management of liquidity risk a transfer price including mismatch, contingency and market liquidity risk is absolutely necessary. It is not sufficient that units in Treasury and Risk Control do a daily gap analysis and gap reporting, or manage this gap by capital markets and money markets instruments. It must be made clear to origination of the business that term-funding is a scarce resource and not all assets can be funded at overnight rates. The costs for a solid maturity structure in funding and appropriate stand-by liquidity must be passed on to the business origination units as it is done for credit and interest rate risk.

The qualitative requirements for liquidity risk are closely connected to the conclusion below, which addresses the issue of managing and controlling liquidity risk and transfer-pricing it.

CONCLUSION

In summary, liquidity risk measurement requires the application of a full kit of qualitative and quantitative tools.

- Liquidity risk addresses uncertainties in the prospective amount and timing of cash flows. As a consequence, managers should use cash flow projections by mapping cash inflows and outflows to maturity buckets and doing a gap analysis.
- Because liquidity risk is scenario-specific, for unexpected cash needs, management should use scenario-based sets of cash flow projections. Liquidity risk measurement and management must

always differentiate between potential bank-specific problems and potential systemic problems.

- A preparation for highly improbable scenarios requires stress testing.
- A variety of measures for stand-by liquidity (for example, holdings of liquid assets) are normally employed.

In addition, qualitative measures are required to reduce the subjectivity in cash flow projections and behavioral adjustments.

NOTES

[1] "Bank Liquidity: Canadian Bank Case Study," Moody's Investors Service (December 2002).

[2] "Sound Practices for the Management of Liquidity Risk at Securities Firms," Report of the Technical Committee of the International Organization of Securities Commissions – OICV IOSCO (May 2002).

[3] Source: "Risikofaktor Liquidität in Kreditinstituten," Renate Wagner, Michael C. Schmeling, Matthias Meyer, and Stefan Kremp, Research in Capital Markets and Finance, Working Paper 2002–03, Ludwig-Maximilian-Universität München (2002).

[4] The net cumulative outflow comprises cash inflows and outflows, however, always resulting in net outflows.

[5] "Sound Practices for the Management of Liquidity Risk at Securities Firms," Report of the Technical Committee of the International Organization of Securities Commissions – OICV IOSCO (May 2002).

CHAPTER 3

Scenario Analysis and Stress Testing

Leonard Matz

INTRODUCTION

S cenarios, as the adage goes, are the language of risk. And liquidity risk is very scenario specific.

Scenarios are far more important to liquidity risk measurement and management than for credit risk, rate risk or operations risk. The need for liquidity arises in many very dissimilar banking situations. The range of potential risk scenarios is far more varied. Both the nature and size of a liquidity event vary by scenario. Customer and counterparty options to withdraw indeterminate maturity deposits, draw-under loan commitments and prepay loans will be exercised differently under different conditions.

Equally important, tactics that work in some scenarios are often constrained and sometimes unavailable in others. For example, it may be easy to renew or replace maturing, unsecured liabilities during some types of systemic funding events, but not in a severe bank-specific funding problem. Marketable assets, on the other hand, may be difficult to sell during a capital market flight to quality. Exhibit 3.1 below illustrates both the source and need variability.

Regulators understand the importance of scenario-specific liquidity risk. The Bank for International Settlement (BIS), for example, emphasizes that: ''A bank should analyze liquidity utilizing a variety of 'what-if' scenarios.''[1]

Consider the following three hypothetical situations:

- A major and unexpected withdrawal of funds happens to occur on the same day as a major and unexpected loan funding. Where could the necessary cash be obtained? What potential sources of funds should be considered?
- Alternatively, suppose that the bank is launching a new consumer lease product, which is expected to grow very rapidly over the

EXHIBIT 3.1   Liquidity in a scenario perspective

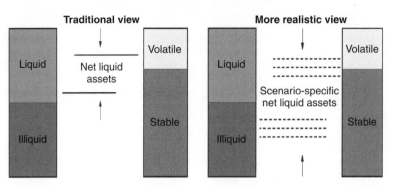

next nine months. Deposits are anticipated to continue to grow at the current sluggish pace, which will barely fund growth in existing loan categories. How should funding be obtained for this new opportunity? Which sources would be available for interim or permanent funding of a new asset type?

- Lastly, consider the case of a bank that is just about to publish its quarterly earnings. For the second quarter in a row, earnings are wiped out by extraordinarily large additional provisions to the loan loss reserve. Those provisions are required because of large loan losses.

Each of these hypothetical situations describes a potential need for liquidity. However, for each of these situations the time period in which liquidity is needed, as well as the available sources of liquidity to meet that need, are materially different. The first is short term and mild. The bank may obtain additional funds easily from almost any source – including additional purchases of overnight Fed funds. The second is long term but mild. The bank might generate the necessary funds from many sources, including a marketing program for new, long-term certificates of deposit (CDs). Cash flows from maturing securities and/or loans may also be a source of funds for the second hypothetical bank. The third is an example of a more severe need scenario. In that case, the bank will probably not be able to borrow new, unsecured funds at a reasonable cost. Indeed, it may not be able to borrow on an unsecured basis at all. The bank in the third situation will have to rely on secured borrowings and/or sales of marketable securities.

As these hypothetical cases illustrate, liquidity sources may be viewed as holdings of short-term salable assets, as the capacity to increase liabilities, and as net cash inflows from all sources. Clearly, some liquidity sources are more useful when liquidity is needed quickly, while others are not available unless the need for liquidity is prolonged. It is equally important to understand that some liquidity sources are available only for low-severity, non-acute liquidity needs, while others are not desirable for non-acute liquidity needs.

Together, the time horizon and the acuteness of the need dictate which of the three previously defined liquidity sources is most suitable. Used in combination, these three groups of liquidity sources meet all of the possible needs described previously.

DEFINING SCENARIOS

Deterministic or probabilistic? Liquidity risk managers tend to feel strongly that only one or the other is appropriate for stress-testing liquidity. As is the case for many other management decisions, this choice is heavily influenced by the preferences and experiences of individual managers. In this chapter, we will evaluate both. The identification of deterministic scenarios is discussed in the following paragraphs. The application of both deterministic and probabilistic scenarios is discussed later in this chapter.

Identifying and Describing Deterministic Scenarios

As we all know, the past is not usually a very good predictor of the future. This creates a particularly significant challenge when developing deterministic scenarios. Take a look at the list shown in Exhibit 3.2. Notice that with one exception, no two consecutive events on the list are similar. The next liquidity event is not very likely to look much like the prior event. (Also note that the list includes 12 events in a 15-year period – an average of one event every 1.25 years.)

Deterministic liquidity risk modelers must, therefore, create and evaluate a wide variety of scenarios. Two standards are: a normal course of business/business as usual scenario, and a bank-specific funding crisis scenario. A selection of systemic crises fills out the list. The two most

EXHIBIT 3.2 Systemic liquidity events (1987–2002)

1987	US stock market crash
1990	Collapse of US high-yield (junk) bond market
1991	Oil price surge
1992	ERM (European Exchange Rate Mechanism) crisis
1994	US bond market crash
1995	Mexican crisis
1997	Asian crisis
1998	Russian default, ruble collapse, LTCM
1999	Gold prices
2000	TMT (telecommunications, media and technology) sector collapse
2001	September 11 payments system disruption
2002	Argentine crisis

Sources: Includes James M. Mahoney, Federal Reserve Bank of New York, presentation entitled "Developing and Implementing Effective Stress Testing Strategies", delivered on June 21, 2001, at the Risk Conferences ALM conference in New York City.

typical systemic crises are a capital markets disruption/flight to quality and a severe recession. A confidential 2005 survey of large US and Canadian banks found that 81% evaluated bank-specific loss of counterparty confidence scenarios, 75% evaluated sector-wide disruption scenarios, 50% modeled other capital markets disruption scenarios, 44% evaluated payment system disruption scenarios, and 19% evaluated country-specific scenarios.

A few tips for creating and evaluating deterministic scenarios include:

- The ordinary course of business scenarios should include any seasonal fluctuations in the bank's liquidity.
- Many bankers like to synchronize their ordinary course of business liquidity scenario with their budget. This avoids the need to explain why business volume or rate forecasts are inconsistent.
- The need to evaluate both long-term and short-term scenarios. Many banks (and regulators) only look at seven- and 30-day hypothetical liquidity events. Historically, liquidity events have led to bank failures in as little as a few days (for example, Barings) or as long as 13 months (for example, Bank of New England).
- Stress levels must not be confused. A mild bank-specific funding problem and a worst case problem are simply one scenario described at two different stress levels.
- Sometimes, a funding problem can build up over months. For example, the impact of a severe recession peaks well after it begins. Other funding problems, for example, capital markets flights to quality, can become severe in one or two days.
- Most importantly, the scenario and its constituent elements absolutely must be relevant to your bank.

  - It must be relevant to the strategic nature of your business. A bank with significant exposure to emerging markets should model an emerging markets melt down; banks with significant equity exposure need to model stock market events, and so on.
  - It must be relevant to the stability or stickiness of your liabilities. A bank that is heavily dependent on volatile sources of funds should create more scenarios and those scenarios should reflect vagaries in counterparty risk tolerance.

Liquidity Events Are Often Global and Have Interrelated Elements

Too many liquidity risk professionals are tempted to look at lists like the one shown in Exhibit 3.2 and say: "Ah, but those are far away and very different from my risks." True, some are specific to one country or one region, while others primarily impact just equity or commodities markets. Complacency may be a mistake.

For several months in the fall of 1998, the collapse of a private hedge fund and the nearly simultaneous melt down of the Russian ruble caused a worldwide disruption in capital markets. Normally, marketable instruments, such as securitized assets, were hard to sell at almost any price. Haircuts for securities with modest risk rose significantly.

Why did two seemingly modest events trigger worldwide disruptions in equity, debt and commodities markets? The hedge fund in question, LTCM, was highly leveraged and did have huge positions in US Treasury securities, but the Federal Reserve stepped in promptly to assure a smooth resolution. The Russian economy at that time was smaller than the economy of the Netherlands.[2]

Changes in oil prices impact on major exporters and major importers. The exporters invest or disinvest in capital markets instruments, altering prices and relative values. Currencies are impacted by cross-border exchanges.

More than ever before, capital markets are globally linked. Sometimes the links are between markets such as commodities and foreign exchange. Sometimes the impact of events spreads because banks and other market participants stub their toes in one place but feel the pain in another. Sometimes changes in confidence are the transmission belts.

Terminology Notes

Scenario analysis and stress testing are two more cases of those unfortunate examples of widely divergent names for the same things. Some risk professionals use the term "scenario analysis" to identify deterministic tests, while "stress testing" refers to probabilistic tests. Some risk professionals define "stress testing" as uni-variant testing, while "scenario analysis" is then defined as multi-variant testing. Sometimes, "sensitivity analysis" is used to refer to uni-variant testing, while "stress testing" refers to multi-variant testing.

In this chapter, the author follows the BIS and defines "scenarios" to be the description of an integrated future view. "Sensitivity tests" are uni-variant tests used to establish the extent to which an outcome depends upon a single variable or single assumption. "Stress tests" are integrated, multi-variant tests that show degrees of severity for scenarios. "Integrated" refers to the fact that assumptions for both independent and dependent variables reflect interrelationships between variables.

STRESS TESTING AND SENSITIVITY ANALYSIS

A stress test, as defined by the BIS, can be either a stress test scenario or a sensitivity stress test. They go on to define a stress test scenario as a multi-variant test that can be either an historical scenario based on a significant previous event, or a hypothetical scenario.[3]

Since we know that no financial institution can afford to hold enough liquidity for a highly improbable event, we use scenario stress testing to understand if we are holding enough liquidity to buy enough time to either outlast the event or implement remedial measures. In a nutshell, scenario stress testing submits a scenario to large, adverse movements. The objective is to determine whether the institution can survive those movements.

Stress testing is an important element for liquidity risk measurement, risk evaluation and contingency planning. Stress testing and sensitivity analysis highlight what can go wrong, when, how badly, and for how long.

Armed with at least approximate answers to those questions, risk managers can identify and implement measures that reduce the impact of hypothetical funding problems. Equally, if not more important, risk managers can identify, in advance, opportunities for effective and rapid responses if such a hypothetical funding problem ever occurs.

Like so many other key elements of liquidity risk management, stress testing deals with the unavoidable fact that banks never hold enough liquidity during normal conditions to survive hypothetical worst case problems. We hold liquid assets to buy time at the inception of non-normal conditions. Stress testing, in that context, enables us to evaluate if we can liquidate assets and implement other remedial actions soon enough and in large enough amounts to survive.

Stress testing serves one other purpose. Forecasting is unavoidably inaccurate. No one can accurately predict future events. We stress that testing can help us refine our forecasts by identifying potential assumption errors and potential misunderstandings of correlations between risk factors.

Sensitivity Analysis

Risk managers often want to know how much of the forecast risk exposure in a scenario is driven by a single independent or dependent variable. Sensitivity analysis is a simple, intuitive way to accomplish that goal.

For systemic liquidity risk scenarios, modelers often perform sensitivity analysis on the following risk factors: prevailing interest rates, credit spreads for financial institutions, market access and time required to unwind specific asset holdings.

For bank-specific risk scenarios, modelers often perform sensitivity analysis on the following risk factors: deposit loss assumptions, assumptions regarding the funding requirements for off-balance sheet commitments, assumptions regarding the availability of new capital markets borrowings, and assumptions regarding the rollover of maturing capital markets funding.

Scenario Stress Test Overview

Scenario-based liquidity risk measurement and stress testing tends to vary key liquidity parameters, while holding credit risk and, in some banks, interest rate risk constant. (Credit risk and rate risk managers often hold liquidity risk constant.) In the real world, extreme events are characterized by both changes: a wide range of risk factors and changes in interrelationships between risk factors.

The central question for stress testing is: What differentiates normal and non-normal or extreme events? We can identify three alternative methods to answer that question: historical Value-at-Risk (VaR) and extreme value analysis, deterministic modeling, and Monte Carlo. Each is explored in the following subsections. A variety of other quantification tools, such as the Loss Distribution Approach (LDA) and the square root VaR model, are not useful for low-frequency/high-severity losses such as contingent liquidity risk, where estimates of loss frequency tend to be highly unstable.

Historical VaR and Extreme Value Analysis

Historical VaR seems to be everyone's favorite stress testing metric. The concepts are simple and easy to apply. The resulting measured quantity of risk is easy to explain. The tools are familiar metrics for trading risk evaluation.

VaR analysis looks at the loss within a selected confidence level. For example, in Exhibit 3.3 if the line indicates a 99% confidence level, we can say that there is a 99% chance that the severity of any loss will fall to the left of that line. The VaR at the confidence level is calculated as a closed form solution based upon the estimation of the two parameters in the distribution. (Don't forget that since liquidity losses result in a non-normal distribution, the normal relationship between standard deviations and percentage confidence levels does not apply.)

EXHIBIT 3.3 Loss distribution

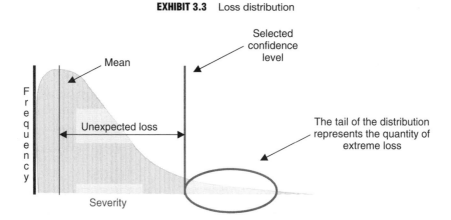

Extreme value analysis attempts to peer into the tail of the distribution to quantify the worst case amount of loss. This is the amount shown in the circle in Exhibit 3.3. Extreme value analysis relies on the fact that the portion of events in a distribution that fall beyond a selected threshold converge asymptotically to a Generalized Pareto Distribution (GPD). Excess tail losses are calculated as a function of the two parameters. Extreme value analysis is often applied to fat tailed distributions like the distributions for liquidity risk.

If the loss threshold, the vertical line in Exhibit 3.3, is low, more data is included but the GPD parameters are biased toward non-extreme data points. Conversely, raising the loss threshold raises the error in the measurement because fewer data points are observed. Yet even a high loss threshold, isolating the extreme tail of the distribution, does not meet our requirements. We have a "Black Swan" problem.

The Black Swan Problem

For liquidity risk managers, the central problem with both VaR and extreme value analysis is that the tail in the distribution of liquidity changes only reveals the most severe changes in the period covering the observations. But for most banks, most of the time, historical data simply do not include the sorts of extreme events that comprise contingent liquidity risk. No matter what statistical tools one selects to peer into the tail, the events that concern can't be seen because they aren't there in the first place. This is an example of what is known as a "Black Swan" problem. The name comes from an observation made by the eighteenth-century Scottish philosopher, David Hume: "No amount of observations of white swans can allow the inference that all swans are white, but the observation of a single black swan is sufficient to refute that conclusion."

Historical VaR Summary

Despite its popularity, historical VaR is a poor tool for quantifying liquidity risk. Like all applications of historical VaR, it relies upon the assumption that historical events are at least approximately reflective of future events. Furthermore, as we just discussed, looking into the fat tail is not insightful either.

Dr. Robert Fiedler in a conversation with the author summed up this issue very succinctly with the following two observations:

- *The Question is not*: "What risk will we get if we push out the quantiles?" – The answer to that question is only a matter of scaling and is therefore meaningless!
- *Instead, the question is*: "Is there a *structural change* that the bank should model?"

The BIS agrees. They note that: "Unlike VaR . . . stress tests simulate portfolio performance during abnormal market periods. Accordingly, they provide information about risks falling outside those typically captured by the VaR framework ... Those [risks] associated with forward-looking scenarios that are not reflected in the recent history ... [are] used to compute VaR."[4]

Some Thoughts About the Use of Hypothetical Assumptions

The best stress tests rely on hypothetical data and assumptions. This is simultaneously beneficial and inaccurate. The primary advantages of hypothetical assumptions are: they can draw from historical experience without necessarily duplicating it, they can be tailored to meet highly customized stress scenarios, and the results help risk managers identify the most important vulnerabilities. The primary disadvantages are that they are inherently subjective and they provide no information about the probability of loss – only the severity.

As one risk professional said: "This type of testing is extremely subjective and rests entirely on the skill and judgment of the risk manger constructing the test. However, *it is probably one of the most important exercises a risk manger can undertake, and will add considerable value to an organization if done well.*"[5] [Emphasis in the original.]

In short, hypothetical assumptions are a flawed but workable alternative. Risk managers should consider them to be a "least worst" solution.

Deterministic Scenario Modeling at Multiple Stress Levels

Useful stress tests for quantifying contingent liquidity risk are deterministic scenarios evaluated at multiple stress levels. Deterministic stress testing simulates shocks that never occurred, or did not occur with sufficient frequency or severity in recent historical data. Robust applications of this approach define current "industry best practice."

As one regulator points out: "International bank supervisors conducted a study of the performance during the market upheaval of banks' risk management systems and the Value-at-Risk models used to calculate market risk capital requirements."[6] The study examined information on the stress testing done by large banks in several G-10 countries and found that *ex ante* stress test results provided a better picture of actual outcomes during the third quarter of 1998, when those tests were based on actual historical experiences of hypothetical scenarios that incorporated simultaneous movements in a range of rates and prices, rather than on large movements in a single market risk factor. Hence, those "firms whose stress testing and risk management systems recognized potential linkages across markets had more realistic estimates of the way events in the fall of 1998 were likely to affect their firms."[7]

Robust deterministic, scenario-based stress testing reflects the following truths:

- Liquidity problems usually do not arise in a vacuum. In previous chapters we have discussed the fact that liquidity risk is a consequential risk. Stress scenarios should be tailored to match expected developments following the triggering event or events.
- As we noted earlier in this chapter, liquidity problems are often mild in the beginning and then either end or progress in stages to worst case levels. Stress scenarios should not overemphasize instantaneous shocks, even though such shocks can sometimes be insightful.
- As we noted above, the duration of funding problems can be a matter of days or more than a year. A range of stress scenarios should be evaluated to understand short, intermediate and long duration events.
- One of the two most important requirements is that robust stress scenarios must reflect the interactions between both independent and dependent variables. For example, the very identification of "marketable securities" needs to narrow as stress levels increase in systemic scenarios. Surprisingly, the 2005 confidential survey mentioned early in this chapter found that only 24% of the responding banks aired the projected quantity of liquid assets to fit the scenario. The stress scenario must have economic and business coherence.
- The second of the two most important requirements is that the most severe stress levels modeled need to be very severe indeed. Time after time, interviews with risk professionals who have actually worked through a major liquidity event include observations to the effect that "our worst case scenario wasn't as bad as it really got." In the good times, bankers tend to forget about previous instances when conditions were less favorable. (This is half facetiously referred to as "disaster myopia.") Managers may also get over-confident in their risk management skills.

In subsequent sections in this chapter we will describe stress test procedures as well as recommendations for selecting data and deriving assumptions.

Using Monte Carlo Modeling to Capture Stress Levels

Of course, deterministic modeling provides no information about the probability of an event – just its severity. Monte Carlo analysis can provide liquidity risk mangers with both. In its purest form, Monte Carlo modeling is as inappropriate for liquidity risk measurement and stress testing as historical VaR. Monte Carlo modeling requires a starting state and parameterization. The key parameters are mean reversion and volatility. Where are these obtained? As the story goes, an economist was once asked the meaning of life. He replied: "It depends on the parameter values."[8] If one uses observed parameters, we simply have a different application of the Black Swan problem. The historical data for most banks simply doesn't include the extreme events. Therefore, it is very unlikely that observed parameters will reflect conditions during extreme liquidity events.

WHERE DO THE NUMBERS COME FROM?

Astute readers may have noticed that our complaint against historical VaR – the lack of data from non-normal conditions – can just as easily be leveled against deterministic stress scenario models. Where do the numbers come from? More specifically, how does a bank with no history of operating under severe stress estimate balance sheet changes for hypothetical funding problems?

Segmenting the Problem

Like most difficult problems, this one is much easier to solve when we break the problem into pieces that can be solved separately. In Exhibit 3.4 on page 48, the influence of four cash flow drivers is illustrated.

The next step is to identify the available quantification tools for each driver. But before we do that, let's take a closer look at two of the most important drivers.

The Impact of Interest Rates on Liquidity Needs

Some potentially material changes in liquidity risk are clearly associated with changes in interest rate levels. Interest rate changes affect liquidity needs in several related ways:

- *The term structure of the bank's assets or liabilities may be affected by changes in prevailing interest rates.* Rate changes can cause fluctuations in demand for rate-sensitive bank assets and liabilities. For example, when prevailing rates seem low, deposit customers may not renew maturing CDs. Instead, they may use the proceeds from those CDs to increase holdings of savings and money market deposit accounts (MMDAs). (That shift actually occurred in 1992.) Such shifts do not reduce the bank's immediate liquidity since the funds remain in the bank. However, shifts like those just described reduce the term of liabilities, which does reduce the bank's potential liquidity because actual liquidity might be less at a future date if the funds are withdrawn. Similarly, customers prefer longer term, fixed-rate loans when prevailing rates are lower, while preferring shorter term and floating-rate loans when rates are higher. As illustrated by the deposit example, the change in term preference for loans does not affect immediate liquidity, but may affect future liquidity since shorter term loans provide more cash flow from cash-scheduled amortization than longer term loans of the same

EXHIBIT 3.4   Bank cash flows viewed from a liquidity perspective

Example cash flows	Cash Flow Drivers			
	Contracts	**Market rates, economic conditions and related changes in credit risk**	**Counter-party confidence**	**Bank management decisions**
Maturity or amortization of CDs, non-callable investments, non-prepayable loans	Entirely			
Loan prepayments	Defining/ controlling	Largely		
Funding of off-balance sheet commitments		Largely	Yes for bank guarantees that must be replaced if the bank's rating falls	
FHLB' loan calls	Defining/ controlling		Entirely	
Withdrawals from indeterminate maturity deposit accounts		To some extent in systemic scenarios	To some extent in bank-specific scenarios	Rate setting has some influence
Renewals of maturing liabilities (sticky)	Defining/ controlling	Some influence	Some influence	Rate setting has some influence
Renewals of maturing liabilities (volatile)		Driver in systemic scenarios	Driver in bank-specific scenarios	Rate setting has influence at low stress levels only
New liabilities		Driver in systemic scenarios	Driver in bank-specific scenarios	Rate setting has influence at low stress levels only
Reductions in stand-by liquidity reserves				Entirely
Other asset sales				Entirely

Note: FHLB (Federal Home Bank Loan).

amount. The higher rate loans are also more likely than lower rate loans to generate principal prepayments and therefore create additional cash flows when prevailing rates subsequently decline.

- *Holdings of bank assets and liabilities with embedded options can be materially affected by changes in prevailing interest rates.*

- *The volume of new bank assets can be directly affected by changes in interest rates.* For example, demand for residential mortgage loans is usually strong when rates are low. When rates are high, loan payments must be larger to meet the same principal amortization schedules; however, as a result, fewer consumers can qualify for the loans. Similarly, unfunded loan commitments for business loans may be drawn down in larger amounts during high-rate environments than during low-rate environments.

- *The volume of the bank's liabilities can be directly affected by changes in interest rates.* When prevailing interest rates are high, customers are more likely to disintermediate the banks – to take their funds out of banks and invest those funds directly in capital markets instruments offering actual or potentially higher yields. Of course, not all, or even a majority of depositors may be that rate sensitive; however, the most rate-sensitive customers are often those with the highest levels of investable funds. When prevailing rates are high, businesses tend to manage their deposit float more aggressively, which may also reduce bank liquidity during those periods.

- *The volume of the bank's assets and liabilities may be indirectly affected as changes in prevailing interest rates track (or cause) changes in business conditions.* During recessions, for example, business demand for credit tends to be much lower. At the same time, employers tend to lay off workers, reduce hiring, or in a few cases go out of business. The associated contraction in business activities creates both direct and indirect incentives for customers to reduce deposits – especially term deposits like CDs. The same factors tend to result in higher loan delinquencies, which reduce the cash flow received from loan payments.

Impact of Credit Risk on Liquidity Needs

Some potentially material changes in liquidity risk are clearly associated with changes in credit risk levels. The level of a financial institution's credit risk exposure, or changes in that exposure, affect liquidity in several related ways:

- The price that the bank pays for funds, especially jumbo CDs and other borrowed funds, will reflect that bank's perceived level of credit risk exposure. For large banks and bank holding companies, the market premium for credit risk exposure is often at least partially based on published credit ratings. However, market participants know that credit ratings often lag behind events. And many financial institutions are unrated. A variety of credit quality indicators, including loan growth rates, the relative size of the loan portfolio, levels of delinquent loans, levels of non-performing loans, and levels of loan losses, are all matters of public record and are often used by funds suppliers to judge credit risk.

- By far the most typical institution-specific funding crisis is a crisis where the availability of funds, especially uninsured funds, suddenly dries up in response to market awareness of credit problems. Typically, a quarterly provision for the institution's allowance for loan losses that is significantly larger than normal triggers a funding crisis. (Too often, a funding crisis following such an announcement is exacerbated because the bank's funding managers are not informed prior to the announcement. Such communications should be required by the bank's liquidity contingency plan.) A commonly seen chain of events starts with credit risk exposure, followed by credit losses, followed in turn by a funding crisis, and then sometimes followed by bank failure. Indeed, while a lack of liquidity has often been the immediate cause of bank failures, credit problems are usually the underlying cause.

Quantifying Contractually Fixed Cash Flows

This is by far the easiest group of cash flows to project. The only variable is time. Liabilities that do not mature before the projected time horizon of one's liquidity forecast are 100% stable. Short-term assets and amortizing assets throw off cash flows. Two key observations:

- First, few liquidity management tactics are more important than managing the maturity profile of your liabilities.
- Second, do not assume that the bank will receive 100% of the proceeds from assets that have contractual maturities within your forecast time horizon. Some assets, like loans with balloon payments, are originally underwritten with the intent of refinancing the outstanding balance at maturity. Some assets, mainly badly underwritten business loans, have to be refinanced at maturity because the borrower's source of repayment has a longer time horizon than the contractual loan term. Some loans and investments default.

Quantifying Cash Flows Primarily Driven by Market Interest Rates, Economic Conditions and Related Changes in Credit Risk

We can estimate the size of some future cash flows reasonably accurately by apply quantitative analysis. Cash inflows from new borrowings and new deposits obtained from capital markets counterparties or serious investors are driven by market rates in normal conditions and in systemic stress scenarios. (This is definitely not true in bank-specific stress scenarios.)

Most loan prepayment options can be forecast to be exercised "rationally." This means that most will fund when prevailing rates fall below the sum of the current coupon rate plus the refinancing costs. In short, these cash flows are correlated with market rates. Liquidity risk managers evaluating systemic stress scenarios with high interest rates can project changes in prepayments using standard rate risk models.

Requirements to fund off-balance sheet commitments can be a major source of cash outflows in stress scenarios. (Accordingly, it is more than a little curious that so many banks do not include these flows when they measure contingent liquidity in stress scenarios.) For liquidity risk analysis purposes, we can divide all off-balance sheet commitments into three groups. (Cash flows from two of those three groups are driven by rates and economic conditions.)

- Funding of some off-balance sheet commitments fluctuates with changes in credit risk that are associated with economic conditions. Examples are bank guarantees, CP backup lines and stand-by letters of credit. These cash outflows are highly correlated with the credit risk of the bank's counterparty.
- Funding of some off-balance sheet commitments fluctuates with the economic cycle. Examples are working capital lines of credit extended to finance business receivables and inventory. These cash outflows are loosely correlated with changes in prevailing interest rates.

Reductions in expected cash flows resulting from loan delinquency and default also fluctuate with changing economic conditions. Accrual accounting obscures the relationship between loan losses and interest rates. However, loan delinquency is at least loosely correlated with changes in prevailing interest rates. For US and Australian banks, this relationship is illustrated in Exhibit 3.5 on page 52.

Quantifying Cash Flows Primarily Driven by Counterparty Confidence

By far the most challenging part of building deterministic stress scenarios is quantifying confidence-driven cash flows. As outlined in Exhibit 3.4, loss of confidence drives some losses in indeterminate maturity deposits, non-renewals of term funding, exercise of Federal Home Loan Bank (FHLB) options, access to new funding, and more.

Exhibit 3.6 on page 52 provides an overview of deposit losses resulting from increases in bank credit risk.

For liquidity risk managers, the obvious problem with the analysis depicted in Exhibit 3.6 is its lack of granularity. Insured deposits are less

EXHIBIT 3.5 Relationship between interest rates and loan delinquency

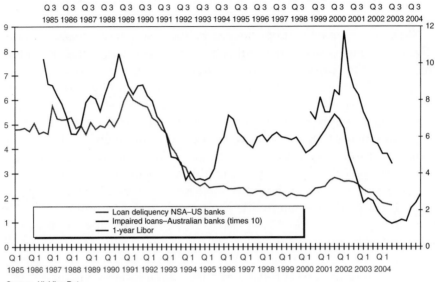

Source: Highline Data

credit sensitive than uninsured deposits. The same is true for secured deposits. Equally important, we know that counterparties who own the funds tend to be less credit sensitive than counterparties who simply manage the funds for third parties.

We can add some rigor to the subjective process of evaluating the credit sensitivity of counterparties. Exhibit 3.7 shows a framework for segmenting funds providers based on three proxies for credit sensitivity: whether

EXHIBIT 3.6 Sensitivity of deposits to changes in bank credit risk (% decline in deposits per 100 bps increase in default intensity)

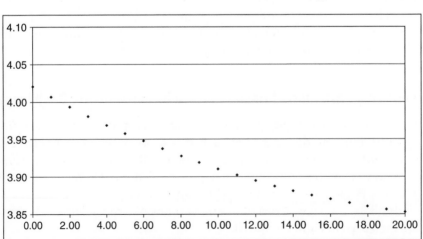

Source: Darrell Duffie, Robert Jarrow, Amiyatosh Purnanandam, Wei Yang, "Model Pricing of Deposit Insurance", *Journal of Financial Services Research*, volume 24, no. 2–3, pages 93–119, 2003, Figure 6, page 115.

EXHIBIT 3.7 Framework for assessing liability stickiness

	Insured or secured	Reliance on information	Relationship with the bank	Overall assessment of stability
Consumers	yes	low	high	high
Small business	in part	low	high	medium
Large commercial	no	medium	medium	low
Banks	no	high	medium	medium
Municipalities	yes	high	medium	high
Capital markets funds providers	no	high	low	low

the liability is insured or secured, whether or not the counterparty relies on public information for decisions, and whether or not the counterparty has a relationship with the bank.

Extrapolating Hypothetical Assumptions from Historical Events

Arguably the best tool for estimating cash flows for high-stress scenarios is to use historical changes as a starting point. Exhibit 3.8 shows selected data from a database of 312 failed banks in the United States during the period 1991 to the first quarter of 2005.

Customer-driven Deterministic Stress Scenario Assumption Summary

We can't get around the fact that hypothetical assumptions are required. Nor can we avoid the subjectivity and uncertainty in hypothetical assumptions. However, as the previous paragraphs make clear, we can develop plausible assumptions. The two keys are:

EXHIBIT 3.8 Historical deposit losses for a selection of failed banks

	Percent of total deposits lost in period T	Percent of insured deposits lost in period T−1	Percent of uninsured deposits lost in period T−1
Largest quartile of "wholesale funded banks"	3.5		23.9
Largest quartile of "retail funded banks"	3.1		7.2

Retail funded banks are defined by the author as banks with insured deposits equal to or greater than 70% of total deposits. Wholesale funded is the converse.
Period T is the time period between the failure date and last quarterly report prior to failure. Period T−1 is the time period between the last quarterly report prior to failure and the next to the last quarterly report prior to failure.
Sources: FDIC and Highline Data with analysis by Michael Matz.

1. By segmenting and grouping the changes we need to predict, we can apply the best tools to estimate the changes in each group. As we have discussed, we can identify drivers for each group of changes. Drivers include contractual restrictions, interest rates, and economic conditions and counterparty confidence. We can further segment liabilities based on variables such as deposit insurance and collateral. The more we look at the problem in individual pieces, the more plausible our conclusions.
2. Careful analysis of historical data from failed banks can be huge, while historical data from our own banks is not useful at all.

It is much easier to appreciate the forecast risk levels when the hypothetical assumptions are grounded in plausible analysis. And it is much easier to explain the forecast risk levels to senior management when plausible assumptions underlie the analysis. An observation from the famous quality control pioneer, W. Edwards Deming, may be overly harsh, but it is still worth considering: "to know what we are doing we need to be able to describe the process involved."

Cash Flows Resulting from Bank Management Decisions

Bank managers can choose from a fairly wide array of potential tactics to increase liquidity. Many of these are discussed in Chapter 5. The two primary tools are selling securities from the bank's stand-by liquidity reserve and, time permitting, selling other bank assets. In some circumstances, tactics may also include new borrowings, using prices to spur new deposits and retain current deposits, or raising prices to discourage new loans. (Of course the effectiveness of each of these tools depends upon both the scenario and the stress level.)

A Serious Problem

A fundamental dilemma applies to our fourth and final group of cash flows – the management-driven cash flows. The problem is as basic as it is serious.

On the one hand, liquidity risk is obscured when stress scenario forecasts include assumptions for future cash flows from management actions such as sales of investment securities and loans. At best, the full extent of the liquidity risk cannot be seen unless the analyst drills down to see the "before management actions" and "after" forecast levels of risk. At worst, it is hidden. "If you are covering today's risk with tomorrow's promises, you are masking risk."[9]

On the other hand, the entire exercise fails to produce meaningful risk measures if we cannot relate a forecast quantity of funds needed to a forecast quantity of funds available to meet that need. How else can we determine whether or not the risk level is acceptable?

The solution is to carefully separate the customer-driven cash flows and bank management-driven cash flows. This point is discussed further in the following section.

STRESS TEST PROCEDURES

Using the assumption tools outlined in the prior section, we can describe stress testing as a nine-step process.

Step 1   Define the scenarios and stress levels you wish to test. A framework or outline for stress scenario development is shown in Exhibit 3.9. *Note*: It is not a good idea to use changes in the bank's rating to define the stress levels. The ratings changes are lagging indicators of trouble and almost always follow the market. Identify and use procurers for ratings downgrades instead.

Step 2   For each scenario, at each stress level, identify the contractual cash inflows and outflows that can be expected to occur in each future time period for your forecast. The net contractual flows for each loan and deposit are clearly denoted in the line item descriptions that can be seen in Exhibit 3.10 on page 56.

Step 3   For each scenario, at each stress level, estimate the cash inflows and outflows resulting from customer behavior. These may be from the exercise of contractual options such as loan prepayment options, or options to withdraw funds from indeterminate maturity deposit accounts. Use the assumption estimation guidelines discussed in the prior section. Customer behavior changes also include non-contractual actions such as new loans. Make

EXHIBIT 3.9   Example scenario and stress level definitions worksheet

	Rates	Access to new unsecured borrowings	Access to new secured borrowings	Counterparty confidence	Changes in loan volume	Changes in credit quality
Ordinary course of business scenario	as per budget	unimpaired	unimpaired	unimpaired	as per budget	as per budget
Bank specific crisis scenario						
stress level 1	as per budget	diminished	unimpaired	mildly impaired	as per budget	mildly impaired
	no current funding problem but an elevated level of risk					
stress level 2	as per budget	none	diminished	severely impaired	increased use of lines	severely impaired
	some funding problems					
stress level 3	as per budget	none	none	worst case	worst case	worst case
	serious funding problems					
Systemic crisis scenario						
stress level 1	up 100	same quantity/higher cost	same quantity/higher cost	unimpaired	as per budget	as per budget
	no current funding problem but an elevated level of risk					
stress level 2	up 200	diminished	diminished	unimpaired	slight decrease	slight deterioration
	some funding problems					
stress level 3	up 300	significantly diminished	significantly diminished	potential diminution	significant decrease	significant deterioration
	serious funding problems					

sure that each customer behavior-driven change in your forecast is appropriate and consistent for the scenario and the stress level.

EXHIBIT 3.10 West Bank cash flow forecast – bank-specific scenario at stress level 2 (Customer-driven cash flows only)

	January	February	March	April
	Month 1	Month 2	Month 3	Month 4
Customer driven				
Installment loan payments (contractual)	862	495	589	481
Installment loan prepayment estimate	451	447	449	450
New loans	(1,080)	(1,071)	(1,076)	(1,077)
Net installment loans	233	(129)	(38)	(147)
Consumer line of credit payments (contractual)	67	67	67	67
Consumer line of credit prepayment estimate	177	186	197	207
Consumer line of credit advances	(950)	(1,002)	(1,057)	(1,115)
New loans	(333)	(351)	(370)	(390)
Net consumer line	(1,039)	(1,099)	(1,163)	(1,231)
Mortgage loan payments (contractual)	370	1,825	137	160
Mortgage loan prepayment estimate	276	276	259	261
New loans	(636)	(636)	(597)	(602)
Net mortgage loans	10	1,465	(201)	(181)
Commercial–non revolving				
Payments (contractual)	1,768	2,248	13,134	9,629
Estimated prepayments	2,108	2,187	2,263	2,195
New loans and rollovers	(9,688)	(10,051)	(10,402)	(10,089)
Net commercial–non revolving	(5,812)	(5,616)	4,996	1,735
Commercial–revolving				
Optional pay downs	3,480	3,845	4,249	4,695
Advances	(9,280)	(10,254)	(11,331)	(12,521)
New loans	(290)	(320)	(354)	(391)
Net commercial–revolving	(6,090)	(6,729)	(7,436)	(8,217)
Demand deposits	764	782	803	822
Regular savings	901	513	524	536
NOW deposits	(2,035)	(509)	(502)	(495)
Other savings	896	550	588	636
MMDA savings	(1,191)	(1,172)	(1,155)	(1,138)
CDs under $100,000 maturing (contractual)	(4,834)	(5,653)	(9,319)	(9,816)
CDs under $100,000 new	6,514	4,849	8,532	11,046
Net CDs under $100,000	1,680	(804)	(787)	1,230
CDs >= $100,000 maturing (contractual)	(6,136)	(9,932)	(5,705)	(4,434)
CDs >= $100,000 new	4,730	8,536	6,318	5,056
Net CDs >= $100,000	(1,406)	(1,396)	613	622
Net income (cash basis)	500	520	540	400
Total customer driven	(12,588)	(13,624)	(3,218)	(5,427)

EXHIBIT 3.11 West Bank cash flow forecast – bank-specific scenario at stress level 2 (total forecasted cash requirement table)

Total customer driven	**(12,588)**	**(13,624)**	**(3,218)**	**(5,427)**
Treasury non-discretionary cash flows				
Investment securities maturing	1,190	3,000	2,500	–
Investment securities pay downs and calls	1,944	2,132	1,754	1,723
Brokered CDs maturing (contractual)	(2,379)	(296)	(3,327)	(3,767)
FHLB borrowings maturing (contractual)	–	(3,000)	–	–
Subtotal treasury non-discretionary cash flows	755	1,836	927	(2,044)
Deficit that must be offset	(11,833)	(11,788)	(2,291)	(7,471)

Step 4   Add the non-discretionary Treasury cash inflows and outflows. These include contractual maturities of investments and borrowings. Note that if you have callable securities, the call exercise needs to be forecast in a time bucket consistent with the interest rate assumption for that scenario at that stress level. Samples can be seen in Exhibit 3.11 above.

Step 5   Sum the customer-driven cash flows and the non-discretionary Treasury flows. This total is the forecast liquidity requirement for each time period in each scenario at each stress level. The bottom line shown in Exhibit 3.11 is this sum.

The same information can be seen in Exhibit 3.12 on page 58. Note that for each time period in our forecast, the exhibit shows a stacked bar with four components. The first component above the zero line in each stacked bar is the sum of the contractual cash inflows. The second component above the zero line is the sum of the cash inflows driven by customer behaviors. The two components of each bar that are below the zero line show the contractual outflows and the customer-driven outflows.

The black line shown in Exhibit 3.12 shows the net cash flow for each time period and its trend. *Note:* The contractual cash flows are shown separately from the assumption-based cash flows. This permits you to easily identify net cash flows that are particularly assumption driven. Also, none of the cash flows depicted in Exhibit 3.12 reflects any discretionary asset sales or borrowings. The black line shows the risk quantity before any management-driven corrective actions are incorporated. Thus the forecasted risk quantity is in no way masked or hidden.

Step 6   Calculate the net cash flow coverage ratio for each time bucket in each scenario at each stress level. This is the amount by which the forecast cash inflows exceed (or fall short of) the forecast outflows. The ratio is typically calculated using the formula shown below, but there are several equally acceptable variations.

$$\text{Cash flow cushion} = \frac{\text{Forecast cash inflows for the period}}{\text{Forecast cash outflows for the period}}$$

EXHIBIT 3.12   West Bank cash flow forecast – bank-specific scenario at stress level
(total forecast cash requirement chart)

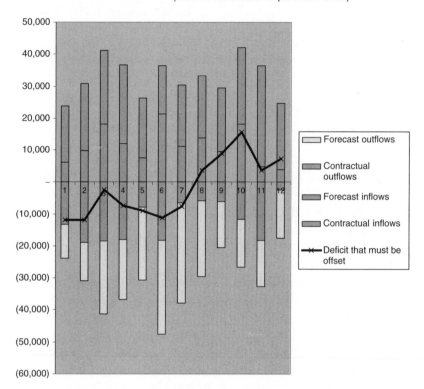

So, for example, a forecast that showed cash inflows totaling 120 and cash outflows totaling 100 would have a cash flow cushion of 1.2:1 or 120%.

Note: First, forecasts for ordinary course of business scenarios and for scenarios at minimal stress levels should always show a cushion. A positive margin for error is required to offset potential model risk. Second, the forecast cash flow cushion for each time period, in each scenario at each stress level can be compared to either required liquidity risk minimums or recommended guidance minimums. These are discussed in Chapter 4. Third, the number of cash flow cushion ratios can quickly get out of hand. For example, if you use 12 time periods for bank-specific scenarios done at each of three stress levels, you will have 36 cash flow cushion ratios just from this single scenario type. The solution is to report these in summary form. An example summary report is shown in Exhibit 3.13. (This example only displays three time periods and scenario stress levels. A typical report actually shows 12 time periods and at seven or more scenario stress levels.) The data in this report can be color coded to call attention to cases where the forecast cushion is very close to

EXHIBIT 3.13 Segment of a cash flow summary report

		March	April	May
Ordinary course of business scenario	actual	1.24:1	1.27:1	1.21:1
	limit	1.2:1	1.2:1	1.2:1
Bank-specific scenario, stress level 1	actual	1.16:1	1.11:1	1.12:1
	limit	1.1:1	1.1:1	1.1:1
Bank-specific scenario, stress level 2	actual	1.02:1	0.94:1	1.04:1
	guidance minimum	1.0:1	1.0:1	1.0:1

the minimum (yellow) and cases where it is below the minimum (red).

Step 7   Determine the quantity of stand-by liquidity available. The quantity of liquidity needed, the black line in Exhibit 3.12, must be compared to a quantity of liquidity available. (The quantity of liquidity needed is sometimes called the "counter-balancing capacity.")

Note: Unless we can compare some quantity of liquidity need to some quantity of liquidity available, it is impossible to answer the central liquidity risk management question: "Is the current level of risk acceptable?"

In order to forecast the quantity of stand-by liquidity available, we need to do four things:

- determine what sources are available in each scenario at each stress level
- determine in what order we plan to access each source. This can be described as a cash flow waterfall
- forecast how long it will take to convert each source to cash
- determine how much cash we can obtain. Haircuts for "marketable securities" can vary significantly with changes in prevailing interest rates and changes in credit spreads. (More information on haircuts, including Exhibit 2.5, can be found in Chapter 2.)

The first two tasks are illustrated in Exhibit 3.14 on page 60. Notice that no new borrowings are forecast in the exhibit projection. That is because this projection is for a bank-specific funding problem scenario at stress level 2. If, instead, we chose to view a forecast for stress level 1, we would see new borrowings included in the projection. Also, notice that the bank's forecast shows that it intends to liquidate its least marketable securities first and its most marketable securities last.

The third task, forecasting how long it will take to convert stand-by liquidity into cash, is illustrated in Exhibit 3.15 on page 60. Notice first that only the unpledged assets are considered – the two wedges protruding from the circle. Then notice that only

EXHIBIT 3.14   West Bank stand-by liquidity available – bank-specific scenario at stress level 2

Deficit that must be offset	(11,833)	(11,788)	(2,291)	(7,471)
New borrowings				
Brokered CDs new				
FHLB borrowings new				
Required change in stand-by liquidity reserve				
Unpledged US Treasuries				
Unpledged agencies (non-MBS)		9,472	2,291	7,471
Unpledged MBS	2,827	2,316		
Unpledged Muni's	9,006			
Total change in cash flow for the period	(0)	0	(0)	(0)
Stand-by liquidity reserve				
Balance at the beginning of the period				
Unpledged US Treasuries	1,989	1,989	1,989	1,989
Unpledged agencies (non-MBS)	21,863	21,863	12,391	10,100
Unpledged MBS	5,143	2,316	–	–
Unpledged Muni's	9,006	–	–	–
Total BOP reserve	38,001	26,168	14,380	12,089

EXHIBIT 3.15   Illustration of stand-by liquidity liquidation

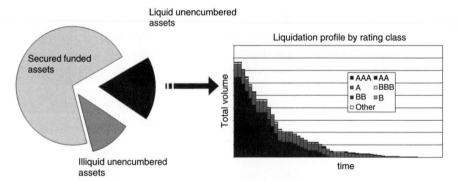

Source: Dr. Michael Reuther, Global Head of Funding and Liquidity Management, Deutsche Bank, "Managing Liquidity Risk in Multiple Currencies and Countries", Risk Training Course, Paris, France, October 17, 2002.

the liquid, unencumbered assets are included in the liquidation analysis. The box on the right-hand side of the exhibit then shows how much the bank thinks it can liquidate in each time period. Notice that they forecast much shorter liquidation periods for the higher rated securities.

The time required to unwind a large position in your stand-by liquidity reserve can vary significantly, depending upon changes in conditions impacting market breadth for each large position. For example, you might assume that on any given day, you can unload a quantity equal to a percentage, say 20%, of average daily trading volume. In that case, you must then make an assumption

EXHIBIT 3.16   West Bank evaluation of the stand-by liquidity reserve bank-specific scenario at stress level 2

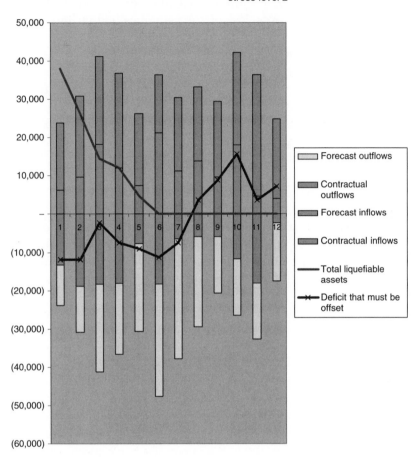

for the change in average daily trading volume that is likely to occur in each scenario at each stress level.

Step 8   Compare the quantity of forecast need to the quantity of fore-cast funds available. The final and most important step is to compare how much cash we think we need to how much we think we can get. Exhibit 3.16 is identical to Exhibit 3.12 with one very important addition. In Exhibit 3.16, we have added another line showing the liquidation of the stand-by liquidity reserve.

The top line on the left shows the amount of the stand-by liquidity reserve. (This is the same amount that we showed at the bottom of Exhibit 3.14.) In order to cover the liquidity cash requirement in period 1, a portion of the reserve is liquidated. Accordingly, the beginning balance for the reserve in period 2 is reduced by exactly the amount of the negative cash flow in period 1.

Notice that for this bank, in this scenario at this stress level, the liquidity reserve is entirely consumed by the end of the fifth month. In other words, West Bank estimates that its liquid asset holdings are enough to "buy" five months.

Note: Traditionally, the quantity of the stand-by liquidity reserve is communicated in either currency units or as a ratio. A bank may say that it has a stand-by liquidity of €100, that its reserve is equivalent to 10% of total assets or that its reserve is equivalent to 60% of volatile liabilities. None of those measures effectively communicates all of the dimensions of risk. Communicating in units of time is far more meaningful to senior managers.

Step 9   Make the management connection. No bank managers intend to preside over the failure of their bank. When we say, as we did for the case illustrated in Exhibit 3.16, that the bank has a large enough stand-by liquidity reserve to survive for five months, we definitely do not mean to imply that at the end of five months management locks its doors and gives the keys to the bank liquidators.

It is essential to view the liquidity reserve survival period as a window of opportunity. It tells the bank's managers how long they would have to come up with additional cash in the event of a scenario like the one projected. It also tells them how much additional cash they have to obtain.

Those last two pieces of information must tie back to the bank's liquidity contingency funding plan. One part of that plan, as discussed in Chapter 6, is a list of potential remedies that management may undertake in the event of a bank-specific funding problem. If the actions on that list do not appear sufficient to raise enough cash in the time available, managers know that they must either reduce the bank's liquidity risk exposure or identify more sources of funds that can be obtained in that situation.

CONCLUSION

The need for liquidity results from many dissimilar banking situations. Funding needs are best understood when split into separate categories. The appropriate amount of liquidity and the appropriate sources of additional liquidity depend on the nature of the need. Because liquidity risk is scenario specific, for unexpected cash needs, management should use scenario-based sets of cash flow projections. Liquidity risk measurement and management must always differentiate between potential bank-specific problems and potential systemic problems.

Stress testing is not an end unto itself. Stress testing is just one part of an integrated, dynamic liquidity risk management process. As we have observed, stress testing and contingency planning fit together. And earlier we discussed integrating stress testing and its limits.

Scenario stress tests are essential for understanding the full scope of liquidity risk exposures. But liquidity is hard to stress test. Stochastic tools are valuable because they can tell us the probability, not just the severity, of liquidity risk exposures. Yet quantitative tools, like historical VaR and Monte Carlo are particularly ill-suited for liquidity risk stress scenarios.

Deterministic stress tests require application of some "least worst" assumptions and methods. The necessary assumptions must be internally consistent. Assumptions must also be varied so that they are consistent with the nature and severity of the scenario under review. Risk managers must segment assumptions, identify what drives the changes, and apply reasonable methods to obtain plausible estimates.

At their best, robust, integrated sets of deterministic stress testing use "plausible" low-probability events to identify key weaknesses, even though we can't know how plausible or improbable they may be. Yet, robust sets of deterministic stress tests are "state of the art." The famous economist John Maynard Keynes once spoke of a preference for being vaguely right rather than being precisely wrong.

NOTES

[1] "Principal 6", *BIS: Sound Practices for Managing Liquidity in Banking Organizations*, February 2000, page 2.

[2] Thomas L. Friedman, "Opening Scene: The World is Ten Years Old," *The Lexus and the Olive Tree*, page xi.

[3] "A Survey of Stress Tests and Current Practice at Major Financial Institutions," report by a working group established by the Committee on the Global Financial System, Bank for International Settlements, April 2001, page 7.

[4] "Stress Testing at Major Financial Institutions: Survey Results and Practice," report by a working group established by the Committee on the Global Financial System, CGFS Publication 24, Bank for International Settlements, January 2005, page 4.

[5] Mike Davies, Head – Risk Management, UFJ International, PLC, "Determining How Effective VaR Type Models Have Been in Increasingly Volatile Markets," Risk Conferences, ALM Europe, Paris, September 23–24, 2001.

[6] Basel Committee on Banking Supervision 1999. "Performance of Models-based Capital Charges for Market Risk." September. Basel, Switzerland: Bank for International Settlements.

[7] Federal Reserve Bank of New York, *Economic Policy Review*, March 2001.

[8] Jeff Thredgold, On the One Hand, page 51 [no further publication information].

[9] Carl Tannebaum, LaSalle Bank, in conversation with the author.

Part 2

Managing Liquidity Risk

CHAPTER 4

Monitoring and Controlling Liquidity Risk

Leonard Matz

The strategies and tactics discussed in Chapter 5 only comprise the nucleus of liquidity risk management. A robust policy can be thought of as the protective shell. Limits are a key component of that shell. Audits and internal control procedures stiffen the management structure. And, of course, the operation of every element must be monitored.

Oversight, policies, limits, reports, internal control procedures and audits are discussed in the following sections.

BOARD AND MANAGEMENT OVERSIGHT[1]

The practical reality in most banks is that daily funding and profit maximization engage almost all of the time and attention devoted to liquidity risk management. Yet funding and profitability can easily be managed sub-optimally when those tasks are not conducted within a consistent, well-designed framework. Managing liquidity risk as a routine task is not a problem as long as the daily management is the distillation of a comprehensive and dynamic management structure.

The Board of Directors (BoD), together with senior management, are responsible for creating the necessary organizational and procedural framework. The primary components of that organizational and procedural framework are described in the following paragraphs.

Liquidity Risk Management Strategy

Each bank should have an agreed strategy for the day-to-day management of liquidity. This strategy should be communicated throughout the organization.[2] The BoD must approve the risk management strategy and is ultimately responsible for every aspect of its implementation and functioning. However, in most cases, the strategies are formulated by senior managers and directors working together. The results then take the form of recommendations submitted to the Board for formal approval.

One of the most important requirements for liquidity risk management strategy is the establishment of risk limits. The liquidity risk strategy should set out the general approach that the bank will take to liquidity risk management, including, as appropriate, various quantitative and qualitative targets. The Board should take reasonable steps to ensure that limits are consistent with the firm's expressed risk tolerance. As discussed later in this chapter, risk limits must be appropriate for the nature, scope and complexity of the bank's activities.

In establishing a liquidity risk management strategy, the Board and senior management need to consider how the bank's liquidity risk management will be coordinated with other strategic planning and risk management objectives. For example, strategic plans to enhance earnings by rapid growth of loans should consider the liquidity risk and funding implications.

Special attention should be given to the critical connection between liquidity risk and reputation risk. As one expert observed: "It only takes a few weeks to ruin a name but a few years to get it back."[3] Before major business initiatives are undertaken, the directors and senior managers should consider key issues such as:

- how the operation of the new business, for example sub-prime lending, might impact the bank's reputation
- how a potential problem with the new business at some future time might attract negative publicity.

Strategy details are generally reflected in the Board-approved liquidity risk management policy, a topic discussed later in this chapter. The strategy for managing liquidity risk should cover specific aspects of liquidity risk management. So far as appropriate to the nature, scale and complexity of the activities carried on, such aspects might include:

- objectives for the management of both short- and long-term funding risk
- objectives for the management of contingent liquidity risk
- the basis for managing liquidity (for example, regional or central)
- identification of appropriate or inappropriate risk management tools
- the degree of concentrations, potentially affecting liquidity risk, that are acceptable to the firm
- ways of managing both its aggregate foreign currency liquidity needs and its needs in each individual currency.

Board Responsibilities

A bank's Board of Directors should approve the strategy and significant policies related to the management of liquidity. The Board should also ensure that senior management takes the steps necessary to monitor and control liquidity risk. The Board should be informed regularly of the liquidity situation of the bank and immediately if there are any material changes in the bank's current or prospective liquidity position.[4]

In addition to approving strategy, an overall risk policy and risk exposure limits, the execution of the Board's oversight responsibilities includes a number of other essential tasks.

One of the most important liquidity risk management actions required from the Board of Directors is ensuring that senior managers establish and maintain an appropriate risk management structure. The risk management structure includes people, procedures and models.

- *People.* Senior risk managers should have authority and responsibility to manage liquidity risk effectively, including the establishment and maintenance of the firm's liquidity risk strategy. The staff should be large enough to effectively measure and monitor the liquidity risk exposures incurred by the bank. Senior risk managers and staff should also possess sufficient experience, knowledge and training to carry out those duties.
- *Procedures.* The bank should have adequate procedures for measuring, monitoring, managing and reporting liquidity risk exposures. It should also have procedures for assuring the integrity of the risk measurement and reporting processes.
- *Models.* The bank should have the data and analytical capabilities to adequately measure and monitor the liquidity risk exposures incurred by the bank.

Additional Board responsibilities for liquidity risk management include ensuring that:

- policy requirements and guidelines are clearly communicated to all affected individuals
- appropriate liquidity contingency funding plans are developed and maintained
- senior managers take reasonable steps to ascertain that liquidity risk is adequately identified, measured, monitored and controlled
- general (as opposed to detailed) monitoring of the firm's overall liquidity risk profile is carried out on a regular basis, as well as any material changes in the firm's current or prospective liquidity risk profile
- senior managers develop and maintain appropriate internal control and audit procedures for liquidity risk management
- senior managers develop and maintain appropriate procedures for monitoring compliance with regulations, Board limits, and other liquidity risk management constraints.

Senior Management Responsibilities

Each bank should have a management structure in place to effectively execute the liquidity strategy. This structure should include the ongoing involvement of members of senior management. Senior management must ensure that liquidity is effectively managed, and that appropriate policies and procedures are established to control and limit liquidity risk. Banks should set and regularly review limits on the size of their liquidity positions over particular time horizons.[5]

Senior management has the responsibility for the establishment and maintenance of policies and processes that translate the objectives and risk tolerance defined by the Board into operating standards consistent with the Board-approved liquidity risk strategy. At large firms there should be a segregation of duties in a *liquidity risk management* function and a *liquidity risk controlling* function for this task.

Liquidity Risk Management Objectives

The objective of a liquidity risk management function is to:

- ensure adequate liquidity at all times
- comply with regulations
- set and comply with liquidity risk limits
- monitor the gap profile structure and the funding sources
- monitor short-term liquidity outflows and their coverage by liquid assets
- ensure a sufficient liquidity reserve of unencumbered liquid assets and the efficient usage of it
- transfer price liquidity risk at a fair market rate.

Liquidity Risk Control Objectives

The objective of a liquidity risk controlling function is to:

- develop, in close cooperation with the liquidity risk management function, an appropriate liquidity risk framework, including procedure and methodology
- independently supervise compliance with these policies and limits
- inform the Board of Managing Directors about the liquidity risk profile of the institution
- calculate the fund transfer costs and allocate them to the business lines and liquidity risk management
- develop (or check on the functionality of) a liquidity risk management system that allows the monitoring and measuring of the liquidity risk profile of the institution
- check and maintain data quality.

In order to achieve the management and control objectives just listed, senior management has responsibility for the organization and function of key tasks, including:

- Oversee the development, implementation and maintenance of procedures and practices for measuring, monitoring and managing liquidity risk.

- Oversee the development, implementation and maintenance of procedures and practices for ensuring that the strategic objectives and risk tolerances approved by the Board are effectively communicated and implemented.
- Understand the size and nature of the bank's liquidity risk exposures, the capabilities (and limitations) of its risk measurement tools, the effectiveness of the bank's risk monitoring procedures, and the tools used to manage liquidity risk exposures.
- Delegate authority and responsibility to a chief risk officer, liquidity risk officer or risk management committee.
- Provide personnel and computer resources sufficient for the amount and complexity of the bank's rate risk exposures. Both the staff expertise and the resources allocated to the risk managers must be sufficient for the complexity and size of the bank's liquidity risk exposures.
- Oversee the development, implementation and maintenance of management information and other systems required for measuring, monitoring, managing and reporting liquidity risk exposures.
- Oversee procedures for managing market access, if applicable.
- Oversee procedures for monitoring and managing intra-day liquidity.
- Oversee the development, implementation and maintenance of adequate processes to follow-up both the execution and the effectiveness of risk management decisions.
- Oversee the coordination of liquidity risk management efforts with other bank risk management activities.
- Oversee the coordination and communication between managers responsible for marketing, pricing, new product development and risk management.
- Oversee the development, implementation and maintenance of effective internal controls over the liquidity risk management process.
- Oversee the development, implementation and maintenance of adequate processes to monitor policy compliance.
- Oversee the development, implementation and maintenance of adequate processes to articulate strategies and management expectations to all relevant functions within the organization.

LIQUIDITY RISK POLICIES

Strategies are translated and organized into guiding principals and rules by policies. Liquidity policies, like all other bank policies, are essential elements in a sound risk management program. They communicate goals and requirements, document limits, assign responsibility, and facilitate coordinated management of all risks. All business units within the bank that conduct activities having an impact on liquidity should be fully aware of the liquidity strategy and operate under the approved policies, procedures and limits.

Yet it is also important to keep in mind that policies are not final goals, but rather one of the key tools for achieving final goals. Merely adopting a policy, no matter how well written, does not by itself reduce or control risk.

The BoD, as discussed above, is responsible for defining the firm's liquidity strategy in line with the institution's expressed risk tolerance and for deploying sufficient resources and staff when delegating these tasks to senior management level and committees. The Board must approve an institution-wide liquidity and funding policy, including procedures and methodologies for the day-to-day measurement, monitoring, and management of liquidity risk in order to fulfill those responsibilities. This policy should also address responsibilities, contingency planning, fund transfer pricing and external regulatory requirements.

General Policy Suggestions

Some of the more important drafting issues are:

- Risk managers should consider crafting policy provisions specific enough to achieve the bank's goals. This means that the policy should be restrictive. It should include risk limits. Risk exposure limits can help management constrain transactions so that overall liquidity management objectives are achieved.
- At the same time, the policy should not be too detailed. Many details of liquidity management may be inappropriate for inclusion in a written policy. Such details are either too petty or too subject to change for them to be made part of a policy. Some banks have written funds management or liquidity management procedures documents that address such details. Other banks include details and provisions subject to frequent change in a separate appendix to their policy.
- The best policy provisions provide clear, focused and practical guidance. Consider, for example, the policy requirement to "maintain monthly average liquidity at or above 2% to 5% of the prior month's average assets" (taken from the actual policy of a large bank). Notice that there is no relationship between the quantity of liquidity to be held to any defined use or need for liquidity. This bank also defined liquid assets for the purpose of calculating its liquidity, but made no allowances for differences in asset liquidity that are associated with systemic or bank-specific need environments.
- The best policies delegate responsibility for developing procedures or assumptions rather than dictating the procedures or assumptions. For example, the policy may require the Asset/Liability Committee (ALCO) (or liquidity risk committee) to establish and monitor guidance or observation thresholds for some risk metrics.

Technical tasks should be delegated to the managers or areas where the technical expertise resides. The additional flexibility alone is a major benefit.

- The best policies are customized. There are significant differences in the types of financial institutions, in their size, and in the nature of their activities. Material differences also exist in the level of expertise of their staff and the extent of their internal controls. Accordingly, it is recommended that the policy reflects each institution's specific risk tolerance, skill level, goals and objectives, and priorities. Each bank can develop the policies and procedures that suit its particular situation. The scope of each policy may vary with the sophistication of the institution.

- The best policies are living documents. As time and circumstances change the bank's business, its risk management, capacity, risk appetite or external conditions, the bank's policies and procedures should change to reflect those developments.

- Policies must reflect constraints resulting from legal entity structure, regulations and international activities. A bank with unencumbered collateral in one legal entity must consider the circumstances or limitations for using that collateral in another legal entity. A bank with stand-by liquidity sources on one currency and potential contingent liquidity requirements in another must consider the market or regulatory limitations for transferring cash – especially in potentially stressed market conditions. Those are just two examples of structural, regulatory and international complexities.

Suggestions for Specific Policy Provisions

Risk managers should consider incorporating some or all of the following policy suggestions:

- A provision for the use of sets of cash flow projections to measure liquidity risk. Standard scenarios should be defined. Ad hoc scenario analysis should be encouraged. Details for defining stress levels, modeling scenarios, assumptions and procedures should be delegated to staff and subject to periodic ALCO (or liquidity risk committee) review.

- A provision for projections of net liquidity cash flow cushions for multiple scenarios.

- Provisions for reporting and management information systems (MIS) guidelines for keeping senior management regularly apprised of liquidity conditions.

- Provisions for limits and/or guidelines delineating minimum appropriate levels of cash flow liquidity cushions.

- Provisions for limits and/or guidelines delineating minimum appropriate levels for holdings of unencumbered, available for sale securities held as a liquidity reserve. The liquidity reserve may not be intended to be sufficient for all potential contingent needs. In such cases, it should be large enough to sustain operations until contingency plans can be implemented and stand-by sources accessed.

- Provisions that articulate a collateral management strategy. These often include internal penalties or incentives to encourage a balance between liquidity risk management objectives and funding and profitability objectives.
- Provisions for other forms of liquidity monitoring and/or limits for applicable risk areas such as reliance on borrowings from capital markets, large off-balance sheet commitments, and so on.
- Provisions that identify the need for periodic review of the bank's deposits and borrowings for any types of undesirable concentrations.
- Provisions that articulate the bank's strategy for holding some deposits and/or borrowings in instruments with maturities considered to be medium or long term.
- Provisions that address liquidity separately for individual currencies.
- Provisions that identify the need for a well-written contingency funding plan that identifies crisis warning indicators and potential action plans.
- A provision that clearly specifies the person or persons authorized to declare that the bank's contingency funding plan is activated.
- Provisions documentation of assumptions used in liquidity measurement.
- Provisions for coordination between concerned bank departments.
- Provisions establishing clear responsibility for decisions, including but not limited to who is responsible for identifying when a problem has escalated to the point where the liquidity environment can no longer be deemed normal.
- Provisions for reviews of both the policy and the contingency funding plan annually, or more frequently when changing conditions warrant.
- Housekeeping provisions: Who maintains the master copy of the policy? What controls or documentation is required for policy changes? Who is responsible for disseminating policy changes?

Policies may also include Board requirements for annual reports from the chief risk officer, or a similar officer, on the adequacy of risk measurement and management resources – systems, staff, expertise and training.

Flaws that Relegate Policies to "Shelfware"

More than a few liquidity risk policies are laboriously drafted, but they are ultimately ineffective. While these policies may not be totally useless, they contain flaws that impair risk management. Common policy flaws include:[6]

- Lack of clear guidance often characterized by platitudes or the use of "maximize" and "minimize" in the same sentence.
- Too many detailed policy requirements resulting from a lack of clarity between Board responsibilities for setting goals and management's responsibility for implanting systems and procedures to achieve those goals.
- Ambiguous delegation of authority. Clarity of ownership can be improved by requiring periodic status reports from the assignee.
- Allocation of responsibility so diffuse that no one takes ownership of inconvenient risk management elements. For example, a risk committee may be responsible for minimizing risk exposure but members of that committee are personally in charge of profit centers that earn more from higher risk exposures. In such cases, committee members may benefit if someone else's area of responsibility reduces risk instead of the committee member's area.
- Weak links between risk management authority and responsibility.
- Policy constraints on actions rather than risks. For example, reliance on certain specific funding sources maybe constrained or prohibited because funds from those sources are deemed "volatile" without regard for the bank's overall reliance on volatile funds.
- Excessive focus on "mechanics." For example, detailed prescription of multiple ratios for measuring liquidity with few details about acceptable risk levels for alternative scenarios and stress levels.
- Limits that are designed more to avoid future violations than to accurately reflect the Board's true tolerance for risk.
- Risk management requirements and/or risk limits that assume more reliable risk reporting than the bank actually has. Detailed risk measurement, reporting, and management requirements without sufficient staff and systems resources are one example. Reliance on reported risk that appears to be precise without understanding the methodological, data or assumption problems that make reported values inherently imprecise is another example. Reliance on reports generated with inadequate controls or testing is yet another.

LIQUIDITY RISK LIMITS

Risk limits are an essential component of prudent risk management. They are also one of the easiest risk control tools to implement. They most certainly require careful analysis. But once that step is complete, they merely need to be approved, communicated to the key players, and incorporated into the risk measurement and reporting procedures.

Meaningful risk limits provide at least three benefits:

1. Carefully established and formally approved liquidity risk limits are a critical risk control tool.
2. Limits are also used to help achieve or maintain other objectives. For example, good limits, along with other risk management

tools, help the bank retain sufficient liquidity to ensure that the bank's external rating does not fall below its targeted rating. And, whether or not an external rating is targeted, limits can help the bank retain sufficient liquidity to be perceived by funds providers as more credit worthy – thereby lowering borrowing costs.

3. Risk limits enable risk managers to clearly communicate to senior managers and directors the relative degree of contentment or concern appropriate for the bank's current risk exposure. A message that says that liquidity is equal to X is not as informative as a message that says that liquidity is below, above or well above our required minimum.

Risk Tolerance

The first of the two most critical risk management questions, as we've discussed in prior chapters, is always: "Is the current risk exposure acceptable or unacceptable?" Answering that question requires identification of risk tolerance thresholds.

In general, as many as nine separate variables should be considered when determining appropriate liquidity risk thresholds. Of course, the relative importance of each variable depends on the unique circumstances and priorities of each bank. What's more, the relative priorities change as those circumstances and priorities change.

The nine limit-determining variables are:

- *The bank's risk appetite.*   Some banks are philosophically inclined to minimize risk exposures as much as possible. Other banks are willing to accept risk positions as long as they represent prudent exposures. The maximum exposure boundaries should reflect the bank's risk philosophy.
- *The bank's level of capital.*   A well-capitalized bank can afford larger risk exposures, since one primary function of capital is to serve as a cushion that absorbs unexpected losses. If the cushion is small, the bank cannot afford an exposure that may lead to potentially large losses.
- *The bank's level of earnings.*   When earnings are strong, a bank can afford to hold larger risk exposure positions. Unexpected losses are less likely to "wipe out" anticipated profits if these are large. Unfortunately, history shows us that financial institution managers are most tempted to increase their risk exposure when profits are under pressure. This is because the largest (but not the only) cost of excessive liquidity risk liquidity is contingent and does not get reported in income statements. The costs of holding liquidity, on the other hand, are mainly costs that do get reported in income statements. When earnings are under pressure, the cost of holding liquidity seems less acceptable and the returns from higher risk exposures are more tempting.

- *The perceived likelihood of an unusual funding need.* If the possibility of higher loan demand, more loan commitment usage, more deposit withdrawals, slower deposit growth, or problems obtaining or retaining funds is perceived to be above normal or growing, banks clearly want less liquidity risk exposure.
- *The confidence in measures of current and projected liquidity.* Unfortunately, liquidity measurement is very much a subjective process. It is both scenario- and assumption-dependent. Liquidity risk managers must always consider that their understanding of risk exposures is approximate. Consequently, we must consider the appropriate level of confidence to associate with our measured risk exposure.

  Confidence in liquidity risk measures is as subjective as the measures themselves. But that does not mean that confidence is unimportant. If we have less confidence in our measured level of risk, we should be less comfortable with small liquidity cushions and low levels of contingent sources. Low confidence may result from either of two circumstances. Confidence in the measured risk may be low because the assumptions used in the measurement process are not well developed. For example, if you base your assumption of loan commitment usage on studies of data from crises at other banks, you can have more confidence in the accuracy of that assumption than if it is based on someone's best guess. However, confidence is also a function of the stability of internal and external conditions. If the bank's balance sheet composition, its markets or the economy is changing, confidence in existing risk measurement assumptions and scenarios should be lower.
- *The bank's level of immediately available liquidity.* The amount of immediately available liquidity enables the bank to buy time at the onset of a funding crisis. That time, in turn, permits the bank to implement contingency plans and to obtain additional funds from slower sources such as loan sales. Whether you define "immediately available" as one day or one week, this is clearly a critical subset of the bank's overall liquidity risk. Therefore, a bank with a high level of immediately available liquidity can more readily accept more long-term and/or more contingent liquidity risk.
- *The ability to quickly and reliably convert stand-by liquidity sources into cash.* As we have seen, many stand-by liquidity sources are more available in some liquidity risk environments than in others. For example, the assets we can expect to sell easily in a bank-specific funding crisis will probably be very difficult to sell during a systemic flight to quality. Therefore, a bank with a diversified mix of stand-by liquidity sources, designed to provide liquidity in a

variety of different potential need environments, is able to justify higher levels of risk exposure.

In addition, as we have also discussed, some stand-by liquidity sources require more effort to convert to cash. For example, putting together a loan securitization, especially for a bank that rarely uses this tool, requires legal, data processing, and loan administration expertise and time. A bank with the experience and resources to implement its stand-by liquidity enhancement tactics smoothly can therefore accept a higher level of risk. Similarly, a bank that does not regularly participate in the repo markets may find it difficult to use the channel in the event of an acute funding need.

- *The relationship between the potential risk and the potential reward.* For a bank that has the capacity to monitor and manage the risk, the most important factor in evaluating the reasonableness or acceptability of risk is the relationship between risk and reward. If the potential reward is small in comparison to the risk, that risk is probably unacceptable, whether we can manage it or not. Philip S. Wilson of the Bank of Montreal said it best: "If you are not trying to pick up nickels lying on the road in front of a steam roller, you aren't in danger of losing your hand." We need to be adequately compensated for the risks that we take. That is the reason for the emphasis on charging liquidity users and crediting liquidity providers. Those charges and credits help create incentives that, in turn, help us manage the size of risk exposures.
- *The other, non-liquidity, risk exposures to which the bank is currently exposed.* Liquidity risk must never be considered in isolation. If credit risk or interest rate risk exposures are large, liquidity risk exposures should be smaller. Obviously, earnings and capital are at risk from both unexpected credit or interest rate risk losses, not just from liquidity risk.

Risk Limits vs Guidance Ratios and Observation Ratios

Formal, Board-approved, risk limits can be difficult to work with. Consider the following:

1. Comparisons of measured risk levels with limits must be evaluated with a healthy respect for the margin of error in our risk quantification. Estimates of the amount of liquidity needed and the amount of liquidity available under various stressed scenarios are highly subjective. In all cases, it is very important to treat these as rough approximations. Liquidity is too assumption-dependent and scenario-dependent to measure precisely.

2. One bank may choose to employ assumptions consistent with highly improbable "worst case" crises. Even in these scenarios, the bank should expect to have positive cash flow coverage in one-day and one-week time periods, but should we expect to have positive cash flow coverage in two months or longer time periods under those conditions? Probably not. On the other hand, banks modeling less severely stressed scenarios might expect positive cash flows in all projected time buckets.

3. If you measure liquidity risk for seven time periods, in three scenarios using three stress levels, you end up with 63 measures of cash flow coverage. If you also have limits for other liquidity-related variables, such as off-balance sheet commitments or maturity diversification, you may easily have 70 or more limits in total. Complying with a limit system comprised of 60 to 70 separate limits is cumbersome at best. It can also be distracting.

Your bank may wish to address all three of these problems by adopting a system that combines a few hard limits with guidance limits and observation ratios. The hard limits are Board-approved minimum liquidity coverage ratios. Hard limits may only apply to the time periods in a single scenario at a single level of stress.

Guidance limits can be minimum liquidity coverage ratios for each time period in the scenarios and stress levels not covered by hard limits. The guidance limits may be established by ALCO (or liquidity risk committee), rather than by the Board. In some cases, the Board-approved policy may simply require that an ALCO (or liquidity risk committee) establish guidance thresholds acceptable to the committee. Violations of guidance minimums or thresholds may merely require closer monitoring, more frequent reporting, and/or additional analysis. Observation ratios may be for ancillary measures of liquidity risk such as maturity distributions.

Selecting Risk Metrics for Thresholds

Limits or guidance thresholds for two types of liquidity risk measurement metrics are essential. One is liquidity coverage ratios, for multiple time periods, multiple scenarios and multiple stress levels. The other is metrics for the sufficiency of stand-by liquidity in different scenarios and stress levels. Targeting risk thresholds for these two metrics is implicitly endorsed by examples provided by the BIS.[7]

Additional liquidity risk limits or guidance thresholds should be employed to fit the bank's circumstances. For example, banks that are heavily reliant on wholesale markets for funding should have risk limits or guidance thresholds for the size of their dependence on purchased funds and diversification of those liabilities. Banks that are primarily funded by time deposits and term borrowings should have risk limits or guidance thresholds for the maturity patterns of those liabilities.

Note: The levels selected for limits or guidance ratios require careful evaluation, but should not be given excessive weight in the risk governance process. The real value in limits and thresholds is often the clarity they provide by identifying the metrics most valued by the bank, subjecting those risk metrics to the monitoring and reporting process created by policy and procedure, and focusing on oversight.

Minimum Size of the Liquidity Reserve

We recommend that each bank establish a Board-approved minimum level for its holdings of unpledged, available for sale (AFS), marketable securities. (In a 2005 survey of US and Canadian banks only 65% reported limits for liquid assets held.[8]) The minimum level established by a bank for its liquidity reserve should reflect both of the following groups of variables:

1. Since bank holdings of marketable securities may not necessarily mature in the next day, week, month or quarter, it is entirely possible for a bank to have low cash flow cushions projected for near-term time periods despite holding large liquidity reserves. Banks with low cash flow cushions in their cash flow projections usually want to hold larger reserves. This is particularly the case for banks projecting small cushions in time periods of six months or less. It is also particularly the case for banks projecting small cushions in mild bank-specific or mild systemic-problem scenarios.
2. Banks with other indications of significant liquidity risk may also want to hold higher reserves. These include, but are not limited to, banks with weak contingency plans, banks heavily reliant on funds providers who are sensitive to the bank's credit worthiness, and banks heavily reliant on short-term borrowings.

Minimum Cash Flow Coverage Ratios

We recommend using Board-approved limits to require minimum cash flow coverage cushions in each time period forecast for normal course of business (going concern) scenarios. The BIS makes the same recommendation: "Banks should set and regularly review limits on the size of their liquidity positions over particular time horizons."[9] The limits or guidance thresholds should reflect all of the key points for risk measurement discussed in prior chapters. (In a 2005 survey of US and Canadian banks, 53% reported that one or more limits were required, 33% reported that one or more guidelines applied, and 13% reported that they were required to monitor forecast cash flow mismatches, even though no limits or guidelines applied.[10])

For each time period, minimum cash flow coverage ratios should at least exceed 1:1. The amount by which they exceed 1:1 needs to be determined on a bank-by-bank basis. Larger cushions are recommended for banks with insufficient holdings of marketable securities as liquidity reserves, banks with weak contingency plans, banks heavily reliant on funds providers who are sensitive to the bank's credit worthiness, and banks heavily reliant on short-term borrowings.

Generally, minimum cushions required for the first week in a forecast period should be larger than those required for weeks two through 12, which, in turn, should be higher than those required for later time periods. Even though the margin of error in the projections is much greater for the later time buckets, the time available to enhance liquidity is also much greater.

Limits or Sub-limits for Subsidiaries, Affiliates, Branches and Currencies

Limits or guidance minimums should be segmented for major currencies and legal jurisdictions. As the BIS notes: "A bank should, where appropriate, set and regularly review limits on the size of its cash flow mismatches over particular time horizons for foreign currencies in aggregate and for each significant individual currency in which the bank operates."[11] Typically, limits are set on a group-level and for each legal entity. Sub-limits are typically set for branches and per regions and currencies.

Scenario-based Risk Limits

Not surprisingly, liquidity risk limits tend to be imprecise or impractical if they don't reflect situational differences for different scenarios and different stress levels. Accordingly, banks need an array or set of risk thresholds. A single limit or guidance minimum for all stress scenarios is not workable. "Banks should analyze the likely impact of different stress scenarios on their liquidity position and set their limits accordingly."[12]

Each bank's philosophy regarding the description of the scenarios will have a huge impact on acceptable or unacceptable minimum amounts. For example, a bank projecting a truly horrific, worst case, bank crisis scenario may not project positive net cash inflows in time buckets for periods beyond six months if it has a good contingency plan for making those ratios positive when needed.

We therefore recommend using ALCO (or liquidity risk committee) approved guidance thresholds, rather than Board-approved limits, to establish minimum cushions for each time period in each forecast stress scenario. Generally, minimum cushions for each time period in low stress scenarios should be larger than those set for higher and worst case stress levels.

Secondary Risk Metrics

It is a good idea for banks that rely on capital markets borrowings, banks that do not hold large liquidity reserves, or banks that have significant off-balance sheet commitments to employ more risk metrics. *Note*: The number of limits or guidance thresholds is not important. The goal is for limits or guidance ratios that enable risk managers and directors to focus on the specific liquidity risk exposures inherent in the bank's activities.

Banks should consider a variety of potentially useful concentration limits. Each should be selected to fit the bank's balance sheet and funding activities. In a jointly released publication, the US banking regulators suggested that: "Limit structures should consider typical behavior patterns for depositors and investors and be designed to control excessive reliance on any significant source(s) or type of funding. This includes brokered funds and other rate sensitive or credit sensitive deposits obtained through the Internet or other types of advertising."[13]

We recommend that, at a minimum, banks limit concentrations of uninsured and unsecured liabilities obtained from credit sensitive types of counterparties – such as trusts, mutual funds and pension funds – where the funds are controlled by agents, trustees or other parties with quasi-fiduciary responsibility for their safety.

Banks that provide credit enhancements to asset-backed securities and banks that provide stand-by letters of credit or guarantees to asset-backed commercial paper SPEs may wish to employ Board-approved limits on the maximum acceptable level for these off-balance sheet commitments.

Banks that rely on short-term deposits or short-term borrowings may wish to consider either a Board-approved minimum for long-term funding or a Board-approved maximum for short-term funding. It is particularly important to control excessive liability maturities on any single day or week.

Banks that issue marketable liabilities may wish to limit the quantity of marketable paper issued and still outstanding. It makes little difference whether that exposure takes the form of jumbo CDs, CP, securitized assets backed by a letter of credit, or any other exposure. We suggest this because the willingness of funds providers to hold exposure to one's "name" can be just as easily filled by secondary market purchases that do not provide any incremental funds.

Last, but far from least, many banks find it useful to establish limits for collateral pledging or minimum requirements for unencumbered collateral. Of course, either of these can be easily treated as sub-limits within limits for the sufficiency of the bank's stand-by liquidity reserve.

Adjusting Risk Limits

Like all other risk management tools, liquidity risk limits can never be treated as static measures. Risk tolerance changes. Strategies change. The size and composition of the bank's balance sheet and off-balance sheet positions change. Market conditions change. Regulatory guidance changes.

It is a good idea to plan on reviewing your bank's liquidity risk exposure limits annually. However, it can be a mistake to adhere to a rigid review schedule. For example, when market conditions become as hostile as they were in the fall of 1998, previously acceptable levels of liquidity risk quickly became unacceptable.

Responses to Limit Breaches

Actual or projected breaches should trigger intensive ALCO (or liquidity risk committee) review. Based on that review, one of the following decisions must be made:

1. The current risk level is temporarily acceptable, even though it is in violation of the limit or guidance threshold. In that case, ALCO should approve a temporary exception if it has that authority, or recommend such a change to the Board. The BIS recommends that: "Management should define the specific procedures and approvals necessary for exceptions to policies and limits."[14]
2. The current risk level is permanently acceptable and the limit or guidance threshold is no longer set at an appropriate level. In that case, ALCO should approve a temporary exception if it has that authority or recommend such a change to the Board.
3. The current risk level is unacceptable. If limits are breached, escalation has to take place. Banks should have policies and procedures in place to ensure that appropriate members of management are notified and that proper actions are taken at the right time. ALCO should approve specific tactics to reduce the risk level and restore compliance with the limit or guidance threshold. Responsibility for implementing those tactics must be clearly assigned. Appropriate follow-up should also be mandatory. Depending upon the nature of the breach and upon the bank's risk policy, reports to the Board may also be mandatory.

Breach Escalation Management Procedures

In banks with a large reliance on money market funding, like securities firms, limit breaches can happen regularly. Hence, it is recommended to have a step-wise escalation process in place. Senior management needs only to be informed if limits are breached persistently, say more than five days in a row.

An example of the breach escalation process is illustrated in Exhibit 4.1 on page 84.

MANAGEMENT INFORMATION SYSTEMS AND REPORTING

More than a century ago, British prime minister Benjamin Disraeli observed that, "As a general rule, the most successful man in life is the man who has the best information." All we have to do is change the wording to apply to both men and women and the observation is as true

EXHIBIT 4.1   Example limit breach escalation process.

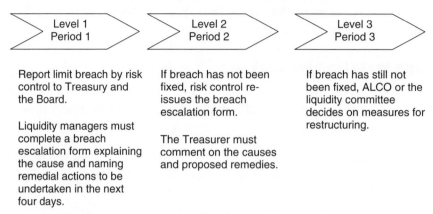

Report limit breach by risk control to Treasury and the Board.

Liquidity managers must complete a breach escalation form explaining the cause and naming remedial actions to be undertaken in the next four days.

If breach has not been fixed, risk control re-issues the breach escalation form.

The Treasurer must comment on the causes and proposed remedies.

If breach has still not been fixed, ALCO or the liquidity committee decides on measures for restructuring.

Source: Dr Peter Neu, "Stress Testing Liquidity," presentation at an Incisive Media Liquidity Training Course, November 2005, Frankfurt.

now as it was then. Liquidity risk cannot be monitored – let alone managed – without robust information systems and reporting. Indeed, this is the fourth BIS liquidity risk management principal: "A bank must have adequate information systems for measuring, monitoring, controlling and reporting liquidity risk. Reports should be provided on a timely basis to the bank's BoD, senior management and other appropriate personnel."[15] A workable management information system is integral to making sound liquidity risk management decisions. Internal bank reports play a key role in the liquidity risk management process.

Under-emphasizing the importance of management information is a serious weakness. As the Office of the Comptroller of the Currency (OCC) points out, management information is a critical component of a bank's overall risk management strategy. Data are necessary to support and enhance the decision-making process and, at a more senior level, are used to help the Board and management make strategic decisions.[16]

Investors, funds providers and rating agencies must rely on published information which, to the say the least, sheds limited light on liquidity risk exposures. Clearly, public information is insufficient for managers and directors responsible for conducting or monitoring liquidity risk. It is almost impossible for anyone charged with conducting or overseeing liquidity risk management to monitor these functions using published data alone.

Characteristics of Best Practice MIS

Almost by definition, the combined information conveyed by all of a financial institution's management reports, in other words by its MIS, must be complete enough to permit effective oversight. Proper oversight requires information. But, more importantly, it requires useful information.

Concise, accurate, comprehensible and timely reports are essential. In this sense, "concise" is just as important as "accurate" and "timely." Effective oversight is impossible if risk management personnel, supervisors, and/or directors have so much information that important details are lost in the clutter. Good management reporting has the following characteristics:

1. The reporting system must be designed to facilitate accurate reporting. The single best method for encouraging accuracy is to keep the reporting system simple. When procedures for generating reports are complex, it is harder to maintain accuracy. Other measures for ensuring accuracy should include training the personnel who prepare the reports and periodically auditing the content of reports.

2. The content of reports must speak plainly to the intended audience. MIS should be designed to ensure that senior managers and directors are shown meaningful information and not overwhelmed with information that might obscure risk. Reports must convey sufficient information to recipients for them to fulfill their management or oversight responsibilities without overburdening them with so much data that the useful information is hard to separate from the merely nice-to-know information. Furthermore, key information should be presented clearly and emphasized appropriately. Management reports should translate measured risks from technical and quantitative formats to formats that can be easily read and understood by senior managers and directors who often do not have specialized technical knowledge of liquidity risks.[17] Data, especially trend data, are more effectively communicated when presented in charts or graphs.

3. The frequency of reporting should provide senior managers and directors with adequate information to judge the changing nature of the bank's risk exposure.

4. The organizational level reflected in reports must reflect constraints resulting from legal entity structure, regulations and international activities. For example, in the United States, consolidated and unconsolidated reports are recommended for "lead" banks in multi-bank holding companies. Liquidity managers at each affiliated bank should be aware of significant funding requirements and liquidity issues at related entities that may impact their entity.

5. The reports must be produced on a timely basis. Good decision making obviously must be based on accurate data. Less obviously, but just as importantly, good decision making requires current information.

   The need for timely information is, in turn, another argument in favor of simple reporting systems. Complex reports are often more expensive to produce and therefore may not be produced often enough to provide managers with timely information.

General Types of Board and Management Reports

Effective liquidity management requires a management information system that allows monitoring, analyzing and reporting of the liquidity profile. Rather than just identifying information that we scatter in reports provided to the various individuals, committees and boards with oversight responsibilities, it might be helpful to consider the three general categories of MIS reports. The three types are:

1. *Position reports*:   These reports describe what we have. The most common are reports detailing holdings of liquid assets. Reports of current off-balance sheet commitments and reports of unused but available borrowing capacity are other examples. Inclusive reports with this type of information are essential; however, they can too easily contain lots of data, yet communicate little information.
2. *Activity reports and forecasts*:   Activity reports and forecasts attempt to capture the dynamics of the bank's risk exposure. The best examples are the multi-period, scenario-specific, stress-level specific cash flow forecasts.
3. *Exception reports*:   Exception-based reporting is often overlooked but can be the most informative type of reporting. Exception-based liquidity reports include reports of limit or guideline violations, reports of other policy compliance violations, and reports of exceptions to established policies and procedures. The value of this type of reporting is that it focuses the attention of readers exactly on those areas that require the most attention.

Most banks, in particular those relying on money markets funding and with large security trading positions, measure their liquidity position daily using a gap analysis or the cash capital framework. In most cases, general ledger balances are used together with front-office systems for securities, repurchase agreement/lending, and derivatives trading.

Report Content, Details, Hierarchies and Frequencies

A management information system for liquidity requires a significant amount of effort for the daily reconciliation of data. In fact, almost all on- and off-balance sheet transactions of a bank need to be aggregated and mapped on liquidity deal-types with specific liquidation cash flow profiles. Problems arise from differences between front- and back-office systems in regards to booking procedures. For instance, at a future settlement date a significant amount of securities are booked in a front-office system two days prior to the cash leaving the bank. Back-office systems and processes, which account for this by internal settlement accounts, are quite often not designed for a daily liquidity gap measurement.

Each bank's MIS must be designed to suit the bank's risk exposures. In the following paragraphs, we provide some best practice recommendations. View these recommendations as a starting point rather than a final plan. The frequency and the contents of your liquidity reports must be customized, based on the degree of sophistication and risk taken by the business. Report content ranges from funding spreads, gap profiles, time-to-insolvency and liquidity ratios, to balance sheet liquidity structure, unencumbered securities and cash capital position. Reporting frequencies might range from daily to weekly for reports to the Treasury and head of Risk Control, to fortnightly or monthly for reports to the Board.

We recommend utilizing three distinct approaches for management reporting.

Reporting for Risk Managers

At the lowest level, risk managers should have detailed information.

- Liquidity risk managers usually require reports that enable them to identify specific risk sources as well as trends. These reports should include information revealing how much of the projected cash flows in each future time bucket – especially unusually large flows – result from current assets and liabilities versus how much results from assumptions. This information may be subdivided into discretionary and customer-driven cash flows, as was illustrated in Chapter 3.
- Separate cash flow forecasts should be prepared for each scenario and at each stress level that the bank has identified for periodic evaluation, as well as any ad hoc scenarios that risk managers believe merit attention.
- Near-term time buckets should be short. Banks with average liquidity risk may choose to view weekly projections for the first four weeks and monthly for the following 11 months. Banks with above-average liquidity risk may choose to view daily projections for the first week, weekly for the next three weeks, and monthly for the following 11 months.
- Net cash flows, in each time period, for each stress scenario, in each currency, should be viewed in currency units and also in ratios such as cash flow coverage ratios.
- Net cash flows, in each time period, for each stress scenario, in each currency, should be compared to limits or guidance minimums.
- Forecast net cash outflows should be compared to the bank's holdings of stand-by liquidity. One or more measures of the sufficiency of the liquidity reserve should be reported. We recommend reporting the length of time, in days, weeks or months, that sales or repos of liquid assets can offset cumulative cash flow short-falls.
- In normal market and funding conditions, cash flow projection sets and liquidity reserve sufficiency reports should be prepared at least

monthly. Large, internationally active banks often do this daily. A confidential 2005 survey of US and Canadian banks found 18% doing daily reporting, 59% doing weekly reporting, and 53% doing monthly reporting. (The percentages exceed 100% because some banks report with more than one frequency.)

- Trends and forecasts for diversification/concentrations should be reported.
- In addition to breaches, instances where the bank is close to a limit or guidance minimum should be researched and reported.
- Liquidity risk mangers should receive monthly indications of credit quality. Each organization should tailor its liquidity reports to meet its own set of liquidity issues and risks.
- Other specific indicators should be selected to fit each bank's balance sheet and funding activities. Additional reports may include reliance on brokered deposits, wholesale funding, short-term funding and negotiable CDs; the outstanding amount of the bank's outstanding negotiable obligations; off-balance sheet exposures; spreads paid for borrowed funds; securities pledged compared to the liabilities that they secure; details of available for sale (AFS), non-pledged securities held for liquidity reserves; and reports of other liquidity risk indicators as appropriate.

Type of Reporting for ALCO or Liquidity Risk Committees

- ALCO or liquidity committee members should receive more summarized information than the liquidity risk mangers, but should be able to receive more detailed data upon request.
- To the extent possible, charts and graphs should be used rather than data tables.
- Data presented in tables should, whenever possible, be color coded to highlight areas of concern.
- Reports should address the three key areas: multi-period, stress scenario cash flow coverage, sufficiency of the liquidity reserve, and diversification. (See examples in Exhibits 4.2 through to 4.4 in this chapter. Also see Exhibits 5.2 through to 5.5 in Chapter 5 for additional examples.)
- Reports of infractions of Board-approved limits, minimums or policy restrictions should be required. (Limits are incorporated in the examples shown in Exhibits 4.2, 4.3, and 4.4.)
- Reports showing activities that are only approaching limits, minimums or policy restrictions are also recommended.
- Reports are generally submitted and reviewed monthly, but should be more frequent whenever market conditions or bank funding appears to be more challenging than normal.

EXHIBIT 4.2 Segment of a cash flow summary report

		March	April	May
Ordinary course of business scenario	actual	1.24:1	1.27:1	1.21:1
	limit	1.20:1	1.20:1	1.20:1
Bank-specific scenario, stress level 1	actual	1.16:1	1.11:1	1.12:1
	limit	1.10:1	1.10:1	1.10:1
Bank-specific scenario, stress level 2	actual	1.02:1	**0.94:1**	1.04:1
	guidance minimum	1.00:1	1.00:1	1.00:1
Numerals are ratios of total forecast cash inflows to forecast outflows.				

EXHIBIT 4.3 Liquidity reserve sufficiency report

	Forecast number of months before negative cash flows consume the stand-by liquidity reserve	Required minimum number of time periods
Normal course of business scenario	24	12
Bank-specific funding scenario		
stress level 1	18	12
stress level 2	7	6
stress level 3	2	4
Systemic-funding scenario		
stress level 1	21	12
stress level 2	11	9
stress level 3	8	6

Reporting for Boards of Directors or Board Committees

- Directors should receive only highly summarized information in standard report packages. Board liquidity risk reports might only include measures that are both straightforward and which simplify the management process for all concerned. *Note*: More detailed information must be presented whenever it helps to explain a key issue, whenever directors ask for more information, and at annual liquidity risk review presentations.
- Reports should be designed to draw attention to limit breaches, other policy infractions, or any other material exceptions. Many banks like to use color to highlight such issues. (See the examples in Exhibits 4.2 and 4.3.)

EXHIBIT 4.4   Reliance on volatile funds

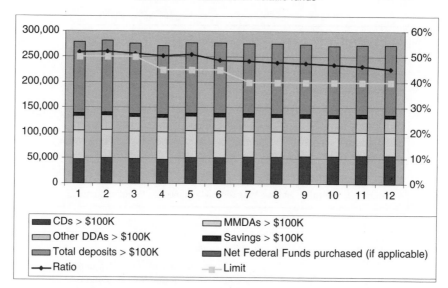

- Explanations and corrective actions (planned or implemented) should be reported for all limit breaches and policy violations.
- Graphs and charts are always preferable to data tables.
- Reports should include summary information on cash flow coverage, the sufficiency of the liquidity reserve, concentrations and exceptions. Supplemental information and/or risk indications should be reported whenever market conditions or bank funding appears to be more challenging than normal.

Supplemental Reports

Bank managers may also wish to employ some or all of the following supplemental reports:

- Reports of other bank activities such as the creation of new products that may impact on liquidity risk and new marketing programs that may impact on liquidity risk. Monitoring bank products with put options is particularly helpful.
- Reports evaluating the assumption dependency of the bank's cash flow projections, the work done to validate assumptions used, and the reasons for major changes in assumptions.
- Reports of national economic conditions such as interest rate trends and forecasts. Reports of economic conditions in the bank's primary trade areas such as unemployment trends and forecasts.
- Reports listing funds obtained through non-relationship, higher cost funding programs such as Internet deposits, and brokered deposits. SR-01-14 recommends that these reports include the amount the rate paid on each instrument, the average rate paid

for each program, information on maturities, and concentration or other limit monitoring and reporting.

MIS Summary

Management reports, like policies and procedures, do not come in standard, one-size-fits-all formats. The descriptions and examples of reports discussed in this chapter are far from exhaustive. The type and amount of information related to liquidity risk depends upon the sophistication of the financial institution's risk measurement system. To some extent, the type and content of management reports varies with the size of the bank, the nature of its activities, and the extent to which bodies such as risk management committees and asset/liability management committees (ALCOs) monitor liquidity risk. Each financial institution must adapt, expand and refine sample reports to fit its specific needs and current situation.

Finally, both the macro and micro scale of MIS requirements are highlighted by the following synopsis:

> MIS should have clearly defined guidelines, policies, practices, standards and procedures for the organization. These should be incorporated in the development, maintenance and use of MIS throughout the institution. MIS is used by all levels of bank staff to monitor various aspects of its overall operations, up to and including, its overall risk management process. Therefore, MIS should be supportive of the institution's longer term strategic goals and objectives. At the other extreme, these everyday financial accounting systems are also used to ensure that basic control is maintained over financial record keeping activities. Since numerous decisions are based on MIS reports, appropriate control procedures must be set up to ensure that the information is correct and relevant.[18]

INTERNAL CONTROLS

Another key component of effective liquidity risk management is appropriate internal controls and audit procedures. Banks should have appropriate systems and controls to deal with both liquidity risk under normal market conditions, and under-stressed or extreme situations resulting from either general market turbulence or firm-specific difficulties.

A robust system of internal controls is critical to the integrity of the liquidity risk management process. Sound risk management practice is founded on strategies, fixed procedures and work flows, measurement methodology, and sound data quality and IT-infrastructure. BIS guidelines state that: "Each bank must have an adequate system of internal controls over its liquidity risk management process. A fundamental component of the internal control system involves regular independent reviews and evaluations of the effectiveness of the system and, where necessary, ensuring that appropriate revisions or enhancements to internal controls are made. The results of such reviews should be available to supervisory authorities."[19]

As a consequence, an effective controlling of liquidity risk, including frequent compliance reviews and regular independent audits is required to:

- establish procedures and policies for liquidity risk management and controlling
- ensure that the liquidity management process follows established strategies and procedures
- independently review data quality and methodologies
- monitor that the liquidity profile is within established limits
- report and, if required, escalate the status of the institution's liquidity profile to senior management and the Board of Managing Directors independently
- test and approve or develop an IT-infrastructure for an efficient liquidity management information system.

In addition, it is a good idea to conduct periodic, independent reviews of the bank's risk management program to ensure its integrity, accuracy, and reasonableness. Items that should be reviewed include: the appropriateness of investment policies, procedures and limits; the appropriateness of the institution's risk measurement system, given the nature, scope and complexity of its activities; and the timeliness, integrity and usefulness of reports to the Board of Directors and senior management.

Internal Control Processes

The controlling process is based on the principle of segregation of duties between a "position managing" unit and a "position monitoring" unit. The task of the liquidity risk controlling unit is not to act as a service center for a liquidity risk managing unit; for example, by taking on the sole responsibility for data quality. In the daily controlling and limit-monitoring process, its task is to independently (from Treasury and business units) assess the validity of a measured liquidity profile and to judge whether on this data basis a limit-monitoring process is possible. Just as liquidity risk managers must know their position to be able to manage the liquidity profile of an institution, liquidity risk controllers must also know the liquidity position of an institution to judge whether the position is within limits or whether he or she is only chasing data problems.

A daily liquidity profile monitoring process could proceed as follows:

- In the first step the liquidity risk controller validates the data quality of the daily feed of the source systems to the liquidity management information system. Steps to be taken are to check on:

- the complete data feed from source systems
- the complete delivery of static data (for example, issue rating, ISIN/CUSIP, maturity, issuer and issuer group) for transactions: the problem could be that, for example, missing rating information leads to wrong judgment on the liquifiability of a security position
- the correct mapping of all transactions to liquidity risk deal-types: problems can arise because off-balance legs of bond/equity financing transactions are not available in general ledger systems. Hence, a cash leg of a repurchase agreement transaction must be recognized as such – and not be treated as a settlement account. The security leg of the transaction must be generated in the liquidity management information system
- new transactions with large volume size: problems could be that for equity positions the quotation in prices or number of shares have been mixed in the system
- implausible changes for each deal-type in the gap profile: problems can arise because in general ledger systems cash and security legs of repurchase agreement/lending or futures transactions are not booked on the same day. At settlement days with large volume sizes (for example, future settlements) this could lead to large swings in internal settlement accounts during the period between spot and value date.

- In the second step the liquidity risk controller validates changes in the gap profile and tracks them back to individual transaction and new businesses. Most changes on the short end of the gap profile will be related to ordinary money markets and short-term funding activities. At the long end of the gap profile, changes will be attributed to new loan business or new capital markets funding by own bond issues.
- After that the liquidity risk controller monitors whether the gap profile is within limits. If limit breaches exist, he or she escalates the breach, together with measures of the liquidity risk manager, to senior management. Since liquidity gap profiles cannot easily be remedied, and since analyzing a limit breach frequently requires in-debt analysis to rule out data problems as a reason of the breach, an escalation process should use a traffic lights system going from yellow to red if the breach is not fixed within a certain time period.
- In the final step the liquidity risk controller reports the gap profile to the liquidity risk managers and requires a sign-off to ensure that the liquidity manager agrees on the position and the liquidity risk profile, and that he or she considers the data quality as adequate for the management and controlling process.

In addition to this daily responsibility of the liquidity profile monitoring there are further duties. These include independent price verification and stripping of funding curves; daily P&L calculation for the liquidity risk manager (fund transfer pricing versus realized funding costs); improvements on policies and methodologies (cash flow mapping, behavioral adjustment); work flows and documentation; testing, approving, and developing systems and infrastructure; and reporting to senior management and Board members.

Key Targets for Internal Controls

A few controls and audit procedures are applicable to all banks. For example, as a general rule, either internal or external auditors should verify compliance with Board-approved policy requirements for liquidity measurement or management. However, most internal controls and audit procedures will vary, based upon the size of the bank, complexity of its business, and the nature of its liquidity risk exposures. For example, in most banks the individuals responsible for managing liquidity risk should not be the same individuals responsible for reporting compliance, but that is an unworkable requirement in the very smallest banks. Most of the suggestions in this section are, therefore, guidance.

An overview of principal internal control categories is provided in the following section.

Validation of Assumptions and Measurement Tools

All prospective measures of liquidity risk require estimates or assumptions about future cash flows. Periodic, independent reviews of those assumptions are an important management control. Similarly, the identified tools for enhancing liquidity, the association of those tools with specific need environments, and the assumptions about the availability of stand-by sources should also be periodically reviewed.

The scope and the frequency of independent assumption and measurement reviews will vary, based upon the size and nature of each bank's liquidity risk exposures. For example, a bank using a simulation model to project liquidity in future scenarios requires a much higher level of model review than a bank using a simple set of reports with relatively few assumptions.

Procedures for Monitoring Compliance with Liquidity Risk Limits and Management Procedures

Compliance with liquidity risk measurement and management policy requirements and procedures should be monitored. Internal control procedures should address the frequency, independence and scope of compliance monitoring. Key risk management requirements include early warning indicators of potentially heightened liquidity risk, compliance with risk limits, compliance with applicable regulations, and compliance with policy requirements. Reviews should be performed regularly. Except in the smallest banks, the reviews should be conducted by persons independent of the funding areas. The bigger and more complex the bank, the more thorough should be the review. Exceptions should be reported to the Board.

Procedures for Monitoring Changes in Liquidity Measurement and Limit Compliance

Internal control procedures should require documentation for all changes in liquidity measurement methods and reporting procedures. Change documentation should note who made the change, when the change was made and the reasons for the change, It is particularly important for internal or external auditors to review whether or not changes resulted in avoiding a policy violation that would have occurred without the change. Internal control procedures should also include a requirement for senior management approval of all changes in liquidity measurement or reporting procedures. Audit procedures should include checks of changes in the way liquidity risk is measured and reported, and checks of the required documentation for those changes.

Other Internal Controls

Banks may wish to consider the additional internal control suggestions listed below:

1. Inexperienced individuals might be required to complete a training program before they are given responsible tasks for liquidity risk measurement or liquidity risk management.
2. Individuals who currently perform responsible tasks in the areas of liquidity risk measurement or liquidity risk management might be given additional training to keep them up-to-date as industry practices, regulations, policies or other constraints are changed.
3. The size of the staff responsible for risk measurement and risk management must be adequate for the size and nature of the risk exposures.
4. The individuals responsible for risk controls must have the resources, including but not limited to data and software, required for them to carry out their responsibilities.
5. Policy exceptions, policy violations or other liquidity risk management failures should be promptly and fully reported to senior managers and to the Board. Periodic management reports should subsequently inform senior managers and directors of all unresolved policy violations, the length of time that violations have been outstanding, and their current status.
6. Periodic management reports in best practice banks also inform senior managers and directors of situations where quantitative policy limits are being approached, even though no policy violations have occurred.

7. Directors should have enough knowledge of liquidity risk, information and training to execute their oversight responsibilities. From time to time, banks might want to provide training for directors.

8. Controls for changes in assumptions used in cash flow projections are an excellent idea. Individuals should not be able to alter assumptions without clear justification that is consistent with ALCO (or liquidity risk committee) strategy. The name of the individual making each change, the date of each change, the nature of each change, and the justification for each change should be documented.

9. Documentation for all assumptions used in cash flow projections should be maintained in a readily accessible, understandable and auditable form. The documentation should include information about how the assumption was generated, the individual(s) who generated the assumption, and the date the assumption was generated.

10. When possible, the individual(s) responsible for auditing reports and policy compliance should be segregated from the individual(s) measuring and monitoring liquidity risk.

11. Differences between book values and market values should be reported to senior managers and directors monthly for all assets considered to be available for quick sale in the event that liquidity is needed.

CONCLUSION

The control and oversight elements explored in this chapter are not independent. Polices and risk limits are shaped by strategies. Oversight occurs at every management link in the risk management chain. Limits, reports and controls are the components of oversight.

Best Practice Features

Best practice liquidity risk control process includes the following steps:

1. Create a liquidity risk-sensitive culture by developing a policy on how liquidity risks are measured, managed and monitored throughout the organization.

2. Define clear-cut responsibilities between Board, senior management, Treasury and risk control.

3. Establish a liquidity risk measurement system and monitor data quality.

4. Develop, together with Treasury, the methodology for cash flow, deal-type mapping and behavioral adjustments.

5. Develop together with Treasury stress scenarios and an appropriate limit system.
6. Monitor limits set by Treasury and report the liquidity status to the Board.
7. Monitor supervisory rules and requirements.
8. Ensure that policies and procedures are continuously updated and improved.

EXHIBIT 4.5   Illustrative flow of responsibility, function, reporting and oversight

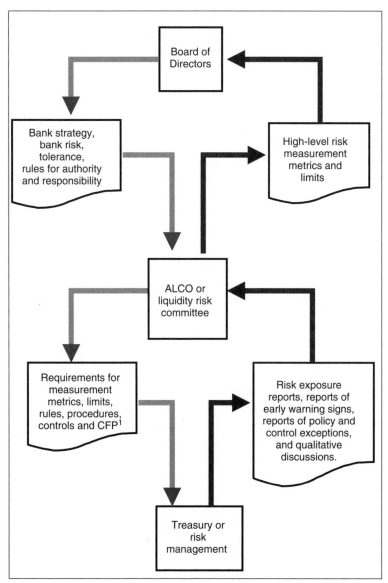

Source: Adapted from a chart created by J. Kimball Hobbs, "Liquidity Policy and Planning Framework", Risk-Waters Liquidity training course, New York, October 20, 2003.
Note: 1 CFP – Contingency funding plan.

Flow of Responsibility, Function, Reporting, and Oversight

Exhibit 4.5 on page 97 illustrates some of the key points discussed in this chapter. The arrows pointing downwards illustrate communication of policy guidance and the delegation of responsibilities. The arrows flowing upwards illustrate reporting and oversight. Risk management guidance – objectives, rules and measurement metrics – become increasingly specific as they flow downwards. Risk reporting becomes more summarized and more qualitative as it flows upwards. At each level, the allocation of authority and responsibility is clear.

Effective liquidity risk management requires strategies, policies, limits, reports and internal controls. Each of these, in turn, requires coordinated efforts of an informed Board, capable management and qualified staff. The tasks are global, but the implementation lies mostly in details.

NOTES

[1] Portions of this section have been adapted from FSA CP 128.

[2] "Principal 1," *Sound Practices for Managing Liquidity in Banking Organizations*, Basel Committee on Banking Supervision, February 2000.

[3] Richard Pattinson, presentation at Incisive Media Liquidity Risk training course, November 2003, London.

[4] "Principal 2," *Sound Practices for Managing Liquidity in Banking Organizations*, Basel Committee on Banking Supervision, February 2000.

[5] "Principal 3," *Sound Practices for Managing Liquidity in Banking Organizations*, Basel Committee on Banking Supervision, February 2000.

[6] J. Kimball Hobbs, "Liquidity Policy and Planning Framework," Riskwaters Liquidity Training Course, New York, October 20, 2003.

[7] Paragraph 18, "Principal 3," *Sound Practices for Managing Liquidity in Banking Organizations*, Basel Committee on Banking Supervision, February 2000.

[8] Private survey conducted by the North American Asset/Liability Management Association.

[9] "Principal 3," *Sound Practices for Managing Liquidity in Banking Organizations*, Basel Committee on Banking Supervision, February 2000.

[10] Private survey conducted by the North American Asset/Liability Management Association.

[11] "Principal 11," *Sound Practices for Managing Liquidity in Banking Organizations*, Basel Committee on Banking Supervision, February 2000.

[12] Paragraph 19, "Principal 3," *Sound Practices for Managing Liquidity in Banking Organizations*, Basel Committee on Banking Supervision, February 2000.

[13] "Joint Agency Advisory on Brokered and Rate Sensitive Deposits," Board of Governors of the Federal Reserve System, Supervision and Regulation issuance SR 01–14, May 31, 2001, page 3.

[14] Paragraph 19, "Principal 3," *Sound Practices for Managing Liquidity in Banking Organizations*, Basel Committee on Banking Supervision, February 2000.

[15] Principal 4, *Sound Practices for Managing Liquidity in Banking Organizations*, Basel Committee on Banking Supervision, February 2000.

[16] "Management Information Systems," *Comptroller's Handbook* series, May 1995, page 2.

[17] *Commercial Bank Examination Manual*, Federal Reserve Board of Governors, Section 2020.1, page 12.

[18] *Commercial Bank Examination Manual*, Federal Reserve Board of Governors, Section 5000.1, page 3.

[19] Principal 12, *Sound Practices for Managing Liquidity in Banking Organizations*, Basel Committee on Banking Supervision, February 2000.

CHAPTER 5

Liquidity Risk Management Strategies and Tactics

Leonard Matz and Peter Neu

T wo fundamental truths shape liquidity risk management. First, we know that we face potentially devastating risks, but that the probability of occurrence for those events is quite small. Second, we know that we simply cannot afford to hold enough liquidity in normal times to survive a worst case problem.

The essence of liquidity risk management is, therefore, reducing liquidity risk to levels deemed acceptable, maintaining the capacity to spot problems quickly and readiness to enhance liquidity promptly as soon as non-normal conditions are observed.

The tools of liquidity risk management are a well-written policy, a comprehensive contingency plan, well-conceived strategies, access to a wide array of management tactics, adequate internal controls and internal audit processes, and relevant stress testing procedures. None of these elements is more or less important than the others. Nor is there any order of precedence. Instead, liquidity risk management involves the coordination of each element in a dynamic process. In this chapter, we will explore liquidity risk strategies and tactics.

While "the capacity to obtain cash when needed" is an accurate definition of *liquidity*, it does not fully articulate the scope of *liquidity management*. At its most basic level, managing liquidity is the process of achieving the following three objectives:

1. *Liquidity management must be prospective.* Historical levels of liquidity are far less important than ensuring that the financial institution has enough cash on hand to meet its future cash flow needs. Like all risks, liquidity risk is prospective. It is the risk that future events produce adverse consequences. Accordingly, backwards looking measurement, like historical ratios, and retrospective management, like plans based upon previous liquidity needs, are of limited value. (In the measurement section

of this chapter, retrospective ratios are considered solely for supplemental reporting of specific risk exposures.) Future funding needs must be estimated. Funding sources (or combinations of several funding sources) must be identified to meet the expected funding needs.

2. *Liquidity management must include provision of a prudent cushion for unanticipated cash flow needs.* Unanticipated liquidity needs can take many forms. Most can be characterized as high probability, but very low severity events. A few can be characterized as very low probability, but high severity events. Maintaining this prudent cushion may be the single most critical aspect of liquidity risk management.

3. *Liquidity management also requires striving to achieve the best possible cost/benefit balance.* Of course, in the event of an extremely severe funding problem, cost is not a factor. In these rare situations, funds are needed at any cost. In all other situations, managers must recognize that even though too little liquidity can kill a bank quickly, too much can kill it slowly. Most, but not all, sources of liquidity cost money.

THE THREE MAJOR CATEGORIES OF LIQUIDITY SOURCES

Liquidity mangers in financial institutions can choose between a number of alternative liquidity sources. In fact, users might identify dozens of alternatives. The simple fact is that all liquidity sources fall into one of three clear groups:

- Cash can be obtained by reducing or liquidating assets kept on hand for this purpose (liquid assets). In other words, cash can be obtained from a liquidity reserve or storehouse on the balance sheet. (Note that "cash on hand" is not listed as a source. Well-managed banks rarely hold much more cash than they require for ongoing operations. Therefore, for a bank that continues in business, cash is a fixed asset.)
- Cash can be borrowed. This is called liability management. Borrowed funds include obvious loans, such as overnight funds purchased and securities sold under agreement to repurchase them (repos). In addition, borrowed funds can include cash obtained from new, interest-sensitive CDs.
- Cash can be obtained from operating cash flows coming into the bank from net interest payments, principal payments from amortizing loans, and investments and net maturities of assets. Managers obtain cash flow liquidity by structuring the timing of cash flows, especially the maturity structure of investment securities, for that purpose.

Each of these three liquidity sources is discussed in the following paragraphs. Some are more useful when liquidity is needed quickly, while others are not available unless the need for liquidity is prolonged. Some are available only for non-acute (low-severity) liquidity needs, while others are not desirable for non-acute liquidity needs. Used in combination, these three groups of liquidity sources meet all of the possible needs.

OVERVIEW OF LIQUIDITY SOURCES

Liquidity sources are probably discussed and written about far more often than liquidity needs. It is not hard to find exhaustive discussions of the potential liquidity provided by various types of investments, loans and deposits. Most of those descriptions of liquidity sources provide help and insight at the transaction level, but less at the institution level. In other words, they tend to provide a lot of value in their evaluations of the liquidity of individual investments, loan portfolios and borrowing practices, but not as much from the perspective of the bank as a whole.

Unfortunately, lists of potential liquidity sources are not by themselves entirely useful to liquidity managers. The fatal weakness here is the assumption that one can evaluate, and even rank, the extent to which an asset provides liquidity or a liability reduces liquidity risk. One can't for the simple reason that any such ranking of available sources in one need scenario is not necessarily the same as the ranking of available sources in a different need scenario.

Several liquidity sources are more available in some circumstances than in others. In fact, liquidity sources that work in some situations may even be completely unavailable in others. The usefulness of a potential source depends very much on the nature of the potential need. The following simple examples of asset and liability liquidity sources illustrate this problem.

First, consider liquidity risk from liabilities. Suppose a bank has an uninsured, unsecured wholesale market borrowing that matures today. In this example, a bank requiring liquidity in the ordinary course of business should have no problem renewing or replacing the maturing borrowing. A bank in the midst of a systemic crisis may or may not have to pay a significantly higher yield to renew or replace the funds – depending upon the nature of the systemic crisis. However, a bank in the midst of a severe bank-specific funding crisis would clearly have difficulty renewing or replacing the maturing borrowing. In fact, it is quite probable that the bank in the midst of a funding crisis would be completely unable to renew or roll over the uninsured, unsecured borrowing. In short, sometimes borrowings are an excellent source of liquidity, but not always.

Next, consider an example of asset-based liquidity available from an Aa-rated, general obligation municipal note that matures in 30 months.

Both a bank requiring liquidity in the ordinary course of business and a bank requiring liquidity for a bank-specific funding crisis would almost certainly consider this security as one of their most liquid assets. For both of those banks, this bond should be salable quickly and with little or no loss. On the other hand, a bank requiring liquidity during the kind of flight to quality experienced in August and September of 1998 would probably find that the municipal bond in this example can be sold quickly only if the bank is willing to take a substantial loss. (During that 1998 experience, market yields for US Treasury securities fell, while yields for intermediate-term, Baa securities actually rose.) In short, sometimes a traded security can be an excellent source of liquidity, but not always. The amount or availability of liquidity often depends to a very large extent upon the circumstances that happen to be applicable.

Liquidity Reserves

Assets that can be readily and reliably sold are variously called liquidity reserves, secondary liquidity reserves, liquidity warehouses or liquidity storehouses. These are almost invariably bank funds invested in securities that are actively traded on capital markets. Because they are actively traded on capital securities markets, investors can reasonably expect that willing buyers will almost always be available (at some price) so that the asset can be sold if liquidity is needed. Since one of the most active securities markets is the secondary market for US Treasury securities, those instruments top most lists for liquid assets.

Liquidity reserves often focus on assets that are both readily marketable and short term – not just on readily marketable assets. Certainly, even the longest term assets can be readily sold in an active secondary market and are therefore liquid. However, the price may not always be attractive and may even be so unattractive that it is a major obstacle to realizing the cash available from the sale of the asset. Shorter term, fixed-rate securities are far less exposed to price volatility. Therefore, a more restrictive definition of liquid assets is those assets that are both readily marketable and short-term assets.

For almost all of the various types of liquidity needs, liquidity reserves are the most reliable source of cash. However, they are not always the most desirable such source. Among other reasons, the lower rates of return earned by those assets makes them less desirable assets to hold. The impact of accounting rules can also reduce the desirability of selling some otherwise marketable securities to obtain liquidity. These are the two main reasons why secondary reserves are not the most desirable sources of liquidity, even though they are often the most reliable sources. The ramifications of this distinction are important.

Since holding short-term, marketable assets as liquidity reserves is not always the most desirable asset management strategy, bank managers tend to minimize their holding of these assets. Asset management strategies that minimize holdings of liquidity reserves are not inherently bad strategies. In fact, to the extent to which they contribute to reliance on a diversified mix of stable liquidity sources, they can contribute to strong liquidity risk management. However, the tension between the requirement for enough liquidity to meet unexpected requirements and the advantages of minimizing holdings of short-term, marketable assets can result in situations where the quantity of liquid assets is smaller than the maximum potential amount of liquidity needed for a crisis. For both of those reasons, liquid assets are an important source of liquidity, but they are rarely the sole source.

Borrowed Funds

Quite a few alternative sources of borrowed funds are available to meet liquidity needs. For short-term, low-severity liquidity requirements, overnight funds purchased are probably the most common type of borrowed funds. Longer term, low-severity funding needs are often met by domestic CDs, Euro time deposits and Euro CDs. Secured deposits and funds borrowed under securities repurchase agreements are also common sources of liquidity and may also be sources available to meet more acute funding needs. Finally, for short-term or the most severe liquidity needs, borrowings from central banks are available.

Liability management tactics for managing liquidity are often very attractive. Sometimes, borrowing funds is the cheapest source of liquidity. Sometimes, mainly for non-severe liquidity needs, borrowing funds is one of the most flexible and most quickly available sources of liquidity.

While unsecured borrowings are not considered reliable sources of funding for acute liquidity needs, secured borrowings may be reliable sources of funds. One major advantage of secured borrowings is that they can enhance the amount of liquidity available from assets. Price or accounting constraints might make it undesirable to sell longer term securities and securities categorized as held to maturity (HTM) when liquidity is needed. However, if one pledges those investment instruments to secure deposits or sells them under agreements to repurchase (another form of secured borrowing), those otherwise illiquid or less liquid assets can provide liquidity. (In this sense, secured borrowings can be seen as either asset-oriented, liquidity reserve tactics, or as liability management liquidity tactics.)

Secured borrowings are often seen as more reliable sources of funds than unsecured borrowings. This is true in some ways. For example, for uninsured deposits a secured depositor may be less likely than an unsecured depositor to pull the funds from the bank in the event of an institution-specific crisis. Similarly, to the extent that uninsured, secured depositors are willing to accept longer term CDs than uninsured, unsecured depositors, the secured borrowing is also a source of liquidity for short-duration funding crises. For example, if secured jumbo CDs have an average maturity of six months, a risk manager might expect that something in the order of half of those funds will not mature and will therefore be likely to remain in the bank during a liquidity crisis that lasts for only two or three months. (In this sense, secured borrowings can be seen as either liability management liquidity tactics or as cash flow liquidity management tactics.) Under both of the two circumstances just described, secured borrowings are less volatile, more reliable sources of funds.

At the same time, experience has shown that it is not always prudent to view even secured borrowings as reliable sources of funds in the event of a funding crisis. There have been situations where funds providers were unwilling to provide repo funding to banks experiencing funding crises, even though the banks were willing to pledge high-quality securities as collateral. One well-known example is the funding crisis of First American in late 1991 and early 1992.

Liquidity managers using liability management strategies to meet some of their liquidity needs must keep the following three issues in mind:

- A realistic understanding of the limits of liabilities as liquidity sources is an absolute imperative. Borrowing can be an excellent source of liquidity under certain circumstances. In the main, these are circumstances in which the bank can project with reasonable certainty that it will either have the cash flow to repay the debt in full when it is due, or that it will be able to renew or replace the maturing debt. Whenever the ability to repay, renew, or replace maturing debt does not seem assured, the reliability of this type of liquidity source is questionable. As a result, borrowings are almost always a very poor source of liquidity in the event of either a bank-wide or a systemic funding crisis. In other words, liability management is a source of liquidity in the ordinary course of business, but may be a source of liquidity risk in the event of an unanticipated funding problem.
- Liability management should be used only to meet actual or potential liquidity requirements when their use is subject to management limits and controls. In large part, this is because the potential for unexpected changes in the bank's ability to repay, renew, or replace debt is a major source of liquidity risk. Even though borrowing to meet non-acute liquidity needs is often reliable, liquidity managers need to control the risk.
- The higher cost of longer term borrowings should not lead managers to overlook the additional liquidity provided by lengthening liability maturities. This is an excellent, if often under-utilized, liquidity management tool.

Operating Cash Flows

One way of viewing the liquidity reserves approach to liquidity management is to view it as the accumulated potential to raise cash in future time periods from the sale of assets. Similarly, one way of viewing the liability management approach to liquidity is to view it as the potential to raise cash by unsecured or secured borrowings in future time periods. Either separately or combined, cash inflows from asset sales and from borrowings can be timed to fund expected cash outflows from new loans, deposit withdrawals, maturing liabilities, and all other expected cash outflows. In addition, either separately or combined, the potential for cash inflows from asset sales and from borrowings can be kept available to meet unexpected cash outflows.

In fact, the distribution of net cash inflows and net cash outflows over future time periods actually constitutes the mismatch liquidity risk faced by banks. That distribution is composed of both the expected cash flows and the unexpected cash flows – the risk of unexpected deviations from the expected distribution pattern. Accordingly, alterations in those cash flow patterns that reduce liquidity risk can constitute some of the most important sources of liquidity.

Once liquidity risk managers begin to see liquidity, whether from asset sales or from borrowings, as a distribution of cash flows over future time periods, they can begin to see liquidity management in a broader context. In this context, measures that defer cash outflows become sources of liquidity. Measures that accelerate actual or potential cash inflows also become sources of liquidity. Thus, a program that reduces the volume of CDs with maturities of one year or less by shifting those deposits to increase the volume of CDs with maturities of one year or more is a liquidity enhancement program. (The higher interest cost of longer term CDs may be a cost of liquidity that the bank is willing to incur to reduce liquidity risk.)

Liquidity is like holding a leaky bucket under a faucet. Liquidity risk managers can measure how much water falls into the bucket in any defined time period – the source of liquidity. They can measure how much water is lost from the leaks in the bucket. The net amount of water retained is their liquidity. Managers can enhance their liquidity by increasing the flow that falls into the bucket or by reducing the flow that leaks out.

Once liquidity is seen as a dynamic process of expected and unexpected cash flows experienced over time, many previously overlooked sources of liquidity become apparent. For example, under traditional bank liquidity definitions, loans are rarely viewed as sources of liquidity. In fact, the notorious loan-to-deposit ratio measures liquidity under the implicit assumption that loans are 100% illiquid. Yet from a cash flow perspective, managers can see that loans can be either sources or uses of liquidity. New loan fundings are uses of liquidity. Net loan repayments are sources of liquidity. Thus, a program that increases holdings of amortizing loans with an offsetting reduction in the growth of non-amortizing loans can be a liquidity enhancement program. Similarly, a program that increases holdings of salable loans with an offsetting reduction in the growth of non-salable loans is a liquidity enhancement program. Salable loans may include loans that can be securitized, such as automobile loans, credit card loans and residential mortgage loans. Salable loans may also include loans with government guaranteed or insured portions that can be readily sold.

In short, liquidity from net cash flows incorporates the liquidity reserves and liability management approaches to liquidity, but incorporates many more potential liquidity sources. At any one time, cash flow sources may be both on-balance sheet and off-balance sheet.

Liquidity risk can be managed from both sides of the balance sheet. Effective liquidity risk management optimizes the use of available liquidity sources on both sides of the balance sheet, while taking into account the risks and costs associated with each type of liquidity source. Effective control of liquidity risk is characterized by a clear-cut segregation of duties between a management unit within Treasury – having the appropriate market access – and an independent risk control unit, which monitors limits, reviews methodologies and does Board reporting. Furthermore, procedures, methodologies (including the definition of stress scenarios), and a contingency plan need to be defined in terms of an institution-wide liquidity and funding policy that is to be approved by the Board.

LIQUIDITY RISK IN DIFFERENT SECTORS OF THE FINANCIAL SERVICES INDUSTRY

Before addressing aspects of liquidity risk management that are common for all sectors of the financial services industry, we will briefly outline specifics and differences of liquidity risk for banks, security houses and insurance firms.

Banks, being highly leveraged, face the risk that wholesale fund providers and depositors will withdraw funds, or do not roll over liabilities as they fall due. As a result they require a certain amount of long-term funding to match their long-term assets in addition to an appropriate reserve of highly liquid securities, which can serve as collateral in case unsecured funding ceases to exist or is sold to meet liability maturities and withdrawals. To measure liquidity risk, banks use cash flow projections, generally under the assumption of going-concern and stressed business conditions, and typically set limits for mismatch gaps in maturity ladder analysis.

Security firms generally fund their assets either unsecured or secured (with a repurchase agreement) in the inter-bank market. They face the risk that the unsecured funding will not be rolled over, and therefore they have to sell their assets at unprofitable market conditions. The magnitude of this risk tends to be higher for firms in this industry because the maturity profile of their liabilities tends to be shorter. To mitigate liquidity risk they hold a certain percentage of their capital in a pool of highly liquid securities that are used as collateral to replace unsecured funding in emergency situations. To measure liquidity risk, security firms compare the collateral value of their unencumbered assets with expected cash and collateral needs from unsecured funding markets.

Insurance firms consider liquidity risk more from an asset/liability cash flow matching point of view. The flow of premiums to the insurer and maturing investments typically contribute to a comfortable liquidity situation. However, insurers face the risk from (1) inadequate technical provisions resulting in uncovered pay-outs; (2) improper management of investments (for example, relying too much on illiquid assets); and (3) insurance risk (for example, catastrophic risk, or options embedded in insurance contracts; for example, triggered by a downgrade); and (4) too strong a mismatch in assets and liabilities. For example, some insurers try to earn a yield pick-up by investing in long-term relatively illiquid assets. This might result in cash flows from assets being received later than required to meet the claims of policyholders. Re-insurers face additional concentration of risk, which might result in a large amount of claims after a catastrophic event.

Insurers' view of mitigating liquidity risk revolves around reducing deviations of actual cash flows from expected cash flows under the assumption of going-concern market conditions. Additionally, they also need to consider holding a liquidity reserve of unencumbered liquid assets and analyze various "what-if" scenarios due to options in their balance sheet. Such options traditionally exist in insurance contracts; for example, surrender options (in some cases at book value, such as after a downgrade of the insurer when trustees act on behalf of large groups of beneficiaries) or options of the policyholder to delay premium payments. In recent years, however, they have become increasingly common in the investment portfolio. Examples are investments with implied short options such as credit-linked notes, in which the insurer is a provider of default protection for a reference asset. Other examples are closeout clauses in derivative contracts (for example, after a downgrade) used for hedging the investment portfolio. In case of asset default the insurer will have to cover the loss and will partly not be repaid its investment. These considerations exemplify how a concentration in assets, customers, and product design can lead to liquidity risk. They explain why rating agencies nowadays incorporate liquidity risk in their overall assessment.

Banks and securities firms are more exposed to short-term cash flow insolvency as they do strong maturity transformations, and rely on volatile funding; for example, wholesale funding and on-demand deposits, which might either not be rolled over or be withdrawn. However, one should note that a large retail funding base provides much more stability even in a funding crisis situation. Insurance companies are less vulnerable to short-term mismatches between the liquidity of assets and liabilities because they receive a steady stream of cash flows from their policyholders and are able to influence the processing speed for claims of the policyholders. As a consequence, banks and securities firms only have a short period to manage a crisis, whereas insurance companies have a longer time frame to recover.

In the banking and securities sector, liquidity risk is often a secondary risk arising due to reputation damages caused by earlier credit, market, or operational risk events. As we observed in Chapter 4, liquidity is a consequential risk. Banks and securities firms manage liquidity risk as a separate risk category by reducing their vulnerability to cash flow mismatches and contingencies under different "what-if" scenarios. Insurance companies, in particular property-casualty insurers, are more vulnerable to liquidity risk caused by catastrophic events – in addition to liquidity risk arising from the investment portfolio. As a consequence, they often consider liquidity risk as a component of insurance or investment risk. Given that catastrophic events are rare, insurance companies focus more on preventing such trigger events than reducing their vulnerability to liquidity risk.

In the following sections we will mainly address generic, sector-independent features for managing and controlling liquidity risk. Due to the greater exposure of banks and security firms to liquidity risk, these two sectors will serve as a model.

LIQUIDITY RISK MANAGEMENT STRATEGIES, TACTICS AND PROCEDURES

An effective liquidity management process is based on established strategies, tactics and procedures, and a solid liquidity measurement and management information system.

Liquidity Risk Management Strategy

The strategic focus of a liquidity management process must encompass the following three requirements:

1. ensuring the institution's ability to generate or obtain cash or a cash equivalent (collateral) in a timely and cost-efficient manner so that obligations can be met as they fall due
2. maintaining market confidence
3. ensuring that profitable business opportunities can be pursued through all market environments for an extended period of time without liquidating assets at undesirable times or raising additional unsecured funding in an unreasonable scale.

In order to meet those requirements, liquidity risk management strategies must address the following questions:

- What risk scenarios does the bank wish to measure, monitor and manage? Capital markets disruption? Payments system disruption? Bank-specific funding crisis?

- What risk exposures concern the bank most? Deposit losses, borrowings, off-balance sheet inflows, off-balance sheet outflows?
- What metrics will be used to measure and monitor liquidity risk? Cash flow projections, measures of stand-by liquidity resources, measures of diversification?
- Under what conditions will liquidity risk be measured and monitored? Short term or long term? Probable stress levels or improbable stress levels?
- What criteria and/or limits will be used to determine whether or not the bank's current level of risk exposure is acceptable or unacceptable?
- If the current risk exposure is not acceptable, how will remediation be addressed and what types of remediation tactics are acceptable?

Well-managed institutions analyze their liquidity profile, ratios, net cumulative outflows and unencumbered securities on a daily basis for a certain time horizon, ranging from 14 days to one year or longer. Short-term funding needs are determined with respect to the current generation of new business and trading positions. Long-term funding needs are reviewed in comparison with strategic business initiatives and in the course of the strategic multi-year planning process. Liquidity management debits or credits (see Chapter 7) funding costs to business units applying an internal fund transfer pricing system that has been established in collaboration with the liquidity risk control unit. The liquidity manager needs not only to analyze the institution's liquidity profile and funding needs under the current market conditions. He or she is also responsible for assessing the impact of adverse market conditions on the institution's business. For doing this, the liquidity manager analyzes the institution's liquidity profile, funding needs and funding access under various "what-if" scenarios. Such scenarios address institution-specific (for example, downgrade, bank-run, loss of access to the unsecured inter-bank market) and systemic crises (for example, the LTCM, decrease in market value of securities used as liquidity reserve, emerging markets crisis, and 9/11).

Based on such an analysis the liquidity manager evaluates whether the current and the forecast liquidity profile of the institution is within an acceptable level compared to the liquidity strategy defined by the Board, or whether additional measures need to be taken.

Liquidity profiles cannot be as quickly changed or turned as the interest rate risk profiles of an institution's balance sheet. Measures taken usually use on-balance sheet instruments like unsecured funding, CP, repurchase agreements, securitization, medium-term notes (MTNs) and bonds. There is no derivative market available for hedging liquidity risk. Committed lines of credit from other banks might indicate wrong security, because, in a crisis of the drawing bank, the committed bank might choose the reputation risk instead of the credit risk and deny the drawdown.

Liquidity Risk Management Tactics

Liquidity risk management tactics fall into four categories:

1. tactics for maintaining a stand-by liquidity reserve
2. other asset management tactics for enhancing liquidity
3. tactics for liability diversification
4. other liability management tactics for reducing liquidity risk.

Each of these four categories is explored in the following subsections:

Tactics for Maintaining a Stand-by Liquidity Reserve

One fundamental point about stand-by liquidity reserves is that liquid assets cannot be considered in isolation. Rather, both the liquid assets and the funding for those assets must be considered together. Exhibit 5.1 illustrates this point. The pair of bars on the left illustrates a bank with a structural liquidity deficit. In response, managers elect to double the quantity of liquid assets. The resulting structure is illustrated by the right-hand pair of bars. Since the bank chose to fund the increase in its liquidity reserve by increasing volatile liabilities, they completely failed to achieve any reduction in their structural liquidity deficit.

The most common tactics for enhancing the stand-by liquidity reserve involve collateral management.

- Manage pledging to avoid unnecessary overuse. Marketable securities are the most reliable sources of stand-by liquidity because they can be sold outright, sold under agreement to repurchase, or pledged to obtain (more stable) secured funding. However, securities already pledged provide no stand-by liquidity at all. The liquidity from those securities has already been "consumed" by the bank.

EXHIBIT 5.1   Change in liquid asset holdings

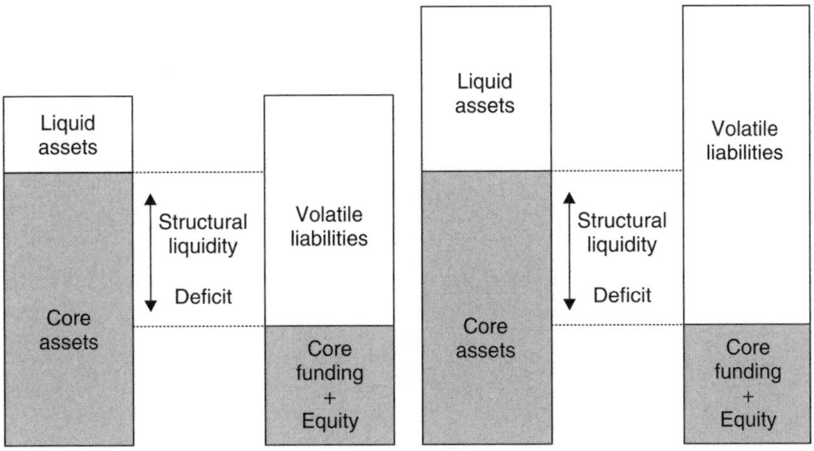

- Stand-by liquidity can be enhanced by monitoring the amount of pledged assets and the amount of the liabilities that they secure. Often, banks fail to reduce the amount of pledged collateral after the volume of funds obtained from a secured counterparty declines.
- Pledging can be managed to use the least readily salable assets acceptable to the counterparty.
- Minimize classification of otherwise marketable securities as "held to maturity." Even though these assets can be repo'd without impairing their accounting treatment, flexibility is reduced because of accounting consequences from outright sales.

Other Asset Management Tactics for Enhancing Liquidity

Asset liquidity beyond liquid securities can be described as the "three S's": syndication, sales and securitization. Given enough time, most bank assets, including fixed assets, can be sold. And, given enough time, most loans can be securitized or syndicated.

Liquidity risk managers need to address some important considerations. For one thing, banks that do not have *recent* experience selling, syndicating or securitizing *very similar* assets, need to allow for more time and expense. Second, banks that sell, securitize or syndicate loans often need to be careful not to diminish the average risk of the remaining assets by selling the highest quality. As one manager noted: "Picking only the low-hanging fruit leaves a very illiquid balance sheet remaining!" Third, banks that model hypothetical, bank-specific crises need to consider that a crisis precipitated by rising loan losses will simultaneously taint the bank's reputation for underwriting and therefore impair its ability to sell loans.

Other tactics include:

- Amortizing assets generate larger cash flows before maturity than non-amortizing assets. A program that increases holdings of amortizing loans with an offsetting reduction in the growth of non-amortizing loans can be a liquidity enhancement program.
- Shorter term investments or loans have final cash flows sooner. Barbell maturity structures for investment securities include, by definition, a large short-term component. Auto loans mature sooner than mortgage loans.
- Asset management strategies, such as laddered maturities for investment securities, can smooth cash flows over time.
- Either separately or in combination, cash inflows from asset sales and from borrowings can be timed to fund expected cash outflows from new loans, deposit withdrawals, maturing liabilities and all other expected cash outflows.
- From time to time, perhaps once a year, liquidity risk managers might rank each major asset type held by the bank from most liquid to least liquid. The percentage of total assets represented by each asset type on the list might also be noted. This ranking should

be understood as a general ordering that is only approximately accurate. A long-term goal for liquidity risk management might then be to shift the mix of assets so that they have more funds invested in assets higher on the ranked list and fewer funds invested in asset types at the bottom of the list.

Tactics for Liability Diversification

The single most important fact to know about diversification is that it is not the panacea it is held out to be. The truth is that diversification can be employed wisely as a strong risk reduction tool or foolishly with the unintended consequence of increasing risk.

The most common and least useful approach to liability diversification is to diversify the number of counterparty names. For example, instead of committed, unsecured lines for overnight funding from two other banks, maintain such arrangements with five or ten other banks. This is not a completely worthless suggestion. The history of liquidity events does include many examples of idiosyncratic responses from counterparties. But it is not a particularly helpful tactic. Wholesale funds providers are brutal arbiters of credit quality. One may take a day or two longer than the others before refusing to extend credit, but that is hardly a source of funding stability.

Diversifying the number of sources for borrowed funds is an effective liquidity risk management tool for a limited number of liquidity risk scenarios. For example, during payments systems disruptions, such as the problems following 9/11, it is helpful to have multiple funds providers in multiple locations.

A far more intelligent approach to liability diversification is to diversify by the type – not the name – of counterparty. This approach is illustrated in Exhibit 5.2 on page 114.

Focusing on diversification by counterparty type, rather than by bank product, is similar but preferable. In reality, almost all institutional funds providers have their own counterparty limits restricting the amount they will provide to any single bank. For those funds providers, it doesn't matter if the bank borrows the money by selling a negotiable CD or in some other form.

Yet even liability diversification by counterparty type is not an automatic benefit. Notice that the largest single category of unsecured liabilities shown in Exhibit 5.2 is retail deposits. Out of the nine types shown, it comprises 25–27% of the totals. Does this concentration pose a heightened level of risk? Not likely. Since retail deposits are more sticky than most other types, that concentration almost certainly reduces risk. A suggestion to improve diversification would, in this example, be counter-productive.

Diversification by counterparty type should focus on ensuring that among the most volatile funding sources, no single counterparty, no group of similar counterparties, and no single market constitutes a concentration. At the same time, concentrations of funds obtained from the

EXHIBIT 5.2   Diversification of unsecured liabilities at Deutsche Bank

External unsecured liabilities by product in € m.

- December 31, 2004: total € 399 billion
- December 31, 2003: total € 357 billion

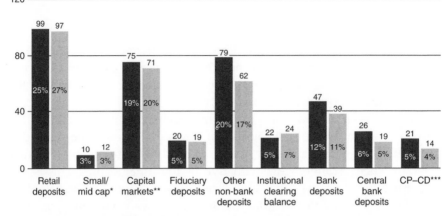

*   Small/mid cap: refers to deposits by small and medium-sized German corporates.
**   Capital markets: harmonization of the definition of capital markets issuances resulted in the exclusion of issuances
      under our X-markets product label.
*** CP–CD: commercial paper/certificates of deposit.

Source: ''Liquidity   Risk,   Funding   Diversification''   Deutsche   Bank,   *Annual   Report
2004*,   http://annualreport.deutschebank.com/2004/ar/riskreport/liquidityrisk.php?-dbiquery=
4%3Adiversification, page 26.

most stable counterparties, types of counterparties, and markets should
be encouraged.

It is also useful to monitor total reliance on the most volatile funding
sources. An example is shown in Exhibit 5.3.

Few, if any, liquidity risk management tactics are more vital than managing the time profile of maturing liabilities. Un-matured time deposits
and borrowings are one of the most stable sources of funding in the event
of a funding problem. Liabilities that do not mature for 90 days or more
are the most stable. Extending liability terms to reduce liquidity risk is one
of the four most important ''best practices'' for liquidity risk management.

Of course, extending liability maturities has a cost. Since yield curves
are almost always positively or upward sloping, rates paid for longer
term funds will almost always be higher than rates paid for shorter term
funds. Just as the case for holding some marketable securities as a liquidity
reserve, this cost must be viewed as part of the insurance cost of liquidity
management. Prudent liquidity risk management requires striking a
balance between the insurance cost and the need for the insurance.

At the same time, liquidity risk managers endeavor to avoid unusually
large amounts of borrowings maturing in any one day or week. The risk
is that the maturity of those borrowings may coincide with infelicitous
market conditions or a decline in the bank's standing in the funds markets.

EXHIBIT 5.3   Forecast trend in large and volatile liability dependency

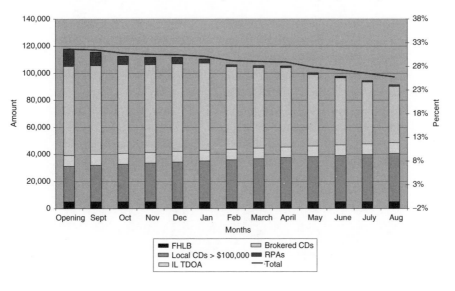

Maturity concentrations in the next one- to three-month quarter should receive prompt attention and remedial action.

Exhibits 5.4 and 5.5 (on page 116) illustrate these points.

Other Liability Management Tactics for Reducing Liquidity Risk

- Emphasizing secured liabilities over unsecured borrowings increases the stickiness of liabilities (as well as reducing funding costs). However, while reducing current liquidity risk, secured borrowings also reduce stand-by liquidity reserves by consuming

EXHIBIT 5.4   An acceptable maturity concentration

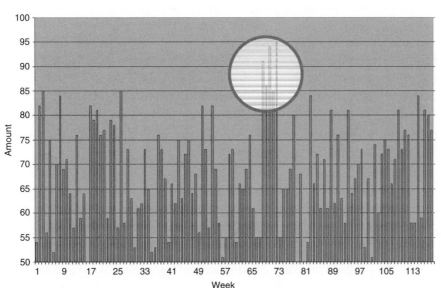

EXHIBIT 5.5 An unacceptable maturity concentration

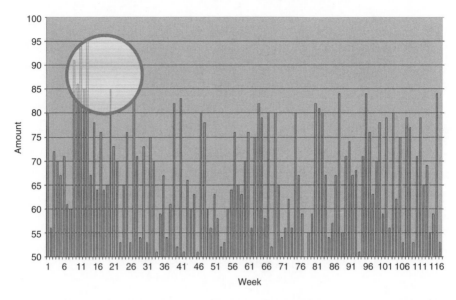

the future liquidity benefit of the collateral. Secured borrowings in normal times reduce the amount of stand-by liquidity available for abnormal conditions.

- Avoid liabilities with put options and/or collateral maintenance requirements tied to the bank's credit worthiness. (Collateral maintenance tied to changes in the market value of the collateral is another matter entirely and cannot be avoided.)

Deposit Retention Programs

Marketing and management tactics known as deposit retention programs can significantly enhance liquidity in two ways. To the extent that they increase deposit holdings and reduce the amount of wholesale market funding the bank uses, they increase liability stickiness and to the extent that they promote the growth of relationship-based deposits as opposed to rate-sensitive deposits, they also increase liability stickiness.

The components of a deposit development and retention program are: a marketing strategy, projections of deposit structure and associated costs, and a formula for comparing results against projections.

To structure a deposit program properly, bank management must consider many factors, some of which include:

1. the composition of the market-area economic base
2. the ability to employ deposits profitably
3. the adequacy of current operations (staffing and systems), and the location and size of banking quarters relative to its volume of business

4. the degree of competition from banks and non-bank financial institutions, and their programs to attract deposit customers
5. the effects of the national economy, and the monetary and fiscal policies of the government on the bank's service area.

The bank's size and the composition of its market determine how formal its deposit program should be. After a bank develops its deposit program, management must continue to monitor the above factors and correlate any findings to determine if adjustments are needed. The long-term success of any deposit program relates directly to the ability of management to make adjustments at the earliest possible time.

Market Access Testing

One facet of market liquidity risk is market access. This is an important element for complex banks and banks that are net purchasers of funds. It is also an important element for banks that make markets in over-the-counter derivatives, or banks that dynamically hedge their positions. Both require constant access to financial markets, and that need may increase in times of market stress.

Regular testing of market access is a common but not entirely useful practice. Some bank liquidity risk managers borrow from each counterparty that has granted the bank a committed borrowing facility. Similarly, the ability to conduct other capital transactions is also tested by periodic transactions. These tests are often done monthly. The inherent weakness of market access tests is that the tests are performed under benign market conditions while the real risk is market access under stressed market conditions. Past experiences indicate that even contractual commitments may not be honored under stressed market conditions. The sole benefit of market access testing is that it helps keep contact information, counterparty communications and procedures up to date.

INTRA-DAY LIQUIDITY RISK MANAGEMENT

The need to consider intra-day calls on liquidity also became an important issue recently. This subject is particularly related to transaction banking and settlement systems.

Questions raised in this context are:

1. Can we fulfill our payment obligations at any time throughout the day?
2. Can we reduce posted collateral?
3. Can we know what a sufficient amount of collateral is?

Intra-day liquidity risk is closely related to operational risk, as it might be caused by system failures in the payment system.

Banks manage intra-day needs for liquidity by increasing the efficiency of their usage of collateral for settlement transactions. This is done by:

1. monitoring real-time currencies, channels, payments, positions, advice and reservations
2. forecasting precise real-time balances for real-time gross settlement (RTGS) and netting channels on one consolidated platform
3. including external channel information from central banks and/or ancillary (netting-/security settlement-) systems
4. matching debit/credit-advice vs debits/credits
5. scheduling outgoing debit payments according to various limits (bi- and multilateral), priorities, algorithms (next best fit, largest first, smallest first)
6. managing currencies, channels and debit payments (start, stop, change priority, change time, change channel/reroute including notification of ledger, and so on)
7. balancing channel positions by automated start-of-day and end-of-day procedures (that is, liquidity transfer)
8. analyzing cash flows and liquidity consumption.

For this, historical cash flows and assumptions on future behavior of other market participants depending on certain market conditions are applied.

The goal is to allow real-time liquidity management ensuring solvency at any time in any channel and any currency, to provide transparency on cash flows and liquidity consumption, to reduce collateral and funding costs without increasing liquidity risk, to improve operational reliance, and so on.

A LIQUIDITY MANAGEMENT PROCESS

Before closing this chapter we will summarize the main steps of a proper liquidity risk management and control process.

It is prudent for liquidity managers to take the following steps:

1. Evaluate the types of environments in which liquidity might be required. We recommend that small banks use three: an ordinary course of business, seasonal or cyclical environment in which going-concern market conditions prevail; a bank-specific (name) crisis; and a systemic crisis. Large banks should use more. For example, one multinational bank defines the following five liquidity scenarios: a market disruption (this is one type of systemic problem), a national macroeconomic disruption (this is another kind of systemic problem), a banking industry-wide disruption, a bank-specific crisis, and normal operating liquidity. Liquidity exposure can stem from both internally

(institution-specific) and externally generated factors. The Federal Reserve Board of Governors describe geographic liquidity risk (for example, premiums required on deposits at many Texas banks in the late 1980s), systemic (for example, the adverse effects upon several large banks caused by the near-failure of Continental Illinois Bank in 1984), instrument-specific (for example, the collapse of the Perpetual Floating Rate Note market in 1986), and internal liquidity risk related largely to the perception of an institution in its various markets: local, regional, national or international.

2. Evaluate the type and size of liquidity needs for each defined environment. For example, in the market disruption scenario, it is unlikely that insured deposits will decline, while in the bank-specific crisis scenario, it is quite likely that bank-insured deposits will be withdrawn. Similarly, in the market disruption scenario, backup lines of credit may have to be funded, but in the normal operating liquidity scenario, backup lines are unlikely to be drawn upon.

3. Evaluate the type and size of liquidity sources for each defined environment. For example, in a market disruption scenario, sales of all but the highest quality, most actively traded types of securities, may only be executed at very unfavorable prices. On the other hand, during a bank-specific name crisis, almost all investment instruments should be readily marketable.

4. Choose the time frame that you feel is most appropriate. Some banks choose to focus on seven and 30 days' liquidity requirements. Experiences of banks in funding crises, however, indicate that 90 days is often necessary. Some crises, such as Southeast Bank and the Bank of New England, last for a year.

5. Determine the maximum amount of liquidity that will be required from each identified source for all of the defined environments. For example, the maximum amount of federal overnight funds borrowed that the bank may want to have available probably comes from the day-to-day or operating liquidity scenario, while the maximum amount of Treasury securities to be held but not pledged will probably come from the bank-specific crisis scenario.

6. Decide how much of the maximum will be held. The best managed banks will probably want to come to this decision in the context of specifically defined environment levels or stages. Crisis stages are often defined in liquidity contingency plans and will be discussed in Chapter 6. For example, under level one, the bank might require at least 50% of the defined maximums; under level two, it might require 75%, and so on. Alternatively, a bank might say that under level one conditions it needs liquidity to

survive a seven-day crisis, but in level two it wants enough for 60 days.

7. Do not focus solely on how much liquidity reserve you want to hold. Evaluate the size of your target liquidity reserve in light of how quickly you will be able to implement contingency plans to obtain new funds.

8. Select an appropriate mix of liquidity tactics to achieve the minimum desired level of liquidity. A balance must be found between finding the lowest cost sources, the most reliable sources, and a diversified mix.

9. Estimate and then acquire an extra quantity of liquidity to serve as a prudent cushion.

10. Take advantage of opportune times to build liquidity when it is cheap or readily available. A market-savvy manager can choose when the cost of carry (the cost of shortening assets or lengthening liabilities) is less than it usually is, and then choose to increase the amount of liquidity from that particularly attractive source at that particularly attractive time.

CONCLUSION: LIQUIDITY RISK MANAGEMENT IS A THREE-LEGGED STOOL

As we have seen, there are a large number of liquidity risk management tactics. Near the beginning of this chapter, we grouped potential tactics based on three targets: liquidity reserves, borrowings and operating cash flows. You may find it more helpful to group these based on the following strategies:

1. Maintain sufficient structural liquidity cushions. Manage forecast cash inflows and outflows in each time bucket, in each scenario, and in each stress level.

2. Reduce contingent liquidity risk to the extent that is practical.
   - Manage potential vulnerabilities such as funding concentrations.
   - Focus on stability, not just the cost, of funding sources.
   - Extend liability terms to reduce liquidity risk.

3. Always maintain the capacity to turn on cash-flow waterfalls from the liquidation of reserves to remedial actions.
   - Always keep some asset liquidity reserves. This is the insurance cost of liquidity management.
   - Be prepared to enhance liquidity quickly at the first signs of increased potential need. But recognize that you cannot and do not want to hold enough for a catastrophe.

All three legs of the stool require a well-trained staff and solid MIS capabilities.

CHAPTER 6

Contingency Planning

Leonard Matz

INTRODUCTION

T he single most important observation about liquidity risk management may be the simple fact that most liquidity risk managers devote
most of their time and attention to day-to-day funding, risk measurement
and compliance tasks. But the really threatening risk lies elsewhere. The
really threatening aspects of liquidity risk lie in the very low probability
but very high severity potential perils. Exhibit 6.1 shows a stylized distribution of the probabilities and severities for liquidity risk threats. Risk
managers "live" in the bottom right quadrant, but get gray hair from
worrying about the top left quadrant.

As a group, all potentially low-probability, but high-severity liquidity
threats comprise the contingent component of liquidity risk. Contingency

EXHIBIT 6.1 Distribution of probability and severity

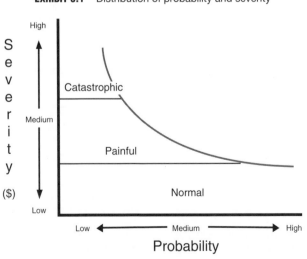

liquidity risk, as we noted in Chapter 1, is the risk that future circumstances may require a significantly larger amount of cash than the bank projects it will need. In other words, contingency liquidity risk is the risk of not having sufficient funds to meet sudden and unexpected short-term obligations.

Unexpected obligations can arise due to unusual deviations in timing of cash flows (*term or mismatch liquidity risk*); for example, non-contractual prolongation of loans. They may also arise from unexpected draws on committed loan facilities or deposit withdrawals (*call liquidity risk*). At the same time, banks are also at risk from unexpected reductions in the availability of cash. Exhibit 6.2 outlines these elements of contingent liquidity risk.

Our knowledge of these contingent cash flows is imprecise. We know that unexpected cash flows result from both endogenous and exogenous factors. The four principal endogenous sources are:

- the bank's estimates of how much liquidity it needs may be too low
- the bank's estimates of how much liquidity it can obtain when needed may be too low
- the bank's estimates of the likelihood of some sort of above-normal liquidity need environment may be too low

EXHIBIT 6.2   Sources of contingent liquidity risk

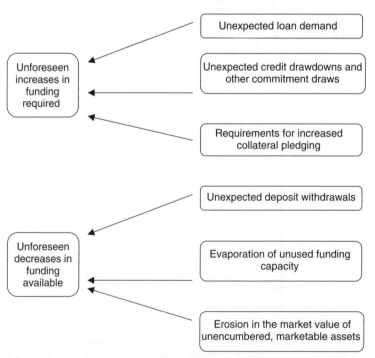

Source: Adapted from a slide created by Werner D'Haese, "Liquidity Contingency Plan: A Case Study at Fortis", Fortis Central Risk Management, ALM Europe, London, October 2005.

- weak management of credit or operations risk that may trigger a liquidity problem.

Exogenous factors include every potential source for a systemic problem (for example, payment systems disruption, capital markets disruption, credit crunch and other examples shown in Exhibit 3.2.) As recently as 2003, a US thrift institution endured a run resulting from rumors spread through its depositors.

Specific information is limited to informed conjecture. We lack advance knowledge of when a low-probability/high-severity threat may materialize. We can't reliably forecast the type of scenario – the shape of that risk. And it is difficult, at best, to know much about either the probability or the severity.

Contingency planning must be driven by a healthy respect for what we cannot know. As the famous economist John Kenneth Galbraith observed: "We have two classes of forecasters: Those who don't know . . . And those who don't know they don't know."[1] After a severe funding crisis that led to the failure of a US regional bank, a senior manger observed that scenarios will be wrong, priorities will be wrong – but advance planning is still invaluable.[2]

Contingency planning, then, is nothing more than a combination of early warning procedures and advance preparation for potential high-severity/low-probability liquidity perils we understand in general, but cannot understand specifically. In the unlikely event of a funding crisis, good contingency planning makes the difference between being in control or reacting to events leading to a downward spiral.

Underlying Risk Characteristics Define the Need for CFPs

The need for robust contingency funding plans (CFPs) is driven by three underlying truths:

- Financial institutions can never avoid liquidity risk. Serving as liquidity intermediaries is one of the main ways that banks add value to the economy. Most contingent liquidity risk is created from the liquidity intermediation function.
- Financial institutions can do little to hedge liquidity risk. Some contingent lending arrangements exist. But only a few remain in place in the event that the borrowing bank's risk increases.
- Most importantly, no financial institution can afford to hold enough liquidity to survive a severe or prolonged funding crisis. Liquidity mismatches are simply too big. Risk managers can't justify the cost of holding a large enough quantity of immediately available liquidity to cover the least likely threats. Yet, since the least likely threats can have devastating consequences, risk managers can't ignore them. From this point of view, contingency planning can

be defined as the bridge between the liquidity the bank chooses to hold and the maximum it might need.

Underlying Risk Characteristics Define the Structure for CFPs

The structure for robust CFPs reflects the way scenarios unfold. CFPs should reflect the fact that funding crises almost always progress in stages. Sometimes the entire progression can be condensed into a very short time period. For example, the final collapse of the Continental Illinois Bank spanned about one week. Sometimes the entire progression can span a year or longer. For example, the Bank of New England failure spanned about 13 months.

As an aside, it is interesting to consider how various national regulators address the duration of potential liquidity threats. In the United Kingdom, the FSA requires banks to report cash flows out to six months, but sets guidelines only for the sight to eight days and sight to one-month time bands.[3] In the United States, the Federal Reserve suggests seven-, 10-, 15-, 30-, 45-, 60-, and 90-day time intervals.[4] More usefully, the BIS guidelines suggest that banks less dependent on short-term money markets look one to three months ahead, while banks dependent on short-term funding only look out to five days.[5]

Note that the unfolding of a funding crisis is often more critical than its duration. The significance of crisis stages arises from the fact that some remedial actions that may be available to funding managers in the early stage of a funding problem may not be available if the problem progresses to a more severe stage. For example, it may be possible to obtained new unsecured funds when experiencing only minor funding problems, new secured funds in an intermediate stage, but no new funds from any source except the Central Bank if the problem becomes grave.

Liquidity contingency planning can benefit from the recognition of two important consequences of the progression phenomena. First, because it is almost impossible to enhance liquidity in the late stages of a crisis, it is important to identify potential problems as early as possible. Second, for the same reason, it is also important to have advance preparations to enhance liquidity quickly.

Accordingly, a major component of liquidity risk management is *being prepared to enhance liquidity quickly at the first signs of increased potential need*. This is one of the most important "best practices" for liquidity risk management. A comprehensive liquidity risk contingency plan is the tool required to maintain that capacity to quickly enhance liquidity.

Key Facts About Stand-by Liquidity and Tactics for Enhancing Liquidity

Beware of overconfidence in market access. Some bankers equate contingent liquidity risk management with market access. They confidently rely on potential access to large quantities of new funds – mainly from their existing counterparties. Sadly, experience shows that those counterparties are very sensitive to bad news and quickly disappear at the first sign of bank-specific funding problems. They do not linger to take prisoners. In some previous situations, capital markets' counterparties have even reneged on contractual obligations in the apparent belief that the risk of being sued by the bank if it survives is less than the risk of losing their money. (These people are not evil. They are simply market professionals with a duty to protect the money they invest for others.) Relying on market access is only logical in normal or mildly disturbed funding conditions.

Do not confuse price with availability. More than a few bankers hold to a critical misconception about contingent or stand-by liquidity sources. The misconception is a belief – often strongly expressed – that obtaining liquidity is just a matter of cost. In other words, no matter how much funding is required, all one has to do is keep raising the price one is willing to pay until counterparties are willing to provide the required amount. Unquestionably, viewing stand-by liquidity as nothing more than a question of cost is valid for very minor funding threats. This is especially the case for mild systemic problems such as interest rate spikes and recessions. But it is quite invalid for more distressed funding environments. Unsecured funds are unavailable in more distressed environments and secured funds are only available until you consume all of your collateral.

In developing a contingency plan, prudent bankers assume that unsecured funding sources are only available under almost benign conditions. Instead, most banks rely on a pool of unencumbered highly liquid securities, which they can either sell or pledge to obtain secured funding during a crisis.

As we observed earlier, a typical bank-specific funding problem progresses from access to funds at a higher cost, to access to secured funds only. Thus managing the bank's holdings of unencumbered, marketable assets ends up being the final determinate between survival and failure. No matter how much you may be willing to pay for new funds, when you have consumed or sold all of your collateral you are pretty much out of options.

Problem Recognition in the Real World

Wasted time, efforts, and opportunities. That is how an executive summed up his experience of managing a funding crisis without a good CFP. What went wrong? In this case, too much time spent in meetings during the first days of the problem, pressure to develop responses under fire, uncertainty about which actions to take first, and being reactive in too may situations. In a very real sense, a robust CFP serves as a partial shield inhibiting sub-optimal decision making.

Recognizing the symptoms isn't hard. Believing them is the problem. "We spent more time coming up with counter arguments – strong regional economy, well-diversified loan portfolios, and so on – rather than considering what if [the symptoms] were right."[6] Other practitioners who have lived through similar experiences tell similar tales. Optimists say that it is just human nature to "look on the bright side." Cynics call it "burying your head in the sand." However you describe it, experience warns us that the first reaction of most managers is to minimize the potential severity of a problem or to assume that it will go away quickly. This is why the triggers discussed later in this chapter are essential components of a robust CFP.

Generating action plans is a lot easier when you are not "under fire." First, it is more productive to identify and consider alternatives when there is no time pressure. Second, evaluating potential action plans under benign conditions avoids the blame assigning and blame dodging that may take place after a problem materializes. This is why the remedial actions discussed later in this chapter are essential components of a robust CFP. Of course, evaluating potential actions under benign conditions lacks focus. We can't know what sort of problem to focus our planning on before a problem materializes. That is why we describe the remedial actions in a CFP as a menu of choices rather than a recipe for responding. If you eventually do come "under fire," it is far better to select from a list than to start from scratch.

Inter-connected Responsibility Flows between Contingency Funding Plans and Liquidity Policies

The CFP cannot stand alone. It must be connected to the bank's liquidity policy in two ways. First, the liquidity policy should not only require a CFP, but it should include general requirements for its basic elements. Typically, the policy will require the identification of both crisis warning indicators and potential action plans without specifying details. Most importantly, the liquidity policy should include a provision that clearly specifies the person or persons authorized to declare that the bank's contingency funding plan is activated.

General Requirements for a CFP

A robust CFP provides bank managers with carefully considered, well-organized action plans for avoiding, minimizing or managing potential funding threats. To achieve that goal, all contingency funding plans must address the following issues.

1. Different kinds of crises require different preparation. Major sources of liquidity are less available or unavailable in some types

of crises. Consequently, it is appropriate that the contingency plan includes separate actions for different need environments.

2. A good early warning system is an essential component. Since enhancing liquidity is nearly impossible after the early stages of a problem, prompt responses are essential. As the BIS observes: "In particular, the first days in any liquidity problem are crucial to maintaining stability."[7]

3. Advance planning is an essential component. Measures and responsibilities to handle a liquidity crisis need to be defined before a crisis situation occurs. Contingency plans should include specific guidance on actions that the bank will take if certain hypothetical events occur. Indeed, this is the main benefit of having a contingency plan. Plans that merely describe crisis management objectives or that only outline general courses of conduct in the event of a crisis may fail to achieve the primary objective of contingency plans. When a crisis hits, busy and stressed managers may not think as clearly or as comprehensively as those same managers can think in calm contingency planning.

4. A contingency plan cannot be a recipe, even though plans must include specific guidance. Instead, it must be a menu of alternative scenarios with a choice of recipes that can be selected to respond to the particular situation at hand. Risk managers cannot predict in advance the exact causes, duration, or seriousness of a liquidity crisis. Providing well thought out alternative actions in advance is essential. Proscribing those actions is an unacceptably inflexible idea.

5. Previous experiences should not be allowed to overly influence contingency planning. The perils that affected other banks are one influence. In the 1982 to 1992 period, bank-specific funding crises were the main threat, while in the years from 1992 through to 1999, a systemic credit crunch and a flight to quality were more influential. After September 11, 2001, the potential for a payment system disruption became the focus of planning. Future crises may not look much like the most recent historical crises. Therefore, contingency plans should not overly weight the most recent scenarios.

6. A careful balance is required for the level of detail for the identification of early warning signals, the assignments of crisis management responsibilities, and the various alternative courses of action. On the one hand, the plan should include enough detail so that the bank can respond early, quickly and effectively to deteriorating liquidity conditions. On the other hand, too much detail can impede decision making. The contingency plan is a formally approved document, and therefore it is not easily changed, and it must be complied with. Details of how liquidity-enhancement measures will be implemented are likely to change – especially

if the actual crisis conditions do not exactly match one of the need environments anticipated in the plan. In short, flexibility, room to maneuver, is just as important as detailed instructions. Once details are locked into a Board-approved plan, the bank's managers lose some of the flexibility they might need to deal with a crisis. Furthermore, it is more cumbersome to update the plan as conditions change. One good idea is to have the Board approve a short, summary contingency plan that leaves most of the details to a plan appendix that can be developed and maintained by senior managers.

7. The contingency funding plan should be a living plan. It should be periodically reevaluated in light of changes in both internal and external conditions. For example, a bank that is entirely funded by retail deposits and a net seller of fed funds may, through growth or acquisitions, become partially dependent on wholesale market funding. Internal changes such as these must be reflected by changes in the contingency funding plan. Similarly, external developments such as the 1998 flight to quality should prompt examinations of the plan. For example, one lesson learned in 1998 was how quickly the market for asset securitizations dried up. Thus, in the months following that event, a contingency plan that contemplated asset securitizations as a source of funds in a systemic crisis might have been revised to de-emphasize that source of funding.

8. The contingency plan should be directly or indirectly coordinated with all of the bank's risk monitoring and risk management activities – especially credit risk. Liquidity management is closely tied to risk management throughout the bank. Liquidity risk managers cannot predict a loss of confidence, nor can they predict its severity or duration. Instead, they should monitor the most likely trip wires.

9. Banks that obtain funding in multiple currencies should create separate contingency plans for the funds' sources and uses in each currency. Under normal circumstances, the cost of raising funds in one currency to meet needs in another currency is usually small. In fact, the cost of funds in one currency may be low enough to represent a cost saving, even after exchange costs. However, when markets are stressed or when the bank's credit rating is under pressure, it can suddenly become much more difficult to accomplish funds transfers between currencies.

10. Banks that are part of organizations that have insurance, real estate or other lines of business should monitor insurance, real estate or other markets in addition to financial markets. Many years ago, a large New York City bank had its name on a real estate investment trust (REIT) that the bank sponsored but did not guarantee. When the REIT experienced problems, the

bank had to help it out despite the lack of a legal obligation to do so. *Counterparty confidence attaches the firm's name – not to its legal structure.*

11. CFPs for banks with subsidiaries, holding companies or other affiliates must also address critically important questions about consolidated and unconsolidated CFP elements.

- Measuring and monitoring liquidity risk should always be done at the top, fully consolidated level. As we just observed in a slightly different context, counterparty confidence attaches to the firm's name – not to its legal structure. A fully consolidated perspective is particularly important for the triggers discussed later in this chapter. Of course, this priority for global reporting does not diminish the importance of legal entity reporting.

- At the same time, potential funding disturbances must be managed by legal entities. Pre-crisis planning, especially the identification and development of potential remedial actions, should be formulated separately for each legal entity under the umbrella of a coordinated, firm-wide plan.

- The CFP must also recognize constraints imposed by the firm's legal structure on the up-streaming funds to parent companies, down-streaming funds to subsidiaries, and cross-streaming funds to other affiliates. This is particularly important for the remedial actions discussed later in this chapter. Pre-crisis planning should include legal agreements between affiliates that clearly authorize the specific types of transfers permitted by law or bank regulations.

SPECIFIC REQUIREMENTS FOR A CFP

The scaffolding for a robust contingency funding plan is constructed with the following components:

Triggers

One of the most important elements in an effective contingency plan is the identification of triggers. Triggers are specific early warning signs for each stage in a liquidity crisis. They are selected in advance. They are described in the contingency plan.

A "best practice" CFP should specify a minimum number of triggers that define when the liquidity environment is no longer normal. For example, the CFP might state that if four out of six triggers are tripped, the CFP is automatically activated. Instead of wasting precious time debating whether or not the liquidity environment has become non-normal, the "tripping" of the predefined triggers automatically shifts management's attention to potential remedial actions.

Note: We recommend employing both quantitative and qualitative triggers. The quantitative triggers help avoid some of the problem recognition problems discussed earlier. The qualitative triggers permit managers to exercise judgment. The absence of quantitative trigger breaches does not necessarily mean that liquidity risk exposures are normal. The tripping of a few quantitative triggers, conversely, should lead to a required meeting and risk review, but does not necessarily mean that liquidity risks are elevated.

Also, notice that ratings downgrades are not mentioned in the first two groups of triggers listed below. They are only discussed in the third group. *Ratings downgrades are lagging indicators.* Instead of watching for downgrades, watch for the procurers of downgrades.

The following events may be considered triggers that identify the onset of a need for more prudent liquidity:

- Example triggers for non-normal funding conditions characterized by no current funding problems, but a heightened level of bank specific liquidity risk.
  - *Increase in the spread paid for uninsured deposits, borrowed funds or asset securitizations.* This is one of the two most widely used triggers at large banks. The spread to monitor is the difference between the funding cost paid by the bank and the funding cost paid by the bank's peers. Actually, it is the trend, rather than the current spread, that is important. Spreads on any one-day are influenced by many factors. Tracking the trend in the cost of funds spread over a short time interval, for example a five-day moving average, is preferable. See Exhibit 6.3 for an example.

EXHIBIT 6.3   Trend in asset swap spreads for six German banks (April 2002 to October 2004)

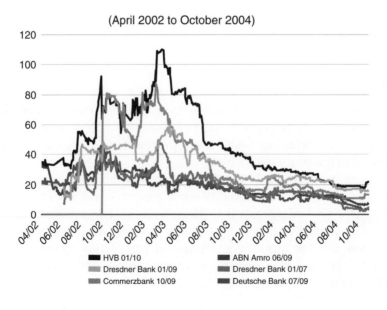

(April 2002 to October 2004)

■ HVB 01/10   ■ ABN Amro 06/09
▨ Dresdner Bank 01/09   ▨ Dresdner Bank 01/07
▨ Commerzbank 10/09   ■ Deutsche Bank 07/09

- *Reductions in tenors lenders are willing to accept.* For example, if the bank asks for a 90-day borrowing and the lender comes back with an offer to lend only overnight.
- *A violation of a liquidity risk limit or multiple measures of liquidity risk approaching limits.*
- *A decline in earnings.* Obviously, an unexpected decline in earnings is not always merely the first in a series. But remember that liquidity is not just having enough funds – it's the perception of having enough funds. Whether or not an earnings decline is really serious, its potential impact on the confidence of funds providers may be serious.
- *An increase in loan delinquency.* Increases in consumer loan delinquency are usually a good leading indicator – particularly if the bank's delinquent loan levels are larger or growing faster than those of its peers. However, business loan delinquency is a less-reliable indicator. Commercial loans tend not to be categorized as problems until the problems are unmistakable.
- *A decline in the bank's stock price relative to the change in stock prices for the bank's peers.* Research has shown that this is an excellent early warning indicator. Since stock prices on any one-day are influenced by many factors, we recommend tracking the price trend over short intervals; for example, a five-day moving average.
- *Significant asset growth or acquisitions.* This can be an excellent, if often underestimated, early indicator of future problems. If the bank's loan assets are growing faster than the rate of growth for the general economy, the bank can be achieving that growth rate only by increasing its market share. But increasing market share requires taking unfamiliar borrowers away from competitors who know those borrowers better. In short, this is well understood to be a high-risk activity.
- *Legal, regulatory or tax changes that either increase risks or make risk management more difficult.*
- Example triggers for non-normal funding conditions characterized by no current funding problems, but a heightened level of systemic liquidity risk.
  - *Large increase in prevailing rates for new liabilities obtained from brokers, via the Internet or directly from capital markets lenders.*
  - *Significant change in the currency exchange rate.* This is an excellent early warning indicator for banks in countries heavily dependent upon either imports or exports.
  - *A strong or unexpected central bank shift from an accommodative to a restrictive monetary policy.*
  - *Changes in unemployment rates or other macroeconomic indicators to levels associated with recessions.*

- *Loss of funds-provider confidence in a major capital markets participant that threatens to spread to other capital markets participants.*
- *A violation of a liquidity risk limit or multiple measures of liquidity risk-approaching limits.*
- *Indications of a potential peak in an asset bubble.* Examples might be "irrational exuberance," speculative trading approaching levels that might be characterized as frenzied, and widespread reductions in or waivers of business standards normally deemed prudent.
- *Political interference in either bank lending or banking supervision.*

• Example triggers for non-normal funding conditions characterized by a mildly abnormal bank-specific funding environment that may deteriorate further.

- *An increase in the level of either non-performing loans or loan losses.* Bank of New England's illiquidity resulted from the reactions of funds providers after the bank's real estate losses became public knowledge. For Continental Illinois, it started with oil and gas loans. Other examples can be cited. Like problem loan levels, however, loan losses tend to be a lagging indicator and therefore not the best early warning trigger.
- *More severe, multiple or uncorrected violations of liquidity risk limits.*
- *A downgrading* by a nationally recognized statistical rating organization *(NRSRO).* This is one of the two most widely used triggers in the contingency plans for large banks. It is a logical trigger because many wholesale market funds providers base their credit decisions on published ratings. Therefore, as a bank's ratings decline, funds providers reduce the amount of funds they are willing to supply, or completely drop the bank from their approved lists. However, ratings should never be the only trigger. Nor should a ratings downgrade be considered to be an early warning trigger. Rating agencies are notoriously slow to react to deteriorating credit quality. By the time a bank's rating falls, the liquidity risk manager may not have enough time to undertake liquidity enhancement measures.
- *Pressure to buy back bank obligations trading in secondary markets.*
- *Customers who normally pay for bank services by maintaining balances shift to paying fees.*
- *Turndowns of borrowing requests.* Turndowns are not uncommon. For example, a particular seller may not necessarily be interested in selling on every single day of the year. But the trend in turndowns is important. If more funds providers begin declining to lend, or if the amounts that they are willing to lend seem to be declining, it may be a sign of deteriorating confidence.
- *Requests for collateral or smaller transaction sizes from lenders previously willing to provide unsecured funds or larger transaction amounts.*

- Example triggers for non-normal funding conditions characterized by a mildly abnormal systemic funding environment that may deteriorate further.
  - *Difficulty selling securities that are normally liquid.*
  - *Indications of a "credit crunch." For example, system-wide increases in loan demand or reduced availability of inter-bank funds.*
  - *Flight to quality in capital markets.*
  - *Spread of a loss of funds-provider confidence from one or more major capital markets participants to numerous other capital markets participants.*
  - *A payment systems disruption that slows or confuses funds transfers between financial institutions.*
  - *A significant increase in the severity and/or duration of a recession.*
  - *More severe, multiple or uncorrected violations of liquidity risk limits.*
  - *Political events that influence either economic activity or confidence. For example, Canadian banks might be affected by Quebec secession, European banks by future EU referendums, and so on.*
  - *A material increase in credit quality at financial institutions caused by a post-bubble decline in asset prices.*

ACTION PLANS MENUS

A "best practice" CFP should address each major category of liquidity-enhancement tactics. Three detailed groups of potential action plans are listed below. (Note that the examples listed are topics for action plans or summaries of action plans. Actual plans must be more detailed. Also note that the following lists include some suggestions that are only suitable for longer term problems.)

Four rules should govern design of your action plans. First, the objective is to identify the components of a controlled process that promotes deliberate orderly behavior. The potential actions must allow for a controlled escalation. The idea is to respond quickly without over-reacting. Second, action plans should be created separately for each crisis stage or stress level defined by the bank. The usefulness of one action compared to another will vary in different circumstances. Third, the potential actions must include responses suitable for a problem that lasts for half a day or one that lasts for half a year. Fourth, an à la carte menu with many choices is much more beneficial than an inflexible menu.

The CFP in general, and the identified action plans in particular, must fit together with the bank's liquidity management and stress testing. In particular, if a stress test indicates that under X scenario the bank may need as much as Y dollars within Z amount of time, the remedial actions suitable for the X scenario should be able to provide at least Y dollars within Z amount of time. Best practice plans list estimated cash raised and time frames for each remedial action designed to raise cash.

Best practice plans include example remedial actions for non-normal funding conditions that are characterized by no current funding problems, but a heightened level of liquidity risk. Under these conditions, the bank simply wants to increase its alert status and take low-cost steps to improve slightly reduce liquidity risk while slightly increasing stand-by liquidity reserves.

- Review opportunities to increase the size of the liquidity reserve (perhaps by switching some asset holdings from less liquid instruments or perhaps by obtaining new term borrowings that can be invested in new liquid assets).
- Intensify collateral management to free additional collateral.
- If possible, substitute surety bonds from third parties for collateral. (More likely to be an available option in a systemic problem than a bank-specific problem.)
- If yield curves are not steep, lengthen average liability maturities as much as possible – especially for unsecured liabilities.
- For systemic liquidity problems, limit reliance on funds borrowed in less liquid markets, instruments and currencies.
- Review opportunities to alter the mix and the terms of either assets or liabilities to increase net cash flow cushions in the overnight, seven-day, 30-day, and 90-day buckets.
- Begin reporting liquidity risk information to senior managers, risk committees, and directors more often and in more detail.
- Update reports, with contact information, listing the bank's largest funds providers.
- Refine cash flow forecasts.
  - In the context of the current funding environment, estimate potential liability withdrawals and runoff by the type of counterparty.
  - In the context of the current funding environment, estimate potential funding requests under existing, off-balance sheet commitments by the type of commitment.
  - Re-review and adjust critical assumptions used for liquidity risk measurement in light of the current funding environment and observable risks.
- Re-review and adjust previously developed plans for obtaining new secured funds and plans for orderly sales of liquid assets. The focus of the re-review should be on how those plans may be impacted on by the potential escalation of currently observable risks.
- Increase the frequency and severity of liquidity stress tests. Stress testing should emphasize potential deterioration resulting from potential escalations of currently observable risks.
- Identify and develop plans to deal with adverse provisions in contracts with funds providers. For example, any triggers or material

adverse change (MAC) clauses that might require collateralization of heretofore unsecured debt, increases in collateral margin
requirements and/or termination of unfunded commitments.

- Implement previously established procedures to ensure that any
  counterparty resistance or unusual pricing for any equity, debt
  or wholesale funding instrument *is immediately communicated to a
  designated officer*.
- If the bank engages in direct marketing of bank or parent company
  paper, consider increasing emphasis on direct marketing. Increasing
  sales incentives or commissions is a popular tactic.

Best practice plans include example remedial actions for non-normal
funding conditions that are characterized by a mildly anomalous bank
funding environment. Under these conditions, the immediate risk may be
higher funding costs or regulatory scrutiny. The main risk is the threat of
further deterioration. This is when the bank must be willing to pay more
for liquidity risk protection.

- Use a combination of observations of current conditions and estimates of the short-term outlook to evaluate the potential scope,
  severity and duration of the problem. Then use that information
  to refine likely and worst case liquidity forecasts. Finally, use the
  information from the forecasts to select tactics for enhancing liquidity, to prioritize those tactics, to assign responsibilities for those
  tactics, and to establish implementation deadlines.
- Continue building a reserve of unencumbered, marketable securities. *Note*: It can be tempting to reduce these holdings as an early
  response when unexpected demand for liquidity first arises. The
  temptation is particularly strong when it is more expensive to sell
  less liquid assets or to add longer term liabilities. Pre-crisis plans
  should include resistance to such temptations. In the early stages
  of a problem, it is better to take actions that may not be available if
  conditions deteriorate further.
- Mobilize a team to manage relationships with the bank's largest
  funds providers. Communicate proactively. Promptly address concerns.
- Brief all personnel likely to receive inquiries from depositors, borrowers, press, industry, or rating agency analysts; regulators or
  capital markets funds providers. (Refer to communications guidelines discussed below.)
- Brief regulators.
- Mobilize a team to identify assets that can be sold or pledged.
  Begin work on stand-by funding capacity from securitizations,
  whole loan sales, and so on. Pre-crisis plans should allow for
  unforeseen delays. (Bankers who worked through previous crises
  report that this can take much longer than expected, even for banks

that regularly do securitizations. Glitches arise with no regard for urgency.)

- Audit the location and eligibility of collateral for central bank borrowings.
- Shift the mix of deposits, as possible, from under-30-day liabilities to over-90-day liabilities. Consider using advertising, as well as higher rates on longer term deposits. Target both maturing deposits and new customers.
- Obtaining as much new, 90-day or longer, unsecured funding as possible, before increases in the intensity of funding problems foreclose that option.
- Adjust pricing and/or marketing to increase holdings of insured deposits.
- Implement previously developed customer retention plans for existing depositors. (Deposit retention programs are described in Chapter 5.)
- Implement previously developed guidelines for responding to requests for early redemption of time deposits.
- Selectively slow asset growth (perhaps by increasing loan rates).
- Curtail trading activities.
- Implement previously established procedures to help maintain an orderly secondary market for bank paper. Procedures should include plans for working with market-makers and plans for determining if negotiable instruments will be retired and/or purchased from anxious market participants. Buybacks should be selective.
- Ratchet up the frequency and detail of liquidity risk information reported to senior managers, risk committees and directors.
- Assign an individual to ensure that decision-makers (or the crisis management committee) have up-to-date and complete information on all regulatory requirements for funds transfers among affiliates, central bank borrowings, minimum holdings of liquid assets, use of deposit brokers, and so on. Information should be for each legal entity and each country or regulatory jurisdiction.

Best practice plans include example remedial actions for non-normal funding conditions that are characterized by a seriously anomalous bank funding environment. These are the actions to consider taking when the risk of not obtaining enough future funding is looming, but opportunities to obtain cash are not exhausted.

- Implement pre-crisis plans for daily cash flow forecasts and supplemental reports.
- Restrict new lending as much as possible *without* risking further reduction in customer confidence.
- Cease trading activities.

- Increase cash held in branches and ATMs merely to avoid a potentially embarrassing shortage.
- Move collateral to the central bank(s) if required.
- Tap alternative funding sources (for example, tri-party repurchase agreements for illiquid securities, MTN-programs in local markets, and so on.)
- Intensify efforts, employee incentives, and/or customer incentives for deposit retention.
- Discontinue any financial support for bank obligations trading in the secondary market.
- Evaluate opportunities to sell illiquid assets or business units if the funding problem worsens.

As noted earlier, the contingency funding plan is generally not desirable for the CFP to require specific actions. (We recommend that the changes in the frequency and detail of liquidity risk reports be the only mandatory actions required in the CFP.) The purpose of the action plans is merely to give the benefit of carefully, calmly and thoroughly considered options to harried managers dealing with a crisis.

Crisis Management Teams or Committees

Many banks elect to define a crisis management team or crisis management committee in their contingency plans. Instead of informal and haphazard communications among senior managers and internal risk experts, a crisis management team serves as a forum where members can avoid duplication of assigned responsibilities, makes sure that everyone isn't assuming that someone else is doing a key task, increases the efficiency of decision making, and improves communications.

When the CFP is invoked, this previously defined group springs to life. (Earlier in the chapter, we noted that the liquidity policy should include a provision that clearly specifies the person or persons authorized to declare that the bank's contingency funding plan is activated. For banks that choose to establish a crisis management team in their CFPs, the team may be automatically activated at the same time.)

The obvious purpose of a crisis management team is to direct the implementation of the CFP. Notice the use of the word "direct" in the previous sentence. Direction is not the same as doing the work. The BoD or a committee of the Board, rather than by the crisis group, may make some decisions. Implementation of decisions is typically delegated to the department or desk that normally manages similar actions. Responsibility for the generation of reports typically remains with the group or department that normally prepares liquidity risk reports. *The crisis management team coordinates the implementation of the relevant CFP provisions, keeps people organized, keeps tasks prioritized and follows up to ensure that decisions were implemented properly.* "The formation of a crisis management team is vital to the success of any contingency funding plan. Experience has shown that a team of highly skilled staff members is necessary to quickly asses the evolving situation, rapidly decide a course of action, implement the actions, monitor the situation, and take corrective actions as necessary."[8]

Membership of the crisis team should be carefully considered. In order to fulfill its assigned functions, the crisis management team needs to be comprised of a mix of senior managers and risk experts. The president and chief financial officer (CFO) should be members so that crisis team decisions are not delayed by the need to receive approval from top management. Executives in charge of deposits and lending are often included because crisis team decisions may involve their areas of responsibility. The Treasurer and any other senior executives responsible for funding obtained from capital markets counterparties should be members. And last, but hardly least, the senior officers responsible for risk management – along with subordinate liquidity risk experts – must be team members. Other personnel, such as media relations managers, may have observer status on the crisis team.

In order to keep the crisis team membership at a workable size, you may wish to have a primary committee with subcommittees. Subcommittees can be organized by type of responsibility (for example, risk monitoring and reporting, communications, and so on) or by geographic regions. Organizations with multiple legal entities should have entity-level crisis teams that report up to a company-wide team. Similarly, organizations doing business in many countries might have country-level crisis teams that report up to a company-wide team.

Pre-assigned duties should be established for legal, electronic data processing (EDP), communications, public affairs, lending, branches and other personnel. The plan should not just address what funding, investment, Treasury and asset/liability will do. Some of those pre-assigned duties may not apply in a given situation while unforeseen tasks will undoubtedly be identified and must be assigned. Each selected remedial action should be assigned. In addition, the plan should specify who is responsible for prompt notification of regulators and who is responsible for providing information and reports requested by regulators. (When we say "who" is responsible, we do not mean to suggest that the CFP should name individuals. Assignments change too rapidly. Rather, the plan should name positions; for example, the CFO, the chief risk officer (CRO), the Treasurer.)

Important tasks should have both a primary and a backup person assigned. On the morning of September 11, 2001, two senior executives of a large regional bank were stuck for hours on the tarmac at LaGuardia airport. Cell phone networks were overloaded. These managers were out of the loop.

The CFP may also state that the crisis team shall meet as often as necessary to monitor and respond to the crisis. The team should continue to function until a designated senior executive, risk management committee or other party determines that the abnormal funding environment no longer prevails.

Reporting

Management reports of potential funding sources and uses should be addressed in the plan. Points to consider include:

- *Increase the frequency of liquidity reports.* For example, from monthly to weekly in the early stages of a potential crisis and from weekly to daily in a crisis.
- *Increase the amount of detail shown in the bank's liquidity reports.* For example, a cash flow gap report that normally shows expected inflows and outflows grouped by month might be expanded to show weekly forecasts.
- *Add supplemental liquidity reports for selected early warning indicators.* For example, the bank may begin daily tracking of the spread between the rates it has to pay for new funds and rates paid by peers.
- *Add supplemental liquidity reports of contingent needs and sources.*

Communications

Both internal and external communications play critical roles in the management of potential funding problems. BIS Principle 13 states that: "Each bank should have in place a mechanism for ensuring that there is an adequate level of disclosure of information about the bank in order to manage public perception of the organization and its soundness."[9] No one likes unpleasant surprises.

Yet it is equally important to realize that risk managers simply cannot have a pre-planned response to every possible rumor or adverse development. Consequently, the contingency plan should be very precise about identifying who will make decisions about communications, the individuals responsible for internal and external communications, and the priority that needs to be given to internal and external communication. At the same time, the plan should not attempt to specify too many other details. Identify individuals by title or position; not by name.

During a crisis, confidence can be further eroded by unclear or inconsistent communications. Communications topics to address include:

- Pre-crisis planning should require an emergency contact list of internal and external contacts. Make sure that the list includes cell phone (mobile) numbers. Keep the list up to date. Key managers should keep a copy of the list in their office, a copy at home, and a copy in their brief cases. Identify backup managers.

- Prompt, proactive communications with major depositors and lenders should be required. Relationship management depends, to a large extent, on confidence. And confidence, in turn, is strongly influenced by communications. Advance plans should include a requirement for regular communications in a crisis, along with procedures that identify communicators and the large liability providers. Line-level contact personnel, such as money desk staff, branch staff and commercial relationship managers, should have assigned roles for communicating with their counterparts at entities that provide funds. In addition, more senior bank managers should have assigned responsibilities for communicating with large depositors and with senior officials at capital markets funds providers.
- Prompt, proactive communication with regulators is equally important. Regulators are likely to be far more cooperative if they are confident that bank managers recognize the potential risks and are promptly implementing contingency plans.
- Pre-crisis planning must carefully address media relations in the event of a bank-specific funding problem. The BIS liquidity guidelines note that: "As part of contingency planning, banks must decide how they will deal with the press and broadcast media when negative information about the bank is disseminated."[10]
  - One critical topic is the control over information. Overly simple plans such as "all media contacts must be approved by X" or "no one may communicate with the media" are counter-productive and likely to fail. Experiences show that when the media does not have access to facts that they can report, they report rumors and market speculations instead.
  - Pre-crisis plans should focus on coordination of media relations rather than on control. The individuals or committee responsible for disseminating information should be identified. The contingency plan should identify a senior-level committee or possibly the chief executive officer (CEO) to make key decisions about the release of important information in the event of a crisis. Separately, a single individual may be designated to handle press and public relations.
  - CFP provisions should provide for employee briefings. Everyone who might be asked, by customers, the media or other outsiders, should know what they are permitted to say as well as what they are not permitted to disclose. The emphasis should be on disseminating accurate and consistent information, rather than on attempting to restrict communications.

Astute communications management can help a bank counter rumors, allay concerns of funds providers, reduce the risk of ratings downgrades, and avoid unwanted regulatory attention. For example, if material adverse information about the bank becomes public, the bank should be prepared to immediately announce corrective actions that are being taken. This will help calm the fears of market participants and demonstrate that the highest levels of management are attentive to the problems that exist.

- Pre-crisis planning should also address the ongoing outflow of information.
  - Maintaining a steady flow of information can be very helpful. "Experience has shown that when there is a more continuous stream of information about a bank, it is easier to manage market perceptions during times of stress. Banks should be certain to provide an adequate amount of information on an ongoing basis to the public at large and, in particular, to major creditors and counterparties."[11]
  - Key internal people must have advance notice of all adverse announcements. When possible, it is also helpful to give advance notice to regulators.
- Internal communications are essential and should not be under-emphasized. In the short term, key managers can't be surprised. For example, the money desk staff can lose important credibility if they learn news about their bank's problems from their outside contacts before they have heard it from inside.
- The contingency plan might also address how the focus of communications might shift over time. For example, regular dialogue with the rating agencies can help in the early stages of a crisis. But ratings are lagging indicators and once rating agencies start to downgrade, it is hard to stop them from overreacting. On the other hand, regular dialogue with regulators is important throughout a crisis, but especially once serious funding problems begin.

Central Bank Borrowings

The contingency plan might address the issue of when the central bank borrowings should be used or avoided. Alternatively, it might simply name a particular senior officer whose approval is required before accessing funds from this source.

Multinational banks also need to address how plans to access central bank borrowings are coordinated with the location of eligible collateral and with liquidity needs in various currencies.

Plan Administration

The CFP should be reviewed and updated at least annually. Feedback from tests and from experiences at other banks should be used to refine the plan. It is particularly important to adjust the plan when the bank's business activities, markets or liquidity regulations change.

Each member of the crisis management team should have three copies of the CFP. One copy to be kept in the office, one copy at home, and one for the briefcase or laptop computer. Contact lists, if not included in the CFP, should be distributed similarly.

Some potential remedial actions require ongoing maintenance. Records of loan commitments must be periodically audited and cleaned of errors (scrubbed). Pledge requirements must be regularly reviewed and pledged collateral must be regularly adjusted. Documents for loans the bank might sell must be audited. While the contingency plan does not need to list each task, let alone name someone responsible, the plan should at least identify the major tasks.

PLAN TESTING

Regular testing is an important part of contingency planning.

Ineffective Tests

Testing liquidity contingency plans is one of the most misunderstood, misapplied aspects of liquidity management. Many bankers and regulators equate the idea of testing contingency plans with testing contingency funding sources. With this in mind, they do things like verifying the availability of fed funds borrowings.

Testing contingency funding sources offers very limited benefits. If a bank rarely uses a particular source of funds, it is a good idea to obtain some funds from that source once in a while just to keep the bank's name on a list or to make sure that the bank's staff has the right contact information. *However, it is a serious error to conclude that occasional use of each potential funding source provides any assurance that funds will be available from that source in a crisis.* On the contrary, funding sources that are plentiful in the ordinary course of business dry up rapidly in a crisis. There is some value in fire drills to test personnel assignments and markets, but the real thing is quite different.

Beneficial Testing and Simulations

Liquidity contingency plan testing can be valuable. The following five uses of tests or simulations should be considered:

1. Banks that rarely sell loans, repo securities, borrow from the fed, or otherwise obtain funds from sources that they hope to use in the event of a liquidity problem need to go through the exercise of using these sources. For all loan sales or secured borrowings, preparation includes ensuring that assets are in good form and arranging custody in a manner that allows for flexibility. It is a good idea to test that preparation from time to time.

2. Large banks can use simulations to test communications, coordination, and decision making involving managers with different responsibilities.

3. Large banks can also use simulations to test communications and coordination between managers with different geographic locations or subsidiaries. Banks operating in three or more different time zones clearly have extra communications challenges. For example, a rumor or an operational failure might cause a funding problem during business hours at a western location after the bank's senior managers at an eastern location are gone for the day.

4. Consider running tests late in the business day. This can highlight specific problems such as difficulty in selling assets or borrowing new funds at a time when business in the capital markets may be winding down. It may also highlight staffing bottlenecks inside the bank, such as clerical departments with less staff in the late afternoon or clerical staff that is unwilling to work overtime.

5. Well-designed simulations give senior managers an opportunity to consider, in advance, the ramifications of decisions that they may have to face during a crisis. This can help familiarize new managers with the issues and interactions that arise during a crisis, and it requires annual discussion of major issues.

CONCLUSION

The vast majority of banks have contingency funding plans. In fact, they are a regulatory requirement in many countries. Yet at the same time, the vast majority of plans fall well short of best practice. A 2005 confidential survey of large US and Canadian banks found that only one of the respondents did not have written CFPs. However, only 62% of respondents who have written plans indicated that they considered their plans to be very realistic. That is down from 73% of respondents to a similar survey in 1997. (The decrease is not likely to be a result of poorer contingency plans. Instead, it probably reflects more awareness of what a best practice plan might include.)

The gap between typical contingency planning and best practice contingency planning may be wide. Fortunately, closing that gap is neither difficult nor expensive.

- CFPs need to have well-defined triggers. In the survey mentioned above, 81% of the respondents said that their CFPs defined triggers.
- CFPs need to have as many well-conceived choices for remedial actions as possible.

- Both triggers and potential remedial actions must be defined and organized to reflect differences in conditions associated with different scenarios.
- Assignments of responsibility must be clear and all-encompassing.
- Plans for both internal and external communications must be realistic and all-inclusive.

Contingency planning may be broad in scope and highly detailed. Yet it is neither complicated nor intricate. This is a planning and organization exercise – not rocket science. Planning and organization produce early detection, prompt reaction and effective responses.

Writing and maintaining a CFP should not be a "gloom and doom" exercise that is done once in a while and then put in a drawer to gather dust. Preparing for the worst is the way to avoid or minimize a worst case experience. A well-written CFP provides the necessary structure, tools, information and response framework. A good plan, by itself, reduces liquidity risk by improving the odds of surviving a crisis.

The advantages of a robust plan go well beyond improving the odds of surviving a crisis. A good plan also improves day-to-day management of liquidity. The process of creating and periodically updating a robust CFP improves the understanding of the liquidity characteristics of bank products, lines of business and funding decisions. Lessons learned can be just as important as the completed plan. A good plan can help the bank optimize, and therefore minimize the cost of, liquidity risk management. A good plan gives directors and regulators more comfort in senior management's awareness of, and preparedness for, potential threats. And a good plan can even boost profits by facilitating better deployment of risk capital.

The best contingency plans are simply well thought out extensions of normal funding and balance sheet management activities. The advantages of a robust CFP are undeniable.

NOTES

[1] Jeff Thredgold, *On the One Hand . . . The Economist's Joke Book*, Thredgold Economic Associates, USA, 2001, p. 17.

[2] Charles Frankle, "Managing Liquidity Contingency Risk, Contingency Plans and Practical Insights," Incisive Media Liquidity Risk Training course, London, 4 February 2002.

[3] Prudential Liquidity, "Interim Potential Source Book: Banks," Financial Services Authority, LM, Section 4, page 2, and Section 5, page 1, June 2001.

[4] Liquidity Risk, Section 2030.1, *Trading and Capital Markets Activities Manual*, Federal Reserve Board of Governors, April 2003.

[5] Principal 5, Paragraph 28, "Sound Practices For Managing Liquidity in Banking Organizations," Basel Committee on Banking Supervision, Basel, February 2000.

6   Charles Frankle, "Managing Liquidity Contingency Risk, Contingency Plans and Practical Insights," Incisive Media Liquidity Risk Training course, London, 4 February 2002.

7   Principal 5, Paragraph 28, "Sound Practices For Managing Liquidity in Banking Organizations," Basel Committee on Banking Supervision, Basel, February 2000.

8   Paul A. Decker, "The Changing Character of Liquidity and Liquidity Risk Management," *The Journal of Lending & Credit Risk Management*, May 2000, vol. 82, no. 8, page 32.

9   Principal 13, Paragraph 5, "Sound Practices for Managing Liquidity in Banking Organizations," Basel Committee on Banking Supervision, Basel February 2000.

10   Principal 13, Paragraph 87, "Sound Practices for Managing Liquidity in Banking Organizations," Basel Committee on Banking Supervision, Basel, February 2000.

11   Principal 13, Paragraph 86, "Sound Practices for Managing Liquidity in Banking Organizations," Basel Committee on Banking Supervision, Basel February 2000.

Market Developments in Banks' Funding Markets

Peter Neu, Armin Leistenschneider
Bernhard Wondrak
and Martin Knippschild

A robust, liquid pricing system is necessary for both optimal pricing of bank products and to create the right balance of internal incentives. Reasonably accurate compensation for the generators of liquidity and charges to the consumers of liquidity are needed to achieve these. For example, without a liquidity transfer pricing system that is robust and reasonably accurate, banks tend to undervalue the liquidity provided by consumer deposits and to under-price the liquidity cost of commitments.

Liquidity pricing is receiving more attention now than ever before. It is the indispensable tool for management to make banks' liquidity risk transparent beyond Treasury and risk management units. Like for credit risk, a proper liquidity transfer price system ensures the origination of new business to be in line with risk management practice.

THE IMPACT OF MARKET DEVELOPMENTS IN THE FUNDING MARKET ON BANK LIQUIDITY RISK

Long-term Funding of Banks

To understand the importance of liquidity transfer pricing, one must consider the development of asset swap spreads of senior debt issued by the major banks over the last decade as shown in Exhibit 7.1. Traditionally, most major banks could issue senior debt below the swap curve. This changed for the first time during the Asian and Russian crises in 1997 and 1998, followed by the LTCM bailout. At that time, investors' and rating agencies' perception of credit risk inherent in major banks' trading books changed. Investors demanded a risk premium when buying banks' debt, and rating agencies downgraded the long-term rating of many banks' senior debt. Despite the soaring equity markets during the following years, it remained a reality for most banks to issue senior debt above Libor, at least for plain vanilla issues.

EXHIBIT 7.1 JP Morgan credit index financial asset swap spreads eurozone

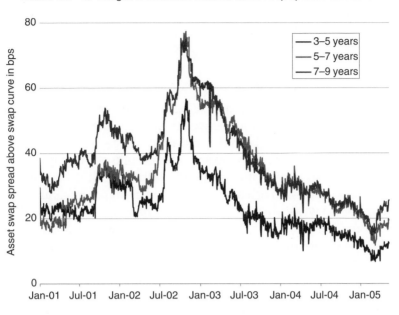

The market perception of banks' debt changed for the second time after the bursting of the new economy bubble, and, in particular, after the Enron and Worldcom defaults in 2002. Investors became skeptical about banks having large loan exposures to corporations subject to fair value accounting. At the same time, banks suffered from large loan loss provisions as a consequence of the economic recession following the bursting of this bubble. Particularly in Europe, both effects led to asset swap spreads of up to 50 to 100 bps for 10-year senior banking debt. During that period, many banks experienced further downgrades of their long-term rating.

After 2003, asset swap spreads of bank debt fell significantly for two reasons. The first reason is that banks had cleaned their loan portfolio and, thereby, had reduced their exposure to credit risk. The second – and more important – reason is a consequence of market effects: after the equity markets had crashed, investors shifted their asset allocation further toward the bond markets and, hence, bond prices soared. At the same time, central banks reduced interest rates to heal an ailing economy. As a result, investors – particularly institutional ones (insurers, pension funds) – who were seeking yield pickups to match their liability cash flows, were increasingly buying bonds issued by the financial services industry. These were considered as still safe and yet offering at least a small yield enhancement compared to Treasuries. Simultaneously, after having strongly reduced their loan book, banks were issuing less new debt.

This market environment was characteristic for 2003 and 2004, and led to a liquidity squeeze for long-term debt and a strong bond bull market. The results were historically low credit spreads for financial services bonds; that is, historically low capital markets funding costs for banks. In early 2005, we saw a slight reversal of this development with an increase of corporate bond spreads; in particular, after the downgrade of General Motors and Ford debt to the "junk" level. Investors have started to value the true credit risk in non-Treasury bonds more rationally.

Short-term Funding of Banks

The liquidity crises in 2002 and 2003 not only impacted on banks' long-term debt, but also strongly influenced their short-term funding capabilities. Some banks – having been downgraded twice – were on the brink of losing their "prime" short-term rating. These banks were confronted with reduced access to money market funds with the result that unsecured cash had to be borrowed on shorter terms and at higher rates, and secured funding (repos) was only given with higher haircuts.

For some banks, it was even clear that they would almost entirely lose their access to unsecured funding, if they did not solve the problems in their loan books.

In this situation, it became necessary for banks to assess and value:

- the liquefiability of the trading assets and the cost of holding those assets
- their capability of replacing unsecured funding by repo funding
- their contingent funding liabilities in committed credit lines, CP-backup lines and derivatives.

UNDERSTANDING LIQUIDITY COSTS IS A MANAGEMENT IMPERATIVE

Clearly, funding spreads of the order of 50 to 100 bps prohibit any profitable loan business, at least to customers with good ratings. As a consequence, liquidity (funding) risk became very visible to everyone working in banks during 2002/2003. It became clear that funding costs for issuing senior debt could no longer be neglected and that they could have had a lasting impact on the business model and the P&L. Senior management became aware that long-term funding costs must be passed on to the asset side when issuing new loans. Term funding costs became widely recognized as an indisputable part of the customer rate.

At the same time, senior management realized that access to secured and unsecured money markets could be seriously limited or, after losing reputation by a short-term downgrade to a non-prime status, could even be impaired. In contrast to the long-term funding risk, which is in the first place a P&L risk, a short-term funding problem puts the solvency of the bank at risk. The result was that contingency and illiquidity in assets had to be accounted for by Treasury by holding a sufficient amount of term-funded liquidity reserve (Treasuries). The opportunity costs for these hedges had to be transferred to asset-holders to make them aware of the (short-term) liquidity risk in their position.

Even after the crises in 2002 and 2003, long- and short-term liquidity risk continued to receive attention by senior management, and it became widely accepted that liquidity risk was a "real" risk and had to be addressed with a proper transfer price system.

Generally, the following drivers of the transfer price are considered:

- *Fixed or floating rate*: For floating rate loans, the liquidity tenor and not the interest tenor determines the liquidity risk portion of the transfer price.
- *Amortization schedule of the notional*: Amortization and repayable instruments can have durations that are significantly shorter than the maturity tenor. Liquidity transfer prices should be based on the expected timing of the cash flows. Hence, amortization cash flows must be rolled out before transfer pricing a position.
- *Notional liquidity outflow*: Liquidity costs are influenced by the amount of the required funding. A benchmark liquidity spread can be applied for standard business, say mortgages or consumer loans. Large ticket loans, however, say above US$10 million, should be priced individually by Treasury as the funding costs for them might be higher than those for small ticket loans.
- *Eligibility as collateral*: Some assets consume liquidity and, in parts, also provide liquidity because they are eligible as collateral at central banks or in repo markets, or are readily saleable. Examples are highly liquid securities; for example, Treasuries, which serve as a stand-by liquidity reserve. A proper liquidity transfer price system accounts for both.

Liquidity pricing is not a one-way road. Liquidity costs are charged to consumers of liquidity, mostly illiquid long-term loans, commitments or illiquid securities and strategic investments, and credited to providers of liquidity, mostly stable core deposits and securities eligible as collaterals at central banks. However, it is important to ensure that the transfer pricing does not give incentive to excess term liquidity; for example, from core deposits or excess holdings of stand-by liquidity, such as short-term, marketable securities. If a bank credits core deposits to its sales units and invests these funds in short-term money market placements, its liquidity transfer price system gives the wrong incentives and leads to a negative P&L impact.

Two guiding principals are very important. One guiding principle is that liquidity costs depend on the scenario (market condition), the bank's balance sheet, and its positioning in the market. Repo, for example, can only be used as a funding source in a crisis, if the bank is already an established repo player and counterparty limits are available at other banks. The second principle is that the higher the liquidity reserve, the lower the liquidity risk, but the higher the liquidity costs. In other words, too little liquidity may kill a bank suddenly, but too much might kill it slowly. First-class management of liquidity needs to maintain the intricate balance between liquidity risk and liquidity costs.

DEVELOPING BEST PRACTICES

Current practices for measuring liquidity costs and benefits are extremely varied. A great many banks know that they have some spending money – mainly associated with carrying liquid assets – but do little or nothing to quantify those costs. While it is reasonable to avoid spending money to measure something that might not be managed much differently with better information, ignorance is not necessarily bliss. For one thing, a weak understanding of explicit liquidity costs and benefits makes it hard to price bank products appropriately. As a result, prices do not provide optimal incentives, and some products, like loan commitments, probably do not capture all of the risk incurred by the bank.

Many other banks have some systems for quantifying liquidity costs and benefits. Two interesting observations can be made about the practices at these banks. First, there is not a lot of consistency in measurement methodology. Some focus on the opportunity costs of holding liquid assets. Some focus on the marginal costs of funds. Some focus on other metrics. There are lots of good ideas, but little consensus about what constitutes best practice. Second, almost unanimously, when interviewed, liquidity managers state that they want to be doing more to measure costs than they currently do. Many bankers are considering advanced pricing methodologies, but few have implemented them so far. There is a lack of connection between what these managers want to do to calculate and price liquidity costs, and what most of their banks are currently able to do. Some are still pondering the issues. Some are using rough or incomplete methodologies.

The problem with virtually all approaches to measuring liquidity costs is that they focus on just one or two liquidity sources or needs. Each has relevance in its context. They are all reasonably accurate and valid in limited applications, but they all break down in broad application.

Good Measurement Requires Segmentation

There exist three types of liquidity risk. Each has associated costs. Each should be addressed in a liquidity transfer price system:

- mismatch or funding liquidity costs
- contingency liquidity costs
- market liquidity costs.

Mismatch liquidity costs refer to the liquidity risk in the bank's current balance sheet position, and, therefore, to the costs of obtaining a follow-on funding at current market conditions. Mismatch liquidity costs are applicable for tenor above 12 months, charged to loans and expected loan commitment draws, credited to stable deposits. The transfer price is calculated under going concern market conditions.

Contingency liquidity costs refer to the liquidity risk of not having sufficient funds to meet sudden and unexpected short-term obligations. The arising costs of maintaining a reserve of unencumbered assets are charged to unexpected loan draws and credited to liquid assets. The price depends on the selected scenario.

Market liquidity costs refer to the inability to sell trading assets at all or only with a haircut to the fair (discounted cash flow) price. Reasons for this can be impaired access to the respective markets (for example, after loss of reputation), general market disruptions following systemic crises, a position in a security that is not actively traded, a position in a security that has suffered a material increase in risk, or, simply, a too big position. The calculated overnight carry has to be corrected by charging market liquidity costs to the trading desk P&L.

From a management account perspective, liquidity costs consist of three components. First, mismatch liquidity costs charged for long-term loan business and credited for stable deposits. Second, contingency liquidity costs charged for open committed lines of credit and other contingencies and credited for liquid assets. Third, market liquidity costs (haircuts) charged for illiquid trading assets. From this perspective, even a self-funding institution has liquidity costs for contingent risks.

A key requirement for pricing of liquidity risk is understanding that these components are very distinct. One of the most practical insights that we can glean from this division is a better understanding of liquidity costs. If liquidity risk has three components – or contributing parts – then it has three associated, but independent costs.

At a minimum, you must have dual methodologies: one for normal/mismatch liquidity and one for crisis/contingent liquidity. Current sources of liquidity and current users of liquidity are usually different from stand-by sources and contingent needs. Indeed, they can be contradictory. For example, holding a five-year Treasury bond uses current liquidity capacity. It contributes to mismatch liquidity risk. But that holding is also a source of stand-by liquidity if the bond is not pledged and can be sold when additional funds are needed. Mismatch liquidity costs arise from liquidity held for normal operating environments, plus some amount of prudential liquidity cushion. Contingent costs are costs incurred for holding "stand-by liquidity" – maintaining the capacity to quickly increase liquidity if necessary. Both the costs of the prudential cushion and the stand-by liquidity are analogous to the costs of an insurance policy. We pay an insurance premium for protection from risks we do not expect to incur, but which can be catastrophic if they do occur.

We can therefore consider the "dual pricing methodologies" concept described in this chapter as one charge for the current funding costs and a separate charge for the insurance costs of holding stand-by liquidity.

Liquidity pricing must recognize both, either with net charges or dual charges. Dual system charges and credits can build. For example, a partially funded long-term credit facility can have a normal liquidity charge allocated to the funded portion and a contingency liquidity charge allocated to the unfunded portion. Similarly, a long-term CD can have a mismatch liquidity credit for reducing liquidity risk in the ordinary course of business, as well as a contingent liquidity credit for reducing liquidity risk in a potential crisis. Dual system charges and credits can offset each other. For example, a two-year Treasury note might receive a normal liquidity charge but a contingency liquidity credit.

A FRAMEWORK FOR MEASURING LIQUIDITY MISMATCH COSTS

In recent years, consensus has emerged among some, but by no means all, of the largest financial institutions. This consensus uses marginal costs of funds to tease out the portion of the yield that is attributable to the liquidity. For example, the spread between the swap curve and banks' costs to issue senior term debt can be used to eliminate the portion of the term premium associated with liquidity risk. Banks decipher these costs by swapping back to floating their fix-rate borrowing costs and observing the difference in the resulting floating rates between each term.

These relationships can be seen in Exhibit 7.2.

The bank issues a 10-year fix-rate bond at 4.30%, which is callable by the bank after six years. Treasury's long-term funding unit, which issues this bond, swaps the fix-rate back to floating by contracting a bank-internal 10-year receiver swap with an interest rate proprietary trading unit, which pays 3.7% fixed. It also sells the call right by going short on a six-year receiver swaption; that is, the rates unit has the right to enter in six years in a four-year receiver swap where it would receive 3.7% fixed, canceling the fix-rate coupon cash flows of the initial receiver swap. The fixed rate of the receiver swap is determined such that the term-funding center receives – together with the annualized option premium – exactly

EXHIBIT 7.2 Liquidity term premiums for a callable bond

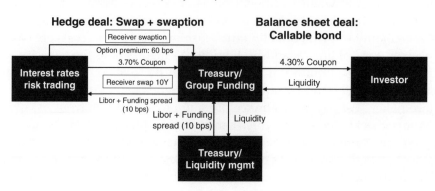

the amount paid fixed to the investor of the bond. The funding costs are defined as the spread above the floating rate, which must be paid by the term-funding center to value the receiver swap par at inception. The funding spread after swap and option premium is charged to Treasury's liquidity management unit, which receives the liquidity generated by the bond issue. This unit then charges the loan departments with liquidity costs for term funding consumption, which are calculated on a funding spread curve derived from such a composition of a structured bond issue.

With this approach, all kind of structured bond issues can be stripped in embedded derivatives and floating rate plus funding spread-denominated cash instruments. Exhibit 7.3 shows a decomposition of a credit-linked note in a credit default swap and a floating rate cash bond.

Making the subtractions between the cash market and swap curves for selected maturities will produce a set of liquidity term costs, such as those shown in Exhibit 7.4.

Of course, the exact figures depend on both the marginal funding costs for each bank – the top curve in Exhibit 7.4 – and also on the level of the yield curve each day. Since these are derived from actual yield curves, they change. Large banks might want to update these costs weekly or even daily. Small banks can do so less often.

EXHIBIT 7.3   Liquidity term premiums for a credit-linked note

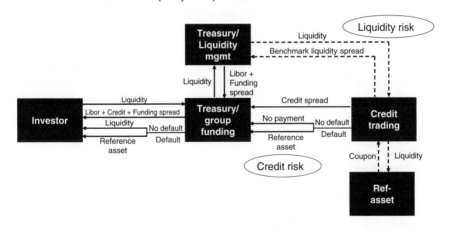

EXHIBIT 7.4   Liquidity premium curve

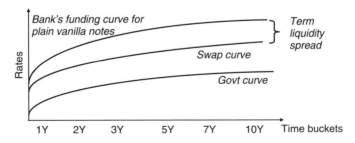

When calculating term liquidity spreads for internal transfer pricing purposes, one should consider that asset swap spreads of individual bonds contain a premium for the credit risk of the issuing bank and a liquidity premium for the particular bond. The latter depends, for instance, on the issuing volume, the time to maturity, or on market specifics, such as that investors consider a particular bond as a benchmark for an entire market segment. The bank does not want to take this bond issue-specific liquidity premium for its internal transfer pricing, but only the credit risk premium. Hence, when calibrating term funding spread for internal liquidity transfer pricing, the bank should average over the asset swap spread of a portfolio of bonds. Such a portfolio can also contain bonds issued by the bank's peers. Furthermore, internal term funding spreads should also consider that the asset swap spread of a large syndicated bond issue is quite different from that of small volume private placements. The bank should account for this by weighting syndicated bond levels and private placement levels according to the historical and future planned issuing volume.

We shall now apply this concept to transfer price mismatch liquidity risk in an amortizing term loan.

Pricing Liquidity Risk in Amortizing Term Loans

The concept that has been described in the last section can most easily be applied to term loans with a fixed amortization structure. In this case all future amortization cash flows are known so that the corresponding term funding spreads can readily be assigned.

There are two approaches that most banks apply to price the mismatch liquidity costs. They are described in the following two sections using a five-year term loan of US$10 million notional and yearly linear 20% amortization rate as an example. Note that for the following considerations it is irrelevant whether the customer rate is fixed or floating.

Tranching Approach

The first approach uses a simple partition of the linearly amortizing loan in individual tranches, each having a different tenor. A five-year loan of US$10 million notional and with a 20% amortization rate p.a. can be stripped in five loans of each US$2 million notional, bullet repayment, and tenors ranging from one to five years.

Exhibit 7.5 on page 155 shows the different tranches and the associated term liquidity spreads derived from the yield curve for the bank's senior debt as laid out in the previous section.

It becomes apparent from this picture that, although the tenor of the loan is five years, liquidity is on average only bound for a period somewhere around three years. Hence, a term funding spread of about 27 bps, and not the five-year term funding spread of 40 bps should be charged to loan origination.

EXHIBIT 7.5 Calculating mismatch liquidity costs for a 5-year linearly amortizing term loan

Usage (mn)

1st tranche: 0 bps
2nd tranche: 13 bps
3rd tranche: 27 bps
4th tranche: 35 bps
5th tranche: 40 bps

1Y   2Y   3Y   4Y   5Y

An exact calculation confirms this evaluation. The mismatch liquidity costs for this cash flow structure and funding spread level is derived from the tenor-weighted term funding spread of each tranche:

Liquidity cost

$$= \frac{1 \times 0\,\text{bps} + 2 \times 13\,\text{bps} + 3 \times 27\,\text{bps} + 4 \times 35\,\text{bps} + 5 \times 40\,\text{bps}}{1 + 2 + 3 + 4 + 5}$$

$$= 29.8\,\text{bps}$$

Internal Rate of Return Approach

Although the previous approach is very intuitive, it becomes very laborious to apply, if amortization schedules are more irregular. To risk transfer pricing such a loan with respect to mismatch liquidity risk it becomes inevitable to roll out individual cash flows exactly. The transfer price is then derived from the difference in the internal rate of return (IRR) or par rate with respect to the swap curve and the funding curve (swap curve shifted by the term funding spreads). Exhibit 7.6 illustrates the approach.

The IRR for the swap curve fixes the fair transfer price paid by loan origination to asset liability management (ALM) as the transfer price for interest rate risk in the loan.

EXHIBIT 7.6 Calculation of mismatch liquidity costs for an amortizing term loan

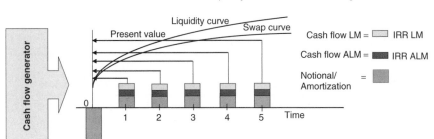

$$\sum_{t=1}^{T}(N_{t-1} \times IRR_{ALM} + A_t) \times e^{r_{swap}^t \times t} = N_0 \Rightarrow IRR_{ALM}$$

N_t denotes the outstanding notional at time t, A_t the amortization amount in period $t-1$ to t, and r_{swap}^t the swap rate at time t.

Analogously, the IRR on the bank's term funding curve is the transfer price for interest rate and mismatch liquidity risk, where BLS_t denotes the benchmark term funding spread above the swap curve, and LM stands for "liquidity management."

$$\sum_{t=1}^{T}(N_{t-1} \times IRR_{LM} + A_t) \times e^{-(r_{Swap}^t + BLS^t) \times t} = N_0 \Rightarrow IRR_{LM}$$

The transfer price for liquidity mismatch risk – relative to the term funding level of the bank and the amortization schedule of the loan – is given by the difference between these two IRR:

$$\text{Liquidity cost} = IRR_{LM} - IRR_{ALM}$$

Exhibit 7.7 shows the result of this approach for the five-year linearly amortizing loan of the previous section.

The transfer prices are:

- *transfer price for ALM*: 4.262%
- *transfer price for LM*: 4.544%
- *mismatch liquidity spread*: 28.2 bps.

The difference to the previous result is a fair value effect.

Pricing Mismatch Liquidity Risk in On-demand Non-maturing Assets and Liabilities

Pricing mismatch liquidity costs become more complicated when less information about future cash flows is known. In this case the bank must estimate the amount and the timing of cash flows based on market scenarios and customer behavior. Products where this applies are

EXHIBIT 7.7 Calculation of mismatch liquidity costs for an amortizing term loan

	1Y	2Y	3Y	4Y	5Y
Swap rate	3.80%	3.90%	4.20%	4.40%	4.50%
Term funding spread	0 bps	13 bps	27 bps	35 bps	45 bps

on-demand non-maturing loans such as current accounts and credit card loans, and on-demand non-maturing deposits such as sight, saving and term deposits.[1]

It is important to note that there is a need to apply the technique described below separately for each type of on-demand credit facility and demand deposit. For example, credit cards need to be analyzed separately from letters of credit and commercial working capital lines of credit. Similarly, sight deposits have a different cash flow behavior than saving deposits. On-demand non-maturing deposits can be modeled on a portfolio basis, because customers might shift between different product-types; for example, between saving and sight deposits. Without that, there is a liquidity outflow from the bank. For the transfer pricing, however, product-specific stickiness must be considered. The allocation of excess core level due to cross-product cash flows within the bank can be done according to the relative volume contribution of each product-type, or, more advanced, according to the product-specific stickiness relative to the total portfolio stickiness (measured, for instance, by the core balance or volatility).

The pricing of on-demand non-maturing products for mismatch liquidity requires an estimation of the balance that will be drawn (loans) or is at the bank's disposal (deposits) on a long time horizon. This balance will either require term funding (credit card loans) or provide term funding. We will call this the "core balance," which will be debited or credited for mismatch liquidity. It has to be determined by a statistical analysis based on the current and historical balance of these products, their drift and volatility; the customer rate; and exogenous factors, such as interest rates, equity indices, GDP growth, and so on. Such an analysis shall not only separate the current balance into a volatile and core part. It shall provide information on the liquidity duration of the core balance. This liquidity duration can be visualized by dividing the core balance in tranches of different maturity.

Consider the following example: ABC bank has US$12 billion of non-maturing deposits. The statistical analysis has shown that US$10 billion are sticky and can be considered as core. Furthermore, the analysis has revealed that the liquidity duration of the core deposits can best be replicated by three tranches with:

- 25%, or US$2.5 billion rolling at a one-year horizon
- 35%, or US$3.5 billion rolling at a two-year horizon
- 45%, or US$4.5 billion rolling at a three-year horizon.

Each tranche is rolling, in our example on an annual basis, so that each year a fraction of each tranche is credited with the current term funding spreads. The remaining balance of US$2 billion between the current balance and the sticky part is considered as a buffer for customers who call their deposits on short notice. Therefore, it cannot be considered

EXHIBIT 7.8 Rolling replicating portfolio to price on-demand products

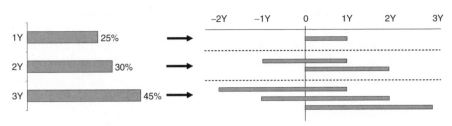

as long-term funding and, consequently, cannot be credited with term funding costs. Exhibit 7.8 illustrates this treatment.

The mismatch liquidity costs are then given by the accrual funding costs of the replicating rolling portfolio. In our example the mismatch liquidity spread is:

$$
f_0 = \frac{Core\ balance}{Current\ balance}
$$
$$
\times \left[\begin{array}{l} 25\% \times BMS_0^1 \\ 30\% / 2 \times BMS_0^2 + 30\% / 2 \times BMS_{-1}^2 \\ 45\% / 3 \times BMS_0^3 + 45\% / 3 \times BMS_{-1}^3 + 45\% / 3 \times BMS_{-2}^3 \end{array} \right]
$$

where BMS_{-n}^j is the bank's benchmark funding spread n years ago ($n = 0, 1, 2, \ldots$) for a j-year term funding ($j = 1, 2, 3, \ldots$). The amount in US dollars credited to the origination unit for these deposits in the management accounts is the current balance in US dollars multiplied by the mismatch liquidity spread f_0.

Exactly in the same way, the sticky parts of sight loans would be charged with term funding costs corresponding to the liquidity duration of each tranche, and the volatile part would be funded overnight. Note that there is also a contingency liquidity risk in sight loans that will be dealt with in the following section.

A FRAMEWORK FOR MEASURING CONTINGENCY LIQUIDITY RISK COSTS

Pricing contingency liquidity risk – both the loan-funding options and the deposit withdrawal options – must be at least as important as pricing the term or mismatch risk. The underlying goal of any well-designed liquidity-pricing methodology must be to appropriately reward the providers of liquidity and penalize the users. At a minimum, a well-designed pricing system should at least motivate the users to use less and the providers to provide more. Pricing contingency liquidity costs and valuing stand-by sources must therefore be essential components of best-practice liquidity pricing. Unfortunately, since the costs of liquidity contingency risk are harder to quantify, this component usually receives less attention than the pricing of liquidity mismatch risk.

The mismatch component of liquidity risk is fairly stable. The contingency risk component, on the other hand, can be very volatile. Most of the "what-if" aspects of liquidity risk fall into this category. Indeed, all of the liquidity need scenarios defined – such as liquidity in the ordinary course of business; liquidity for a bank-specific crisis; and liquidity for cyclical, market and other systemic disruptions – impact the bank in the form of liability losses or asset increases. Those liability losses or asset increases are, in turn, simply the exercise of customer options – both contractual options and franchise-related options.

Liquidity contingency risk includes most of the risks we have described as low-probability/severe-consequence events. In large part, what we defined as low-probability/severe-consequence events are those that involve the exercise of liquidity options. Options related to loan funding are certainly a part. In addition, there is also a whole set of options related to deposit withdrawals. Early in the 1990s, for example, we saw the customers of a major US bank lined up outside the branches to withdraw their insured deposits. Another instance happened on a smaller scale in 2003. In short, almost all of the bits of liquidity risk that we worry about most are included in the contingency risk component.

How do we estimate the costs of the borrower's right to exercise a loan commitment or the depositor's right to withdraw funds? Both opportunity costs and yield curve spread-derived liquidity premiums fail to capture the liquidity costs of off-balance sheet risks such as unfunded lines and other commitments.

Some mathematically inclined bankers hypothesize about how to apply option-pricing theories to liquidity. One banker speculated that: "In theory, one way to charge for this would be to value the option that is implicit in this structure. I view it as maybe an option on a spread lock. The customer can draw money at some point in the future for some amount of time at some rate. That means we have to fund some amount of money at some point in the future for some amount of time at some spread. We would want to buy an option to guarantee a spread on this borrowing."[2] We will give an example on how this approach can be used for pricing contingent liquidity risk in committed credit lines.

In the meantime, back on the ground, we need a practical solution. We want to be able to quantify some charges to reflect the option risk in liabilities that can be withdrawn and the option risk in commitments that can require funding. At the same time, we want to quantify credits for the stand-by liquidity provided by liquid assets and sticky liabilities.

In the following sections, we will consider methods for quantifying the major elements of contingent risks and stand-by sources. Following those discussions, we will take a look at combining these quantities.

Quantifying the Opportunity Costs of Stand-by Liquidity Provided by Liquid Assets

One of the easiest to calculate components of stand-by liquid asset costs are the opportunity costs of holding liquid investment securities and funding them unsecured. Such assets are held as a liquidity buffer for emergencies in case of reduced access to the unsecured funding market or requirements exceeding market supply; for example, financing of drawdown on committed credit lines. Secured funding being generally cheaper than unsecured funding, the banks pay opportunity costs to the market for holding this liquidity reserve of unencumbered liquid assets.

These can be seen in Exhibit 7.9.

Quantifying the Costs of Loan Commitments

An important impetus of contingency liquidity costs is that granting loan commitments generates liquidity risk and stand-by liquidity costs money for the banks.

To communicate this message to the sales departments and to make them pay for contingencies will significantly impact the sales process and bring it in line with liquidity risk considerations. Clearly, the exact amount depends on various scenarios and factors like product-type, tenor of drawdown or facility, and customer behavior. In some banks, however, management might find the communication of a full model approach too complicated and too assumption-driven. From this viewpoint, the initial step when implementing the concept of contingency liquidity costs is not the clarification of *"how much* a credit line will be charged", but *"that* a credit line will be charged." The methodology can be improved afterwards when the concept has been accepted by the sales department, and when the costs are part of the customer rate for an open line of credit.

Hence, during the course of first implementation, for the sake of transparency, management should restrict itself to one scenario, neglect the volatility of term funding spreads, and use one drawdown factor for all products (very simplified) or one per product type. Denoting by Δ the drawdown factor, with Δs the spread between secured (repo) and unsecured short-term funding, with f_T the term funding spread for

EXHIBIT 7.9   Liquidity premium curve

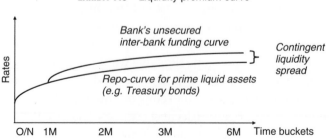

end-of-facility T, and with L the limit and U the current usage, the annual contingency liquidity CLC costs can be calculated as:

$$CLC = \Delta \times (L - U) \times (\Delta s + f_T).$$

The first term proportional to Δs counts for the opportunity costs of stand-by liquidity of amount $\Delta \times (L - U)$. The second term proportional to f_T is the term funding cost of the stand-by liquidity.

Following the first implementation, the methodology can systematically be improved. The customer can draw money at some point in the future for some amount of time at some rate. That means the bank has to fund some amount of money at some point in the future for some amount of time at some spread. For pricing that option of the customer one first defines more scenarios and then determines a risk premium for the guarantee on the spread of a future borrowing.

Denote by Δ_{ij}^s the drawdown factor (or hedge ratio) for each product-type i and counterpart-type j under scenario s, and denote by p_s the probability weight for scenario s to occur ($\Sigma_s p_s = 1$). The spread guarantee is of the nature of a US option on the funding spread with volatility determined by the historical volatility of the bank's term funding spreads and strike price equal to the guaranteed spread that is determined by the current term funding spread for the borrowing. The maturity of the funding spread option is the end of the loan facility T. Standard option price theory for a US call option can be applied, if wanted. However, there is no separate trading for funding spread options and hence no secondary market with settled prices and hedging possibilities. Accordingly, no implied volatility exists. Instead of using option pricing a simple risk premium set by the historical annualized volatility σ_s of the term funding spread f_T can be used. All together this provides the following formula for pricing the annual cost of contingency liquidity risk for product-type i and customer-type j:

$$CLC_{ij} = \sum_s p_s \times \Delta_{ij}^s \times (L - U) \times (\Delta s + f_T) + (L - U) \times \alpha \times \sigma_f \times f_T.$$

Here, α is scaling factor for the risk premium of order 1.

We shall now apply this concept to price the liquidity risk in a revolving loan facility.

Example for Liquidity Transfer Pricing a Revolving Loan

The liquidity transfer price of a revolving loan facility contains two components: mismatch liquidity costs for the usage and contingency liquidity costs for the open limit. In the following we will treat these two components separately.

Mismatch Liquidity Costs for the Usage of a Revolving Loan Facility

The current usage of a revolving loan facility is characterized by the drawn amount and the tenor of the drawdown. For the bank only the current usage, the current open line and the current tenor of a drawdown is known. When hedging the mismatch liquidity risk of individual draws under the loan facility, for example, by buying maturity-matching term funding, Treasury faces the challenge of generating a large number of funding tickets that have to be adjusted upon each change of the drawn amount. Furthermore, Treasury would neglect that many short-term draws under a loan facility will be rolled over so that a core amount will be drawn permanently until the final maturity of the facility.

Instead of hedging mismatch liquidity risk of each individual draw, it is more appropriate in practice to hedge it on a portfolio level. For this purpose the current usage is separated in a core usage, which will remain drawn for the entire lifetime of the facility, and a volatile usage, which fluctuates on short terms. The volatile usage (haircut) is funded on short notice, whereas the core usage is funded until the end of the facility. The core usage can be defined in various ways; for example, by matching the average or expected usage of revolving loan facilities in this portfolio.

Contingency Liquidity Costs for the Open Limit

Having separated the current usage in a core and volatile part, the potential future drawdown on the open line has to be estimated. The bases for this are usually historical experiences of the bank on the customer behavior and the contract type. For instance, for a revolving loan the contingent drawdown ratio can be linked to the default or downgrade probability of the customer. This assumes that customers will extensively draw on the line, if they come into financial difficulties. Other examples are commercial paper (CP) backup lines for a conduit that issues asset-backed commercial papers (ABCP) to fund its assets. In case that the commercial papers cannot be rolled over, the conduit will draw on the CP-backup lines. Here, the drawdown ratio is linked to the likelihood of a systemic market disruption in the ABCP market or the liquidity bank's specific downgrade probability.

Clearly, product-type and counterparty-specific drawdown factors need also to be modeled under various systemic and bank-specific scenarios. However, although this might be conceptually sounder, it requires estimating the different probability weights of each scenario. For simplicity, we restrict ourselves to one scenario in the following example.

Exhibit 7.10 shows the pricing of a five-year revolving facility with US$10 million, US$3 million current usage thereof, and US$2.5 million core usage (25% of limit). The five-year term funding spread is at 40 bps p.a. and the spread between the bank's secured and unsecured funding curve is 8 bps p.a. The volatility of the term funding spread is 5% p.a. The hedge ratio is 20% of the unused limit, which is US$7 million (70% of limit).

EXHIBIT 7.10   Pricing liquidity costs for a revolving loan

Term funding at end of facility × Expected draw	Mismatch liquidity costs	40 bps × 25% = 10 bps
+		+
(Cont. liquidity spread + Term funding) × Hedge ratio × Current open line + Funding spread risk premium	Contingent liquidity costs	(8 bps + 40 bps) × 20% × 70% + 40 bps × 5% × 70% = 8.12 bps
		Liquidity spread on limit = 18.12 bps
Liquidity spread × limit	Total costs p.a.	Liquidity costs = 18.12 bps × US$10 mn = US$18 120 p.a.

The liquidity costs of the revolving loan amount to 18.12 bps p.a. of the limit.

FRAMEWORKS FOR MEASURING THE COST OF MARKET LIQUIDITY

Usually, a trader's security position is valued against an overnight carry rate when calculating the daily P&L. To estimate the market liquidity costs for such a position, one must therefore estimate inasmuch that the overnight costs of carry have to be corrected for necessary term funding. There are two dimensions to be considered:

- how easily the position can be sold on the street
- which part of the position can be funded by repos and which part needs unsecured funding.

One should proceed in three steps:

In the *first step*, the liquefiability of a security position should be assessed. Criteria to do this are, to name a few: rating (high investment grade, investment grade, non-investment grade), issuer group (government, bank, corporation), country group and country rating (OECD, G7, emerging markets), listed at a major exchange, currency, own position relative to outstanding volume, degree of structuring (plain vanilla vs ABS), and so on.

According to these criteria, in a *second step* the securities should be grouped in different liquidity classes, each of which has a different liquidation horizon associated with it. For example, for prime liquid assets, such as G7 Treasuries, say 35% of the position can be liquidated overnight, another 35% within one week, and the final 30% within two weeks. More illiquid assets are assigned a respectively longer liquidation horizon. One could also include a haircut, which would be mapped at the final maturity of the security. In the liquidity gap analysis, cash inflows from security holdings are modeled analogously. In this way, the necessity of term funding is naturally documented for each security position.

In the *third step* the share of possible repo-funding and necessary remaining unsecured funding is determined for each security type. As an example, a G7 Treasury position can be repo-funded up to 97% and needs only 3% unsecured cash. For a corporate bond, the relations might be 60% repo and 40% unsecured funding. Obviously, these percentages are not assigned for each individual security position (which would mean assigning 100% or 0%): they can only be attributed for a portfolio and relative to the bank's position as a repo-player in the market. If the bank is not an active repo-player, that is if it has no large counterparty limits available at other banks, a trader cannot claim a high repo-funding ratio for a large volume position, even if there is a liquid repo market for such securities.

Based on the cash flow profile derived from step two, the unsecured funded and haircut parts of the positions are charged with term funding costs. The "repo'able" share is charged with contingency liquidity costs, which account for the probability that the repo funding cannot be rolled over and the opportunity costs for holding the corresponding amount of highly liquid stand-by liquidity.

Let us look at the following example of a US$10 billion corporate bond trading position. For this position, a 10% haircut is assumed, which is modeled as a cash inflow at final maturity of the bond, say in five years, and charged with the corresponding term funding spread, say 25 bps. For the remaining US$9 billion bond position, it is assumed that 60% can be funded via repo and 40% needs unsecured funding. Liquidating the unsecured funded part of the position is assumed to be possible by selling 10% overnight, a further 20% between overnight and eight days, a further 20% between one and two weeks, a further 30% between two weeks and one month, a further 10% between one and three months, and the final 10% between three and six months. These cash flows are charged with the corresponding spreads for unsecured funding, which are in this example: zero bps below one month, two bps for one month, five bps for three months, and 10 bps for six months. Finally, the secured funded part of the position is charged with one bp contingency liquidity costs, which is derived from a 10% probability that repo funding cannot be rolled over and 10 bps opportunity costs for holding stand-by liquidity for the secured funded fraction of the bond position. This calculation is laid out in Exhibit 7.11 on page 165. Together, all components lead to a charge for market liquidity of 3.8 bps p.a., which is *pro rata* allocated to the trading desk for each day of holding this trading position.

A CASE STUDY: TECHNICAL DESCRIPTION OF THE FUND TRANSFER PRICING PROCESS

In traditional banks, loan systems usually are well established and often do not meet the full range of demands that are made from modern risk

EXHIBIT 7.11 Example costs for market liquidity

Corporate bond		'000 US$
Trading position (MtM)		10,000
Haircut	10% of trading position	1,000
Unsecured	40% of position after haircut	3,600
Repo	60% of position after haircut	5,400

Time band		Cost of market liquidity p.a.		
	Liquidation cash flows%	'000 US$	bps p.a.	US$ p.a.
O/N	10%	360	0.0	0
8 days	20%	720	0.0	0
2 weeks	20%	720	0.0	0
1 month	30%	1,080	2.0	216
3 months	10%	360	5.0	180
6 months	10%	360	10.0	360
Unsecured	40%	3,600	2.1	756
Secured	60%	5,400	1.0	540
Haircut (5Y)	10%	1,000	25.0	2,500
Total p.a.		10,000	3.8	3,796

management concepts. One solution is the implementation of supplement systems, which use data sources from booking systems and cover all the requirements from risk management systems.

In the following we want to outline how a technical implementation of a liquidity transfer pricing system could be designed.

Interfaces to Booking Systems

A bank typically faces several booking systems distributed across its IT landscape that need to be connected to the data warehouse. Of course, all systems use different technical platforms and different internal data models. Not one system had a database function so the only way to download the data from the booking systems was to import the total data stock or an excerpt of the original data storage.

Most of the booking systems are batch systems, where a data download by database functionality cannot be applied. The pragmatic solution should be the establishment of daily data downloads within the daily batch processing in the booking systems. To avoid the download of data masses that would not be used in the later analysis a technical documentation for each data system needs to be created in which the necessary data fields and contents of each booking system to the data warehouse have to be specified for the transfer process. The challenge will be to locate and to combine special product know-how from business divisions and technical know-how from IT divisions for each particular booking system.

For each booking system a set of filters must be implemented to reduce the number of records that have to be transferred and to reduce the number of data fields in each data record. Some booking systems contain internal data sets, which are not relevant for market risk and liquidity risk purposes. These data records can be filtered out for the data transfer. Additionally, historical data records were not transferred from the booking systems to the data warehouse. By this the necessary traffic on the internal data net for data downloads could be reduced significantly.

Another way to reduce data volume could be a filter on the data record fields. A full data record in a loan booking system for domestic loans contains far more than 400 fields. For market risk and liquidity risk purposes only less than 100 fields were relevant. The filter function for data record fields would reduce the data volume by the factor four.

Usually the data type for the transfer from the booking system to the data warehouse is a text file. In the data warehouse all text files should be stored as source files to keep track functionalities. This enables the user to check original data entries when the mapping process or the clearing process do not generate correct or expected data inputs.

Not all data sources for the market risk and liquidity risk analyses are available on the bank's platforms. Domestic and foreign subsidiaries use their own IT platforms and again different booking systems. For some subsidiaries the data delivery will be subject to legal and tax-related restrictions that need to be solved in advance before designing the interface to the data warehouse.

Mapping

After implementing interfaces to the different source systems the next task is to standardize the heterogeneous data import and to define a common data model for all source systems, which contains all information that is needed to perform the calculations. The vast amount of data need to be organized around an analytical framework that classifies the data and permits the understanding of variables not only at the lowest level of granularity, but also at higher aggregation. In its simplest form this means looking at aggregates or organizing the data, so that they can deliver better intelligence. A view of data, which has been collected from several source systems, has to be synchronized.

For each booking system individual mapping rules have been defined. The implementation of these rules requires an in-depth knowledge of all relevant products. In most cases the information of several fields has been combined and new variables have been defined because some data for the calculation of cash flows and yield figures were not available in some of the booking systems.

Clearing Section

Besides the integration of various booking systems into a homogeneous data model the quality of the imported data is also a big issue. Mistakes in data or missing data can cause, at worst, a crash of the whole data warehouse. It complicates the correct interpretation of the data and prevents the data from being calculated.

After mapping, a sub-process is needed where the imported data are examined to find typing errors, as well as to deduce from other fields the value of missing ones and therefore to prepare the imported data as input for the calculation engine. The sub-process described is called clearing.

The tasks could include:

- to verify the type, range and length of the data fields
- to complete missing or incorrect fields by default values or inference values from data redundancies
- to add those fields, which are necessary to run the calculation engine
- to validate single and inter-field consistency requirements
- to label the contract as compatible or incompatible, thereby clearing the records for the calculation engine

Market Data

Several different types of market data are needed for the calculation. The interest rate curves, FX-rates, implied volatilities and volatility smiles, as well as spread information (liquidity and credit spread) for various currencies and several products could be extracted from front office systems; a manual input should also be possible, especially for performing simulations or stress tests.

Results and Reporting

A liquidity transfer pricing system should provide all figures and results for the calculation of liquidity costs for each particular contract. To allow an easy communication with the front office system of liquidity management it should be made sure that the most common data structure with the front office data model is implemented.

Depending on the daily data mass in the system it can be necessary to delete results from the database after calculating relevant risk- and profit and loss (P&L) figures. Cash flow data for each particular contract require lots of storage space. It can be appropriate to clean cash flow data after calculating liquidity costs. For certain key dates (end of month, end of quarter, year-end) a full data set should be kept.

A data warehouse with a broad range of banking book products stored in one consistent data format will soon reveal an ability to support not only liquidity risk analyses, but also to serve market risk and P&L analyses.

Other examples of banking book systems are the market risk analyses for interest rate risk in banking books where sensitivity figures can be calculated from cash flow data, or where cash flows are used for gap profiles. The present value functionality can be used to calculate present values for banking book products, like fixed rate loans to support the hedge accounting process according to IAS 39 or SFAS 133, or to provide results for fair value disclosure.

Relevance for "Sarbanes Oxley" (SOX) and Certification

In order to achieve ongoing SOX compliance, CFOs must be able to guarantee that financial information is consistently and accurately tracked from source to disclosure, while providing insight into any changes and adjustments that might occur along the way. In this process not only the working processes and their interfaces are focused by SOX rules. The systems that produce data or analyses for SOX-relevant reports have to be SOX-approved as well. The following steps of a software development process have to be in the focus of SOX documentation:

- *development and support of software*: problem analyses, software design and test design, realization, and system integration
- *test and implementation of software systems*: V/I tests, test documentation and formal approval
- *ensuring system reliability*: to make arrangements for hardware, software and staff reliability
- *hand over in the production environment*: documenting this procedure, user concept, monitoring of tools in production, and problem management
- *configuration management*: creating software packages and archiving, changing requests, and version management by standard software
- *quality assurance*: adjustment due to law and policies, implementation of a test concept, status reports, and a user forum.

The adherence to all steps has to be documented through key controls. The effectiveness of these controls will be tested by a walk-through process of internal and external auditors.

Besides verifying a clean software development process, the bank has to assure that the system generates the expected outcome. Consistent test documentation from first implementation to the current applied version is necessary to get the approval in the SOX baselining process. For systems that were implemented years earlier, and where initial test documentation in a SOX-compliant form is not available, all active system functions have to be tested and documented in the current version to comply with current SOX requirements.

CONCLUSION

Liquidity risk transfer pricing is an indispensable tool for management to make banks' liquidity risk transparent beyond treasury and risk management units. As for credit and market risk, transfer pricing ensures that the risk inherent in client transactions is transparent to the sales units. It ensures proper risk-adjusted pricing.

In this chapter we have laid out that liquidity risk transfer pricing must not only consider long-term mismatch risk, but also contingent liquidity risk and associated market liquidity risk for securities held as collateral against short-term unexpected liquidity drawdowns. A proper liquidity transfer cost system needs to address all these components of liquidity risk.

In practice, the implementation of a liquidity transfer price system requires a lot of technical effort and is best linked to other treasury- and controlling-related topics, like interest rate risk management of the banking book, IAS 39/SFAS 133, fair value disclosure, and SOX compliance.

NOTES

[1] Term deposits have from a liquidity point of view a certain rollover rate, although from an interest rate risk viewpoint the customer rate can always be fixed at each rollover. From this perspective a certain fraction of the term deposit balance is "non-maturing" and can be modeled like sight and saving deposits.

[2] Robert Crowl, vice-president, National City Bank.

Part 3

Case Studies and Alternative Views

CHAPTER 8

A Concept for Cash Flow and Funding Liquidity Risk

Robert Fiedler

Although illiquidity and insolvency have always been issues of utmost importance for senior management, during the decades since the development of basic asset liability management (ALM) tools like the liquidity gap analysis, there has only been weak convergence towards a standard for measuring liquidity risk. However, there has been some movement during the last years: leading global banks have developed internal methodologies for the quantitative measurement of liquidity risks. Both as a consequence of that and independently, regulators under the umbrella of the BIS in Basel have drafted direction signs and rudimentary standards for the measurement and management of liquidity risk,[1] and have begun to transpose them locally; not everywhere at the same speed. Nonetheless, these methods are far less established than the analogical ones used to measure market and credit risk. Merely the formulation of commonly accepted methods for operative risks is of comparable intricacy, especially if one takes into account that Basel II requires explicit capital adequacy – unlike liquidity risks – for operative risks, thus forcing the development of a methodology. Below we first examine what makes it so difficult to find a consistent liquidity methodology and then try to sketch a possible solution.

All problems start with the various understandings of the notion "liquidity," respectively "liquidity risk," but the biggest problem is the fact that this is regarded as a rather "academic" problem. The "liquidity risk" of not being able to sell a bond in a timely fashion at a fair price matches with the "liquidity risk" of a bank not being able to generate enough funds in order to meet its payment obligations, which might collocate with the "liquidity risk" in the sense of lack of central bank funds.

The insufficient differentiation between *liquidity risk management* and *liquidity management* (in the sense of *cash management*) is another problem. In the cash management perspective the liquidity of the bank is condensed in a single number at the end of the day: the central bank balance. This view reduces complexity enormously, but in an inadmissible way for the purpose of liquidity risk management. For cash management purposes the quality of a liquidity forecast is determined by its ability to anticipate this single *ex post* number – which is only the product of a complex netting of collateralization, payment, funding and cash management processes – the *management of the term structure of liquidity*. The cash management view intrinsically assumes that all these processes that have worked in the past, will work in the future as well. This is appropriate in a going concern situation, but it will not work in a future environment where, for example, market liquidity or own credit ratings have deteriorated – which is the view liquidity risk management must take.

Furthermore, liquidity risk in the sense of liquidity-induced losses and insolvency risk are seen as linearly coupled processes – because too little liquidity is bad (high insolvency risk) and more liquidity is better (lower insolvency risk) it is deduced that much more liquidity is better. But in practice too much liquidity can be bad as well. A bank, for example, which takes an "over-prudent" approach might end up "always-liquid" and therefore will experience opportunity losses because the surplus funds can only be placed at unfavorable rates. In addition, the bank could eventually attract unwanted credit risk when lending out the surplus.

Due to the traditional dominance of credit risk, risks are in general perceived to be on the asset side of the balance sheet. Although market risk has moved the focus toward a more balanced point of view, liquidity risk is still out of the focus, because it resides mainly on the liability side. Also, the traditional buy-and-hold portfolio view in market and credit risk is usually transposed to ALM, making it hard to detect continuity funding risk. This is part of the more general problem in ALM, which is the unaltered transformation of market risk methods. The usage of risk-free or risk-neutral forward yield curves is especially problematic. In an arbitrage-free world it does not make a difference if *ex ante* forecast yield curves turn out *ex post* as poor estimations of the actual future interest rates: if deals are done at generally accepted market prices they can (in this theory) always be fully immunized against interest rate changes by selling or hedging. The evidence, however, can only be checked indirectly: if the immunization is not possible, price arbitrage is possible – this cannot be.

In reality, a hedge or sale is often unwanted or impossible, but risk-neutral forward curves are nevertheless used to conjecture future cash flows – with obviously bad results if interest payments or cash liquidity are forecast. All in all, many bankers regard liquidity risk management as an art rather than as a science. This should be changed.

We will first try to systematize the different usages of the term "liquidity" and establish a consistent view on one particular part of the problem: the cash flow or funding liquidity risk of a (financial) institution.

MARKET LIQUIDITY

Financial instruments such as bonds or equities are liquid if they can be easily sold "at market price"; a liquid market consists of liquid financial instruments. Bond traders, for example, would characterize a liquid bond as trading with little or no "liquidity premium." The first problem arises when we try to describe liquidity risk in terms of a liquidity premium. In a naive understanding of liquidity, we assume that there is a proper quantitative relationship between the amount of "free bonds" in the market and the liquidity premium. However, the liquidity premium is often used to explain "other" price effects as well.[2] Market liquidity is also a function of transaction size; transactions in tiny amounts as well as indigestible big blocks trigger the inclusion of a liquidity premium in the price.

Classic VaR is about the cost of liquidating traded portfolios in an adverse market, but it does not separate market risk and liquidity risk. Market liquidity effects are not excluded *per se* – they are already built into historical market prices. However, the weakness of the VaR concept in this regard is that the risk of a portfolio is measured independently from its size, thus assuming constant market liquidity independent from its size. This effect could be included in VaR calculations by adjusting the holding period to take size into account: a range of "low liquidity premium" has to be identified, quantifying the smallest as well the biggest amount of securities where "normal", not liquidity-affected, market prices can be assumed. If a position is too small or too big in that sense, the holding period should be longer than the standard one-day period. This raises the question about the right "standard" holding period for VaR. Unfortunately, the amount of guesswork needed to initialize such quantitative models makes it very hard to achieve better results than those which rules of thumb would have given anyway.[3]

CASH FLOW LIQUIDITY RISK

Cash flow liquidity risk of a bank could be characterized as the bank's risk of being unable to meet its contractual payment obligations (insolvency). As insolvency itself is binary (a bank is either solvent or not, there is nothing in between), the risk could be expressed as the probability of being insolvent. The ability of an institution to remain solvent depends on its counterbalancing capacity, its ability to generate cash by the sale (or repo) of assets, as well as to create new liabilities. The rate, at which cash can be generated, by whatever means, is a critical aspect in the management of cash liquidity.

Cash liquidity risk arises from different sources:

- *systemic*: the shortage of central bank funds due to a regulatory action or a failure of the market redistribution process (not enough credit limits available, lack of information about potential "long" counterparties, and so on)

- *individual*: the bank's credit rating is cut or is at least rumoured to be doubtful
- *technical*: the "forward payment structure" (the cumulated net cash inflows and outflows of the institution) is biased, or the uncertainty about its anticipated values is too high.

The *systemic liquidity risk* is often regarded as being inevitable – most banks take the position that the regulators will act to preserve the integrity of the system. In such a case the internal management of cash liquidity risk by the institution is all but immaterial: if there is an absolute lack of funds in the market even the best quality liquid assets will not help to produce cash liquidity – funding costs can rise to "infinite" levels.

In the case of an *individual credibility crisis*, the counterbalancing capacity is distorted. It is difficult to raise deposits even at a premium; assets are difficult to sell at a fair price because the market expects to pay a distressed price. An ample and well-shaped liquidity portfolio has in many cases allowed institutions to survive temporary problems and restored market confidence.

Finally, in a *technical liquidity crisis*, the solvency of the institution could be seriously affected, simply because there are much more outflows than inflows in a certain period. It does not matter that "technically" after the end of this period the bank will have a cash surplus. There are no systemic events and no crises in individual credibility. The counterbalancing capacity is fully available but simply inadequate. However, if the reserve would be higher, it would compensate the excess of outflows. This raises the essential question: "What is the ideal size and structure of the liquidity reserve?" Simply stated, higher liquidity reserves result in a greater likelihood of staying solvent – unfortunately these reserves are not available for free.[4]

What is crucial is how the funding of the liquidity reserve is structured in time:

- the net liquidity effect, which can be generated from a short-term funded reserve, might not last long enough[5]
- long-term funded reserves that produce stable amounts of cash consume the overall funding capacities of the bank, eventually a permanent over-funding of the bank, at high costs.

Cash flow liquidity risk can be defined as the danger of possible losses stemming from "unwanted" liquidity situations:

- the bank's funding rates are too high, or it repo's or sells its assets at prices which are too low, measured against "normal" market rates/prices[6]

- the bank places surplus funds at rates which are too low, measured against previous funding rates
- the bank loses money by holding excessive liquidity reserves with respect to its actual needs.[7]

Practical Needs

Prudent liquidity risk management starts with identifying the bank's most *probable future liquidity situation* (the anticipated forward payment structure) plus quantifying its possible counterbalancing capacities – this could be called *"structural – liquidity risk."* The additional risk arising from an adverse change, both to the projected position as well as to the assumed counterbalancing capacity, could then be called *"extended liquidity risk."*

The structural risk can be measured with a classic liquidity gap analysis in which credit risks and operational risks are disregarded: expected cash in- and outflows are netted and accumulated in time. This is straightforward, if the expected cash flows are known – such as interest inflows from a straight government bond. The problem is more complex for contingent cash flows.

There are different sources of uncertainty:

- if the expected cash flows of a financial instrument are solely a *function of market parameters*, they can be estimated with the forward curve, respectively with stochastic simulation. Most traded contingent financial instruments are of this type
- financial instruments that depend on *counterparty decisions* only can be modeled under the hypothesis that historic behaviour can be extrapolated into the future (this is the usual treatment of volatilities in VaR modeling). Core deposits, for example, are usually modeled in this way
- financial instruments that are *mixed* in the above sense can be modeled using a modified arbitrage-free argument, thus assuming economic behaviour of the counterparties (a cash flow from a short option requires certain market conditions to prevail, as well as a customer decision to execute the option).

Other Comments

A pure retrospective analysis of the payment profiles of certain balance sheet positions will sometimes result in cash flow forecasts with low volatility, whereas it is clear that these balance sheet positions can produce huge cash flows in certain market events. Contrarily, parts of the balance sheet with high volatility might turn out to produce less dramatic turbulence in beleaguered situations. For example, the swing in the balance of savings deposits has remained moderate, sometimes for decades, but during a bank run they could fall near to zero almost immediately.

On the other hand, short-term repo business, which has been responsible for the biggest cash swings during the last years, will in a crisis
produce more desirable than adverse cash flows. So both normal and
extended liquidity risk can be further divided into stable and distressed,
subject to market conditions.

It is an art to dynamically manage an institution's balance sheet items
in the light of moving markets: volatility is smoothed where necessary as
well as increased if appropriate. Nevertheless, prudent banking requires
understanding the behaviour of the bank's cash situation in normal
markets as well as the boundaries of possible outcomes in the case of an
event. In the case of a liquidity crisis, it will be very hard for a potential
lender to judge whether the bank's liquidity crisis is just the result of a
technical cash shortage – or if it is part of a much bigger problem.

A CONCEPT FOR CASH FLOW AND FUNDING LIQUIDITY

The Concept in a Nutshell

There are different types of *liquidity risk*:

- *insolvency risk of a bank* – the potential disability of a bank to raise
  enough cash timely (in order to meet payment obligations)
- *funding cost risk of a bank* – potential increased comparable funding
  costs (immediate or deferred) leading to profit erosion, inability to
  do new business or losses on existing business
- *liquidity risk of a currency or a payment system* – potential lack of
  funds (central bank money) or the disability to distribute these
  funds to the seekers of cash
- *liquidity risk of a financial instrument* – risk of not being able to
  sell/buy or repo this instrument in volume and time, without
  affecting the market price ("too much").

We will start with the *insolvency risk of a bank*; later the other types of
liquidity (risk) will be integrated into the concept. In the beginning we do
not look at cash-flow projections from a cash manager's view, but take
the liquidity risk manager's point of view.

In this first stage of the insolvency risk concept the decisive question
is:
    "Will the bank be solvent in the future?"
or,
    "What is the likelihood of the bank being solvent in the future?"
or,
    "How 'far' is the bank from insolvency (distance to default)?"

The risk of future insolvency rises as the surplus of future outgoing cash flows over incoming cash flows increases and the uncertainty of the cash flows increases. Consequently, the aim is to have a surplus of cash – with high probability. Unfortunately, a surplus of cash is costly in general, because the surplus liquidity will usually be dispensable at the end of the day and thus has to be given back to market, incurring opportunity costs together with unwanted credit risk.

The equilibrium between avoiding insolvency and preventing unnecessary costs and risks should be determined and controlled if the "most probable" future liquidity situation is implemented in our concept:

- starting from the set of all *contractual deals*, it is straightforward to determine the *deterministic cash flows* (with no optionality)
- next, the *expected values of non-deterministic cash flows* need to be estimated
- finally, the *model risk* in the computation of the non-deterministic portion has to be reflected.

The fundamental problem is the treatment of cash flows that are either not contractually fixed (or known today) or stem from yet non-existing business. Should, for example, the principal cash flow of a tradeable bond be mapped to its maturity (because this is "contractual" for the bond) or should it be put into a quite short time band (because it can be sold "immediately")?

The preferred solution is based on the fact that in liquidity management future cash flows can stem from three types of "liquidity optionality":

- *no liquidity option* – both counterpart and bank must exercise contractual payments
- *short (passive) liquidity option* – the bank must accept the counterpart's decision to exercise this option (the counterpart can, for example, withdraw savings deposits or call an additional loan tranche)
- *long (active) liquidity option* – the bank itself can exercise this option (for example, call on a liquidity facility, sell a bond against cash or "store" surplus cash in a fungible security, and so on).

First Step

All cash flows are grouped into classes, depending on the liquidity-optionality type they stem from. *Expected cash flows* (*ECFs*) consist of all cash flows stemming from a "no liquidity option": all fixed cash flows, including the cash flows that would be known if the underlying reference rates would be known (like a floater coupon if the forward Libor rate is known).

Next, the *contractual* cash flows are collected. These consist of:

- *fixed (determined)* cash flows
- *variable* cash flows (where through the design of the underlying financial instrument the actual future cash flows can vary from their current values)
- *hypothetical* cash flows stemming from yet non-existing business (once these deals exist, they may have known cash flows).

Next Step

The *expected cash flows* have different grades of uncertainty: from almost none (fixed cash flows) to hypothetical cash flows where we do not even know if the underlying deals will ever exist. We will regard this uncertainty only as risk, if it leads to detrimental cash flows. "Detrimental" has to be taken against the liquidity situation of the bank and means therefore not necessarily "greater outflows/smaller inflows".[8]

So if we want to capture all types of potential liquidity risks, we need to capture all potentially detrimental effects stemming from the uncertainty of cash flows; however, as in a first step to measure the downside risk of becoming insolvent (and not the risk of being "over-liquid"), we take a biased approach insofar as we consider only:

- *short* liquidity optionality, leading to lower inflows or higher outflows and consequently only as a result of net cash flows, which are detrimental in an insolvency view
- *long* liquidity optionality, leading to higher inflows or lower outflows.

As a result, the *cash flow at risk (CFaR)* adjusts the bank's expected liquidity situation by making allowance for potential changes of anticipated cash flows. There are, as in VaR, two possible views: downside CFaR takes only changes into account which are detrimental for the bank's liquidity profile (in an insolvency risk view); two-sided CFaR captures both lacking and surplus cash flows, as an extreme positive deviation from the expected liquidity situation it can be a risk as well (in a broader ALM view).

Intrinsic CFaR reflects uncertainties within existing contracts stemming from changes of market indices and counterparty decisions (short liquidity options). For example, a client decides to withdraw a call deposit or opts for a deferred payment. However, exercising a prepayment option would be "not detrimental" in the sense of insolvency for the bank's liquidity situation and would therefore not be included in CFaR.

Extrinsic CFaR should capture as well incertaities like distorted payment processes, credit risk of a counterparty, own operational risk, and so on.

The *counterbalancing capacity (CBC)* finally captures all "long liquidity options", which result in the hypothetical cash flows the bank could generate in order to improve a potentially detrimental liquidity situation. For example, sell or repo assets, especially securities, acquire additional liabilities in the market (for example, from liquidity facilities with other banks or other unsecured funding in the market).

We can now formulate the decisive question: "Will the expected liquidity situation, with the probable passive optionality deducted, be more disadvantageous than the headroom of the bank (active optionality) – or not?"

Or, in another form:

$$ECF - CFaR + CBC > 0$$

resp.

$$CBC > -(ECF - CFaR)$$

Here the bank remains solvent (in this concept) only if the above inequality holds. That means in the future expected cash flows (ECF), risk-adjusted by the cash flow liquidity at risk (CFaR), cannot be dominated by the bank's ability to hypothetically counterbalance (CBC) this shortage. Hence, the bank becomes insolvent.

If we go back to the example: a bank has a tradable bond in its investment portfolio. In this concept, the cash flows at maturity plus the interest cash flows are put into ECF (in the first instance); further, assume CFaR = 0 (no optionality in the cash flows).

The CBC is estimated by making salability assumptions for this bond (for example, like 30% in two days, 50% in three days, the rest within two weeks). By this the "contractuality" of the bond's cash flows is reflected in ECF. ECF itself is not distorted by the uncertainty stemming from the salability of the bond, which is reflected by the "active optionality", CBC.

In regard to the above equation: ECF and CBC cannot simply be added (for example, component wise, like vectors). If the bond is sold before maturity, interest payments after the sales date and final repayment would be double counted in CBC and ECF.

Formally, the cash flows in ECF are conditional. ECF is firstly calculated assuming the bond is held until maturity; assuming that CBC is generated (the bond is sold as in the example), ECF is recalculated, omitting the doubled cash flows.

Nomenclature

The following nomenclature is in Exhibit 8.1 on page 182. We will try to be as consistent as possible, without giving up readability. Therefore, slight inaccuracies can happen: in ECF_t the dependency of ECF on the time is

EXHIBIT 8.1   Nomenclature and abbreviations used in this liquidity risk concept

Nomenclature

ECF_t Expected cash flow CF^+_t Inflow CF^-_t Outflow $..._t ...$ in $t = 0, 1, ..., T$	LaR^α liquidity at risk $...^\alpha...$ confidence level α	CBC	Counter- balancing capacity
$ECF = ECF_D + ECF_{ND}$ ECF_D deterministic ECF_{ND} non–deterministic	$CFaR^\alpha$ Cash flow-at-risk	A	Asset liquidity
	$ELaR^\alpha$ Expected liquidity at risk (cash flow risk)	S	Sale liquidity
$ECF_{ND} = ECF_F + ECF_V + ECF_H$ ECF_F floating ECF_V virtual ECF_H hypothetic		R	Repo liquidity
	$VLaR^\alpha$ Value liquidity at risk (NPV risk)	S + R	Balance sheet liqudity
FLE Forward liquidity Exposure (cumulated) $FLE_t = FLE_{t-1} + ECF_t$ $FLE_0 = $ Nostro balance		CBC	$= A + S + R$

MCO	Maxmium cash outflow:	FCE_t	$< MCO_t$
AMCO	Adjusted MCO:	$FCE_t + CBC_t$	$< AMCO_t$

denoted the subscript t; however, we might use a notation like a function f(t) as well, if this is easier to read: $ECF_D(t)$.

EXPECTED CASH FLOWS (ECF)

In the following section the fact that ECF is a function of time ECF(t) is suppressed in our notation. ECF for *deterministic cash flows* ECF_D contains capital and fixed interest cash flows from *all contractual deals*. Credit or operational risks which could lead to the customer's inability to pay are not considered in ECF_D. Since the non-deterministic behaviour of ECF can result from many elements of uncertainty, *non-deterministic cash flows* are include by calculating the expected values of the following variables:

- *Floating cash flows (ECF_F)* are determined by *market indices* that are not yet known, such as:
  - variable interest cash flows forecast with the risk-neutral yield curve or other yield curves
  - cash flows depending on exchange rates and so on.
- *Virtual cash flows (ECF_v)* are the estimates of the deviation of "real cash flows" from their original projections such as:
  - savings deposits – in practice the contractual cash flows are substituted by the cash flows of a replicating portfolio
  - early repayments stemming from counterparties exercising repayment options

- deferred or lacking payments due to the inability of the customer to repay loans on time
- *Hypothetical cash flows (ECF$_H$)* stem from future, yet unknown new business such as:
  - "non-performing loans" – hypothetical new loans are generated leading to outflows that (partially) offset the contractually guaranteed but improbable inflows
  - cash flows from new deals that are regarded as unavoidable; for example, drawings from loan facilities
  - anticipated rollover of repayments.

Note: principally all types of non-fixed or non-existent deals can be modeled and included in the concept of hypothetical cash flows. However, the modeling of very insecure deals leads to high dependency on assumptions and returns ECF values that might be inappropriate for practical purposes. Under this liquidity risk concept, expected cash flows originating from active options should be collected in CBC and not in ECF.

FORWARD LIQUIDITY EXPOSURE (FLE)

Liquidity can only be created or dissolved by central banks. If a bank is long a certain amount of liquidity on a certain day, it will either leave this amount on its central bank account until the next payment day, or eventually place it in the market until it is paid back on a day further in the future. In both cases the initial amount will be compounded with the inflows and outflows of that future payback day. For the sake of simplicity we make the assumption that the funds are always placed until the next payment day – and further, that there are no interest payments as they are too small to matter in the context of solvency.

If the bank is short, it will raise the money in the market or get it via repo from the central bank – we make the assumption that the bank is able to do so.

We can now forecast the liquidity situation of this bank by cumulating net positions from day to day into the future. More formally, if we look at the end of a certain day t: the net cash flow ECF(t) is the sum of all inflows $CF_k^+(t)$ and outflows $CF_m^-(t)$, $ECF(t) = \Sigma_k[CF_k^+(t)] + \Sigma_m[CF_m^-(t)]$.

If ECF(t) is positive, the bank will either lend out this amount to other banks or keep it at the central bank account. If ECF(t) is negative, the bank needs to raise this amount from other banks or from the central bank. We assume, that in both cases, ECF(t) will be received/paid back on the next day and suppress interests here. Therefore, the bank will start in $t + 1$ with the cash position ECF(t) plus all in-/outflows on that day:

$$ECF(t) + \Sigma_k[CF_k^+(t + 1)] + \Sigma_m[CF_m^-(t + 1)].$$

In order to account for this cumulative effect, we introduce the *forward liquidity exposure* FLE(t) or FLE_t at a day t:

In t = 0 : FLE(0) = balance of the nostro account
In t + 1 : $FLE(t+1) = FLE(t) + \Sigma_k[CF_k^+(t+1)] + \Sigma_m[CF_m^-(t+1)]$

As we now account for the time structure of liquidity and the cumulating effect of net cash positions we can give a better answer to our original question, "Will the bank be solvent in the future?"

The decisive inequality turns to:

$$FLE(t) - LaR(t) + CBC(t) > 0$$

Which has to hold for all days t of our chosen future time horizon.

This shows an essential characteristic of solvency: it is not time-insensitive but has a term structure. It is not sufficient that the inequality holds for certain days, or on average, it must hold for all days. A surplus of liquidity on day t + 1 is useless if the bank has gone insolvent on day t. The FLE(t) describes the term-structure of solvency appropriately.

Below we must work out how to forecast the term-structure effects of the model risk LaR(t) and the counterbalancing capacity CBC(t) as well.

LIQUIDITY AT RISK (LaR)

Non-deterministic cash flows (ECF_F, ECF_V, ECF_H) can be forecast, but these forecasts will usually differ from the reality – *ex post*. However, a forecast error can be estimated *ex ante* to estimate the expected quality of the future forecast.

- If the forecast cash flows only depend on market parameters (for example, interest payments linked to EURIBOR), the market parameters are changed (simulated) and the effect on the resulting cash flows is determined.[9]
- In the next step, all the probable changes in the yield curve are derived from their behavior in the past. If this is applied to the above, the result is LaR.
- The changes resulting from CFaR impact more than insolvency risk. Every change of ECF could have detrimental economical effects such as increased cost of funding, decreased return on funds placed, or higher risks. In order to separate these risks from insolvency risk itself, we consider *value liquidity at risk* (VLaR).

ECF is first calculated for variable cash flows in a standard market scenario (risk-neutral forward yield curve), then ECF' is newly calculated under the assumption that the yield curve was shifted by 25 bps (for example, as a result of a rating downgrade). The difference between ECF′ and ECF gives us the sensitivity to changes in the market.

Interpretation

With a probability of α (which must be defined in advance), the cash flows will vary between ECF − LaR and ECF + LaR.

In addition, if cash flows change and thus ECF, this deviation will also affect the present value (NPV). In order to be able to distinguish between these effects, the following naming conventions are used.

EXPECTED CASH FLOW (LIQUIDITY) AT RISK (CFaR)

This is the possible changes of ECF "downwards", caused by possible changes in the underlying cash flows.

Interpretation

With probability α, the net cash exposure at a future time interval will be floored by $CFaR_\alpha$.

VALUE LIQUIDITY AT RISK (VLaR)

This is the possible change in the discounted value ($CFaR_\alpha$) of the changed cash flows.

Interpretation

With probability α, the "downward value change," $NPV(CFaR_\alpha)$, will not be greater than $VLaR_\alpha$.

Both CFaR and VLaR result from the uncertainty of ECF. In modeling, for reasons of practicability, one usually begins with the estimation of the non-deterministic cash flows and calculates the potential deviation of the floating cash flows from this estimate. Then, the risks are considered when simulating the virtual/hypothetical deal. For example, the volume paths of the savings deposits are simulated stochastically in the model from the University of St. Gallen; that is, the expected value (ECF) and the α-quantile ($CFaR_\alpha$) can be determined.[10] In the next step, the cash flows which were assumed to be deterministic before, and deviations resulting from the effects of the credit risk and operational risk, can be taken into account (extended scenario building).

COUNTERBALANCING CAPACITY (CBC)

Measuring possible negative developments (downside risk) is one thing, quantifying the risk exposure which a bank can bear is quite another. Even if opinions vary and may differ in this respect, for VaR-type problems there is a common denominator: *The possible detrimental value change must not be greater than the capital available (to offset this possible loss).* This is especially the point of view of the supervisory authorities (regulatory risk capital) for market, credit and operational risks. It can be applied to VLaR but not to CFaR: if CFaR would indicate a possible insolvency of the bank, in the logic of capital as a risk buffer this funding gap would have to be filled with equity – this is not available for such a purpose since it has already been included in the calculation of FLE. For this reason, a substitute for capital is required for the CFaR case: the CBC.

Initial Situation

At a future point in time, t, there is a shortage of liquidity – $E_t := \text{CFaR}_\alpha(t)$.

Question

Is the bank able to fund at least E_t; that is, will it be possible to avoid insolvency?

Answer

This is achieved by analysing the possibilities of the bank to create counterbalancing liquidity:

- F – balance sheet extension acquisition of additional non-secured funding
- R – balance sheet neutral sale/repurchase of assets in return for temporary liquid funds (until the repurchase date)
- S – balance sheet contraction sale of assets against liquid funds.

If the maximum liquidity that could be generated by F_t, S_t and R_t until a certain point in time t, was known (with probability α), it would be possible to determine if it would be sufficient (with probability α) to fund the liquidity shortage E_t in t. Thus the CBC is defined as follows:

$$\text{CBC}_t = F_t + S_t + R_t.$$

With probability α, a possible future liquidity shortage E_t could be counterbalanced by a combination of acquiring unsecured funding as well as repo'ing and selling assets; that is, $E_t + \text{CBC}_t$ is non-negative – or, in other words, with probability α, it will be possible to keep the bank solvent at the future t.

NON-SECURED FUNDING

F_t, *funding liquidity* (liquidity-by-funding), is a "soft" value resulting from a self-analysis that may be based on historical funding by counterparties. It is normally negotiated between the unit of the bank that sets the liquidity limits and the units that utilize the liquidity limits. If an agreement has been made, these amounts must of course be reduced by the amounts already funded in the market.

REPO/SALE OF ASSETS

First, before assumptions about repoability/salability can be made, it is necessary to clarify which assets can be used:

- All assets that are available for liquidity management are marked as *eligible assets* and grouped in the so-called *box position.*
- The maturity structure of the box position (assets as of value date) is described as *forward asset inventory* (FAI).
- Each asset is analysed – individually or as element of an asset class – with regard to its salability: the highest possible amount S^A_t that can be sold out of the forward asset inventory until t is determined or estimated. The sum of the values S^A_t across all eligible assets is called *liquidity by sale*, S_t.
- Each asset is analysed – individually or as the element of an asset class – with regard to its repoability: the highest possible amount R^A_t that can be generated by repos out of the forward asset inventory until t is determined or estimated. (FAI must, of course, be reduced by S^A_t because the assets already sold are no longer available for repos.) The sum of the values R^A_t across all eligible assets is called *liquidity by repo*, R_t.
- The sum of liquidity by sale plus liquidity by repo is called *balance sheet liquidity*, $BSL_t = S_t + R_t$.

INTERNAL LIMIT SETTING

The BIS requires limitation per currency depending on the deal term.[11] There are two main methods for setting liquidity limits with the aid of FLE (which may be LaR-adjusted):

- maximum cash outflow (MCO_t)
- adjusted maximum cash outflow ($AMCO_t$).

MAXIMUM CASH OUTFLOW

Per time interval $[t, t + 1]$, an amount MCO_t is set as a lower limit. The limit has been breached if:

$$FLE_t < MCO_t$$

Interpretation

The business area that utilises the limit must control future cash flows so that the minimum cash position MCO_t does not fall below the amount allowed – independent of its ability to actually offset shortages; that is, it must be possible to assume that the limit-setter can always compensate for all liquidity shortages.

Advantage

This is simple, clear and no CBC is required. The concept is appropriate if limits can be allocated according to requirements.

Caveat

If limits can only be assigned, depending on the available liquidity resources, first, the CBC of the business area that wants to utilize the limit must be estimated. If this capacity changes (for example, if realisable assets are sold), the limits must be reallocated and the complete limit-setting process must be carried out again.

ADJUSTED MAXIMUM CASH OUTFLOW

Per time interval $[t, t+1]$, an amount $AMCO_t$ is set as a limit. The limit has been breached if:

$$FLE_t + CBC_t < AMCO_t$$

Interpretation

The business area that utilizes the limit must manage their future cash flows in such a way that the minimum cash position, $AMCO_t$, does not fall below the amount allowed. At the same time, it must take into account that it has to offset a possible shortage by itself without outside help.

Advantage

Changes in the CBC of the business area that wants to utilize the limit are adjusted automatically – without it being necessary to carry out a reallocation process.

Caveat

CBC is required, its effects must be clear.

LIQUIDITY RISK MEASUREMENT: PRACTICAL IMPLEMENTATION OF A CONSISTENT METHODOLOGY

The aim of this section is to show how consistent measurement of liquidity risks can be implemented in a practical way. A refined stochastic analysis is not dealt with here.

General Procedure for Liquidity Risk Measurement

The *liquidity risk* is the risk that the bank may not be able to undertake the necessary borrowings (*insolvency risk*) or could do so only at higher costs (*funding cost risk*). The potential liquidity exposure in this context is calculated by determining or estimating the cash flow profile (or EFC) over time.

EXHIBIT 8.2 ECF and forward liquidity exposure (FLE) on an overall level

	Date	ECF overall							
		Expected : E				Quantile : E_α			
		ECF^+	ECF^-	ECF	FLE	$ECF^+{}_\alpha$	$ECF^-{}_\alpha$	ECF_α	FLE_α
O/N	19.07.2005	31.95	−40.04	−8.09	−8.09	31.95	−40.04	−8.09	−8.09
T/N	20.07.2005	38.77	−18.49	20.28	12.19	38.72	−18.53	20.19	12.10
S/N	21.07.2005	14.47	−35.91	−21.44	−9.25	14.45	−35.95	−21.50	−9.40
1 w	26.07.2005	15.94	−32.97	−17.03	−26.28	15.87	−33.15	−17.28	−26.68
2 w	02.08.2005	43.16	−17.28	25.88	−0.40	42.92	−17.39	25.53	−1.15
1 m	21.08.2005	24.68	−27.72	−3.04	−3.44	24.59	−27.98	−3.39	−4.54
2 m	20.09.2005	37.60	−34.15	3.45	0.01	37.09	−34.55	2.54	−2.00
3 m	21.10.2005	47.14	−28.27	18.87	18.88	46.44	−28.65	17.79	15.79
6 m	21.01.2006	19.14	−24.62	−5.48	13.40	18.76	−24.89	−6.13	9.66
1 y	21.07.2006	21.42	−24.62	−3.20	10.20	20.52	−25.45	−4.93	4.74
2 y	21.07.2007	31.51	−33.41	−1.90	8.30	29.93	−34.21	−4.27	0.46
3 y	21.07.2008	29.68	−16.95	12.73	21.03	27.88	−17.57	10.30	10.77
5 y	21.07.2010	26.02	−18.35	7.67	28.70	25.73	−19.32	6.41	17.18
7 y	21.07.2012	17.88	−24.43	−6.55	22.15	16.29	−26.09	−9.81	7.37
10 y	21.07.2015	38.15	−14.62	23.53	45.68	35.34	−15.33	20.01	27.38
15 y	21.07.2020	28.43	−33.69	−5.26	40.42	27.10	−35.32	−8.22	19.16
30 y	21.07.2035	30.43	−18.65	11.78	52.20	27.91	−21.24	6.67	25.83
> 30 y		25.98	−42.16	−16.18	36.02	23.13	−48.47	−25.33	0.49

In a period grouping (time buckets) to be fixed by the user in accordance with the requirements (here from O/N up to 30 years in increasing steps), the expected cash flows (incoming cash flows ECF^+ and outgoing ECF^- cash flows) are mapped. The sum of cash inflows and outflows results in the balance for each period (ECF). The balance that has been accumulated over time (FLE) indicates if a liquidity surplus or liquidity shortage is estimated (see Exhibit 8.2).

Since the cash flows are contractual; that is, are assigned to already existing deals, but are not necessarily all predetermined, it must be possible to display the degree of uncertainty in estimating non-predetermined cash flows. If this uncertainty ($CFaR_\alpha$ – cash flow at risk, the α-quantile) for a predefined probability of occurrence α has been determined (more details later on), the expected "cash flows with haircuts" are known; then:

- $ECF_{\alpha+}$, the expected cash inflow, decreased by the haircut $CFaR_\alpha$
- $ECF_{\alpha-}$, the cash outflow, increased by $CFaR_\alpha$.

The balance ECF_α and the accumulated balance FLE_α result correspondingly "with haircut" (see Exhibit 8.3 on page 190).

THE CASH FLOW TYPES AND THEIR UNDERLYING DEALS

Contractual cash flows can be divided into *deterministic* (predetermined and thus already known) ECFD and *non-deterministic* ECFND. Of course, even deterministic cash flows are not absolutely "safe"; for example, due

EXHIBIT 8.3   ECF and α-adjusted expected cash flows ECF$_\alpha$

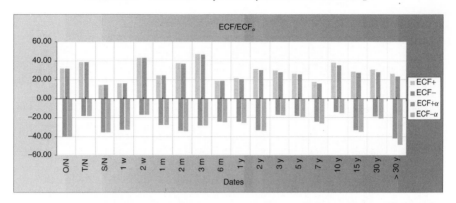

EXHIBIT 8.4   ECF$_D$ and FLE – expected values and quantiles

| | Date | ECF$_D$ – deterministic | | | | | | | |
| | | Expected : E | | | | Quantile : E$_\alpha$ | | | |
		ECF$^+$	ECF$^-$	ECF	FLE	ECF$^+_\alpha$	ECF$^-_\alpha$	ECF$_\alpha$	FLE$_\alpha$
O/N	19.07.2005	15.11	–6.99	8.12	8.12	15.11	–6.99	8.12	8.12
T/N	20.07.2005	12.77	–3.34	9.43	17.55	12.77	–3.34	9.43	17.55
S/N	21.07.2005	0.90	–13.79	–12.89	4.66	0.90	–13.79	–12.89	4.66
1 w	26.07.2005	4.58	–4.20	0.38	5.04	4.58	–4.20	0.38	5.04
2 w	02.08.2005	12.30	–1.09	11.21	16.25	12.30	1.09	11.21	16.25
1 m	21.08.2005	14.18	–8.72	5.46	21.71	14.18	–8.72	5.46	21.71
2 m	20.09.2005	8.06	–8.41	–0.35	21.36	8.06	–8.41	–0.35	21.36
3 m	21.10.2005	9.27	–6.41	2.86	24.22	9.27	–6.41	2.86	24.22
6 m	21.01.2006	6.95	–14.82	–7.87	16.35	6.95	–14.82	–7.87	16.35
1 y	21.07.2006	4.94	–8.70	–3.76	12.59	4.94	–8.70	–3.76	12.59
2 y	21.07.2007	8.60	–20.35	–11.75	0.84	8.60	–20.35	–11.75	0.84
3 y	21.07.2008	8.31	–4.43	3.88	4.72	8.31	–4.43	3.88	4.72
5 y	21.07.2010	11.31	–7.00	4.31	9.03	11.31	–7.00	4.31	9.03
7 y	21.07.2012	5.31	–1.41	3.90	12.93	5.31	–1.41	3.90	12.93
10 y	21.07.2015	14.74	–5.95	8.79	21.72	14.74	–5.95	8.79	21.72
15 y	21.07.2020	9.21	–19.00	–9.79	11.93	9.21	–19.00	–9.79	11.93
30 y	21.07.2035	18.09	–7.84	10.25	22.18	18.09	–7.84	10.25	22.18
> 30 y		6.43	–9.22	–2.79	19.39	6.43	–9.22	–2.79	19.39

to operational risk or credit risks that are, however, not taken into account here. Thus, the quantile portion is "trivial" in that it is always zero (see Exhibit 8.4).

The non-deterministic cash flows are split into three types (see Exhibit 8.5) according to the level of difficulty in predicting them:

- *floating* cash flows, which only depend on a future index; for example, a floater with interest payments that are uniquely determined by EURIBOR
- *variable* cash flows, which can show more complex dependencies (both the point in time and amount of the cash flow are not

EXHIBIT 8.5 Hierarchy of deterministic and non-deterministic ECF

ECF overall			
ECF_D deterministic	ECF_{ND} non–deterministic		
	ECF_F floating	ECF_V variable	ECF_H hypothetical

determined), but they can at least be assigned to deals that already exist (a call option of the floater)

- *hypothetical* cash flows, which belong to a deal that does not yet exist (for example, deposits that are expected to roll over).

Floating Expected Cash Flows (ECF$_F$)

They can be mapped as a time-dependent function of an index, which is fixed in the future/is not known for the time being. In the case of an underlying interest rate (for example, EURIBOR), the forward rate y^F (which has been implicated from the par yields/zero yields) is used as an estimate of future interest, but it is also possible to use other curves.

The risk or sensitivity is then determined by forecasting the risk of the forward interest rate curve (the deviation between the interest rate curve actually occurring and the current forward interest rate curve). If these deviations are estimated statistically *ex ante* using methods such as Forecast-at-Risk (FaR), the result is the *cash flow at risk, CFaR*.[12] A shift of the current interest rate curve y^F by σ^F results in the sensitivity of the cash flow relative to the changed interest rate curve $y^F + \sigma^F$.

In Exhibit 8.6 on page 192, the classic VaR for the interest rate curve (holding period one day) was used – scaled by the square root of the days until the future date.

Variable Cash Flows (ECF$_V$)

Both the size and the start date of variable cash flows may be unknown. They originate from existing deals.

Example

€100 fixed-term deposit for one year, six-monthly 2% with call right after six months. The contractual/deterministic view without the call option:

$$€ \ 1.00 \text{ in } t_{+6 \text{ m}}$$

$$€ \ 101.00 \text{ in } t_{+12 \text{ m}} \text{ capital plus interest}$$

The following variable cash flows (which replace the deterministic cash flows) result from the historic derivation that 30% of the depositors

EXHIBIT 8.6   ECF$_F$ and FLE – expected values and quantiles

Date	ECF$_F$ - floating							
	Expected : E				Quantile : E			
	ECF$^+$	ECF$^-$	ECF	FLE	ECF$^+$	ECF$^-$	ECF	FLE
O/N 19.07.2005	2.82	−9.51	−6.69	−6.69	2.82	−9.51	−6.69	−6.69
T/N 20.07.2005	7.85	−0.51	7.34	0.65	7.85	−0.51	7.34	0.65
S/N 21.07.2005	9.85	−11.57	−1.72	−1.07	9.85	−11.58	−1.73	−1.08
1 w 26.07.2005	4.19	−8.53	−4.34	−5.41	4.19	−8.54	−4.35	−5.44
2 w 02.08.2005	5.44	−4.67	0.77	−4.64	5.43	−4.68	0.76	−4.68
1 m 21.08.2005	3.56	−2.30	1.26	−3.38	3.55	−2.30	1.25	−3.43
2 m 20.09.2005	10.70	−9.75	0.95	−2.43	10.67	−9.78	0.89	−2.54
3 m 21.10.2005	14.39	−6.22	8.17	5.74	14.34	−6.24	8.10	5.56
6 m 21.01.2006	2.00	0.00	2.00	7.74	1.99	0.00	1.99	7.55
1 y 21.07.2006	1.20	−1.59	−0.39	7.35	1.19	−1.60	−0.41	7.14
2 y 21.07.2007	4.24	−2.03	2.21	9.56	4.20	−2.05	2.15	9.29
3 y 21.07.2008	0.00	−7.49	−7.49	2.07	0.00	−7.58	−7.58	1.71
5 y 21.07.2010	13.84	−2.15	11.69	13.76	13.63	−2.18	11.45	13.16
7 y 21.07.2012	0.00	−10.84	−10.84	2.92	0.00	−11.03	−11.03	2.13
10 y 21.07.2015	6.80	−4.64	2.16	5.08	6.65	−4.74	1.92	4.04
15 y 21.07.2020	13.49	−6.94	6.55	11.63	13.14	−7.12	6.02	10.06
30 y 21.07.2035	3.62	−3.78	−0.16	11.47	3.49	−3.92	−0.43	9.63
> 30 y	8.40	−14.21	−5.81	5.66	8.09	−14.74	−6.65	2.98

exercise their right to call:

€ 31.00 in $t_{+6\,m}$ 30% capital repayment plus interest

€ 70.70 in $t_{+12\,m}$ 70% remaining capital plus interest

The distinction from hypothetical cash flows (these belong to the deals that do not yet exist) is not always clear cut; for example:

- for an individual savings deposit, future cash flows are to be assigned to the existing deal (variable cash flows)
- on the other hand, cash flows can exist in a portfolio of savings deposits belonging to savings deposits that do not yet exist (hypothetical cash flows).

Example

Savings deposits, nominal amount $= 100\%$. At the set time structure $(t_1, \ldots, t_N)$, fictional cash flows are assumed: $(x\%_1, \ldots, x\%_N)$ the determination of which is not dealt with here.

Hypothetical Cash Flows (ECF$_H$)

Hypothetical cash flows result from deals that do not yet exist (today). They are therefore non-contractual and should be disregarded in our methodology. For practical reasons, however, it is sometimes inevitable to regard them. In order to do this, hypothetical deals are generated, for example, by renewing existing deals. Overlapping with variable cash flows (for example, savings) is not always avoidable (see above).

Example 1

Historically, a portfolio of loans ("bad-performing loans") shows the characteristic that only about 20% of the contractual capital cash flows actually flow. On average, repayment is "postponed" by three months. In the deterministic view, the following results are obtained for a loan of €100 with a three-month interest rate of 6%:

€ 101.50 in t_{+3m} capital plus interest

Assuming that 80% of the capital repayment is not flowing, but has to be considered as a "bridging loan" for three more months at 8%, we obtain in total:

€ 101.50 in $t_{+3\,m}$	capital plus interest	(deterministic)
€ − 80 in $t_{+3\,m}$	bridging loan	(hypothetical)
€ 80.40 in $t_{+4\,m}$	remaining capital + interest	(hypothetical)

Example 2

Historically, a portfolio of six-month deposits shows the characteristic that – after interest re-pricing – about 60% of the deposits are reinvested. In the deterministic view, the following results are obtained for a deposit of €100 with a six-month interest rate of 3% (= 3.5% reference rate minus 0.5%):

€ − 101.50 in $t_{+6\,m}$ capital plus interest

Assuming that 60% is reinvested for a further six months at the forward rate (4.5%) minus 0.5%, in total, we obtain:

€ − 101.50 in $t_{+6\,m}$	capital plus interest	(deterministic)
€ 60.00 in $t_{+6\,m}$	reinvestment at 4%	(hypothetical)
€ − 61.20 in $t_{+12\,m}$	remaining capital + interest	(hypothetical).

The question now remains as to how consequently this view is to be applied. For instance, the same reinvestment assumption can also be applied to the cash flows in $t + x + 6m$ (forward rate 5%):

€ −101.50 in $t_{+6\,m}$	capital plus interest	(deterministic)
€ 60.00 in $t_{+6\,m}$	reinvestment at 4%	(hypothetical)
€ − 61.20 in $t_{+12\,m}$	remaining capital + interest	(hypothetical)
€ 36.00 in $t_{+12\,m}$	reinvestment at 4.5%	(hypothetical)
€ − 36.81 in $t_{+18\,m}$	remaining capital + interest	(hypothetical)

and so on.

Limitation

Measurement of the liquidity/liquidity risk is one thing, its management is quite another (see Exhibit 8.7).

Who, Whom, How, by What Means, What Exactly?

Who: First of all it must be determined who is responsible for the management of the solvency or the liquidity risk of the bank: the limit-setter (for example, the Treasury).

Whom: It must be determined who will be limited: the limit recipients (for example, the business areas, legal sub-units, local units, currency areas, and so on).

How: It must also be considered whether limits are supply or demand driven:

- *Demand-oriented*: The historical liquidity utilization by the limit recipients is captured and set as a limit. This implies the assumption that what succeeded in the past will also succeed in the future (going concern). If, however, the demand changes, it is unclear what will happen with this approach.
- *Supply-oriented*: The bank's ability to bear liquidity risks is determined (for example, by making assumptions about the liquifiability of tradable assets and estimating the amount of unsecured funds that could be raised) and distributes this bearing capacity to the limit recipients via limits.

By what means: In principle, different ratios describing the liquidity situation can be limited: the maximum net cash outflow in a period, the ratio of short-term liabilities to long-term assets, and so on. *In practice*, the cumulated liquidity gap FLE(t) is limited over time because it shows the liquidity shortage (or the liquidity surplus) in future periods. As a *refinement*, the risk-adjusted liquidity gap FLE_α (t) (the expected gap reduced by the cash flow risk) should be limited, if it is available for calculation.

EXHIBIT 8.7 Typical limit setting for insolvency risk respectively funding risk

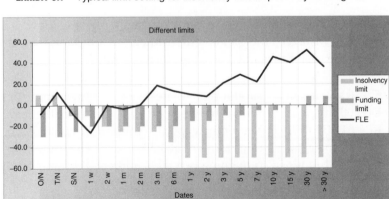

EXHIBIT 8.8   Combined limitation of insolvency and funding risks (via FLE)

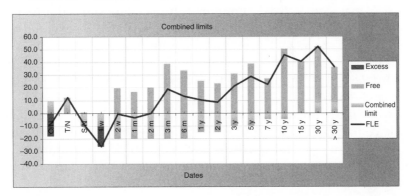

EXHIBIT 8.9   Combined limitation via risk neutral FLE or via risk-adjusted FLE$_\alpha$

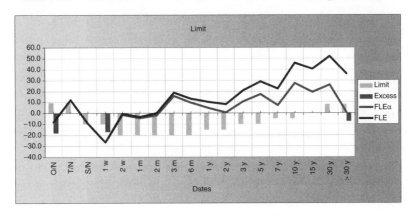

What Exactly is Limited?

- If the *insolvency risk* is to be limited, always sufficient liquidity (positive FLE or at least narrow negative limits) has to be ensured. Liquidity shortages in the future, however, are "less dramatic" since there is enough time to cover the shortages (typical limits: see Exhibit 8.8).

- However, if the *funding risk* is to be limited, it is (almost) the other way round: the close periods are less interesting because no dramatic changes in the funding costs are to be expected. However, this does not apply to the long-term area; furthermore, the periods are longer and the yield effects are greater (typical limits: see Exhibit 8.9).

FROM UNADJUSTED TO ADJUSTED LIMITING

There are two major ways to set liquidity limits on the basis of FLE (which is or is not LaR adjusted). First, per time bucket T, a so-called MCO$_T$ (*maximum cash outflow*) amount is set as the limit. This limit is breached if:

$$\text{FLE}_T < \text{MCO}_T$$

Interpretation: the limit-taking entity has to steer its future cash flows in a way that a given fixed minimum future cash position (MCO$_T$) is not violated – independently from the entity's capability to counterbalance this potential shortage. For example, the limit-setting entity can always act as lender of last resort, sometimes even in a going-concern situation.

Advantage: it is simple and clear, especially if limits can be allotted "demand-driven."

Caveat: if the limit has to be allotted "supply-driven," an estimation of the counterbalancing capacity (CBC) of the limit-taking entity has to be implicitly incorporated – this can change quickly (for example, if an entity sells liquefiable assets after the limit setting), an adaptation to the new situation has to be made by a reallocation of limits, running through the limit-setting process, which is usually slow and cumbersome.

The more advanced way of limiting is to set per time bucket T, a so-called AMCO$_T$ (*adjusted maximum cash outflow*) as the limit. This limit is breached if:

$$FLE_T + CBC_T < AMCO_T$$

Interpretation: the limit-taking entity has to steer its future cash flows in such a way that a given fixed minimum future cash position is not violated. It has to manage its capability to counterbalance this potential shortage, which means that the entity acts as "its own lender of last resort" – at least partially or in going-concern situations.

Advantage: it is more supply-driven, and changes in the counterbalancing capacity of the limit-taking entity are automatically adjusted without going through reallocation processes.

Caveat: it cannot be implemented without CBC.

The following example illustrates the difference between both methods.

MCO

The group treasury of internationally operating Alwayssolvent Bank wants to allot a liquidity limit to its New York branch. The forward liquidity exposure (FLE) should not fall below −1.0 bn within the next two months.

$$MCO_T = -1.0 \text{ bn}, T = (\text{from today, to two months ahead})$$

However, Alwayssolvent Bank NY thinks it should have a liquidity limit of MCO$_T$ = −3.0 bn. It argues that 0.4 bn should come in emergency from the portfolio that is eligible for the FED window. Then 0.6 bn could be raised unsecured in the money market and the rest would come from repo'ing a special portfolio of liquid assets of 2.0 bn, which are 100% repoable, as the New York branch claims.

After some bargaining, both parties agree on MCO$_T$ = −2.8 bn. After three months a watchful controller finds that the New York special portfolio has been sold down from 2.0 bn to 0.1 bn. The free funding has obviously been invested in loans as these have gone up from 2.7 to 4.6 bn.

On the previous week's average, New York has had an FCE of around -2.7 bn, but always within the limit of -2.8 bn. As treasury has only reserved a portfolio of 1.2 bn US government bonds exclusively for New York, they decide to make a proposal to the Board to restructure the New York limit to $\mathrm{MCO_T} = -1.0$ bn.

The following morning, a large fund in Singapore collapses. At midday the largest lender of the fund, Neverworry Bank, in Rome, is no longer able to execute payments. At noon in New York, repo markets have doubled interest rates and sharpened haircuts to almost 10%, but are more liquid then ever.

At Alwayssolvent Bank NY, yesterday's forecast of the previous day FLE turns out to be accurate: New York is -2.6 bn short. Group treasury immediately turns its US government portfolio in 1.1 bn cash and finds another 0.1 bn from various sources. The market for unsecured funds has dried out completely, but friendly banks in New York collect another 0.2 bn. In the late afternoon Alwayssolvent Bank NY finds itself $-2.6 + 1.1 + 0.1 + 0.2 = -1.2$ bn short. Assuming, that another 0.4 bn should come from the FED window, Alwayssolvent Bank NY would end up with a final deficit of -0.8 bn.

AMCO

In the beginning, group treasury sets the adjusted liquidity limit to $\mathrm{AMCO_T} = -1.0$ bn. This means that the FLE plus the CBC should not fall below -1.0 bn within the next two months. As under-current calculations the portfolio of liquid assets of 2.0 bn generates a CBC of 1.9 bn. New York *de facto* owns the desired headroom of $-1.0 - 1.9 = -2.9$ bn, which is almost fully used, until after one month, 0.6 bn of the liquid assets are sold. Both the negative exposure and the CBC go down in parallel by 0.6 bn, leaving the situation unchanged. However, as New York pays out an additional 0.5 bn loans, it has to report a limit excess of 0.4 bn.

Group treasury decides to increase their US government bond portfolio from 1.2 bn to 2.0 bn, and enlarges the New York limit to $\mathrm{AMCO_T} = -1.8$ bn; however, the New York branch has to pay 30 bps for the additional 0.8 bn. After that, New York decides not to swap more than 0.3 bn liquid assets against new loans.

When Neverworry Bank gets into trouble, New York is short 1.6 bn. After repo'ing the 1.1 bn liquid assets portfolio against 1.0 bn of cash, group treasury can cover the remaining 0.6 bn shortage by repo'ing only one-third of its US government portfolio against cash.

Liquidity at Risk

We will discuss both the liquidity at risk effects on cash flows, *CFaR*, and the value liquidity at risk, *VLaR*.

Cash Flow Liquidity at Risk (CFaR)

Assume that:

- we are looking at a portfolio P, which consists of financial instruments F
- the time horizon is $t = 1, \ldots, T$
- the expected values of the deterministic cash flows of each instrument F are generated directly by computing:

$$\mathrm{ECF_D}(F) = (\mathrm{ECF_D}(F)_1, \ldots, \mathrm{ECF_D}\ (F)_T)$$

  where the vector $\mathrm{ECF_D}(F)$ consists of numbers $\mathrm{ECF_D}(F)_t$
- the non-deterministic cash flows are generated by simulations S_k, $k = 1, \ldots, K$, with a matrix as result:

$$[\mathrm{ECF_{ND}}(F)_{t,k}]_{t=1,\ldots,T;k=1,\ldots,K}$$

- the kth row $(\mathrm{ECF_{ND}}(F)_{t,k})_{t=1,\ldots,T}$ represents the term-structured outcome of the kth simulation S_k. This can be regarded as a linearized distribution of the cash flows
- the arithmetic mean of the results of the simulations on a fixed day t (the tth column) gives the *expected cash flow in t*:

$$\mathrm{ECFN_{ND}}(F)_t = 1/K \cdot \Sigma_{k=1,\ldots,K} \mathrm{ECF_{ND}}(F)_{t,k}$$

- the term structure of the expected values of the non-deterministic cash flows are:

$$\mathrm{ECF_{ND}}(F) = (\mathrm{ECF_{ND}}(F)_1, \ldots, \mathrm{ECF_{ND}}(F)_T)$$

- for given $\alpha \in (0, 1)$ and t, the lower quantile $Q^-_{\alpha,t}(\mathrm{ECF_{ND}}(F))$ is determined by reordering the tth column:

$$(\mathrm{ECF_{ND}}(F)_{t,k})_{k=k,\ldots,K}$$

  so that:

$$\mathrm{ECF'_{ND}}(F)_{t,k-1} \overset{\leq}{=} \mathrm{ECF'_{ND}}(F)_{t,k}$$

  holds and stopping at the $K \cdot \alpha^{\mathrm{th}}$ element:

$$Q^-_{\alpha,t}(\mathrm{ECF_{ND}}(F)) = \mathrm{ECF'_{ND}}(F)_{t,K\cdot\alpha}$$

- the quantile can be interpreted as lower limit under which the expected cash flows will only fall with probability α.[13]

We can now define CFaR as the difference between ECF and the uncertainty of their appearance, reflected by the above quantile:

$$CFaR_t \overset{def}{=} ECF_t - Q^-_{\alpha,t}(ECF_{ND}(F))$$

We have not specified how the simulations are generated. They might be stochastic (for example, Monte Carlo methods), historic, or manually created.

In practice, we will look at:

- the *expected cash flow situation*, ECF_t, respectively
- the *risk-adjusted expected cash flow situation*, $ECF_t - CFaR_t$.

In the cumulated view, the *forward liquidity exposure*, we start with the nostro account balance as FLE_0 – where we do not have uncertainty. Next we determine $FLE_1 = FLE_0 + ECF_1$. If we use the risk-adjusted cash flow situation $ECF_1 - CFaR_1$ instead, we get $FLE_1 = FLE_0 + ECF_1 - CFaR_1$, the *risk-adjusted forward liquidity exposure*. Going on like that $FLE_{t+1} = FLE_0 + ECF_t - CFaR_t$ means that we will cumulate the CFaR portions as well:

$$FLE_{t+1} = FLE_0 + \sum ECF_t - \sum CFaR_t.^{[14]}$$

Example

In the following example we take up a somehow inverse method: we assume that a potential stochastic simulation of the future will be essentially driven by the historic distribution of the cash flows and therefore simplify the procedure and estimate the CFaR straightforward by the quantile of its historic distribution (see Exhibits 8.10 to 8.12).[15]

Once the cash flows are ordered by size, we get the quantile simply by counting: in this example, the sample size is 250, with $\alpha = 10\%$, Q^+_α is the 25th smallest inflow (Q^-_α is the 25th largest outflow), and so on.

EXHIBIT 8.10 History and average of inflows and outflows

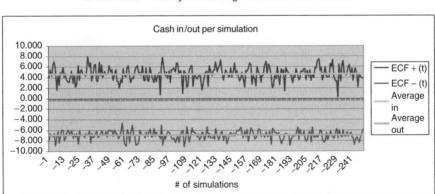

EXHIBIT 8.11 History of outflows ordered by simulation/by size of cash flow

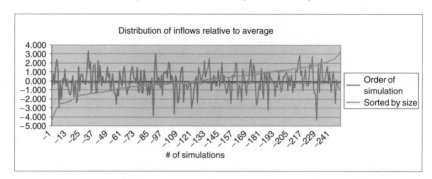

EXHIBIT 8.12 History of outflows ordered by simulation/by size of cash flow

	Inflows							Outflows					
			to average			=10%				to average			=10%
Sim s	$ECF^+_t(s)$	Average ECF^+_t	In order of simulation	Sorted by size	$CFLaR_t$	Q^+	Sim s	$ECF^-_t(s)$	Average ECF^-_t	In order of simulation	Sorted by size	$CFLaR_t$	Q^-
-1	4.044	4.670	-0.626	-4.359	-1.629	3.040	-1	-7.815	-6.954	-0.861	-2.158	-1.132	-8.086
-2	5.512	4.670	0.842	-3.916			-2	-6.575	-6.954	0.379	-2.011		
-3	4.287	4.670	-0.383	-3.636			-3	-7.059	-6.954	-0.105	-1.994		
-4	6.485	4.670	1.815	-3.218			-4	-7.128	-6.954	-0.174	-1.945		
-5	7.008	4.670	2.339	-3.033			-5	-6.580	-6.954	0.374	-1.889		
-6	5.833	4.670	1.163	-3.022			-6	-8.948	-6.954	-1.994	-1.835		
-7	1.648	4.670	-3.022	-2.678			-7	-6.919	-6.954	0.035	-1.825		
-8	4.656	4.670	-0.013	-2.558			-8	-6.236	-6.954	0.718	-1.689		
-9	2.612	4.670	-2.057	-2.523			-9	-8.390	-6.954	-1.435	-1.685		
-10	4.955	4.670	0.285	-2.488			-10	-7.144	-6.954	-0.190	-1.668		
-11	4.494	4.670	-0.176	-2.468			-11	-5.895	-6.954	1.059	-1.605		
-12	5.951	4.670	1.281	-2.436			-12	-6.088	-6.954	0.866	-1.572		
-13	4.052	4.670	-0.618	-2.416			-13	-7.876	-6.954	-0.922	-1.564		
-14	4.860	4.670	0.190	-2.360			-14	-7.508	-6.954	-0.554	-1.447		
-15	3.573	4.670	-1.096	-2.280			-15	-6.631	-6.954	0.323	-1.445		
-16	3.157	4.670	-1.512	-2.270			-16	-5.905	-6.954	1.049	-1.435		
-17	3.126	4.670	-1.543	-2.257			-17	-6.631	-6.954	0.323	-1.406		
-18	4.317	4.670	-0.353	-2.074			-18	-6.545	-6.954	0.409	-1.350		
-19	5.288	4.670	0.618	-2.057			-19	-6.073	-6.954	0.881	-1.348		
-20	2.918	4.670	-1.752	-1.991			-20	-7.423	-6.954	-0.469	-1.345		
-21	4.673	4.670	0.004	-1.952			-21	-6.731	-6.954	0.223	-1.333		
-22	2.234	4.670	-2.436	-1.904			-22	-7.228	-6.954	-0.274	-1.312		
-23	2.595	4.670	-2.074	-1.752			-23	-6.594	-6.954	0.360	-1.293		
-24	6.258	4.670	1.589	-1.724			-24	-8.622	-6.954	-1.668	-1.187		
-25	3.517	4.670	-1.152	-1.629			-25	-6.013	-6.954	0.941	-1.132		
-26	5.310	4.670	0.640	-1.611			-26	-7.082	-6.954	-0.128	-1.072		
-27	5.468	4.670	0.799	-1.604			-27	-6.945	-6.954	0.009	-0.993		
-28	4.642	4.670	-0.028	-1.603			-28	-6.806	-6.954	0.148	-0.977		
-29	4.484	4.670	-0.185	-1.543			-29	-7.403	-6.954	-0.449	-0.975		
-30	4.308	4.670	-0.362	-1.538			-30	-6.561	-6.954	0.393	-0.922		
-31	5.373	4.670	0.703	-1.513			-31	-6.922	-6.954	0.032	-0.912		

Value Liquidity at Risk (VLaR)

Here, one method is presented to describe the value liquidity risk (VLaR) resulting from the (general) liquidity risk (LaR).

First, the liquidity gap FLE is determined. Then, the *normal funding costs* in the periods with liquidity shortage (*"liability buckets"*) are calculated, using the bank's specific forward interest rate curve $f(t) + \sigma(t)$, which is composed of the risk-neutral forward interest rate curve $f(t)$ plus the bank's specific funding spread $\sigma(t)$. Next, the funding spreads are extended to $\sigma'(t)$ and the *extended funding costs* are recalculated with $f(t) + \sigma'(t)$ for the liability buckets. The difference between the normal and the extended funding costs represents the funding component of VLaR. In order to transform this term-structured result into one figure, the respective NPVs can be calculated (see Exhibits 8.13 and 8.15).

EXHIBIT 8.13 VLaR via normal and extended funding costs

	Time		Forward	Spread	ReFi	Spread	ReFi'	FLE overall			
	Date	Years	f(t)%	$\sigma(t)$%	f(t)+$\sigma(t)$%	$\sigma'(t)$%	f(t)+$\sigma'(t)$%	FLE	γ(CF)	γ'(CF)	$\Delta\gamma$
O/N	06.10.2005	0.00	2.00	0.00	2.00	0.00	2.00				
T/N	07.10.2005	0.00	2.10	0.00	2.10	0.00	2.10	17.40	0.00	0.00	0.000
S/N	08.10.2005	0.01	2.20	0.00	2.20	0.00	2.20	22.43	0.00	0.00	0.000
1 w	13.10.2005	0.02	2.30	0.01	2.31	0.01	2.32	−7.33	0.00	0.00	0.000
2 w	20.10.2005	0.04	2.40	0.01	2.41	0.02	2.43	−5.39	0.00	0.00	0.000
1 m	08.11.2005	0.09	2.50	0.01	2.51	0.03	2.54	3.44	0.00	0.00	0.000
2 m	08.12.2005	0.17	2.60	0.01	2.61	0.03	2.64	9.91	0.00	0.00	0.000
3 m	08.01.2006	0.26	2.70	0.01	2.71	0.05	2.76	7.88	0.00	0.00	0.000
6 m	10.04.2006	0.51	2.80	0.01	2.81	0.10	2.91	−3.54	−0.02	−0.03	−0.001
1 y	08.10.2006	1.0	3.00	0.01	3.01	0.15	3.16	−10.77	−0.16	−0.16	−0.008
2 y	08.10.2007	2.0	3.50	0.05	3.55	0.25	3.80	−24.60	−0.81	−0.87	−0.057
3 y	08.10.2008	3.0	4.00	0.10	4.10	0.32	4.42	−8.25	−0.30	−0.32	−0.023
5 y	08.10.2010	5.0	5.00	0.20	5.20	0.38	5.58	−14.50	−1.17	−1.26	−0.085
7 y	08.10.2012	7.0	6.00	0.30	6.30	0.50	6.80	−8.78	−0.72	−0.78	−0.057
10 y	08.10.2015	10.0	7.00	0.40	7.40	0.70	8.10	5.64	0.00	0.00	0.000
15 y	08.10.2020	15.0	7.50	0.50	8.00	0.90	8.90	10.73	0.00	0.00	0.000
30 y	08.10.2035	30.0	8.00	1.00	9.00	1.70	10.70	9.77	0.00	0.00	0.000
> 30 y			8.00	2.00	10.00	3.20	13.20	4.65	0.00	0.00	0.000

Sum −0.232

EXHIBIT 8.14 Forward liquidity exposure (FLE), normal and stressed funding curves

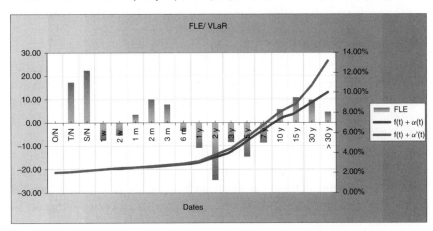

EXHIBIT 8.15 Difference $\Delta\gamma$ between normal and stressed funding costs as a result of the stressed funding curve

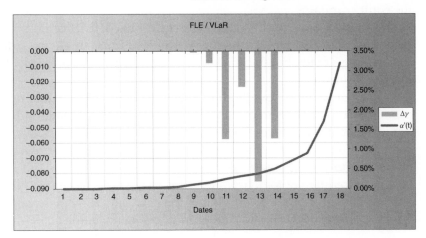

NOTES

1 BIS No. 69 paper.

2 Sometimes high liquidity (in the sense of a large amount of available securities) even results in a high-liquidity premium: shortly after the introduction of German Jumbo Pfandbriefe, large MBS issues, the yield-spread rose from −10 bps to +6 bps (against Libor) during six months. The market was obviously unable or not willing to digest the new issue's large number of available bonds; the bonds could only be sold at price discount. On the contrary, before the delivery date of a future, cheapest-to-deliver issues trade above their theoretical price. Selling them at the "fair price" would mean to give up additional income resulting from repos at lucrative rates – they are not very liquid. This is a first hint that liquidity risk is two-sided.

3 For example, during the LTCM crisis the yield spread between the 30- and 29-year US Treasury rose from under five bps to over 25 bps in two months, reflecting a different appreciation of the benefits of liquid securities rather than a change in the liquidity situation itself. Even if the premium were solely a function of market liquidity, it would not be a fair measure of liquidity itself, it could at best measure the perceived value of liquidity.

4 It is not contradictory that liquidity portfolios sometimes produce positive returns if benchmarked to funding levels. This is because the return is normally not high enough to meet the economic capital targets of the shareholders.

5 If a liquidity portfolio is funded with, say, weekly deposits, the net liquidity effect will shrink to zero after a week. If – not unlikely in such situations – haircuts rise, even negative liquidity impacts are possible. In a liquid repo market no additional liquidity can be created, but if the repo market dries out the bank is left with a possibly illiquid asset without funding.

6 Insolvency can be regarded in this framework as the limiting case where funding rates rise to infinity, or at least the funding loss exceeds the equity capital.

7 Note: there is no liquidity risk inherently linked to a certain deal or portfolio; for example, a high cash outflow from an equity index arbitrage deal could be beneficial for an institution with a permanently high cash surplus.

8 Assuming the bank is "overliquid," then the decision of a highly rated counterpart to execute an option not to roll over the drawing under a liquidity facility produces "positive cash flows," but it increases the problem of the bank to place the surplus funds at a competitive rate and avoid unwanted credit risk.

9 In a pure trading book environment this risk would be simple NPV-risk: the different present values of of the changed cash flows, valued with the corresponding yield curves produce a distribution of NPVs; as

usual the risk is the α-quantile. But, as we are in an ALM environment, we need to take a less static approach and identify, for example, the necessary funding transactions of forward short positions: if these gaps increase (CFaR) and funding rates go up in absolute terms (because of an increase in yields) or relatively (because of a detrimental credit event of the bank) the result is economic loss.

[10] Karl Frauendorfer and Michael Schürle 2005, "Dynamic Modelling and Optimization of Non-maturing Accounts," Working Paper, University of St. Gallen.

[11] "Sound Practices for Managing Liquidity in Banking Organisations," *Basel Committee Publications No. 69* http://www.bis.org/publ/bcbs69 .htm#pgtop

[12] Unfortunately, the forward curve gives only bad forecasts for future actual interest rates. With techniques like FaR this problem can be circumvented. See Robert E. Fiedler, *Using Forecast-at-Risk Techniques to Improve the Prediction of Future Yield Curves*, ALMLab paper, 2005.

[13] The potential correlation of the non-deterministic cash flows *in time* is disregarded here.

[14] This means that we do not take into account potential correlations between the non-deterministic cash flows in time as well.

[15] Furthermore, we distinguish between inflows and outflows; it can be discussed, if this is appropriate, or if one should always look at the historical distribution of net flows.

CHAPTER 9

The Liquidity Impact of Derivatives Collateral

Louis D. Raffis

INTRODUCTION

T he global derivatives market continues to expand at a rapid pace. This growth can be attributed to the development of new derivative types, such as credit derivatives, as well as continued growth in the more mature interest rate derivative market. Most large regional banks utilize derivatives for their own balance sheet with the intention to mitigate various types of risk, and find them an inexpensive and effective risk mitigator. Unfortunately, discussion of derivatives in both trade journals and the popular business press tends to focus on the vague probability of a system-wide disruption that leads to the collapse of major institutions, results in terrible financial losses on the part of investors, and massive intervention by the overseers of our financial system.

This commonplace hand wringing about derivatives never dwells on another, albeit more mundane concern to the bank treasurer, which is the focus of this chapter. Specifically, we want to review the liquidity effect that the use of derivatives collateral can have on a financial institution. While collateral may mitigate credit risk to varying degrees, collateral outflows can, under extreme scenarios, place stress on the institution's liquidity position.

This chapter will briefly review the current state of the derivatives market, and touch upon the various types and purposes of derivatives collateral. We will then develop a framework for analyzing the liquidity effects of derivatives collateral, with special attention given to the potential impact of ratings triggers on collateral flows. Background on the increased scrutiny behind ratings triggers analysis is also provided. The broader discussion on ratings triggers will hopefully divulge to the reader potential impacts of ratings triggers beyond the scope of this derivatives-focused analysis.

Last, we provide an approach to stress testing the liquidity effects of derivatives collateral and illustrate how a collateral stress test model can be developed for integration into an institution's overall stress test analysis. This is not intended to be a one-size-fits-all approach because every bank will be driven by the composition and structure of its derivatives position and its use of collateral. Nor is this intended to be an exhaustive discussion on the topic; however, for banks involved in the derivatives market, it is hoped that this material will help to jump-start your own efforts at collateral stress testing.

BACKGROUND ON THE CURRENT USE OF DERIVATIVES COLLATERAL

The International Swap and Derivatives Association (ISDA) Margin Survey 2005 of 109 firms, prepared by the ISDA Collateral Committee, reported $854 billion of collateral was in use by respondents at the beginning of 2005. ISDA used this figure to estimate that $1.21 trillion of collateral was in use worldwide, representing a 19% increase from the $1.02 trillion reported in the 2004 survey.[1]

Respondents had over 70,000 collateral agreements in use, with cash, primarily denominated in US dollars and euros, as the most common asset employed by firms, representing 73% of total collateral. US dollars collateral made up about 43% of all collateral in use, while euros represented about 29% of the total. Sterling and the Japanese yen made up 40% of all collateral in use. US government securities comprised about 8.5% of the total, and the remainder consisted of UK, Japanese, and other government securities, government agencies, supranational bonds, covered bonds, corporate bonds, letters of credit, equities, and metals and commodities.

Respondents to the survey also reported that approximately 55% of their derivative transactions were secured by collateral agreements, as measured both by trade numbers and mark-to-market exposure. This number is significant compared to the 30% figure reported by respondents in 2003 and 50% reported in 2004.

The ISDA Collateral Committee noted that the key underlying drivers supporting this growth are a continuing increase in the number of collateral programs, an increase in the number of collateral agreements (driven in part by the development of the hedge fund industry), an increase in the use of derivatives (particularly equity and credit derivatives) by all players, and a growing awareness of the importance of managing counterparty credit exposure, reinforced by a number of significant market disruptions in the not so distant past.

Surprisingly, according to the Collateral Committee about 77% of the large and medium-sized respondents to the survey indicated that they rehypothecate, or re-use, collateral received from counterparties to satisfy their own collateral needs. While the rehypothecation process can increase operational risk and back-office expenses, many firms have found that this dynamic use of collateral reduces liquidity burdens or can even make a collateral program self-funded.

COLLATERAL AND CREDIT RISK MITIGATION

Credit risk is risk due to uncertainty in a counterparty's ability to meet its obligations. It is the risk that a bank will not receive the money it is owed because the counterparty that owes the money is unable to pay and must default. Because there are a wide array of potential counterparties in the market, from individuals to sovereign governments, and many different types of obligations, the underlying cause of credit risk can vary greatly from counterparty to counterparty. For a derivatives position, credit risk can be defined as the bank's net replacement cost in the event that a counterparty in a negative position versus the bank fails to meet the payment terms of its outstanding positions. Credit exposure is the maximum amount of the potential loss that would be suffered if a bank's counterparty were to default on its obligations. There are two components to credit exposure as it pertains to derivatives.

Current credit exposure, also referred to as mark-to-market position (MTM), is the amount you would lose if a default occurred right now. For example, consider an interest rate swap between two banks, X and Y. The terms of the swap agreement require Bank X to pay Bank Y a floating rate of interest tied to three-month Libor. Bank Y agrees to pay to Bank X a fixed rate of interest over the life of the transaction. By simply calculating the sum of the present value of the stream of all future projected payments for the swap at today's interest rates, we can calculate its current MTM. In other words, we can calculate how much each bank would have to pay in order to unwind, or terminate, the swap today. This is also commonly referred to as the replacement cost of the swap. Typically, at the beginning and at the maturity of the transaction, this value is zero for both counterparties. In fact, it is theoretically feasible, though highly unlikely, for the MTM to remain at zero for the duration of the transaction.

A positive MTM is also the value that one party loses if the other party were to default right now. Given the simple fact that there are two parties to the transaction, the positive MTM from one party's perspective is the negative MTM from the perspective of its counterparty. In practice, the calculation of the replacement value may involve several other factors, such as whether there are relative credit spread differences between Bank X and Bank Y. Since the current MTM value of a swap is the net present value of all future floating rate cash flows netted against all future fixed-rate payments, the credit risk at inception should be minimal because the MTM is zero.

Since the MTM of a swap is dependent upon the number of future payments and the level of future interest rates, as the swap approaches maturity the MTM will approach zero. This amortization effect becomes stronger as the swap approaches maturity and it eventually overwhelms any effect caused by changes in interest rates.

Potential future credit exposure is the theoretical amount that one would lose if a counterparty default occurred at some future date. For certain types of transactions (for example, a term bank loan with a fixed rate of interest and a principal balance due at maturity) this amount is quite predictable. For an interest rate swap, or other type of derivatives transaction there are several variables depending on the type and terms of the derivative, such as the level of foreign exchange rates for FX transactions, or the level of future interest rates for interest rate swaps. Sophisticated estimation techniques based upon statistics and probability theory have been developed to generate a range of potential outcomes, with varying probability of occurrence. An experienced analyst can use such data to derive an accurate estimate of credit exposure over some defined time frame.

Collateral is used to offset or mitigate the MTM exposure in a transaction, since the bank can claim the collateral in the event that its counterparty defaults on its payment obligations at some point during the life of the derivative. If the MTM exposure is fully secured or over-collateralized, the bank only retains the risk of deterioration in the value of the collateral from the time of default to the time the collateral is sold off (assuming non-cash collateral is used). If the MTM is partially secured, the bank will lose only the difference between the MTM and the value of the collateral. In a volatile market environment a non-cash collateral position that was over-collateralized yesterday may not be sufficient to cover the MTM exposure today, and this market risk must be accounted for as well. Typically, full coverage of the MTM exposure is not mandated by the terms of the ISDA agreement and residual MTM exposure for any counterparty is rarely zero. The bank's credit department must determine what the right level of residual exposure is for every counterparty.

RATINGS TRIGGERS IN THE POST-ENRON WORLD

Ratings triggers are clauses in financial contracts and other legal arrangements that are designed to protect one party in an arrangement from the negative consequences of financial deterioration incurred by another party. The financial deterioration is signaled by a downgrade in credit rating typically assigned by a nationally recognized statistical rating organization (NRSRO).

Rating triggers are commonly found in credit agreements covering bank loans and credit lines loan securitizations and in bond indentures. Triggers may turn up in other agreements; often unbeknownst to bank management until the time a negative credit event occurs. A rating trigger typically provides a counterparty with certain rights in the event that a borrower's credit ratings fall to certain levels identified in the document. The financial impact of ratings triggers can vary in severity from small increases in loan pricing and commitment fees in credit facilities, to a loss of revenue from securitization servicing arrangements, to outright events of default that may enable a creditor to put a piece of outstanding debt back to a borrower. In this way the very presence of rating triggers may result in increased downward rating pressure on the distressed firm. In addition, ratings triggers are most often applied to lower rated credits – where they typically pose the biggest risk. For most financial services firms, ratings triggers are viewed favorably because they can be used as a means of reducing credit exposure and improving the risk-return tradeoff in dealing with larger commercial clients at the lower end of the credit spectrum. But for the bank's treasury staff, dealing with the effects of triggers on the flip side of the equation, the view of ratings triggers is similar to the view held by their corporate clients.

Often, such triggers can strike when a company is already under financial distress at just the time when it needs all of its available sources of liquidity.[2]

Rating triggers are also commonly found as part of the standard documentation supporting a derivatives trading arrangement. For example, counterparty agreements between a bank and its trading counterparties might incorporate rating triggers that call for the bank to provide collateral should its rating fall to certain predetermined levels. Such triggers are commonly found in the credit support annex to the ISDA master agreement. It is this topic that we will cover in greater depth here.

The collapse and bankruptcy of Enron in late 2001 and the financial distress of several other firms during the same time frame represented a watershed event in the financial markets that is still being felt in corporate boardrooms and treasuries throughout the country. As we know, a number of financial institutions were severely affected by the fallout, but a more subtle effect has indirectly impacted a much larger number of financial service firms. As has been well documented, in the years prior to 2001, Enron had entered into a number of extremely complex financial transactions that were really understood by few individuals outside the financial markets. Several of these transactions had ratings triggers embedded in them, which in some cases accelerated the financial decline of Enron. Other corporations during these go-go years entered into what appeared to be benign transactions that also contained ratings triggers. Financial distress, or in some instances even the rumors of financial distress, coupled with severe ratings triggers embedded in these various legal arrangements, led to the near collapse of these firms.

In the wake of these events, the rating agencies responded with a closer look at the financial consequences of ratings triggers. For example, Moody's Investors Service published a commentary entitled, "The Unintended Consequences of Ratings Triggers" in December, 2001, and began an annual survey process, requesting firms to research and provide them with all known embedded ratings triggers throughout their respective organizations. You can imagine what a sizable, albeit insightful, undertaking this proved to be for many organizations, particularly for larger, far-flung, and decentralized operators. It was this process that inspired bankers to look closely at the impact that ratings triggers might have on liquidity, affording many a fresh look at their credit rating exposure, and ultimately leading some to a closer examination of the ratings triggers embedded in collateral arrangements.

LIQUIDITY STRESS TESTING

A sound bank liquidity management program will utilize some form of a stress test analysis in an attempt to model negative liquidity effects and management's attempts to rectify the problem. Such events include, but are not limited to, the default of a major market player, a major political event, a natural or human disaster, a company-specific event such as a ratings downgrade, or negative publicity about the bank that causes a run on deposits. One common method to define these effects on the bank is to translate them into a ratings downgrade simulation.[3]

Using available historical industry information, company-specific balance sheet information, and current information on the availability of market-sourced liquidity at various ratings levels, you can calculate the potential liquidity shortfall that may result from a negative liquidity event. The chart in Exhibit 9.1 on page 210 shows one format of a stress testing exercise, incorporating a net cash capital calculation, along with specific management-defined targets for the calculation under different ratings assumptions and response time frames, such as 30, 90, 180 and 360 days. In this way, you can reflect on the increased liquidity that can come with large-scale transactions that have long lead times, such as loan sales and securitizations.

A crucial benefit of the stress-testing exercise is to require bank Treasury personnel to think "out of the box" and look for potential sources of liquidity, such as asset sales, securitizations, secured lending arrangements, and sale/leaseback transactions, to name just a few. Perhaps even more importantly, you need to have a solid grasp of potential drains on liquidity in a stressed situation. Most bankers closely measure and track the most common ones, such as a loss of "hot money" deposits and loss of access to the wholesale funding markets, but a truly thorough stress testing exercise must include the impact of the hidden liquidity drains caused by ratings triggers.

MEASURING THE CONTINGENT LIQUIDITY EFFECTS OF DERIVATIVES COLLATERAL

The use of collateral to mitigate derivatives credit risk offers us an interesting interplay between the bank's credit risk, as captured by its senior unsecured credit rating; interest rate risk (captured by changes in the MTM of its interest rate swap book); and other market-oriented risks, such as FX, equity, credit, energy, and commodity risks.

EXHIBIT 9.1 Net cash capital stress test, December 31, 2005

Bank rating:	**30 day**		**90 day**			**1 year**			
12/31/05	**A1**	**Baa1**	**A1**	**Baa1**	**Ba1**	**A1**	**Baa1**	**Ba1**	**B1**
Net cash capital position	**P1**	**P2**	**P1**	**P2**	**P3**				
Total assets									
Total managed assets									
Adjusted bank ratios:									
Debt issuance									
Loan securitizations									
Total loans:									
Loan growth/Draws on commitments									
Escrow deposits									
Derivatives collateral									
Discount window									
Adjusted net cash capital position									
Adjusted ratio to total assets									
Adjusted ratio to total managed assets									
Preferred range:	15%–20%	10%–20%	20%–30%	15%–20%	10%–20%	35%–45%	25%–35%	15%–25%	5%–15%
	30 day		90 day			1 year			
Bank rating:	A1	Baa1	A1	Baa1	Ba1	A1	Baa1	Ba1	B1

While the use of collateral may substantially reduce a bank's credit exposure, it will transfer some of this exposure into increased liquidity and market risk, effectively converting other forms of derivatives risk – interest rate, credit, foreign exchange and commodity – into potential draws on the bank's available cash and collateral resources. Fortunately, in many instances, these multiple exposures across product lines can offset each other. The effective use of netting arrangements, which allow a bank to consolidate multiple positions with the same counterparty, will use these moderate to low correlations between certain product lines to reduce total collateral flows. Nevertheless, any effective and comprehensive liquidity stress testing regimen requires the bank treasurer to factor in the extreme events that, when combined with the ratings triggers, may manifest themselves through an increase in collateral requirements.

As stated by ISDA in their 2005 Collateral Guidelines, "Collateral agreements can also be a significant liquidity drain on a firm, especially if the firm has executed many agreements with credit rating dependent thresholds. It is essential to have a simulation of the liquidity change impact of such agreements. To accomplish this, some firms simulate the additional liquidity requirements in the event of a downgrade."[4]

The flow chart in Exhibit 9.2 on page 212 shows an approach to stress testing a bank's derivatives collateral position. Obviously, this process cannot be successful unless a strong collateral management reporting effort is already in place. In fact, if bank management decided not to make the necessary up-front investment in collateral reporting, it's highly unlikely that a stress testing requirement will drive management to incur the necessary expense of an upgrade. Perhaps a more likely situation is that you will find the reporting for certain derivative types, such as interest rate swaps, well ahead of newer derivatives products that have yet to be fully integrated into the collateral reporting function. Also, the use of different systems for different products can complicate the information-gathering process.

This becomes even more crucial when the bank employs cross-product netting of counterparty collateral. However, the netting of collateral positions in your liquidity analysis will occur only after you have stressed the individual derivative products.

After gathering your data, the next step in the process is the use of Monte Carlo or other simulation techniques to enable you to predict the demands on collateral, and your bank liquidity position, given adverse movements in interest rates, currency exchange rates, equity prices, credit and commodity prices, and so on. For many banks, exposures beyond interest rate risk may be deemed to be immaterial to warrant the time and effort of a simulation, in which case you should probably conduct a periodic evaluation of the position risk to ensure that your materiality threshold is not crossed. Also, keep in mind that a significant benefit of the more integrated approach is a better understanding of the correlations between various derivatives markets. For most banks, movements in

EXHIBIT 9.2 Derivatives collateral stress test

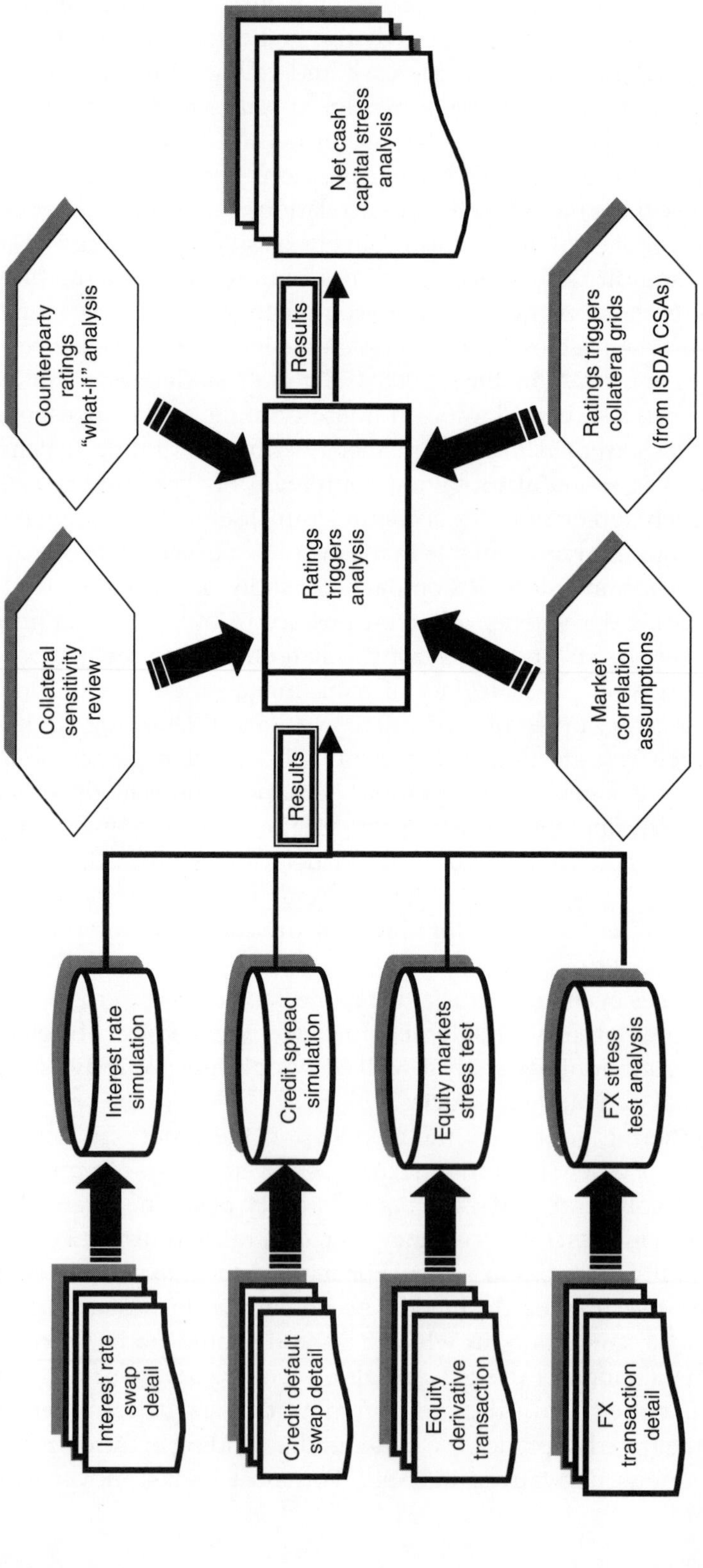

interest rates will be the primary focus of any simulation. You can focus the interest rate simulation on interest rate shock scenarios, and will be consistent with those scenarios your bank is probably already using in its interest rate risk management. In this way you can avoid incremental work by piggybacking on the bank's existing interest rate simulation effort.

It may be appropriate to analyze the behavior of derivatives collateral under multiple rate scenarios, such as curve steepening, flattening, curve inversions, and curve twists (multiple, simultaneous up/down shifts in the curve). Again, it may be possible to piggyback the analysis into an existing rate risk "what-if" analysis.

These interest rate simulations will probably be run using the bank's interest rate risk software, but the results will need to be brought back into a spreadsheet program to allow you to integrate the rate risk analysis with any other simulation work you do. Additional simulations may be appropriate for other products within the derivatives portfolio, either in isolation or in conjunction with other valuation changes. The decision to do this additional work should be based upon the relative size of these other portfolios versus the swap portfolio, the potential incremental collateral exposure generated by the portfolio, and the additional expense incurred in generating the information. The interest rate swap analysis can serve as a template for additional portfolios. For example, for the FX derivatives portfolio, you may analyze the collateral requirements under different percentage changes in the US$/euro relationship, or a broad, significant increase or decline in the drop of the US dollar versus all other currencies. Taking the review further, you can employ a Monte Carlo simulation to evaluate the effects of multiple, random events on the portfolio. For the credit derivatives portfolio, you can determine the nature of the stress test by determining whether the bank is predominantly a net seller or buyer of credit protection. If the bank is a net buyer of protection, the analysis would most likely focus on a general credit spread tightening, which would result in a deterioration in the value of the bank's credit derivatives portfolio, or an improvement in selected industries where a risk concentration may exist. Sufficient historical data exist to facilitate the creation of a robust simulation and a worst case analysis. A comprehensive analysis also requires testing the collateral position against a broad credit spread widening, or a deterioration in selected companies or industries. For the bank that may be short credit exposure, this information would not add to the stressed position, but would be incorporated into the comprehensive liquidity stress position as a potential offset to the stressed liquidity requirements in the interest rate swap book. For other derivatives positions, such as equity derivatives and commodity exposures, you can employ similar techniques to analyze their potential liquidity impact.

Following the stress testing some work will be required to bring these different analyses together. At this point you will probably develop an spreadsheet as the most flexible and cost-effective way to integrate your work so far. It will also facilitate your next step, the introduction of the ratings trigger matrices from your various counterparty agreements. Now, finding and then integrating the ratings trigger information can be a frustrating and time-consuming process if it is not already well documented by your collateral management team or your credit support staff. Fortunately, you will find that such information may be standardized across a large number of counterparties and derivative products, which certainly simplifies to some degree the additional modeling that you require. Exhibit 9.3 on page 216 to 217 shows a matrix of changes to the derivative collateral requirements under different interest rate and ratings-level scenarios. The model allows you to immediately see the liquidity impact of a ratings downgrade of your bank, along with changes in interest rates. Similar tables can be created for other derivatives types and then the impact of ratings triggers can be examined across product lines.

The completed spreadsheet model, which includes the fully integrated ratings trigger information, current MTM information, and interest rate simulation data, can be handed over to senior management to perform a simple "what-if" analysis. You may be surprised to find that for changes in interest rates of 100, 200 and 300 bps parallel shifts in the yield curve will typically tend to far outweigh the impact of even a multiple ratings downgrade for an investment-grade bank.

Combining these multiple portfolio analyses into one liquidity review can provide you with the liquidity impact of complex economic scenarios. You can simulate various points in the economic cycle and couple this work with bank-specific credit information. For example, here is an analysis that calculates the funding demands in the following "economic expansion" scenario:

- a rising interest rate scenario, coupled with a steepening of the yield curve
- widening credit spreads caused by increased corporate borrowing needs
- rising equity and commodity prices
- a one-notch ratings downgrade for the bank, caused by a major acquisition in the not too distant future.

Alternatively, specific market events can be simulated, such as the Asian Crisis, the Russian debt default, Long-Term Capital Management, 9/11, and devaluation of the Mexican peso, just to name a few.

The next step in the liquidity analysis is to evaluate the liquidity effect caused by changes in the market value of individual instruments that your bank uses as collateral. Firms devote considerable time and energy to valuing different types of collateral, so it may be worthwhile for you to capitalize on work already done in this area at your bank. For example, an increase in interest rates would lower the market value of a US government security used as collateral, perhaps resulting in a requirement that the bank calls for additional collateral, or that the bank delivers additional collateral to its counterparties. Or, you might model how a devaluation in the Mexican peso might impact on the collateral value of derivatives agreements collateralized by peso securities. Ideally, you should not choose collateral that is highly correlated with the underlying transaction, but occasionally these situations cannot be avoided. If you only use cash and money market securities as collateral, you may not want to bother with this analysis. Again, whether or not you undertake this additional work will be determined by the potential liquidity exposure you may face.

If you have the ratings trigger information in an easily accessible spreadsheet format, you may want to also look at the impact on liquidity that may result from an upgrade of a major counterparty. Additional modeling effort may be required, and once again you will have to determine whether this additional feature is worth the time and cost of developing and maintaining the model.

Lastly, an additional refinement that you may want to consider is the segregation of liquidity risk for the bank holding company (BHC). In fact, it's easy to conclude that the liquidity risk is greater at the BHC than at the bank subsidiary. Several reasons exist for this:

- limited funding sources for the typical BHC
- significant dependence on subsidiary bank dividends for a substantial portion of its funding, which can disappear if the bank becomes financially distressed
- derivative exposure concentration often limited to just interest rate swaps, foregoing the opportunity to take advantage of cross-product diversification benefits.

You might find as a result of your work, that the BHC is liability sensitive and uses interest rate swaps, that a rising interest rate scenario will increase its interest expense, increase its collateral outflows, while also potentially reducing the dividend flows from its liability-sensitive subsidiary banks.

You can incorporate the results of the BHC liquidity stress test scenarios into your BHC's funding projections. Choosing to incur the additional funding cost by "pre-funding" some or all of a worst case funding need may be regarded as a reasonably prudent measure by your holding company liquidity manager.

Once you complete the collateral analysis, you can pick one or several selected scenarios to place into your comprehensive stress test. As we saw in Exhibit 9.1, the impact on overall bank liquidity resulting from collateral flows will be but one small component of the entire test. If you utilize the ratings erosion approach, you will want to pick the collateral test results that match the ratings scenario. In addition, if your erosion testing employs a time dimension you may choose to utilize multiple

EXHIBIT 9.3 Ratings trigger analysis, bank only ($ in millions)

Moody's		Up 300	Up 200	Up 100	Base	Down 100	Down 200	Down 300
	Aaa	$150	$206	$255	$267	$357	$452	$553
	Aa1	$142	$194	$244	$245	$328	$419	$521
	Aa2	$142	$194	$244	$245	$328	$419	$521
	Aa3	$112	$169	$234	$229	$311	$403	$502
	A1	$100	$155	$219	$211	$290	$381	$478
	A2	$91	$144	$209	$203	$282	$372	$470
	A3	$57	$117	$195	$199	$278	$365	$452
	Baa1	$22	$86	$158	$174	$250	$327	$408
	Baa2	($11)	$55	$133	$157	$230	$305	$386
	Baa3	($11)	$55	$133	$157	$230	$303	$382
	Ba1	($12)	$54	$132	$157	$230	$303	$382
	Below	($12)	$54	$132	$157	$230	$303	$381
S&P		**Up 300**	**Up 200**	**Up 100**	**Base**	**Down 100**	**Down 200**	**Down 300**
	AAA	$164	$212	$255	$271	$365	$464	$571
	AA+	$156	$199	$244	$249	$336	$432	$539
	AA	$156	$199	$244	$249	$336	$432	$539
	AA−	$126	$174	$234	$233	$319	$416	$520
	A+	$113	$160	$219	$215	$299	$393	$496
	A	$106	$152	$211	$207	$290	$385	$488
	A−	$70	$123	$195	$202	$286	$378	$470
	BBB+	$35	$91	$158	$177	$258	$340	$426
	BBB	$2	$61	$133	$161	$239	$317	$404
	BBB−	$2	$61	$133	$161	$239	$316	$400
	BB+	$1	$60	$132	$160	$239	$316	$400
	Below	$1	$60	$132	$160	$239	$315	$399

EXHIBIT 9.3 (continued)

		Moodys	S&P
Bank		A1	A
Holding Co.		A2	A−

Collateral positions ($)

	Up 300	Up 200	Up 100	Base	Down 100	Down 200	Down 300
Bank	$98	$149	$206	$202	$284	$373	$469
Holding Co.	($28)	$13	$70	$131	$215	$317	$443
Total Collateral	$70	$162	$276	$333	$500	$690	$912
Variance	($263)	($171)	($57)	$0	$166	$357	$579

scenarios with market volatility increasing as a function of time, such as a 100 bps interest rate shock scenario for a 30-day time frame, and a 300 or more bps increase for the one-year time frame.

CONCLUSION

A thorough stress test of derivatives collateral requires the ability to access and integrate large sets of disparate information before you can execute a comprehensive liquidity analysis. Any institution must ask if the costs, management attention and staff time required to develop and maintain the analytical tools will be outweighed by the potential liquidity risks imposed by its collateral positions and the desire by bank management to develop a thoroughly robust liquidity stress test analysis. External stakeholders, such as rating agencies or regulators, whose demands may trump the simple cost-benefit analysis, may drive this decision as well. When trying to determine how far to push this analysis, do not forget the fact that relatively benign derivatives markets can lead to complacency when evaluating what is truly the bank's potential worst case scenario. And, that the purpose of a liquidity stress test is to test not only the theoretical limits of a bank's capacity for surviving unexpected events, but treasury management's creative ability to extend those limits.

NOTES

[1] International Swap Dealers Association (ISDA), "2005 Margin Survey," pp. 2–9.

[2] Moody's Investors Service, Special Comment, "The Unintended Consequences of Ratings Triggers," December, 2002, pp. 3–5.

[3] The net cash capital framework was developed by Moody's Investors Service and is described in detail in Moody's Investors Service, Special Comment, "How Moody's Evaluates U.S. Bank and Bank Holding Company Liquidity," July, 2001, pp. 6–7. Net cash capital accounts for the stability of deposits and long-term debt, the salability of mortgage loans and home equity loans, and haircuts securities based on their assumed market value. This analysis focuses on the rating agency view of how an institution would manage through a liquidity crisis.

Net cash capital equals long-term funding less illiquid assets and illiquid securities. Long-term funding equals total equity, all borrowings excluding borrowings with less than original maturity. Illiquid assets are defined as fixed assets plus intangibles, other assets and loans. Residential mortgage assets are considered liquid, subject to a 20% haircut due to market price risk. Illiquid securities include haircuts applied to different securities holdings. Moody's considers MBS 100% illiquid, while they consider Treasuries only 2% illiquid.

[4] International Swap Dealers Association (ISDA), "2005 Collateral Guidelines," p. 71.

BIBLIOGRAPHY

Davenport, Penny (ed.), *A Practical Guide to Collateral Management in the OTC Derivatives Market*, New York, Palgrave Macmillan, 2003, pp. 102–9.

International Swap Dealers Association (ISDA) 2005, Margin Survey, ''2005 Collateral Guidelines.''

Moody's Investors Service, Special Comment 2002, ''The Unintended Consequences of Ratings Triggers,'' December, 2001.

CHAPTER 10

Modeling Non-maturing Products

Martin M. Bardenhewer

Previous chapters in this book have shown that liquidity managers face big challenges. To accomplish sound liquidity risk management, a considerable amount of data has to be collected. Cash flows in particular have to be determined for each financial instrument and for each financial product sold to customers. There are basically two sources of randomness in future cash flows of balance sheet products. The first source is how expiring contracts are replaced by new business. The modeling of new business is rather difficult because, for example, customers may replace a fixed-rate product by a variable rate product, they may switch to an off-balance sheet product, or even switch to another bank. In contrast to the calculation of changes in present values and cash flows of existing business in the near term there is only little information about new business available that can be exploited by a quantitative model. The second source is how the notional of products without a contractual specified maturity evolves.

In this chapter we focus on the latter source of randomness in the cash flow projection. In a deposit such as a simple savings account the liquidity risk manager wants to know how long the deposits will stay, assuming that the deposit rates are adjusted appropriately when market rates change. The manager seeks a model that projects the joint evolution of the deposit rate and of the balance of the deposits based on some forward rates and their respective volatilities quoted in the market. A deposit contains complex options that make the modeling challenging. In a simple savings account, for example, customers have the right to withdraw all their money or some part thereof at any point in time, possibly due to a short notification period. Of course, customers have the right to never amortize or withdraw at least some part of the balance. Except for very extraordinary situations, some core balance can be expected, which is a lower barrier of the balance even in the long run. Such a product is called "non-maturing," though this term is somewhat misleading. Each single contract matures at some future date. The crucial point in a non-maturing product is not a perpetual duration, but rather that the maturity is not determined because the customer can freely choose it. As another example for a non-maturity (or indeterminate maturity) product, overdraft facilities are very common in Europe and within a given limit customers can freely choose their amortization schedule. Moreover, there are mortgages available that have amortization and rate characteristics very similar to deposits. These very common products turn out to be quite complex at closer inspection. The customers' option to choose any desired schedule of principal cash flows is in fact a highly nested option. The amount that can be withdrawn from a savings account in two months from now depends on the withdrawals within the next month. Furthermore, the drivers for the decision to withdraw money are not readily identifiable. To balance the customers' options, the bank has the choice to adjust the rate paid or received on the product. Whereas interest rate cash flows are less important for liquidity risk management than principal cash flows, this option is nevertheless essential, because the rate received on a savings account can be expected to be a major driver for withdrawals. Hence, we expect the options in a non-maturing product to be closely interconnected.

We will discuss the modeling of non-maturing products and show how these models can be implemented in a liquidity risk management framework. As a starting point we formulate the questions that we will try to answer:

- What are the characteristics of the embedded options? What drives amortizations and withdrawals?
- Which criteria should be used in the assessment of different modeling approaches?
- Are there significant differences between cash flow estimates in different models? Can they be quantified and what is their impact on liquidity risk management?
- Should the same models be used for liquidity risk management and interest rate risk management?
- Should the same models be used for existing and for new business?
- Should the same models be used in a liquidity stress situation and in a normal situation?

The answer to the last question is clear: No! There is no need for sophisticated cash-flow models in a liquidity stress situation. The focus in this case is on management processes in the near term and on the use of all available liquidity facilities, hopefully according to a well-prepared contingency plan. All this is described elsewhere in this book. In what follows, we focus on normal market situations and the projection of cash flows that helps to establish a sound funding program.

NON-MATURING PRODUCTS

As pointed out, the main feature of a non-maturing product is the customers' option to choose any desired amortization schedule. At any point in time they can amortize some percentage of the outstanding notional, possibly due to a short notification period. The maturity of a contract is not specified and is at least from the issuer's point of view indeterminate. This option only makes sense if the issuer has the option to adjust the interest rate paid or received on the product. For example, in a fixed-rate non-maturing deposit customers would immediately withdraw the whole outstanding notional as soon as interest rates rise, because they would now have the possibility to invest it at a higher fixed rate. If the bank however raises the rate paid on the saving accounts, investors are more reluctant to switch to a new fixed-rate investment. The structure of the embedded options differs from other cancelable products. Many fixed-rate products have prepayment options, too, but these contracts always have a maximum maturity. In most cases a prepayment fee has to be paid, if a contract is terminated before maturity. In a fixed-rate mortgage, for example, prepayment options are rather common and customers have the right to amortize some portion of the nominal at some specified points in time. But they have either to pay a penalty in the case of amortization, or the option premium is explicitly calculated and charged to the customer. Such a fee is not explicitly applied in non-maturing products.

On the liability side of a balance sheet, savings accounts and current accounts are well-known examples of non-maturing products. On the asset side, overdrafts and credit card loans are non-maturing. The same structure may also apply to other instruments. In Switzerland, for example, a non-maturing mortgage is the standard real estate financing product. This type of mortgage differs from a simple adjustable rate mortgage with prepayment, because adjustable rate mortgages have a maximum maturity, the prepayment option is usually linked to a penalty payment, and the interest rate is periodically adjusted with respect to T-Bill or Libor plus a spread. As at least some non-maturing products are on the balance sheet of virtually any bank, they represent a significant part of it for retail banks in particular. It should be noted that a non-maturing product on the asset side is likely not to be a good hedge for such a product on the liability side, because customers tend to exercise either the option on the asset side or the option on the liability side, but not both at the same time.

What is the structure of the embedded options? How could it be modeled? For ease of exposition we discuss the economics of the embedded options in the setting of a savings account in a rising interest rate environment. This example can easily be extended to other scenarios and other products. If interest rates rise, a bank tends to raise the rate paid to its customers on the savings accounts. In general, these adjustments will not be larger than the change in the market rates. It is rather observed that the rates paid to the customers are far less volatile than the market rates and that they are adjusted quite reluctantly in a rising interest rate environment. Thus in this scenario a savings account is less favorable than, say, a one-year money market deposit and we expect more money to be withdrawn. Overall, the customer's option to withdraw money seems to be deeper in the money if interest rates are expected to rise than if they are expected to fall. To learn more about the economics of the embedded options, we have to know which financial instruments are a substitute for saving accounts. Where do customers invest their money if they withdraw it from their savings account? In most cases, an investment in money market products yields more than a short-term deposit in savings accounts. For an investor it is therefore not a good idea to use a savings account as a short-term investment. Most customers regard savings accounts as a medium-term investment and they substitute it in a rising interest rate scenario with some other medium-term investment, rather than with a short-term investment. For a bank, however, at least some significant fraction of the deposits on savings accounts is a substitute for short-term financing due to liquidity considerations. Generally, the two options in a non-maturing product are linked in a non-trivial way and both depend not only on a specific interest rate, but also on some part of the term structure. To make things even more complicated, we cannot assume a market with perfect information because the knowledge of financial markets varies significantly between the customers. Whereas some customers react very quickly on rate changes, others are almost insensitive to them. We expect on an aggregated level that some money is virtually never withdrawn; that is, we expect some lower bound on the balance. For current account deposits, for example, a bank would invest some percentage of the money at a medium-term maturity, although all money could theoretically be withdrawn at any time within some limit. But experience shows that, except for some stress scenario like a bank run, some money will always be in the account. Such a core balance is obvious for current accounts, but it holds true for all other non-maturing products as well.

A model of non-maturing products should take into consideration at least these economic characteristics. It should also focus on customers' options because cash flows are mainly driven by this option. Holding all other things equal, customers' options have an impact on both principal and interest cash flows, while the issuer's option has a direct impact on interest cash flows only. The customers' options can be seen as a portfolio of highly nested options. If they, for example, withdraw in the next month 10% of the outstanding notional, they can withdraw one month later at almost 90% of the outstanding notional as of today, and so on. It is obvious that the dimensionality of the problem quickly explodes and a numerical approach has to be applied to look at the option as a whole rather than modeling each nested option on its own.

MODEL OVERVIEW

The models of non-maturing products fit into two main classes: the replicating portfolio models and the option-adjusted spread (OAS) models. In the former approach, a non-maturing product is replicated by a portfolio that mimics the evolution of the interest rate of the product and the evolution of its amortization schedule. For non-maturing assets and liabilities, such a replicating portfolio can be seen as a financing portfolio or as a real-world investment of the funds, respectively. The OAS model has a different starting point. Term structure models are used to apply option pricing theory to non-maturing products. The embedded options are explicitly modeled and their value is part of the present value of the product, or added or subtracted implicitly as a spread to its coupon. Of course, this simple classification cannot perfectly capture every model. We will also discuss a model that incorporates stochastic optimization based on a term structure model in the replicating portfolio framework. It can be seen as a combination of elements of both basic approaches. This model is explored in more detail in the next chapter. As shown in later sections, the cash flow forecast from different models may differ significantly. Different cash flow forecasts should lead to different funding programs, thus leading to different liquidity gaps. Model choice should therefore be a deliberate decision. The most important quantitative benchmark is the result of model back testing. We discuss two approaches to back testing in a later section. Furthermore, we need some qualitative criteria to assess the quality of a model to reach a decision. Such criteria are now discussed.

- *Flexibility*: Non-maturing products have a rich structure of embedded options that should be covered by a model. The separation of customers' and bank's behavior is obviously a desirable model feature. Changes in the specification of a non-maturing product, or constraints on the volumes of specific hedge instruments, for example, are easily built into a flexible model. However, flexibility is typically accompanied with complexity.
- *Complexity*: This has three dimensions. First, a complex model is hard to communicate. This is a crucial point because the models for non-maturing products are part of risk management on an enterprise level and are used in funds transfer pricing to split the earnings between Treasury and the sales departments within a bank. Even if financial engineering specialists develop these models, they still have to be explainable to senior management and to senior sales people. Otherwise they simply will not be accepted and will not be used. Second, a too simplistic model can lead to wrong decisions in risk management, which can have a significant impact on the earnings in both normal and stress situations. But sophistication in modeling is not a good thing for its own sake. In many cases, we observe a tradeoff between the explanatory power

that a model has at least at a theoretical level and the amount of work to implement it. The possibility of implementation failure rises with rising complexity. A very sophisticated model may have even less power in practice than a simpler one! Third, the models have to be integrated in balance sheet risk management processes and often also in funds transfer pricing systems. Models for non-maturing products, however, affect the balance sheet as a whole and are used in funds transfer pricing to separate earnings between the front departments and the bank's treasury. In this regard, they differ from most models used in trading that affect only a single trading department.

- *Implementation*: Whereas storage costs are not strong criteria for model assessment, calculation time still is an issue. In a balance sheet simulation, for example, the balance sheet has to be revalued for each simulated path. If some probabilistic approach is applied for the generation of the simulation paths of the balance sheet, and at the same time for the modeling of the non-maturing products, we quickly run into what is called the curse of dimensionality. Simulating the balance sheet with only 100 paths, and pricing the products in a valuation model with 1,000 paths, for example, will end up with a total of 101,000 valuation paths. The second issue is the maintainability of the implementation. A model should be calibrated periodically to new data and this should be accomplished with little work. Finally, the implementation code itself should be easily maintained.

In what follows, we first give a description of the models and their implementations. Then each model is assessed with respect to the three criteria discussed. Finally, the implications for liquidity risk management are discussed.

REPLICATING PORTFOLIO MODELS

The replicating portfolio approach was developed by Rod Jacobs in the 1980s for modeling the prime rate and Tom Wilson extended its use to the modeling of non-maturing products.[1] This approach aims to transform the complex non-maturing product into a portfolio of simple plain vanilla instruments, which has very similar characteristics. Such a replicating portfolio consists of money market instruments and coupon bonds traded in liquid markets. The cash flows of this portfolio replicate the cash flows of the non-maturing product as closely as possible. This approach has a straightforward economic interpretation. The money from a non-maturing liability can be invested in liquid plain vanilla instruments at any time and a non-maturing asset is likewise refinanced by plain vanilla instruments. If a bank is seeking, for example, a strategy that yields a constant margin for the savings accounts, it looks for a replicating portfolio that yields the interest rate paid in the savings accounts plus a constant margin. A replicating portfolio can therefore be a real investment or refinancing portfolio respectively for a non-maturing product. This highlights the real importance of models for non-maturing products. A change in the model for savings accounts is equivalent to a change in the investment portfolio of the bank with a direct impact on current and future earnings.

For ease of exposition, we continue to focus on a replicating portfolio of savings accounts, but the concept can equivalently be applied to other non-maturing liabilities or to any non-maturing asset. In a first step we suppose that the volume of the savings accounts is stable over time. Of course, this assumption is far too simplistic, but it will be relaxed in a second step. The volume of the savings accounts can be invested in different buckets, say one month, three months, six months, 12 months, two years, and five years. For the latter two it is a reasonable strategy to use par-coupon bonds or equivalent swaps because they are liquidly traded. Thus the yield of a replicating portfolio is determined from Libor and swap rates from one month up to five years. Each of these buckets is then divided in monthly maturities. The six-month bucket consists of six different contracts with monthly maturities. The five-year bucket consists accordingly of 60 contracts. As time goes by, every month one contract per bucket matures and is replaced by a corresponding new contract at par; that is, a six-month money market instrument in the six-month bucket, and a five-year par-coupon bond in the five-year bucket. This idea of such a dynamic investment strategy in the replicating portfolio is shown in Exhibit 10.1.

The coupons of its constituents determine the yield of a replicating portfolio. The yield of the replicating portfolio in this example is given by current one-month, three-month, six-month, 12-month, two-year, and five-year rates, and by a set of historic rates. The historical Libor and swap rates are the coupons of the instrument bought in the past, like

EXHIBIT 10.1   Replicating portfolio strategy

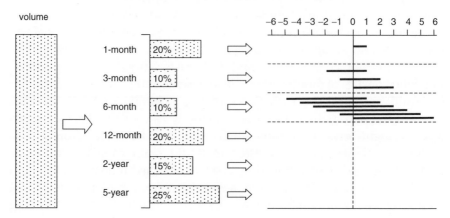

the three-month money market instrument bought one month ago, which has still two months to maturity. The historic rates used are therefore in the three-month bucket, the three-month Libor as of one month ago and as of two months ago, in the six-month buckets the six-month Libor as of one, two, three, four and five months ago, and so on. Adding up all maturities in all buckets, the replicating portfolio in this example consists of 106 contracts $(1 + 3 + 6 + 12 + 24 + 60)$ and the yield of the replicating portfolio is an average of these 106 rates. The weights are determined such that this yield is as close as possible to the rate paid on savings accounts plus a constant margin over time.

In general, a replicating portfolio does not trade at par because interest rates have changed since the inception of at least some of the contracts. This has an interesting impact on the setup of a new replicating portfolio if, for example, a new non-maturing savings product is introduced. The simple fact that the money invested in the new replicating portfolio must equal the money paid by the customers in the new product implies that a new replicating portfolio can only be set up in two ways. First, the money may be invested in a replicating portfolio described as above, which either has a higher nominal than the non-maturing product if it trades below par, or which has a lower nominal if it trades above par. Second, the money may be invested in a replicating portfolio that trades at par and has the same nominal as the non-maturing products. Such a new replicating portfolio consists only of newly issued instruments. The six-month bucket, for example, would consist of six newly issued contracts with maturities ranging from one to six months. Each month the maturing contract is replaced by a new six-month contract, such that the six-month bucket consists only of six-month contracts not before five months from now, and the five-year bucket consists only of five-year contracts not before 59 months from now. The first approach has the advantage of being fully equipped from the first day on, whereas the second approach has the highly desirable feature that its nominal value equals the nominal value of the non-maturing product.

The unrealistic assumption of a constant volume can now easily be relaxed. If on average a constant volume is expected, each change in volume can be seen as a random fluctuation around the mean. A balancing volume that aligns the volume of the replicating portfolio with the volume of the non-maturing product covers the fluctuation. If the balancing volume is positive, it is invested in the shortest maturity available in the replicating portfolio, the one-month bucket. If it is negative; that is, if the actual volume is less than the expected average, it is withdrawn from this bucket. The one-month bucket in a replicating portfolio can therefore be seen as a money market account that serves as a buffer for random volume fluctuations.

But even with this extension of the replicating portfolio approach, the model structure is not rich enough to deal with realistic situations. Typically, some trend is assumed. A rise in volume is expected for, say,

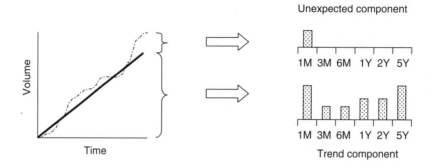

EXHIBIT 10.2   Decomposition of volume changes

the next year, while for others constant or even declining volumes are expected. The latter not only applies to a product at the end of its life cycle, but also to savings accounts in a rising interest rate environment, for example. A replicating portfolio model has to account for those trend assumptions to be used in real-world applications. Volume changes can be decomposed in a deterministic component explained by the trend assumed and an unexpected component such as a fluctuations around this trend. The replicating portfolio model presented up to now has to be extended to include these two components of a trend. As shown in Exhibit 10.2, the deterministic component is distributed over the buckets according to their weightings, while the balancing volume again is covered by the money market account.

The bucket weights are the final output of the estimation of a replicating portfolio model. Given these weights, the number of all contracts and their maturities are fixed and the yield of the portfolio can be calculated as a simple average of all coupons in the portfolio. The inputs to the estimation procedure are the trend assumed, historical data of interest rates, and historical data of the volume of the non-maturing product. These data are collected for an estimation period that covers, say, the last five years, and the parameters are estimated from these data.

In a first step, the form of the trend function is determined either by estimation or by expert knowledge. The latter approach is useful for new products or significant redesigns of a product. Product managers and sales people are asked for their expectations on the evolution of the volume. These expectations can directly be used as a trend or fitted to some trend function. In the former approach the trend function is estimated with regression techniques if sufficient historical data applicable to the current situation are available. Typical trend structures are linear, quadratic, exponential or a combination of these.

$$\text{Linear trend}: \quad V_t = \beta_0 + \beta_1 \cdot \Delta_t + \sum_i \kappa_i \cdot (r_{i,t} - \overline{r_i})$$

$$+ \delta \cdot (cr_t - \overline{cr}) + \varepsilon_t$$

$$\text{Quadratic trend}: \quad V_t = \beta_0 + \beta_2 \cdot \Delta_t^2 + \sum_i \kappa_i \cdot (r_{i,t} - \overline{r_i})$$
$$+ \delta \cdot (cr_t - \overline{cr}) + \varepsilon_t$$

$$\text{Exponential trend}: V_t = \beta_3 \cdot \exp(\beta_4 \cdot \Delta_t) + \sum_i \kappa_i \cdot (r_{i,t} - \overline{r_i})$$
$$+ \delta \cdot (cr_t - \overline{cr}) + \varepsilon_t$$

where

$i \in \{1, \dots, I\}$	Maturity of buckets in months
V_t	Total volume at time t
$r_{i,t}$	Interest rate with maturity i at time t
$\overline{r_i}$	Average interest rate with maturity i over estimation period
cr_t	Customer's rate at time t
$\overline{cr}$	Average customer's rate over estimation period
Δ_t	Time in months between time 0 and t
$\beta_i, \kappa_i, \delta$	Parameters to be estimated
ε_t	Residual at time t

According to the quality of the data the coefficients of the trend function can be estimated using the simple ordinary least square (OLS) approach or a robust approach. The former equally weights all data points, while the latter puts less weight on outliers and is less sensitive to small changes in the underlying data set. Robust techniques make weaker assumptions on the distribution of the residuals than the OLS regression. Depending on the approach chosen, the estimation can be implemented in a statistic software package or in spreadsheet software.[2] Note that these trend functions do not incorporate a random component. They are fully deterministic and any deviation from the trend observed in reality is put into the one-month bucket *ex post*.

Given a specified trend function, the weights of the buckets are determined such that the yield of the replicating portfolio mimics the rate of the non-maturing product plus or minus a fixed spread during the estimation period. This can be seen as an optimization problem. The optimal weights of the buckets minimize the volatility of the spread between the yield of the replicating portfolio and the non-maturing product. In other words, the optimal portfolio weights would have kept the fluctuations of the margin in the past as small as possible. Of course, the weights sum up to one. This optimization problem can be easily formulated as an OLS problem with constraints. Any statistical package or advanced spreadsheet software can be used to determine the portfolio weights. Using a trend function determined above, the estimation problem can be written:

$$cr_t = \theta_0 + \frac{F_t(.)}{V_t} \cdot \sum_j \alpha_j \cdot ma_{j,t} + \frac{A_t(.)}{V_t} \cdot r_{1,t} + \eta_t$$

$$\text{s.t.} : \alpha_j \geq 0, \quad \forall j$$

$$\sum_j \alpha_j = 1$$

where

$j \in \{1,3,6,\ldots,60\}$	Maturities of buckets in months
cr_t	Customer's rate at time t
V_t	Total volume at time t
$F_t(.)$	Trend volume at time t; $F_t(.)$
	$= F_t\left(\Delta_t, r_{i,t}, \bar{r}_i, cr_t, \overline{cr}; \hat{\beta}_0, \ldots, \hat{\beta}_4, \hat{\kappa}_i, \hat{\delta}\right)$
$A_t(.)$	Balancing volume at time t; $A_t(.) = V_t - F_t(.)$
$ma_{j,t}$	Moving average interest rate with maturity j at time t; $ma_{j,t} = \frac{1}{j} \cdot \sum_{i=0}^{j-1} r_{j,t-i}$
$ma_{j,t}$	$= \frac{1}{j} \cdot \sum_{i=0}^{j-1} r_{j,t-i}$
	$r_{1,t}$1 − month rate at time t
	$\theta_0, \ \alpha_j$Parameters to be estimatedη_t
	Residual at time t

This estimation problem can be explained economically as follows. The rate of the non-maturing product is expressed as the yield of the replicating portfolio and a spread. The yield of the replicating portfolio consists of three parts. The first part is the weighted average of the coupon rate of each instrument in each bucket ($\sum_j \alpha_j \cdot ma_{j,t}$), scaled by the ratio of the trend volume and the observed volume.[3] The second part is the yield of the balance volume invested in the one-month bucket. The remaining part, $\theta_0 + \eta_t$, is the spread consisting of a constant factor and of a time-variant factor that allows for fluctuation over time. It is often observed that very large positive and negative weights are calculated if they are not restricted. For this reason, we rule out short positions in the replicating investment portfolio to avoid spurious results. Only the one-month bucket can become negative over time due to its function as a buffer for unexpected fluctuations. A non-zero buffer indicates model misspecification. The estimation of the weights of the buckets should be based on a period that comprises at least one economic cycle. However, this estimation period may not yield a reasonable trend function. Using a shorter estimation period for the trend function than for the estimation of the weights implies the assumption that no trend different from the volume has been observed in earlier periods. In sum, the calibration of the replicating portfolio model to historic data, as well as to an assumed trend, requires a careful implementation.

Market Mix

The optimization procedure focuses on the margin of the non-maturing product only; that is, on the yield of the replicating portfolio and on the rate of the non-maturing product. It takes only the issuer's option to adjust the rate into account and ignores the customers' option to withdraw the money. This may lead to undesirable results for non-maturing liability products. Suppose that a significant portion is invested in long maturities as a result of the optimization, but money is withdrawn quickly in a rising interest rate environment. Then the maturing volume in the replicating portfolio may be less than needed to cover additional withdrawals. In other words, the bank runs out of cash and faces a severe liquidity crisis. For this reason, the customers' option, which actually dominates the characteristics of a non-maturing product, has to be taken into account. Since the idea of replicating portfolios relies on the stability of the margin, the risk of running out of cash is incorporated as a constraint. Based on historical data, the estimated bucket weights are adjusted if the maturing volume in the replicating portfolio had not covered the withdrawals at any time in the past. This can be done in a simple matrix called "market mix."

In a market mix, the bucket weights calibrated to the time series of the customers' rate are compared with the bucket weights calibrated to the time series of the volume of the non-maturing product. There are several ways to calculate the latter ones. In a simple approach, these weights are set equal to the maximum historical volume changes for each maturity bucket in the estimation period. For the one-month bucket, for example, the maximum relative reduction over one month of the volume is calculated, for the three-month bucket the maximum relative reduction over a three-month period, and so on. In a more complicated approach, an optimization problem is formulated like in the calibration to the customers' rate and solved using regression techniques. For liquidity risk management, however, the first approach is sufficient. Once these weights are calculated, they are related to weights driven by the customers' rate. If the volume-driven weights dominate the rate-driven weights, the former are used to assure enough liquidity in the replicating portfolio, otherwise the latter are kept. Exhibit 10.3 explains this procedure in detail.

EXHIBIT 10.3 Market mix

	1M	3M	6M	Buckets 12M	2Y	5Y	10Y
(1) Optimal weights	5%	10%	25%	15%	20%	0%	25%
(2) Liquidity constraint	20%	10%	5%	25%	10%	30%	0%
(3) Row (1) cumulated	5%	15%	40%	55%	75%	75%	100%
(4) Row (2) cumulated	20%	30%	35%	60%	70%	100%	0%
(5) Market mix	20%	10%	10%	20%	15%	25%	0%

Suppose that the optimization procedure yields the weights as shown in row (1). Row (2) shows the maximum historical volume changes in the same estimation period, which are cumulated in rows (3) and (4). These numbers are compared, starting with the shortest maturity bucket: The market mix weight is chosen for each bucket such that the maximum cumulated weights are met. For example, the maximum cumulated weight in the six-month bucket is 40%. The weights of the preceding buckets in the market mix portfolio add up to 30%. Thus the weight of the six-month bucket in the market mix portfolio is 10%. Having done this for each bucket, the market mix provides the final bucket weights for the replicating portfolio. The numbers above show a typical pattern. The weights of the optimal replicating portfolio calibrated to the evolution of the customer's rate only tend to be low for short maturities and tend to be high for long maturities. The relatively small volatility of the customers' rate puts more weight on long maturities than on shorter maturities, because long rates are typically less volatile than short rates. On the other hand, the liquidity constraint puts more weight on the short maturities to ensure that at every point in time enough money from the investment portfolio is available to meet the customers' withdrawals. Of course, the impact of the liquidity constraint on the market mix leads to a less stable yield spread between the resulting replicating portfolio and the non-maturing product. We actually face a tradeoff in the model between a stable margin and a low liquidity risk, and that is exactly what is observed in the real world. No model can solve this puzzle. However, the basic approach can possibly be improved as shown below.

Stochastic Optimization

A main characteristic of non-maturing products is that their cash flows are random. It is difficult to anticipate how much money will be withdrawn from the savings accounts in one year from now. However, experience certainly helps to estimate this amount. In other words, a bank operates with expected cash flows. The determination of the expected cash flows in a replicating portfolio approach is rather simple. It is basically assumed that the interest rates evolve in the future as they did in the past; that is, no source of randomness is modeled. Instead of simulating possible future scenarios, the optimal weights are calculated only with respect to the single realized scenario in the estimation period. For example, if the estimation period has been dominated by low interest rates and by a stable rate paid on the savings accounts, the replicating portfolio tends to have more weights on long than on short maturities. In such a situation, a bank may expect rates to rise quickly in the near term, forcing it to raise the rate paid on the savings accounts, too. But the replicating model does not account for this expectation. If the expected scenario becomes true, the margin is quickly wiped out because the bank is still heavily invested in long maturities at low rates while paying higher rates to its customers. Furthermore, more money will be withdrawn in a rising interest rate environment, forcing the bank to sell some portion of the low-yield replicating portfolio at unfavorable terms to avoid liquidity problems. Constant portfolio weights are a further drawback of the standard replicating portfolio. The maturing contracts are renewed according to the same rates, which is also true if a trend is assumed. The model implies that these weights are never adjusted. However, in a practical application of the model new weights will be calculated after, say, one year, which clearly violates the basic assumption of constant weights. What can be seen at first glance as a simple calibration of the model to new information on volume and interest rates makes the model inconsistent. Anticipated adjustments of the weights in the future should influence the determination of the weights today. The standard replicating portfolio approach, however, specifically excludes adjustments of the weights in the future.

In Chapter 15 Karl Frauendorfer and Michael Schürle improve the standard replicating portfolio approach significantly to avoid its short-comings. Their extension is twofold. First, they introduce randomness by modeling the dynamics of the interest rates and possibly other factors. Second, they apply a multistage optimization procedure to calculate the weights of the replicating portfolio. The first extension abandons the simple view of the future described by a single scenario only. The second extension explicitly accounts for adjustments of the portfolio weights in the future. This enrichment of the standard model is in fact the determination of optimal weights with respect to a non-deterministic world; that is, the techniques of stochastic optimization are applied to non-maturing products. The differences between the standard replicating portfolio approach and its extension with stochastic optimization is the same as the difference between a simple buy and hold investment strategy and a dynamic investment strategy. In a buy and hold investment strategy the holdings are chosen once at inception of the investment horizon and kept constant no matter what happens in the future. The standard replicating portfolio approach is like a buy and hold strategy, which is chosen based on the assumption that prices will evolve in the future exactly as they did in the past. A dynamic portfolio strategy is based on a set of possible future price evolutions. It takes into account that the holdings will repeatedly be adjusted in the future according to then prevailing prices. The application of stochastic optimization is therefore a substantial enrichment of the standard replicating portfolio approach. It introduces a couple of new components into the modeling of non-maturing products. First, the optimization problem is specified. A minimization or maximization function is then combined with some constraints. For example, the volatility of the margin could be minimized with respect to restrictions on changes in the weights to avoid expensive major reallocations of the replicating portfolio. Other specifications can easily be incorporated. Then the dynamics of possible future outcomes of interest rates and other driving factors is modeled and appropriate scenarios are generated. The idea of the trend is extended to a volume function in the next step. A simple trend function is identical to the assumption of a single scenario of the evolution of the volume of the non-maturing product. A volume function describes the evolution of the volume as a function of driving factors like interest rates or macroeconomic indexes, for example. The application of the volume function to the scenarios of the driving factors yields scenarios of the volume evolution. A rate function specifies the evolution of the rate paid or received on the non-maturing product. Putting it all together, the weights are determined from an optimization procedure based on the future evolution of the volume and the customers' rate. This is obviously a non-trivial task. To look at stochastic optimization in modeling non-maturing products in more detail, we proceed in three steps. In the first step we analyze how randomness is modeled. Then the optimization problem is discussed. Finally we show how this problem is solved. It is not hard to imagine that the move from the deterministic world to the stochastic world introduces more advanced mathematical concepts that we omit here for ease of exposition. These are well documented, for example, in the references given in Chapter 15. We will defer the discussion of the volume function and the rate function to the analysis of the option-adjusted spread approach below.

Randomness is introduced in the model through interest rates, which are assumed to fluctuate in some reasonable way. To model the evolution of a swap curve, for example, some economic constraints have to be taken into account. In a world where cash exists, interest rates cannot become negative because money would be earned simply by holding cash otherwise. On the other hand, interest rates could become infinitely large at least in theory, but we expect them to revert to some long-term mean. Furthermore, not the evolution of a single interest rate has to be modeled, but the evolution of an interest rate curve at whole. If interest rates of different maturities are modeled independently, arbitrage opportunities are likely to exist in the model, which cannot exist in reality. To model the evolution of a term structure of interest rates is therefore far more than throwing a die, and term structure models have been developed to account for these restrictions. These models are crucial for what follows and we therefore discuss their idea in brief.[4] In the most general setting, the evolution of a forward curve is modeled, either expressed through forward rates with an infinitesimal interest rate period or through forward Libor rates as observed in the market. As in the Black–Scholes setting the evolution of the rates is composed by a deterministic drift and a stochastic diffusion component. The drift can be seen as an expected evolution and is usually modeled mean reverting for interest rates; that is, rates above a specified mean tend to move down towards this mean and rates below tend to move up. The diffusion component encapsulates all randomness in the model and is driven in practical implementations by some appropriate random numbers. The diffusion component is driven by a number of factors, typically between one and three. Empirical analysis shows that in most cases 90% or more of the movement of a term structure can be explained by three factors. The structure of these two components, the drift and the diffusion, drives the possible outcomes of interest rate curves in the future. A term structure model is calibrated to historical or current market data by estimating the parameters of the two components. At this point we have to distinguish whether such a model is used for liquidity risk management or for interest rate risk management. In the latter case, the focus is on the present value of an instrument whereas the focus is on cash flows in the former case. If the present value and its possible change have to be calculated, the basic reasoning of the seminal ideas of Black and Scholes has to be applied. All calculations have to be done under an artificial risk neutral probability measure. The mathematical notion of a probability measure has a simple economic interpretation. To calculate the present value, cash flows can either be discounted with a discount factor that is fully known today, or, for example, month by month with the future one-month money market rate, which is random as seen from today. Hence a simulation must be adjusted in a way that discounting with simulated rates yields the same present value as discounting with the discount factor calculated from the current yield curve. For this reason, the drift component is adjusted appropriately in a term structure model according to the discount instrument chosen, and it has been shown that it is fully driven by appropriate forward rates and the parameters of the diffusion component. However, such an adjustment would not be a good idea for liquidity risk management. In this case we are not interested in a risk neutral expectation of the evolution of the interest rates and of the cash flows, but in our specific expectations of future cash flows. Technically speaking, the drift parameter is not a function of diffusion parameters, but has to be specified on its own to express our subjective expectations about future outcomes. In summary, term structure models are used for interest risk management under a risk neutral measure, while for liquidity risk management they are used under a subjective probability measure. Simulated cash flows under two different measures may differ significantly and it is thus a serious mistake in risk management to use the wrong measure by accident.

Given the evolution of interest rates and possibly other driving factors, the evolution of the volume and the customers' rate is simulated. Then an optimization problem is specified and connected to the simulated scenarios. The techniques of stochastic optimization are flexible enough to allow for a wide range of possible formulations of the optimization problem. Minimizing the volatility of the margin as it is done in the simple replicating portfolio approach may lead to replicating portfolios, which are unprofitable. It is likely that there are situations where the minimal variance margin is too low to cover overall costs, which include operating costs and possible capital charges. Minimizing the variance is therefore a rather risky strategy! Frauendorfer and Schürle propose the minimization of the downside deviation of not meeting the overall costs. They impose several restrictions on this optimization; for example, regrouping of the replicating portfolio is restricted to avoid huge transaction volumes. Another restriction is imposed on the volume of the replicating portfolio for non-maturing liabilities to meet withdrawals in each scenario. This is superior to the market mix in the standard replicating portfolio. It is both theoretically sound and more efficient because it avoids the calibration to a single historical worst case scenario. The solution of the optimization problem with respect to the randomness is a non-trivial problem. The dynamics of the driving factors and the optimization procedures have to be combined in such a way that the solution of the stochastic optimization can be approximated by a solution of a deterministic optimization. For this reason, the evolution of the driving factors is approximated by a non-recombining tree as depicted in Exhibit 10.4. The full distribution of the factors is replaced by nodes. A node can also represent a decision on the reallocation of the replicating portfolio. For each decision node the optimization problem, including the restrictions, is duplicated and solved given the values of the driving factors in that node. Such a tree approximates the randomness by a deterministic structure and the optimization problem can be solved with respect to this structure by linear programming techniques. It should be noted that the number of steps in the non-recombining tree is limited. Applying the optimization procedure to every scenario and every future point in time, we quickly run into a curse of dimensionality. The number of nodes in every step grows exponentially and adding an additional step may become computationally very expensive. The discrete approximation of the continuous distribution has to be chosen carefully in practical implementations.

OPTION-ADJUSTED SPREAD MODELS

Option-adjusted spread (OAS) models describe the spread that, for example, is received by a holder of a callable bond above the yield of the corresponding non-callable bond. The issuer has the right to call

EXHIBIT 10.4   Approximation of the dynamics of stochastic factors in a non-recombining tree

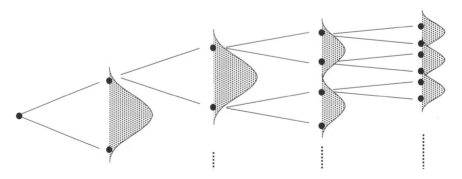

the bond and the bondholders are short an option for which they receive a fee. This fee is easily accrued over the lifetime of the bond if it is assumed that the option will not be exercised. An early application of OAS models to balance sheet management has been published by Rigsbee, Ayaydin and Richard.[5] OAS models for non-maturing products capture the highly complicated embedded options in these products by models for the evolution of the customers' rate and for the evolution of the volume of the non-maturing products. The value of the options embedded in a non-maturing product cannot readily be accrued over a lifetime as for a callable bond because this lifetime would be infinite. No corresponding instrument without these options is available in the market, and in this sense the term OAS is misleading for modeling non-maturing products. The key component of an OAS model in asset–liability management is an amortization or volume model, which projects future prepayments in a mortgage or withdrawals in a deposit, respectively. Expected future amortizations are estimated from historical data. For a mortgage, for example, amortizations are expressed as a function of contract-specific factors, pool-specific factors, and market interest rates of different maturities. The contract-specific factors include date of origination or age (an old mortgage is more likely to be repaid than a new one), and loan size (larger loans tend to prepay faster). Pool-specific factors include seasonality and the so-called burnout effect that some borrowers are very reluctant to prepay. The level and the steepness of the interest rate curve, possibly with some time lag, is probably the main driver of a specific mortgage. Other macroeconomic factors could also be incorporated. Note that the discounting of cash flows to calculate present values restricts the driving factors to prices and yields of liquidly traded instruments. As long as cash flows are not discounted, the dynamics of any driving factor can be modeled. Another component is a rate model. It is a function of driving factors like the volume model, but the customer rate is typically modeled as a function of interest rates only. Finally, a term structure model as described in conjunction with stochastic optimization is a main component of an OAS model as well. Hence the components of an OAS model are also part of the stochastic optimization for non-maturing products, but both models differ significantly in the application of these components. This is shown in the following sections.

The Jarrow–van Deventer Model

Jarrow and van Deventer have developed a model for the valuation of demand deposits and credit card loans that can be classified as an OAS model.[6] They start with a simple term structure model and two equations, which describe the evolution of the rate and of the balance of the demand deposits. A money market rate drives both variables, the rate paid on the deposits and their balances. This specification allows for a closed form solution for the value of a demand deposit. The model is applied to Federal Reserve aggregated data on rates and volumes of negotiable orders of withdrawal accounts, passbook accounts, statement accounts and demand deposit accounts. The restriction on a money market rate as a single driving factor for the volume and the customers' rate makes this model unrealistic for more complex products like savings accounts. Additionally, the feature of a closed-form solution for the value based on risk-neutral expectations is of no importance for liquidity risk management, which concentrates on simulated cash flows based on subjective expectations. Even for interest rate risk management a closed form solution is advantageous in practice only if the instrument to be valued is frequently hedged. However, for non-maturing products the time between the adjustments of a hedge is typically much longer than the time to calculate risk measures in a simulation-based model. For this reason, we focus in what follows on the general approach of OAS models. In contrast to the specific case of the Jarrow–van Deventer model the general approach needs a simulation framework that is more flexible in the modeling of the economics of non-maturing products.[7]

The General Approach

As shown above, a volume model, a customers' rate model, and a term structure model are the three key components of an OAS model. Term structure models have been discussed above and now the latter two models deserve closer attention.

The bank sets the rate that it pays to or receives from the customers in a non-maturing product according to prevailing market rates. The bank's option to set the rate is driven by market interest rates, either directly or indirectly through customers' behavior. Some stickiness of the customers' rate is typically observed. The rate of a demand deposit, for example, is very stable over time (if non-zero at all), and the rate paid on savings accounts changes from time to time, depending on the evolution of the interest rates. But even in the latter case the customers' rates are adjusted with some time lag, which should be incorporated in a model. For savings accounts, for example, we expect dependence on both Libor and swap rates. Some fraction of the volume can be expected to be more or less insensitive to changes in the customers' rate, while well-informed customers quickly withdraw their money if rates rise. Thus, one portion is a long-term financing for the bank, whereas another portion is similar to short-term financing. Overall, we expect different functions for the customers' rate for different products. It may simply be a constant for demand deposits, but for savings accounts the customers' rate could be a function of a Libor rate, say the one-month Libor rate, and the five-year swap rate as a medium-term capital market rate. To incorporate the time lag, the customers' rate is assumed to depend not on current market rates but on market rates observed in the past. A model for the customers' rate of savings accounts, for example, may have the form:

$$
\begin{aligned}
\textit{Customer's rate}(t) = {} & \beta_0 + \beta_1 \cdot \textit{average of 1M Libor over the last 6 months} \\
& + \beta_2 \cdot \textit{average of 5Y swap rate over the last 6 months}
\end{aligned}
$$

where $\beta_0, \beta_1, \beta_2$ are parameters that are estimated from historical data. If β_1 and β_2 are positive, some lower bound β_0 for the customers' rate is assumed. The use of the average rate instead of a single rate accounts for the stickiness of the rate.

As discussed above, the customers' rate is not the most important driver of the cash flows. We expect that the customers' behavior is a more significant driver for them. For this reason, a specification of the amortizations or withdrawals is a cornerstone of every OAS model. Such a specification is called "volume model" or, more technically, "volume process." For a demand deposit we may expect some stable volume over time. Virtually no customer will use it as an investment product, because the rate paid is typically very low. Demand deposits are rather used to hold cash for liquidity purposes. A volume model for a demand deposit will be simply that; for example, 50% of the volume at the beginning of the month will be withdrawn by the end of month, while the remaining money is held for liquidity reasons for, say, two years. If risk management is done on a daily time grid, the volume for each day may be interpolated between the beginning of month and the end of month. For savings accounts, however, the volume model has to be more sophisticated. We may observe that in a rising interest rate environment, withdrawals of some customers are mainly driven by money market rates, while other customers see savings accounts as a medium-term investment and withdraw their money not before swap rates have moved up significantly. The time lag for the withdrawals is possibly shorter than for the rate adjustments, because the volume is far less stable than the customers' rate. Finally, seasonality factors could be incorporated. It may be observed, for example, that less money is withdrawn in autumn than in the months of and before summer vacations. A volume process for savings accounts could therefore look like:

$$
\begin{aligned}
\textit{Withdrawals}(t) = {} & \alpha_0 + \alpha_1 \cdot \textit{average of 1M Libor over the last 6 months} \\
& + \alpha_2 \cdot \textit{5Y swap rate}(t-2) \\
& + \sum_{i=3}^{4} \alpha_i \cdot \textit{dummy for quarter}(i)
\end{aligned}
$$

Both models can be formulated as autoregressive models (AR), instead of relying on averages. In an AR model the withdrawals at time t, for example, depend on the withdrawals of recent periods. If a model is AR(1), it depends only on the withdrawals of time $t - 1$.

A similar analysis can easily be done for other non-maturing products. For non-maturing mortgages other economic variables like house prices, gross national product, and so on can be used as long as only cash flows have to be estimated under a subjective probability measure.

The interaction of the components of an OAS model is illustrated in Exhibit 10.5. In a first step, realizations of future interest rates are simulated in a term structure model. The output is a set of scenarios, in which each scenario describes a specific evolution of interest rates over a given time horizon in multiple time steps. The volume model and the customers' rate model are applied to each time point in each scenario. The volume and the customers' rate at time t yield the interest rate payments at time $t + 1$. The volume at time t and the volume at time $t + 1$ yield the principal cash flows. Thus, all cash flows are fully specified by the term structure model, the volume model and the customers' rate model. This is sufficient for liquidity risk management. If an OAS model is used to value a non-maturing product and to manage its interest rate risk, the simulation has to be set up under a risk neutral measure. Appropriate discount factors can then be extracted from the term structure model and the value of the product is easily obtained by summing up the discounted cash flows.

Estimation

The parameters of an OAS model have to be estimated in each of the three sub-models. If the OAS model is used to project cash flows only, drift and diffusion components of the term structure model are independently calibrated to interest rate data, or own expectations are used. If, on the other hand, the model is used for valuation, drift and diffusion components are jointly calibrated to interest rates and their volatilities.

EXHIBIT 10.5   Functionality of an OAS model

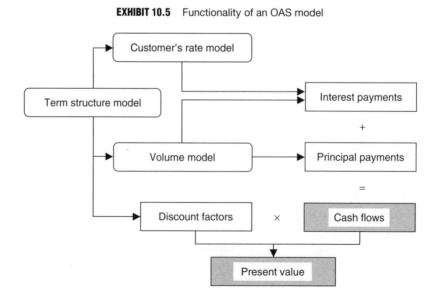

Again, we refer to the literature for a detailed exposition of the calibration of term structure models.

The customers' rate model is calibrated to historical interest rate data and historical customers' rates. The volume model is calibrated accordingly to historical interest rate data and historical volume changes. Whereas the models can be estimated with standard regression techniques, the comparison of different model specifications is more complex. Does the customers' rate on a savings account depend on the one-month Libor and on the five-year swap rate, or on the six-month Libor only? Should an autoregressive volume process be modeled? How should seasonality factors be incorporated? At a first glance, as many driving factors as possible should be built into the model. But on the other hand, over-parameterization has to be avoided. As more variables lead to a higher R-squared, but do not necessarily improve the explanatory power of the model, a regression model with many independent variables may provide spurious results. The calibration of too many variables to historical data bears the risk that the structure observed in the past is artificially closely matched, but the future is not explained very well. It is therefore strongly recommended to use advanced tests to assess the statistical quality of a model.

Beyond regression techniques we should address two more questions of the estimation of a volume model. First, should the volume model be calibrated to the balance of a non-maturing product or to its withdrawals and amortizations only? Second, should a volume model be estimated from aggregated data for the whole market, on a position level for the bank, or even on a contract level? The answer to the first question is ambiguous and actively discussed among practitioners. Liquidity risk management focuses on the balance of a non-maturing product. This balance can either be modeled directly or split into volume from existing business and volume from new business. If the balance is modeled directly, the parameters are estimated from the historical evolution of the balance, which is easily available in virtually any bank. If the balance is split, models are calibrated to historical amortizations and withdrawals, whereas new business is projected by another model. A simple model for the projection of new business is the use of expert knowledge from sales people. We favor the second approach – that is, to split the balance into existing and new business – because this accounts for the possibly very different sources of information for the forecast of the two parts of the balance evolution. We may even use two different models for the withdrawals and amortizations of two different non-maturing products, but use a single model for the new business generated in these products. It should be noted that the answer to the question of new business is even more evident for interest rate management. If interest rate management is meant to stabilize present values, that is equity capital, the models should incorporate existing business only, because anticipated new business is usually not hedged. If interest rate management is meant to stabilize cash flows, however, both modeling approaches can be used.

Now we address the second question, which is closely related to the first. In the academic literature on non-maturing products the models are typically calibrated to aggregated data provided by some regulatory authority. These data help to give an understanding of the market as a whole and of how a model works, but it is almost meaningless for risk management. Banks and their products differ significantly with respect to region, brand, business model, and so on. A model for non-maturing products used in risk management should therefore never be calibrated to aggregated data, but rather to proprietary data. If the models are calibrated to existing business only, data are not publicly available. It is even hard for some banks that have good proprietary historical data for withdrawals and amortizations. But should we go even one step further and estimate a volume model using data on the contract level? This is common in the modeling of adjustable-rate mortgages where contract-specific factors are used, like age of the contract and the loan-to-value ratio. This information on the contract level is essential for credit risk management, but the information added to liquidity and interest rate risk management is less valuable. The reason for this is twofold. First, liquidity and interest rate risk management are done on a pool level, using aggregated data and averages, and most of the contract-specific factors can be averaged. Second, and more importantly for liquidity risk management, it is computationally very costly to simulate the cash flows of thousands of individual contracts.

Implementation

The main challenge of the implementation of an OAS model is the simulation of interest rate scenarios in a term structure model. Building it up from scratch, serious knowledge on interest rate modeling is needed. At least basic term structure models are implemented nowadays in many risk management systems that cover non-maturing products. However, the calibration of these models to yield curves and volatilities awaits further development in many systems. Interest rate scenarios are generated by a Monte Carlo simulation because the volume and rate functions typically introduce path dependency in OAS models. As shown above, time lags in adjusting the customers' rate and in withdrawals and amortizations are observed in the market, and these features are covered in the corresponding models by the dependence on past interest rates. Beside Monte Carlo, such a path dependency can be implemented only using a non-recombining tree, but as shown above, such a tree is exposed to the curse of dimensionality because its dimension grows exponentially while Monte Carlo grows only linearly. Nevertheless, Monte Carlo simulations still require significant calculation costs. It has to be kept in mind that an expected value calculated with a numerical method is only an estimation of the true, unknown value, and therefore exposed to a variance. If only a few scenarios are used to calculate an expected value, two different seeds for the random number generation will likely generate very different expected values. Thousands of scenarios are needed in practice to calculate stable expected cash flows and values. Given a time horizon of, say, 20 years and a monthly time grid in 5,000 scenarios, 1.2 million valuations have to be performed. However, using powerful systems it is possible in practice to model the cash flows of a whole balance sheet with several non-maturing products using OAS models on a daily basis.

The implementation of the estimation of the term structure model can be cumbersome but can principally be done in a spreadsheet if no specialized software is available. The estimation of the other sub-models is likewise computationally not challenging. As in the case of the replicating portfolio approach, standard regression analysis as well as more advanced tests can be done with virtually any standard statistics software. Once a customers' rate and a volume model are identified, they can be estimated using appropriate regression techniques. It should carefully be tested whether the requirements of simple techniques like OLS are met. More advanced methods like robust techniques have to be used otherwise. Overall, the estimation of the customers' rate and the volume model is easier than the estimation of the optimal weights in a replicating portfolio model because no constraints are involved.

MODEL ASSESSMENT

Up to now, our analysis has been focused on the characteristics of each model approach. We have discussed how a non-maturing product can be replicated by a portfolio of money market instruments and par bonds. Then we have shown how this approach has been notably extended by the introduction of randomness, where the optimal replicating weights are determined dynamically with respect to scenarios of possible future realizations of the driving factors. Finally, we have described how the embedded options in a non-maturing product can be modeled in an OAS approach. The models obviously exhibit major differences. Which approach should actually be used to model, for example, savings accounts? Model choice is actually the crucial point in practice. As theoretically argued above, and as it will be shown empirically in the last section, different models lead to different risk management decisions that have a considerable impact on earnings. Is there any model in general superior to others? The bad news is *no*! The good news is that we can mostly identify a superior approach for a specific situation, given the characteristic of the product and data availability. In what follows, we assess the models in three steps. In a first step we give a qualitative assessment of the models with respect to the criteria we have defined above: flexibility, complexity and implementation issues. Then we move to a quantitative assessment and show how the models can be back-tested. This concludes our theoretical analysis. Finally, we study the models empirically and show for a real-world example the impact that different models have on liquidity and interest rate risk management in a bank.

Flexibility

Both approaches, which incorporate randomness, are very flexible compared to the standard replicating portfolio approach. In the latter, the economics of the customers' and the bank's option, which differ significantly, are not adequately transformed into the model. The replicating weights are determined mainly by fitting the model to the historical evolution of the rate paid or received on a non-maturing product, although the customers' option to amortize is far more important for the expected cash flows than the bank's option to adjust the rates. To avoid the worst, that is to run into liquidity problems, at least for non-maturing liabilities a method to account for extreme withdrawals has to be integrated. As an example we have shown the approach of a market-mix portfolio, even though it is not an intrinsic part of the replicating portfolio model. On the other hand, the stochastic optimization method and the OAS approach both allow for many characteristics of the embedded options. Through the specification of a volume and a rate model, the different characteristics of the bank's option and the customers' option, as well as their interdependences, can be reasonably well covered. The stochastic optimization has even more flexibility because extra economic properties can be incorporated like liquidity constraints on hedging instruments, for example. It uses the main components of an OAS model, but adds a flexible optimization procedure. A flexible model should also allow for the separation of existing and new business. We presented the above arguments for modeling new and existing business either jointly or separately. This flexibility is only offered by the OAS approach, which can be calibrated to changes in balances as well as to changes in amortizations. The standard replicating approach can also be used for both variants at least in its simplest form where no volume function enters the model. The stochastic optimization approach has been applied so far only to the joint simulation of new and existing business.

Complexity

We mentioned above the three dimensions of the complexity criterion. First, the models for non-maturing products must be communicable to senior management because they lay the foundations for funding programs and hedging strategies. Second, the probability of failures in operating a model rises with its complexity. Finally, it is difficult to integrate a complex model into regular risk management, funding and pricing processes. The most complex model presented here is undoubtedly the stochastic optimization approach. Even if the replicating portfolio approach is well known to senior management, this approach seems to be difficult to communicate. The mathematics involved is rather complex and the mechanics inside the model are difficult to explore, most notably the impact of a change in the constraints of the optimization problem. This may result in a trial and error approach in the specification of the model. If constraints are set too tight, the solution is mainly determined by the input. If constraints are set too loose, the resulting weights may be unrealistic for practical use. A correct implementation of the model and its daily, weekly or monthly use can be cumbersome, and its integration in risk management processes can be difficult. However, it should be kept in mind that this complexity is basically the flipside of the coin of the high flexibility of the model. The deterministic replicating portfolio approach is by nature far less complex. Difficult questions don't arise until the model is analyzed in depth. This approach and its basic idea are therefore easy to communicate. It is observed that a replicating portfolio model is well accepted, as long as the amortizations of the replicating portfolio are in line with the amortizations of the non-maturing product. Finally, this approach is easily integrated in risk management and management accounting procedures. Due to its simple and non-stochastic structure, an understanding of the mechanics inside the model comes naturally. The OAS approach is more complex. The idea of a term structure model and of the volume and rate models are reasonably easy to communicate, but it is more difficult to understand the impact a parameter change has on the output. Overall, we regard an OAS model as simple to include in a bank's management processes.

Implementation

Implementation is of course closely related to complexity. A model that is difficult to implement is complex and vice versa. We focus here on two aspects of an implementation: calculation costs and maintainability. A replicating portfolio model, for example, is very cheap in terms of calculation time and storage demand. Since no randomness is modeled, a replicating portfolio is simulated only for one scenario – the observed scenario of the estimation period. The OAS approach requires the calculation of thousands of scenarios to obtain reliable results. On top of simulated scenarios, the stochastic optimization approach adds the solution of a multi-step optimization problem that boosts calculation costs. The simple replicating portfolio approach is most suited in terms of calculation costs, followed by the OAS approach. The stochastic optimization approach has the highest implementation costs. In terms of maintainability our assessment may be surprising. The OAS model turns out to be simplest to maintain. The estimation of the volume and rate models is straightforward. However, it should be kept in mind that data for withdrawals and amortization must be available to estimate the volume. The rate model, as well as the replicating portfolio approach, only needs interest rate and customers' rate data. The implementation of a term structure model and its calibration to swap curve and volatility data is common knowledge nowadays, and should be readily available in an up-to-date risk management system. The maintenance of a replicating portfolio model can be tricky at a closer inspection if it is not available at your fingertips in a risk management system. As shown above, the replicating portfolio requires continuous re-balancing of all instruments along the trend function assumed, as well as in the one-month bucket to meet the divergence from the trend. This can turn out to be difficult to customize. The estimation of the portfolio weights is more complex than the estimation of the parameters of an OAS model, too. Finally, the implementation of a stochastic optimization approach is apparently difficult to maintain.

Which model should be chosen? A replicating portfolio model is easy to communicate but not very flexible. Its implementation can be tricky, but data requirements are extremely low and its output is calculated fast. A drawback is its theoretical inconsistency. Weights are calculated based on the assumption that they are never adjusted, which is obviously not valid in practice. Additionally, the embedded options are essentially not modeled, since no randomness is assumed. The stochastic optimization pushes up the flexibility of the model significantly at the cost of very high complexity and time-consuming calculations. The OAS model seems to be overall a good choice at first glance, but it has a lower degree of freedom than the stochastic optimization approach. Thus model choice depends on the specific situation. To model a current account, for example, which has a very stable customers' rate and whose volume is rather deterministic, the replicating portfolio approach may be a good choice. The same is true even for more complex non-maturing products, as long as the differences in the amortization schedule implied in the replicating portfolio and the customers' behavior observed in reality differs not too much in absolute terms and balances are not too volatile. The power of the stochastic optimization lies in its flexibility. If the complexity of the model can be handled, we may expect results superior to the standard replicating portfolio approach. The OAS model tends to be a very good choice for the liquidity risk management of major non-maturing products, where withdrawals and amortizations are heavily driven by movements in the interest rates or other economic factors for which interest rates can be used as proxies. It balances usability with theoretical soundness.

A model choice should not rely on theoretical considerations only. Different models and their specifications should be assessed empirically, and even once a model has been chosen its performance should be checked regularly using back-testing techniques. If a model is used for liquidity risk management only, the back testing focuses on cash flows. The expected cash flows are calculated in a model as of, say, one year ago and compared with the cash flows observed in reality since that date. This is actually a joint test of the theoretical model and the scenarios that are plugged into the model. If subjective probabilities are used for scenario generation, the specific scenarios and their drift may have even a higher impact on the model output than a change of the model itself. To separate these effects the model should be run in a first step of the back test, not on the estimated interest rate scenarios, but on the evolution of the interest rate observed in the back-testing period. This helps to break up deviations in an effect of model choice and in an effect of scenario choice. But the back testing of cash flows has a serious drawback. Suppose that the output of a replicating model is a single forecast of the monthly cash flows over the next three years. In almost any case, cash flows observed in reality in the subsequent months will differ from the forecast by some degree. It is impossible to quantify the severity of the deviation of real cash flows from projected cash flows based on a single observation. What is the model risk if observed cash flows are somewhat lower than the projected cash flows for the first half of the back-testing period and higher for the second half? Should we use modeled cash flows that exhibit severe deviations from real cash flows in the short term to assess a medium-term funding program? We would need a large amount of subsequent back-testing periods to assess the quality of the forecasts, which is clearly unfeasible for a three-year period. The same reasoning basically applies to scenario-based models like the OAS or the stochastic optimization approach, although they provide some information of the quantiles of the cash flow distribution. Overall, the back testing of cash flows depends more on a subjective assessment of the fit of modeled cash flows than on strict quantitative criteria. The application of back-testing procedures that are used in interest rate risk management could be a remedy for this problem. These procedures indirectly test the goodness of cash flow forecasts of a model in a single measure. The main step in the aggregation to a single measure is the discounting of the modeled cash flows to calculate their present value. As a starting point, the present value of the non-maturing product is calculated in the model for some date in the past. The key interest rates of that date are shifted by a small amount and the present value is recalculated. A key rate delta profile is obtained in this way, which shows the sensitivity of the present value with respect to small changes in the key rates. Then, the corresponding hedge for each key rate bucket is constructed with forward rate agreements and interest rate swaps, which totally offsets the sensitivity. The portfolio of the non-maturing product and the hedge instruments, which is risk-less for an arbitrarily small time period within the model, is now rolled over for a small time period in reality, and the present value of the non-maturing product and the hedge instruments is calculated, given the interest rate observed at that day. This is done for several time steps in the back-testing period. The deviation of the observed yields of the theoretically perfectly hedged non-maturing product from the risk-less rate is a clear indicator for the quality of the model, since it explicitly shows the risk of poorly specifying model parameters. This back-testing procedure is a direct application of the basic argument used by Black and Scholes to derive the option pricing formula. It should be noted that through the use of an appropriate discounting procedure the cash flows are forecast under the risk neutral probability measure. But for liquidity risk management the subjective probability measure should be applied to model real-world cash flows. This back-testing procedure nevertheless provides some useful information about the model quality. The main difference between the risk neutral measure and the subjective measure is the time weighting of the future cash flows. While the time weights are implicitly given through market discount factors under the former measure, they have to be explicitly chosen under the latter measure. This translates into a different drift between both measures. The volatility of the cash flow estimates, however, does not differ between both measures. We therefore conclude that there is little chance that a model will perform very well for cash flow forecasts if it has only a few degrees of freedom and performs poorly in risk neutral back testing. Of course, in this back-testing procedure we do not test the quality of the subjective scenarios plugged into the model. But this is exactly the economic assumption common to all models, which has to be made by a liquidity risk manager rather than a testable part of a specific model. From our experience, the OAS model is superior to the replicating portfolio model for all major non-maturing products, with significant changes in customers' behavior over time. To our knowledge, no back-testing results for the stochastic optimization approach are published yet.

IMPLICATIONS FOR LIQUIDITY MANAGEMENT

The very first implication of a model for non-maturing products of liquidity risk management is the structure of the projected cash flows. In a first step, we deal with amortizing and withdrawals cash flows only. The models are used to calculate expected withdrawals of deposits or amortizations of loans. Subsequently, new volume is modeled separately. These two kinds of cash flow projections may even have two distinct sources of information. While the former is estimated from historical data in general, the latter may be extracted from expert knowledge of the marketing department, or from sales people who know best the bank's current strength to attract new customers and raise their on-balance assets under management. The reason for this is straightforward. Amortization schedules of existing business are mainly driven by expected interest rates, whereas acquisition of new loans and new deposits is strongly affected by marketing and sales initiatives like promotion, introduction of new products, or some benefits compared to competitors. We focus on the modeling of existing business in this case study, assuming that new business is projected independently from model choice. We have calibrated a replicating portfolio model and an OAS model to the same data of a savings product. The data consists of volume and withdrawals of a sub-portion of a real product and its customers' rate, and covers a 186-month period from January 1990 to June 2005.

Exhibit 10.6 shows a typical pattern for the cash flows projected in a replicating portfolio model. The replicating portfolio consists of buckets of one month, 12 months, two years, five years and 10 years. The bucket weights are 4%, 31%, 7%, 34% and 24%, respectively. The cash flows exhibit a step profile that is produced by virtually any replicating portfolio. In the first month, all buckets contribute to the cash flow. Afterwards, the contract in the first bucket has matured and only the remaining buckets contribute to the cash flows. For every bucket, one contract per month matures and causes a slight jump in the cash flow profile. This jump is typically substantial at the boundary of a bucket because, for example, in the 12-month bucket only 12 contracts carry a weight of 31%, while in the 60-month bucket 60 contracts carry a weight of 34%. Due to the high number of contracts in a long maturity bucket, the contribution of the single contract to the bucket weight tends to be lower than the contribution in short maturity buckets. This is valid as long as the bucket weight for a long maturity is not substantially higher than that of a short maturity. As expected, the principal cash flows dominate the cash flow profile. This profile is both conservative and risky at the same time. The first bucket carries a significant portion of the replicating portfolio and therefore almost 8% of the volume is expected to be withdrawn within the next month. In other words, the replicating investment portfolio provides enough liquidity to meet a very high portion of withdrawals. On the other hand, a significant portion is still invested in the 10-year bucket. This can be seen as rather risky, since the replicating portfolio

EXHIBIT 10.6 Projected cash flows in a replicating portfolio model

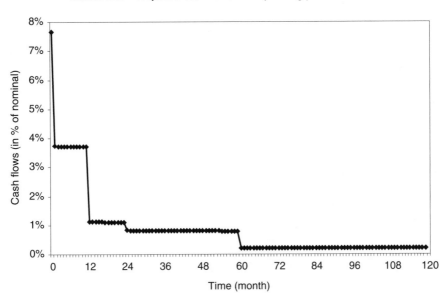

provides not enough liquidity if less than 24% is actually invested by the customers for more than five years. We have used the market-mix approach to calculate these weights. The weights could either be calibrated to maximum withdrawals or to maximum changes in the balance. The calibration to withdrawals would be consistent with the modeling of existing business only, whereas the calibration to changes in the balance would be compatible with the modeling of new business. From a theoretical point of view, calibrating to changes in balance without modeling new business is not perfectly consistent. However, we favor the second approach in any case and accept this slight inconsistency. In a real-world application, the investment portfolio would always be chosen while taking new business into account. We have checked that the replicating portfolio has enough liquidity to meet changes in the net balance even in the worst case observed in the past. If we had used withdrawals only, instead of the net balance to determine the market mix, the replicating portfolio would have had even more short-term weights, resulting in a shorter duration.

Exhibit 10.7 shows the pattern for an OAS model. The OAS approach models uncertainty explicitly. This enables a risk manager to focus not on average expected cash flows, but on bad events that rarely occur. High withdrawals from a savings account are such a bad event in liquidity risk management. We have modeled the dynamics of the interest rates in a term structure model in 10,000 scenarios and have looked at the aggregated withdrawals up to 12 months ahead.[8] The cash flows shown in Exhibit 10.7 are from the particular scenario with aggregated withdrawals for one year, which are exceeded only by 100 out of 10,000 scenarios. This scenario represents therefore the 99% confidence interval for high cash

EXHIBIT 10.7   Projected cash flows in an OAS model

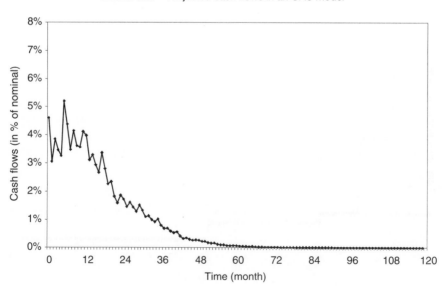

flows. The peaks in the cash flows, which are obvious for the near-term, stem from the incorporation of seasonality effects. As discussed above, the probability measure under which the dynamics of the interest rates and the cash flows are modeled is a crucial point. We have used the subjective probability measure because we deal with cash flows directly, rather than with their present values. The drift of the evolution of the term structure has been calculated from proprietary estimates of the yield curve one year ahead. The diffusion component has been calibrated to volatilities implied in liquidly traded interest rate options.[9] The cash flows are mainly driven by two factors, given a specification of a volume function and a rate function: drift and volatility, or equivalently expectation of future interest rates and uncertainty. The expectation of future cash flows results directly in the drift of the dynamics and drives the level of the average expected cash flows. The spread between the average expected cash flows and the cash flows at the 99% confidence level is driven by the expected uncertainty in the market. High volatility leads to a high spread between average cash flows and extreme cash flows. There are some remarkable differences between the projected cash flows in the replicating portfolio approach and the OAS approach. Projected cash flows in the long term are less in the OAS model than in the corresponding replicating portfolio model. More cash flows are expected in the medium term in return, whereas in the near term they are approximately equal. Though seasonality effects are very evident, the cash flow profile is smoother and exhibits no structural jumps at all. In addition, the duration of the savings accounts is lower in the OAS approach than in the replicating portfolio approach. This stems from the fact that the former is directly calibrated to principal cash flows, while the latter is basically calibrated to the customers' rate, which is rather stable over time. This difference of the duration between both models is even more evident if cumulative cash flows are considered. Regardless of the approach chosen, the principal cash flows must add up to unity because in the long run all money will be withdrawn. There may be differences in the interest cash flows in different approaches, but interest rate cash flows are very small compared to principal cash flows. Exhibit 10.8 on page 252 shows the aggregated principal cash flows in the replicating portfolio approach and in the OAS approach. The money is withdrawn much quicker in the OAS approach than in the replicating approach, indicating again the shorter duration of the existing business in savings accounts in our specific example. It should be noted, however, that the difference between both approaches strongly depends on the subjective expectation of future interest rates. We draw the conclusion from this analysis that the different model approaches yield very different cash flows. But we do not state that, for example, the cash flows in an OAS model are lower than in a replicating portfolio model in general, although this is the case in the specific example discussed. The basic message is that these differences in projected cash flows lead to very different funding strategies. In our example the gap between the outstanding volumes of existing business

EXHIBIT 10.8   Projected aggregated cash flows

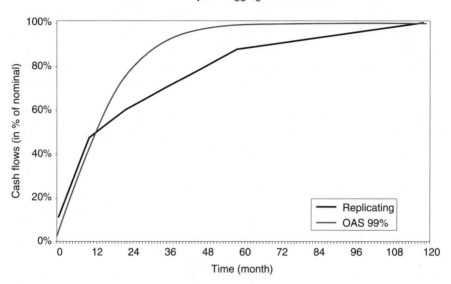

three years from now is 22% of the volume as of today. If the same new business volume is assumed in both models, a funding program based on the OAS model would include for every billion of volume the raising of additional funds of 220 million, compared to a funding program based on the replicating portfolio model. Even if netting effects from non-maturing assets and liabilities, and the flexibility in the design of a funding program, are taken into account the differences are very significant.

As a side step we now look at the impact that model choice has on interest rate risk management. This is directly linked to the back-testing procedure described above. In asset liability management the interest rate risk is typically hedged with derivatives, mainly interest rate swaps. The volume of payer and receiver swaps in the hedge portfolio depends largely on the risk profile of the product to be hedged, which in turn is calculated in a model. For this reason, we have calculated delta profiles for both the replicating portfolio and OAS models. A delta profile shows the sensitivity of the present value with respect to a change of Libor and swap rates. For the replicating portfolio approach we have used the same model as above. For the OAS approach we have to use the risk neutral probability measure; that is, the drift is calculated from forward rates and volatility quotes instead of proprietary expectations of future interest rates. In addition, average cash flows are used instead of cash flows at the 99% confidence level. Exhibit 10.9 on page 253 shows the key delta profile for savings accounts in both models, given a small drop in the key rate. For example, if the two-year swap rate drops by one bp in the next moment, the present value of the savings accounts will drop by roughly 0.2 bps of its current balance in the replicating model. The intuition for this sensitivity is simple. The savings accounts are replicated by a portfolio of short positions in bonds and their present value drops because their

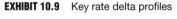

EXHIBIT 10.9   Key rate delta profiles

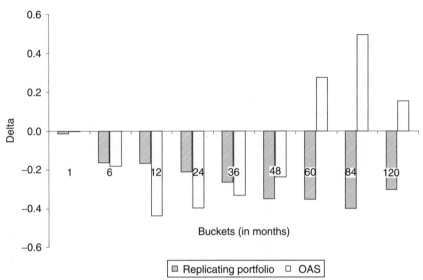

coupons are not adjusted instantaneously and the bank cannot profit immediately from more favorable financing rates. The same key rate delta is almost twice as big in the OAS model. It is not surprising that the models differ with respect to the delta profiles produced, but exploring the structure of these differences gives some further insights into how the models work. There are two main differences. In the one-year and two-year buckets the sensitivity of the non-maturing product to changes in interest rates is much higher in the OAS model than in the replicating model. Second, and possibly more difficult to explain at first sight, the sensitivities with respect to long-term rates have opposite signs! The first observation is easily explained by the fact that the OAS model, at least in this example, puts relatively more weight on the medium-term cash flows than on short-term cash flows or long-term cash flows. For longer terms the replicating portfolio still has a negative sensitivity. The sign of the sensitivity is the same for all buckets because the possibility of negative weights has been excluded in the optimization problem to avoid an artificial fit. But how can we explain the positive delta for the swap rates of five years and above in the OAS model? As shown above, this approach explicitly models the embedded options in a non-maturing product where the customers' option to withdraw the money typically dominates the bank's option to adjust the customers' rate. The data used in this example tell us that customers' behavior is largely driven by the evolution of the five-year swap rate. For example, expected withdrawals in one year from now are mainly driven by the expected evolution of the five-year swap rate up to this date. Beside the volatility, which is incorporated through the calibration of the term structure model, the option embedded in the non-maturing product is therefore driven by the series of five-year forward swap rates whose start dates range from one month to the end of the model horizon. This finding is consistent with option pricing theory in general because the value of an option depends not on the spot price of the underlying, but on its forward price. In contrast to the replicating portfolio model, a drop of the swap rates with maturities of five years and beyond has a positive impact on the value of the non-maturing product. This is because less money is withdrawn and from the bank's point of view, more business can be refinanced at a relatively cheap rate. To look at the flip side of the coin, rising rates result in higher withdrawals and thus lower the value of the savings accounts.

Each key rate delta can be hedged with a corresponding fair swap. A positive seven-year delta, for example, can be hedged with a seven-year payer swap because its value drops if interest rates fall, which offsets the rising value of the instrument to be hedged. Using the replicating portfolio model in our example, savings accounts are hedged against changes in the seven-year swap rate with a seven-year receiver swap, as opposed to the OAS model, which tells us to use payer swaps. Given the numbers above, each billion of volume in savings accounts is fully hedged against the seven-year rate with an 80 million payer swap in the OAS model. A 60 million receiver swap is required to hedge the same risk in the replicating portfolio model. Summing up these different hedge strategies over all key rates, all products and total volume, this has a significant impact on expected cash flows and, of course, on interest rate risk management. The fundamental differences in the key rate delta profile between the OAS model and the replicating portfolio model suggest very different back-testing results. As mentioned above, the OAS model typically provides higher hedge efficiency than the replicating portfolio model.

CONCLUSION

Non-maturing products, although more complex than most instruments traded frequently on the markets, represent a significant part of the balance sheet of most banks. Nowadays customers react smartly to economic changes and quickly alter their balances by withdrawing funds or adjusting the amortization schedule of their debt. This makes modeling the cash flows of non-maturing products difficult and exposes a bank to significant liquidity risk. Potential liquidity gaps have to be discovered early to reduce the risk of a liquidity crisis. Models for non-maturing products play, therefore, a significant role in liquidity risk management. No standard has evolved yet and due to the differences in the design of non-maturing products, availability of data, and applications there will probably never be the one model that covers all. In fact, we stress that it may be worthwhile in practical applications to use different models for different tasks, even though only one model should be used for all tasks in theory. It appears that the use of an OAS model for the risk management of savings accounts, for example, and the use of a replicating approach for fund transfer pricing, or even two different specifications of the same approach, can improve the accuracy of the management of the savings accounts even if the different models are not consistent with each other. The stochastic optimization approach can be powerful in the management of selected non-maturing products. The empirical analysis has shown that a simple replicating model results in an unrealistic cash flow pattern and is consequently not appropriate for liquidity risk management. Instead, an OAS model would probably be used to calculate expected cash flows for the time period that matters for liquidity risk management. We recommend different models for different purposes in liquidity risk management, interest rate risk management and fund transfer pricing.

It should be noted that the models presented here are based on the assumption of normal markets and are not well suited for stress management. To work in a normal market environment, models are calibrated to some historical time series and possibly some expected volatility. For stress tests, however, this is completely wrong: The change of economic factors and the people's reaction to it differ from the past, and calibrating stress scenarios to time series would not be a good idea. A complete risk management covers both, normal markets and stress events. Stress scenarios either reflect historical events, probable future shocks or hypothetical severe events. The evaluation of appropriate scenarios is driven by economic considerations alone, and for non-maturing products stress scenarios are directly applied to their volume in liquidity risk management. The calculation of expected cash flows in normal market situations, however, relies much more on statistical techniques, and the models are therefore complex and technically demanding. But in contrast to a complex product in the trading book, not only highly specialized financial engineers have to deal non-maturing products. The main challenge in the application of such models to non-maturing products is to meet the different requirements of a broad spectrum of stakeholders, including senior management, sales people and highly specialized financial engineers.

NOTES

[1] Wilson, T.C. (1994). "Optimal Values," *Balance Sheet*, Vol. 3 No. 3, Autumn, pp. 13–20.

[2] The OLS approach is implemented in any statistics package and in some spreadsheet software. The robust techniques are implemented in advanced statistical software, including the package "R" freely available under the GNU license.

[3] It should be noted that the estimation of the moving average could be cumbersome. In a proper setup, the weights of the interest rates from which the moving average is calculated have to be balanced according to the trend function. Nevertheless we recommend the estimation with

constant weights to avoid the difficulties in implementing the estimation with non-constant weights, in particular with regard to the estimation period of the trend function, which turns out to be quite short in practice.

[4] A sound theoretical treatment in interest rate modeling from a practitioner's point of view is given by Brigo, D. and Mercurio, F. (2005), *Interest Rate Models*, Springer, Berlin.

[5] Rigsbee, S. R., Ayaydin, S. S., and Richard, C. A. (1996). "Implementing 'Value at Risk' in Balance Sheet Management – Using the Option-adjusted Spread Model," in Fabozzi, F. and Konishi, A. (ed.), *The Handbook of Asset/Liability Management*, McGraw-Hill Companies, Chicago.

[6] Jarrow, R.A. and van Deventer, D. R. (1998). "The Arbitrage-free Valuation and Hedging of Demand Deposits and Credit Card Loans," *Journal of Banking and Finance*, 22, pp. 249–72. In a subsequent paper the model has been slightly extended and discussed empirically. Cf. Janosi, T., Jarrow, R. A., and Zullo, F. (1999). "An Empirical Analysis of the Jarrow–van Deventer Model for Valuing Non-Maturity Demand Deposits," *The Journal of Derivatives*, Fall 1999, pp. 8–30.

[7] The Jarrow–van Deventer model is extended to the general case with simulation in Kalkbrener, M. and Willing, J. (2004), "Risk Management of Non-maturing Liabilities," *Journal of Banking and Finance*, 28, pp. 1547–68.

[8] A one-factor Libor market model with time-invariant constant forward rate volatility has been used to model the dynamics of the term structure in this case study. The diffusion component has been calibrated to CHF at-the-money cap volatilities. From our experience, the general results discussed here hold true even if another term structure model is used.

[9] It should be noted that the specific cash flows shown in Exhibit 10.7 could be expected to be unstable with respect to implementation issues: A slightly different confidence level or even another random number seed yields another scenario with possibly very different cash flows. Using different specifications we have found, however, that the differences of the cash flows do not weaken the general results presented here. Nevertheless, this instability is a problem that has to be dealt with in practice if a high confidence level is used.

CHAPTER 11

The Net Cash Capital Tool in Bank Liquidity Management[1]

Louis D. Raffis

T he banking industry has been faced with deposit disintermediation as an increasingly sophisticated client base has been offered an ever-increasing array of savings and investment alternatives. As a result, bank liquidity managers have found it necessary to develop ever more sophisticated measures of liquidity beyond just the loans to deposits ratio. A number of ratios have been designed to measure a bank's dependence upon credit-sensitive or "hot" money. These include, but are not limited to, ratios such as the following:

- wholesale funding to total assets
- market-sourced funding to managed assets
- short-term funds dependence
- stable assets to stable funding
- 30-/90-day crisis liquidity coverage ratios %
- overnight position to total funding.

While each of these ratios may provide a valuable piece of additional information for the manager, our bank found that none of these alone provided a comprehensive look at our bank's liquidity position. Our search for such a comprehensive measure led us to the net cash capital position, a tool developed and utilized by Moody's Investors Service. This tool, which was originally developed to analyze securities firms, simply attempts to determine whether a bank's long-term funding is greater than its illiquid assets, assuming that a bank will not be able to roll over its short-term funding and will have to unwind its liquid assets to continue to remain solvent. The value of the tool is that it provides us with a consistent and externally accepted framework to quantify, analyze, and then communicate our liquidity position to rating agency and regulatory analysts.

THE MOODY'S NET CASH CAPITAL TOOL

As Moody's describes it, this liquidity analysis is designed to compare the cash demands from a bank's contractual obligations with the issuer's inflow of cash, excluding the cash generated from refinancing debt. The bank net cash capital tool attempts to measure cash demands today using information pulled from a bank's call report. The tool is a conceptually straightforward measure:

$$\text{Net cash capital} = \text{Long-term funding}$$
$$- \text{Illiquid assets}$$
$$- \text{Illiquid securities}$$

A positive result indicates that the bank would be able to continue operating from its currently available resources, even with a temporary disruption in the unsecured wholesale funding markets.

To facilitate peer comparisons, Moody's will divide the net cash capital measure by total assets, or managed assets. The components of the calculation include a number of items that can only be found in a bank's regulatory reports:

Long-term funding within the cash capital context includes equity capital, hybrid capital securities, long-term debt and non-brokered insured deposits:

> **Total equity capital**
> *Plus*
>> Subordinated notes and debentures
>> Other borrowed money
>> Hybrid capital securities
>> Deposits in domestic offices
>> Brokered deposits originally denominated <$100 K
>> Time deposits >= $100 K: 1–3 years
>> Time deposits >= $100 K: >3 years
> *Less*
>> Total time deposits of $100 K+
>> Other borrowed money, FHLB advanced <= 1 year
>> Other borrowings <= 1 year
> **= Total long-term funding**

While one can debate the relative "stickiness" of some of the deposit categories above, with Federal Deposit Insurance Corporation (FDIC) insurance in place, it is assumed that most deposits will stay in place because most sophisticated depositors recognize the credit of the US government stands behind them. Brokered deposits are not included because the bank regulators can quickly shut down the bank's access to this funding source, particularly if the bank does not stay "well-capitalized" within its crisis period.

Illiquid assets include fixed assets, intangibles, other assets and loans. (Residential mortgage liquidity is subject to a 20% haircut due to market price risk.)

Premises and fixed assets
Plus
> Other real estate owned
> Investment in unconsolidated subsidiaries
> Customers' liability on acceptances
> Intangible assets
> Other assets
> Loans and leases, total net not held for sale

Less
> 80% of home equity loans
> 80% of all other 1–4 first lien loans
> Loans to US branch of foreign banks
> Loans to other commercial banks, US
> Loans to other depository institutions
> Loans to foreign branches, other US
> *Loans to other foreign banks*

= Total illiquid assets

Moody's also deducts loans provided to other depository institutions as these funds can quickly be called and replaced by funding elsewhere within the banking system.

Illiquid securities are deducted from long-term funding also. Mortgage-backed securities (MBS) are haircut 100% as Moody's views these as highly illiquid. This measure hurts a number of banks as many investment managers view MBS as possessing attractive risk/return profiles.

Investment securities haircuts
100% haircut (of fair value available for sale)
FNMA, FHLMC, and all other MBS, ABS, credit card receivables, home equity lines, automobile loans, other customer loans, commercial and industrial loans
33% haircut (of fair value)
Other domestic debt securities and foreign debt securities
15% haircut (of fair value)
Mutual funds and other equity securities
10% haircut
Fair value of Munis available for sale, Munis held to maturity, and the fair value of MBS pass-thru GNMA, MBS pass-thru FNMA, and other MBS pass-thru
2% haircut (of fair value available for sale)
US Treasury securities, US government agency obligations,
All other US government-sponsored agencies
Total value of these haircuts = Total illiquid securities

SHORTCOMINGS OF THE MEASURE

While the measure is somewhat comprehensive, several simplifying assumptions employed to keep the measure simple and useful for most banks also reduce its precision:

- The measure does not incorporate unfunded loan commitments, which the bank is generally obligated to fund at any time. Not only does it exclude unfunded loan commitments, but also commitments that banks make to asset-backed commercial paper programs.
- It includes long-term debt that is maturing within one year as long-term funding.
- It excludes cash earnings expected to be generated by the bank's normal operations.
- The haircuts could be too low and may increase at a time of greater illiquidity. Also, the supply of secured financing by type of collateral can change regardless of the haircut, depending on the counterparty's appetite for collateral.
- Certain haircuts, such as 100% for all types of MBS, are perhaps too onerous, because no distinction is made between the more liquid, shorter duration securities with a proven track record of market liquidity, and less liquid and more interest-rate-sensitive bond structures.
- The measure gives no credit to a bank that can readily realize cash from loans other than residential mortgages. Considering the well-developed loan sales market and broad securitization market, the current framework could underestimate the true liquidity held by those banks that have in place loan sale capacity and/or securitization capacity.
- Some of the items are rather obscure to bank management since they are often regulatory descriptions of asset categories.
- Finally, no single snapshot measure can fully capture all the mitigating activities that can be undertaken by bank management to enhance liquidity in a crisis.

HOW THE ADJUSTED NET CASH CAPITAL MEASURE IS USED BY ONE BANK

Originally developed at our bank prior to the acceptance of the net cash capital framework, the crisis liquidity funding analysis was used to evaluate the bank's ability to withstand a short-term funding crisis of up to 90 days. The analysis looked forward at 30-day intervals, introducing transactions that could be used to alleviate a liquidity problem, but also required a certain amount of lead-time, such as asset securitizations. The framework also allowed for an effective simulation of incremental liquidity draws, such as a loss of customer deposits, reduction of credit lines from certain credit-sensitive counterparties, and increased draws on customer lines of credit.

In other words, by introducing a key variable – time – we captured a number of items that the more static net cash capital measure failed to pick up. Next, we used the crisis liquidity framework under multiple ratings scenarios. This allowed us to simulate various scenarios, such as a gradual deterioration in the bank's credit over time. We recognized that our bank's funding capacity would correlate closely with our rating, and that the rating scenarios could serve as a good proxy for various bank-specific funding crises. In addition, the ratings migration analysis inspired us to contemplate the implications of ratings triggers embedded in lending agreements, securitization documents, and other contractual arrangements. The liquidity effects of these triggers were factored into the analysis as well.

We found that a crucial component to the analysis was determining what our market access would be under deteriorating ratings scenarios. Considering that we had no experience with much weaker ratings, we turned to Wall Street capital markets personnel to help us develop a picture of the bank's ability to access such varied markets and investor bases, which included fed funds, repo, CP, MTNs, euro-MTNs, subordinated debt, hybrid capital, and preferred and common equity. We found that periodic updates to these scenarios are necessary to address changes in investor appetite, economic conditions and the development of new funding sources.

Now while we realized that we had a dynamic tool available to us, we found it also possessed several limitations, including no value in peer analysis, time requirements for updating, and inconsistency with the rating agency snapshot view of liquidity as captured in the net cash capital tool.

After considerable discussion, we felt that the most appropriate way of capturing the best features of these two liquidity tools was to take the multi-period, dynamic view of the crisis liquidity framework and integrate it into the net cash capital framework, which facilitated peer group analysis (by downloading bank regulatory reports into our calculation model) and communications with the rating agencies.

This "syncing up" of the two frameworks required extending our 90-day crisis liquidity analysis out to one year, the time frame utilized by Moody's net cash capital framework. This opened up some additional funding sources to be reviewed for us. For example, we identified some asset portfolios that can be securitized with longer lead times. Factoring in potential loan growth from commitment draws is a further enhancement that can be easily incorporated. Finally, and perhaps most importantly, we layered in debt issuance capacity under different market conditions, time frames, and ratings scenarios. This feature of the tool required that we revisit our market access analysis and it also drove us to introduce

EXHIBIT 11.1   The multi-dimensional measurement tool

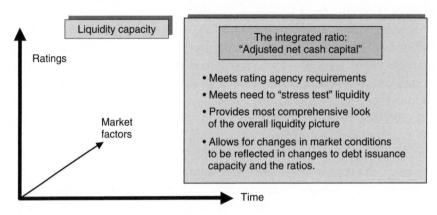

additional ratings variations. The illustration in Exhibit 11.1 was used as a communication device as we introduced the new measure.

The integration of the two frameworks required us to convert the net cash capital framework into 30-day, 90-day, and one-year time frames, and then introduce the declining credit scenarios onto these time frames. The model produces a net cash capital position for each time period/rating scenario, which is then converted into ratios by dividing by total assets and/or managed assets. The 30-day scenario ratios should tie to published Moody's numbers and can be used for peer comparisons also. Exhibit 11.2 on page 263 shows how we converted the net cash capital framework into a multidimensional analysis.

After these ratios were calculated, we then adjusted the net cash capital position with the various crisis funding plan items mentioned above. Discount window borrowings are assumed to only be available in the shorter time frames. The cash capital positions for each time/rating scenario are recalculated and compared to established internal guidelines (see Exhibit 11.3 on page 265). We found that these adjustments demonstrate to our external constituencies that our liquidity position is much stronger than it appears to be under the simple snapshot look. Over time we found some significant benefits from this integrated framework:

- reduction of the number of snapshot liquidity measures
- simplification of the measurement and reporting process
- development of consistent funding "triggers" driven by one set of ratios
- enhanced discussions with regulators and rating agencies, including more effective peer comparisons.

The establishment of recommended guidelines for the calculations was based upon available peer group information, primarily from rating agencies and regulatory reports. We chose to establish positive guideline

EXHIBIT 11.2 The net cash capital framework in three dimensions

Net cash capital & crisis analysis

Moody's rating:	30 day				90 day				1 year			
	A1	Baa1	Ba1	B1	A1	Baa1	Ba1	B1	A1	Baa1	Ba1	B1
BANK ratios:												
LONG-TERM FUNDING												
Total equity capital	2,141,890	2,141,890	2,141,890	2,141,890	2,141,890	2,141,890	2,141,890	2,141,890	2,141,890	2,141,890	2,141,890	2,141,890
Plus: Subordinated notes & debentures	913,927	913,927	913,927	913,927	913,927	913,927	913,927	913,927	913,927	913,927	913,927	913,927
Plus: Other borrowed money	3,723,326	3,723,326	3,723,326	3,723,326	3,723,326	3,723,326	3,723,326	3,723,326	3,723,326	3,723,326	3,723,326	3,723,326
Less: Oth brwd money, FHLB adv: <= 1 Yr	6,942	6,942	6,942	6,942	6,942	6,942	6,942	6,942	6,942	6,942	6,942	6,942
Less: Other borrowings, <= 1 Yr	2,117,375	2,117,375	2,117,375	2,117,375	2,117,375	2,117,375	2,117,375	2,117,375	2,117,375	2,117,375	2,117,375	2,117,375
Plus: Deposits in domestic offices	16,762,817	16,762,817	16,762,817	16,762,817	16,762,817	16,762,817	16,762,817	16,762,817	16,762,817	16,762,817	16,762,817	16,762,817
Less: Brokered dep orig den <100 K	55,839	55,839	55,839	55,839	55,839	55,839	55,839	55,839	55,839	55,839	55,839	55,839
Less: Total time deposits of $100 K	1,701,273	1,701,273	1,701,273	1,701,273	1,701,273	1,701,273	1,701,273	1,701,273	1,701,273	1,701,273	1,701,273	1,701,273
Plus: Time deps >=$100 K: 1–3 Yrs	393,122	393,122	393,122	393,122	393,122	393,122	393,122	393,122	393,122	393,122	393,122	393,122
Plus: Time deps >=$100 K:>3Yrs	186,575	186,575	186,575	186,575	186,575	186,575	186,575	186,575	186,575	186,575	186,575	186,575
Total long-term funding	**18,843,342**	**18,843,342**	**18,843,342**	**18,843,342**	**18,843,342**	**18,843,342**	**18,843,342**	**18,843,342**	**18,843,342**	**18,843,342**	**18,843,342**	**18,843,342**
ILLIQUID ASSETS												
Premises & fixed assets	196,073	196,073	196,073	196,073	196,073	196,073	196,073	196,073	196,073	196,073	196,073	196,073
Other real estate owned	23,376	23,376	23,376	23,376	23,376	23,376	23,376	23,376	23,376	23,376	23,376	23,376
Investment in unconsol subs	186,797	186,797	186,797	186,797	186,797	186,797	186,797	186,797	186,797	186,797	186,797	186,797
Customers liability on accept	13,814	13,814	13,814	13,814	13,814	13,814	13,814	13,814	13,814	13,814	13,814	13,814
Intangible & other assets	1,957,206	1,957,206	1,957,206	1,957,206	1,957,206	1,957,206	1,957,206	1,957,206	1,957,206	1,957,206	1,957,206	1,957,206
Loans & Leases, Total net not held sale	20,495,526	20,495,526	20,495,526	20,495,526	20,495,526	20,495,526	20,495,526	20,495,526	20,495,526	20,495,526	20,495,526	20,495,526
Less 80% of Home equity loans	3,160,657	3,160,657	3,160,657	3,160,657	3,160,657	3,160,657	3,160,657	3,160,657	3,160,657	3,160,657	3,160,657	3,160,657
Less 80% of all other: 1-4 first liens	2,188,917	2,188,917	2,188,917	2,188,917	2,188,917	2,188,917	2,188,917	2,188,917	2,188,917	2,188,917	2,188,917	2,188,917
Less other loans & accept	15,239	15,239	15,239	15,239	15,239	15,239	15,239	15,239	15,239	15,239	15,239	15,239
Total Illiquid assets	**18,577,894**	**18,577,894**	**18,577,894**	**18,577,894**	**18,577,894**	**18,577,894**	**18,577,894**	**18,577,894**	**18,577,894**	**18,577,894**	**18,577,894**	**18,577,894**

EXHIBIT 11.2   (continued)

Net cash capital & crisis analysis

Haircut	Moody's rating:	30 day A1	Baa1	90 day A1	Baa1	Ba1	1 year A1	Baa1	Ba1	B1
	ILLIQUID SECURITIES									
100%	MBS	2,297,827	2,297,827	2,297,827	2,297,827	2,297,827	2,297,827	2,297,827	2,297,827	2,297,827
100%	Other	121,829	121,829	121,829	121,829	121,829	121,829	121,829	121,829	121,829
2%	Govt securities	3,542	3,542	3,542	3,542	3,542	3,542	3,542	3,542	3,542
10%	Munis/MBS passthru	197,269	197,269	197,269	197,269	197,269	197,269	197,269	197,269	197,269
33%	Fairval of other debt secs	25,808	25,808	25,808	25,808	25,808	25,808	25,808	25,808	25,808
15%	Fairval of mutual funds/Equities	41,805	41,805	41,805	41,805	41,805	41,805	41,805	41,805	41,805
	Total illiquid securities	**2,454,319**	**2,454,319**	**2,454,319**	**2,454,319**	**2,454,319**	**2,454,319**	**2,454,319**	**2,454,319**	**2,454,319**
	LTFNDG	18,843,342	18,843,342	18,843,342	18,843,342	18,843,342	18,843,342	18,843,342	18,843,342	18,843,342
	ILLIQA	18,577,894	18,577,894	18,577,894	18,577,894	18,577,894	18,577,894	18,577,894	18,577,894	18,577,894
	ILLIQLIQ	2,454,319	2,454,319	2,454,319	2,454,319	2,454,319	2,454,319	2,454,319	2,454,319	2,454,319
	Net cash capital position	**(2,188,870)**	**(2,188,870)**	**(2,188,870)**	**(2,188,870)**	**(2,188,870)**	**(2,188,870)**	**(2,188,870)**	**(2,188,870)**	**(2,188,870)**
	Total assets	**29,565,512**	**29,565,512**	**29,565,512**	**29,565,512**	**29,565,512**	**29,565,512**	**29,565,512**	**29,565,512**	**29,565,512**
	Total managed assets	**31,134,637**	**31,134,637**	**31,134,637**	**31,134,637**	**31,134,637**	**31,134,637**	**31,134,637**	**31,134,637**	**31,134,637**
	Net cash capital ratio to total assets	−7.40%	−7.40%	−7.40%	−7.40%	−7.40%	−7.40%	−7.40%	−7.40%	−7.40%
	Net cash capital ratio to managed assets	−7.03%	−7.03%	−7.03%	−7.03%	−7.03%	−7.03%	−7.03%	−7.03%	−7.03%

EXHIBIT 11.3 Net cash capital: ratios and preferred ranges

	30 day		90 day			1 year			
	A1	Baa1	A1	Baa1	Ba1	A1	Baa1	Ba1	B1
Beginning net cash capital	(2,188,870)	(2,188,870)	(2,188,870)	(2,188,870)	(2,188,870)	(2,188,870)	(2,188,870)	(2,188,870)	(2,188,870)
Debt issuance	1,382,353	829,412	2,347,826	1,408,696	117,391	1,956,522	1,173,913	97,826	–
Loan securitizations	–	–	765,988	765,988	765,988	3,214,661	3,214,661	3,214,661	3,214,661
Total loans: $18,444,412									
Loan growth/Draws on commitments	(553,332)	(553,332)	(922,221)	(922,221)	(922,221)	(1,154,781)	(1,154,781)	(1,154,781)	(1,154,781)
Discount window	5,180,449	4,662,404	5,180,449	4,662,404	1,709,548	–	–	–	–
Adjusted net cash capital position	3,820,600	2,749,614	5,183,172	3,725,997	(518,164)	1,827,532	1,044,923	(31,164)	(128,990)
Adjusted ratio to total assets	12.92%	9.30%	17.53%	12.60%	–1.75%	6.18%	3.53%	–0.11%	–0.44%
Adjusted ratio to total managed assets	12.27%	8.83%	16.65%	11.97%	–1.66%	5.87%	3.36%	–0.10%	–0.41%
Recommended range guidelines:	17% 22%	12% –22%	25% –35%	17% –22%	12% –22%	45% –55%	30% –40%	20% –30%	10% –20%

ratio ranges for even the most stressed funding scenarios, even though we understood that meeting these hurdles would be a challenge. We also recognized that a degree of uncertainty exists with all of these scenarios, but particularly for those in the one-year time frame. Nevertheless, the resulting weaker results under certain time period/rating scenarios led us to embark upon certain actions designed to enhance our funding capacity, including the following:

- increasing our wholesale funding sources into Europe, Canada and Asia
- expanding our securitization capabilities into new asset categories
- developing a strong loan sales function
- divesting less profitable loan portfolios
- expanding our funding capacity at the Fed window,
- expanding deposit-gathering initiatives, including brokered CDs
- seeking out and cultivating new investors within our existing funding programs.

CONCLUSION

It has been our experience that bank liquidity management "best practices" are shaped not by Treasury management so much as by external stakeholder groups, primarily the regulators and rating agencies. Treasury's task is to develop the analytical tools that efficiently satisfy these external constituencies while providing strong, meaningful decision-making capability to the Treasury staff. It is not uncommon to find that these groups don't agree on a common approach to the analytics.

Our bank's answer to this challenge is the adjusted net cash capital measure. The measure allowed us to eliminate several redundant or obsolete liquidity ratios, thus increasing staff efficiency, while more effectively meeting the informational needs of our external constituencies. We have successfully shifted our focus away from simple "measurement management" toward a greater emphasis on strategic decision-making, with an emphasis on contingency planning.

And while we can never say that we are prepared to handle all potential contingencies, we have found that thorough, periodic reviews of the underlying assumptions embedded in the adjusted net cash capital measure, coupled with the appropriate action items, serve as an excellent way to ensure the continuous enhancement of our bank's liquidity position.

NOTE

[1] Editors' note: While many large banks around the world have chosen to deal with the Moody's cash capital view of liquidity as a type of compliance burden, one bank has adapted the concept and applied it

as a practical tool for viewing crisis liquidity risk. Even if you prefer to use a more nuanced measurement approach, this application of the cash capital concept is worth reviewing.

BIBLIOGRAPHY

Moody's Investors Service, Ratings Methodology, ''How Moody's Evaluates US Bank & Bank Holding Company Liquidity'', July, 2001.

CHAPTER 12

Managing a Funding Crisis: Citizens First Bancorp, a Case Study 1989–1994

Bruce W. Mason[1]

THE MAKING OF A CRISIS

No two recessions are ever caused by the same reasons. There are always circumstances such as changes in accounting, regulatory and economic variables that come in a unique fashion to cause a crisis. The banking problems of the early 1990s in the northeast US were a result of the region's real estate problems. Fueled by a strong regional economy, both residential and commercial real estate markets had ballooned during the 1980s. New Jersey's strong economy made it one of the most desirable banking areas in the country. Banks had expected a soft-landing; however, the ballooning real estate market values led to an eventual over-building, widespread speculation, and eventual collapse. Late in the decade, when the regional economy weakened, and the high volume of new construction projects coincided with falling demand, the ballooning prices burst. Increasing loan defaults became the key ingredient in the banking crisis of the early 1990s. Despite the sound condition of the region's banks in 1986 and 1987, conditions changed drastically by 1989. The pendulum had swung to higher levels of conservative wariness, and new accounting terms had surfaced such as "performing non-performing loans" and "in-substance foreclosures" to identify classes of loans that now required loan loss reserves, unlike in the past.

Financial institutions were clamoring to obtain adequate accounting guidelines for restructured loans. Some bankers resisted the new accounting guidelines as an overreaction by regulators stemming from the recent Texas, Oklahoma and New England banking crises. These accounting rules mandated that banks charge-off loans that were being restructured, with the rationale that these loans may result in a foreclosure at a later date. This accounting rule coincided with examiners moving into the New Jersey region from the troubled geographic areas of New England

and Texas. These seasoned regulators were committed to preventing the repeat of mistakes that led up to the savings and loans (S&L) bailout. The S&L crisis had grown out of government deregulation that practically eliminated the distinction between commercial and savings banks. Deregulation caused a rapid growth of savings banks and S&Ls that could tap into the huge profit centers of commercial real estate investments. As the 1980s wore on the economy surged. Interest rates continued to go up as well as real estate speculation. The real estate market was in what is known as a "boom" or "bubble" mode. Many S&Ls took advantage of the lack of supervision and regulations to make highly speculative investments, in many cases lending more money then they really should have. When the real estate market crashed, it did so in dramatic fashion and many S&Ls were crushed. The S&Ls now owned properties that were worth a fraction of what they had originally paid. Many S&Ls went bankrupt, losing their depositors' money, along with it. In 1980 the US had 4,600 thrifts, by the mid-1990s less than 2000 survived. The S&L crisis ended up costing about $600 billion of taxpayer money in "bailouts."

This was a recipe of financial woe for many banks. Banks under increased scrutiny by regulators were hesitant to make additional loans and credit dried up even further. Market values plummeted even faster with developers not able to get additional funding. CAMEL ratings deteriorated and non-performing loans where increasing significantly. In the northeast, 16 banks failed in 1990, 52 in 1991, and 42 in 1992. Total losses from these bank failures approached $10 billion.

CRISIS BREWING

The Citizens management discussion published within the 1989 Annual Report showed only the smallest evidence of events that were to unfold. In fact the management discussion placed a positive tone on the financial condition of the bank.

> We are happy to report that in 1989, Citizens First again attained its goals for asset growth and, more importantly for net income and earnings per share. Citizens finished the year with total assets of $3.08 billion [see Exhibit 12.1 on page 270], and loans of $2.1 billion [see Exhibit 12.2 on page 271], a 14.8 percent and 11.2 percent increase respectively over 1988. These gains continue to underscore how asset growth had accelerated in recent years. It took the bank 84 years, from its founding in 1899 to 1983, to reach its first $1 billion. Three years later in 1986, we reached $2 billion, and in another three years, we have exceeded the $3 billion mark. Net income also reached a record level of $37.2 million [see Exhibit 12.3 on page 271] and earnings per share grew 18.2 percent and 16.4 percent, respectively in 1989. Our return on assets was 1.33 percent, above the average of our peer group of banks in New Jersey. Return on shareholders' equity was 20.52 percent, again outperforming industry norms. At a time when many banks are reporting disappointing results for 1989, it is reassuring that Citizens First had solid

EXHIBIT 12.1   Total assets (year-end, millions)

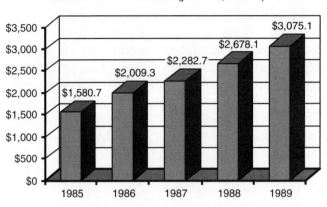

gains in assets and earnings. This is a positive sign that our management strategies are working well.

... There has been a great deal of press coverage regarding nonperforming real estate loans in the nation and in New Jersey. At year-end, our nonperforming loans amounted to $77.7 million or 3.63% of total loans [see Exhibit 12.4 on page 271], up from $45.6 million at year-end 1988. Loan losses for 1989, net of recoveries, were $5.3 million, compared with $2.4 million in net losses in 1988.

... Although we are obviously not insulated from the problem, this total is at a manageable level. Each problem loan has been identified, and a plan has been implemented to work toward an orderly reduction of the debt. We believe that there are adequate reserves in our loan loss allowance to cover all present and future problems. At the end of 1989 the allowance totaled $18.1 million. We continue to evaluate our loan portfolio by using early warning signals to classify loans where signs point to deteriorating quality. All classified loans were previously identified, and no additions have been made by regulatory examinations or outside audit reviews. We are following our traditional conservative lending practices to minimize future risk. Almost all of the commercial properties we finance are owner occupied or substantially leased. Residential construction loans to builders are limited to two homes ahead of sale, and borrowers must have a strong net worth. While there had been a significant increase in nonperforming loans, management believed that it would not negatively impact earnings to any large degree.

Citizens continued to perform in line with the strongest and most profitable banks in the state. Liquidity ratios of cash and cash equivalents, and securities maturing in one year to total assets were 20.28%; net loans to total deposits was 78.00%; and shareholders' equity to total assets was 6.27%, all very comfortable levels. Primary and contingent liquidity were also at very satisfactory levels. The economy, however, did not hold its ground and continued to deteriorate in the year that followed.

EXHIBIT 12.2   Total loans (year-end, millions)

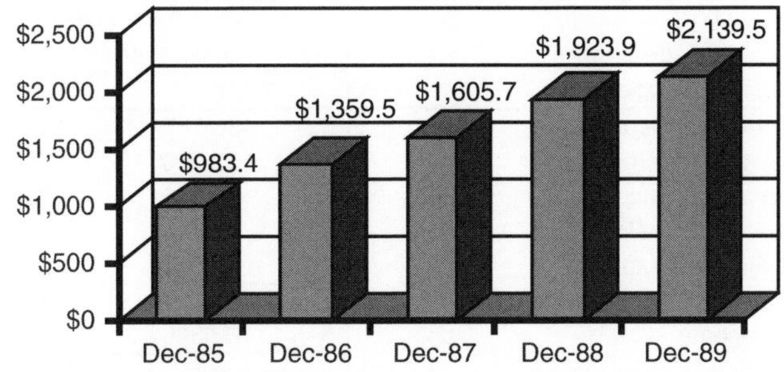

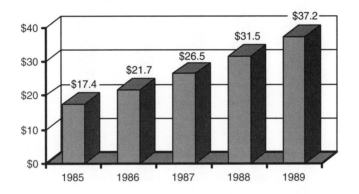

EXHIBIT 12.3   Net income (millions)

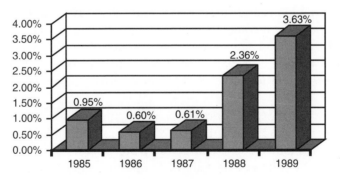

EXHIBIT 12.4   Total non-performing loans to total loans

CRISIS MANIFESTED: SUMMARY OF 1990

Citizens recorded a loss of $102 million in 1990 with an ROA of −3.46% and an ROE of −59.21% (see Exhibit 12.5 on page 272). This loss, the bank's first in 20 years, was caused by a higher level of non-performing assets made up of $152 million in non-accrual loans and $100 million in foreclosed real estate. These assets were made up primarily of real estate loans that were the result of a declining real estate market, as well as a weak local economy, and totaled

EXHIBIT 12.5   Citizens 1990 loss

($'s in 000's) Consolidated Summary of operations:	For years ended December 31,	
	1990	1989
Net interest income	$ 86,767	$ 111,566
Provision for credit losses	153,250	6,600
Non-interest income	10,876	9,228
Net security gains	28	–
Non-interest expense	73,059	64,826
Income before income taxes	(128,638)	49,368
Net income	$ (102,366)	$ 37,190
Return on avg assets	–3.46%	1.33%

EXHIBIT 12.6   Stockholders' equity (millions)

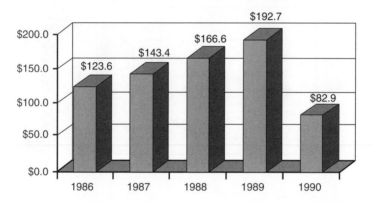

13.74% of total loans and foreclosed real estate. These non-accrual loans ceased to provide income to the earnings stream, thereby negatively impacting the net income of the bank. In addition, Citizens First provided $153 million to its allowance for loan losses in 1990 to protect against current and future losses on loans, further negatively impacting earnings.

Liquidity ratios of cash and cash equivalents and securities maturing in one year to total assets fell to 16.09%; net loans to total deposits also fell to 74.69% (mainly due to charge-offs). Stockholders' equity fell $109.8 million to $82.9 million (see Exhibit 12.6) and equity to total assets fell to 3.09%, again because of increased provisions for loan losses thereby reducing earnings and capital levels.

This dramatic downturn in Citizens' financial picture was further compounded by the resignation of the Chairman of the Board, unfriendly press articles, and of a possible conflict of interest with the bank's outside auditors. On October 17, 1990, the BoD consented to a cease and desist regulatory order issued by both the OCC and The Federal Reserve Bank of New York. The regulatory order mandated the bank to undertake certain measures and refrain from certain other actions. These regulatory actions required Citizens to achieve stated capital ratios, strengthen internal policies and procedures, and improve asset quality. Deterioration of liquidity trends was apparent as some depositors moved funds out of the bank due to FDIC insurance coverage concerns, while others left the bank entirely, in favor of stronger competitors. Contingency liquidity sources were affected by the closure of most unsecured correspondent bank lines of credit. The regulators weren't the only ones seeing a rising incidence of banks in trouble. The First National Bank of Toms River was forced into insolvency in 1991. Their 1990 loss of $165.3 million had completely wiped out the company's capital. Depositors had seen the handwriting on the wall and were withdrawing tens of millions of dollars per day.

Citizens First was forced to start taking steps in 1990 to avert this kind of crisis and to meet their regulatory agreements by submitting a capital plan detailing steps to be taken to improve capital ratios, monitoring liquidity levels on a daily basis, suspending dividend payments, cutting non-interest expenses, and reducing certain asset categories.

The actions taken in 1990 to protect and safeguard the bank's position were:

- A "Special Assets Group" was formed to focus exclusively on problem loans and to resolve them in the best interest of the bank.
- Expenses were reduced in many areas, including salaries and benefits, occupancy, travel, entertainment, and advertising.
- A comprehensive plan to increase the bank's capital ratios was developed with the assistance of an investment banking firm.
- Tax-exempt securities were sold at a gain to improve liquidity and capital ratios.
- A new Chairman was named.
- New auditors were engaged.

With these conditions the external auditing firm of Deloitte & Touche issued a cautionary opinion in the annual report, "... these regulatory matters raise substantial doubt about Citizens' ability to continue as a going concern."

SUMMARY OF 1991

Citizens recorded a profit of $2.9 million for the year with an ROA of 12% and an ROE of 3.50%. The significant factors contributing to Citizens return to profitability were a $129.2 million reduction in the provision for loan losses, investment securities gains of $7.5 million and a $5.9 million gain on the sale of loans. Total non-performing assets declined to $212 million (13.68% of total loans and foreclosed real estate) down from $252 million (13.74%). The amount of non-performing assets continued to put a drag on earnings. Liquidity ratios of cash and cash equivalents and securities maturing in one year to total assets continued its decline to 14.16%, net loans to total deposits declined to 70.13%, and shareholders'

EXHIBIT 12.7 Summary of operations

($ in 000s) Consolidated	For years ended December 31,	
Summary of operations:	1991	1990
Net interest income	$ 78,806	$ 86,767
Provision for credit losses	24,000	153,250
Non-interest income	11,791	10,876
Net security gains	13,398	28
Non-interest expense	76,792	73,059
Income before income taxes	3,203	(128,638)
Net income	$ 2,956	$ (102,366)
Return on avg assets	0.12%	–3.46%

equity to total assets improved to 3.45%. Equity ratios were able to improve as footings fell $200 million while equity improved marginally. Citizens continued to economize by reducing the number of employees by the second 5% reduction in a little over a year. Liquidity continued to be affected as bank customers reduced deposits over $100,000 at a slow but continuous rate, and correspondent lines of credit all but disappeared. There were also some loan sales that took place to produce profits to help bolster earnings. These loan sales, while contributing a profit, reduced the amount of contingency liquidity. The difficulty of this period can also be seen in the volatility in the share price of Citizens' stock. Citizens was listed on the American Stock Exchange as CFB and had fluctuated from a high in 1989 of $15.625 to a low of $1.75 in 1991, erasing over $308 million in shareholder value. The precipitous fall of Citizens' stock price served only to raise the alarm to shareholders/depositors.

Citizens was struggling to maintain its financial destiny (see Exhibit 12.7).

LIQUIDITY REPORTING PRIOR TO IMPLEMENTATION

Liquidity monitoring in the past did not address all of the categories on the balance sheet that could change. The original liquidity report merely reported on current liquidity levels, it did little to bring management into a discussion on what was to be done about the liquidity position. Prior to implementation of the new liquidity funding report, liquidity had been plentiful and was seldom the topic of much discussion either at Asset/Liability Committee (ALCO) or at the BoD meetings. Deposits had always been readily available to fund any level of loan or investment activity in the past, and there was little reason to quantify liquidity in great detail.

A liquidity report was included in the financial packet presented to the BoD monthly. This report was enough to give the directors the feeling that there was sufficient liquidity; however, it did not serve to quantify the real sources and uses of primary liquidity.

IMPLEMENTATION OF LIQUIDITY REPORT

The Federal Deposit Insurance Corporation (FDIC) gave a clear mandate to management to revise, monitor and communicate the liquidity position to management and to the FDIC on a daily basis. The FDIC examiners asked the ALCO manager to present them with the composition of all funding and deposit sources.

The examiners were also presented with the ongoing trends, as well as the seasonal trends for those deposits sources (see Exhibits 12.8 and 12.9 on page 276). Following implementation of the liquidity funding report, liquidity has become a topic of discussion at ALCO at least monthly. The importance of reviewing and discussing liquidity levels had risen in the last few years. ALCO was reminded that liquidity always comes first; without it a bank doesn't open its doors; with it, a bank may have time to solve its basic problems. Each department manager was called to a meeting with the regulators and was asked to speak on the categories under their responsibility. Discussions included the current status and projections for deposit growth and composition, loan growth, investment maturities and reinvestment, contingency liquidity sources and uses, and how much total liquidity is available. The BoD also was more aware of the importance of liquidity with recent articles in the press of banks that had deposits fleeing various banks. The BoD was presented with a monthly review of the liquidity position of the bank. These reports were presented in the Board packet of information and provided improved and up-to-date information.

DEPOSIT COMPOSITION

Citizens had continued its relationship with its core deposit base. Those relationships that had been built in the past had become one of Citizens' most valuable assets. Those depositors so far had stuck with the bank through its recent difficulties in 1990 and 1991. This loyalty can be attributed to the service, convenience and community involvement that have been continuously offered by Citizens.

Citizens had shown that in 1991 its financial condition has stabilized. Citizens' management had been able to stop the earnings decline of 1990 and with the help of some security and loan sales was able to show a small profit for the year (see Exhibit 12.7). The ability to maintain profitability in the future largely depended on Citizens' ability to reduce non-performing assets and lower the provision for loan losses further, which would be influenced by the condition of the real estate market and the local economy.

During 1991, Citizens continued to move toward full compliance with the regulatory agreements with the Comptroller of the Currency and the Federal Reserve Bank of New York, implementing improved monitoring and reporting systems to manage more effectively. Citizens

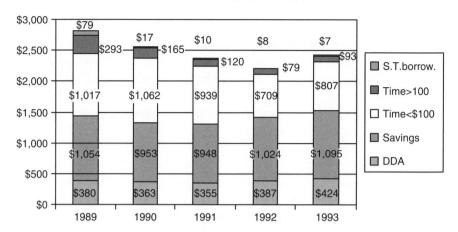

EXHIBIT 12.8   Deposit mix (millions)

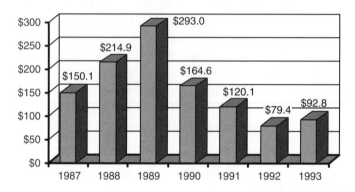

EXHIBIT 12.9   Time deposits >$100,000 (millions)

moved through a period of turbulence that has shown the importance of being able to monitor, forecast and manage liquidity.

Citizens was forced to get back to the basics of providing adequate liquidity for any situation that may arise. Liquidity represents the ability to accommodate decreases in deposits and other purchased liabilities and fund increases in assets. Funds must be available at reasonable prices relative to competitors and in maturities required to support prudently medium- to longer term assets. Liquidity is essential in all banks to compensate for expected and unexpected balance sheet fluctuations and to provide funds for growth. Citizens has shown that it can accommodate decreases in deposits and maintain adequate liquidity levels. With the help of Citizens' core depositors, management and its staff has shown that it can dig in and overcome difficult economic and financial setbacks and land on its feet.

The most important step that Citizens can take at the current time is to continue to increase its capital levels through earnings and capital acquisition. Citizens engaged an investment firm to raise $50 million in new equity capital. The acquisition of capital will serve to improve capital ratios, bank ratings, earnings, and both primary and contingent liquidity levels. Depositors and other account relationships were being reassured that Citizens would continue as a going concern and management would continue to work toward restoring the bank back to financial health.

MEASUREMENT OF LIQUIDITY

Citizens' general philosophy on liquidity was to match cash inflows and outflows within the bank's natural market for loans and deposits. Citizens luckily had never funded itself with brokered or purchased funds, and historically Citizens had been a net seller of Federal Funds. Citizens continued to be able to attract deposits through its strong diversified community deposit network. Citizens had its beginnings in the late 1800s and had lived up to its community bank image. It attracted deposits from the community, hired employees from the local community, and was involved in all aspects of the community. The bank had cultivated a very attractive marketplace. The bank was seen as safe and depositors were confident in the bank's management. The bank's main office even had a vault door design with the same specifications as the main vault at Fort Knox.

Federal Funds was an important tool in helping to provide a ready pool of liquidity to fund loan growth and seasonal fluctuations in deposits. Federal Funds sold took on another role as an insurance fund to withstand any quickening of deposit outflows. The problem for a net seller of Federal Funds is that when it wants to borrow from the Federal Funds market it cannot always count on being able to do so. Therefore the bank must keep its liquidity resident in their assets. Citizens' recent reporting of a drop in earnings and a decline in asset quality may have made it very difficult to borrow in the Federal Funds market. The Federal Funds rate is typically the lowest possible rate in the marketplace, and certainly does not compensate the lender bank for the increased credit risk that may be involved.

Liquidity historically was provided through a variety of sources. Important liquidity sources for Citizens were the stable core deposit bases of its local marketplace. Deposits were acquired over a range of type and maturity categories, including savings, time and checking deposits. Funds were also received from the repayment of loans, and regular maturities of investment securities held in the investment portfolio also supply liquidity. Additional liquidity also could be obtained by converting marketable investment securities to cash by selling them to investment brokers. Citizens was able to secure temporary funding through the Federal Funds market by borrowing from correspondent bank lines of credit. This, as Citizens has found, may turn out only to be a fair weather funding source once the magnitude of loan losses were reported.

Citizens First National Bank as a member of the Federal Reserve System had access to the discount window operated by the Federal Bank Reserve. In practice the discount window still exists and banks are allowed to borrow on a limited basis. Borrowing there does create slack in the Fed's ability to exert control over bank reserves. The Fed therefore had made borrowing at the discount window a privilege to be used sparingly and on a temporary basis. Senior management of Citizens was notified of this policy by meetings with the Fed. Results of these meetings were that the Fed had requested to be notified in advance of any anticipated discount window borrowing. Additional meetings with a liquidity specialist from the Office of the Comptroller of the Currency (OCC) strongly suggested that Citizens' liquidity funding and monitoring report be redesigned to incorporate discount window borrowing as a last resort. The rationale for this suggestion is that the Fed gives borrowing rights sparingly and on a temporary basis. The other major reason was to show that a cushion of liquidity was available should a contingency situation occur. This building up of an adequate cushion was to allow a bank to survive an unexpected event or period of events. Once a bank had to borrow from the discount window for an extended period of time, the likelihood is that it would never be able to stop its need for borrowing.

ADEQUACY OF LIQUIDITY

The adequacy of a bank's liquidity will vary from bank to bank. In the same bank at different times, similar liquidity positions may be adequate or inadequate, depending on the anticipated need for funds. Forecasting liquidity during normal and adverse conditions should be a regular course of action for management. Forecasting future events is essential to liquidity planning. Management must consider the effect those events are likely to have on funding requirements. Therefore extra liquidity must be held against the possible inaccuracy of forecasts. Information that management should consider in liquidity planning includes asset quality, capital adequacy and regulatory agreements. Adequacy of liquidity represents the bank's ability to ensure sufficient cash flow to accommodate increases in the loan portfolio and other asset categories, while meeting decreases in deposits and other liability categories.

LIQUIDITY RESPONSIBILITIES OF ASSET/LIABILITY COMMITTEE

One of the mandates in the cease and desist regulatory order was an update to the liquidity policy of the bank. ALCO was to address liquidity at least monthly to decide if the liquidity position of the bank was adequate. ALCO was to review liquidity levels on a more frequent basis as the need arose. Liquidity has always been a bit of a paradox – conceptually easy to understand, yet difficult to quantify. This paradox makes it necessary to monitor and review liquidity continuously. It therefore is the duty of ALCO to be on top of the entire liquidity process. Without ALCO the liquidity funding report would not produce any meaningful monitoring or trigger any management decisions. Management would be making decisions in the dark.

ALCO was to review the current and future liquidity position, including the following:

1. the current and forecast liquidity position and its' adequacy
2. the trend, composition, and dependency of the bank's funding sources for evaluation. Changes in savings, time and demand deposits to be reviewed in detail
3. the current magnitude, composition and trend of the bank's loan production; it had to be determined if the trend of loan production was going to be adequately funded through deposit sources
4. the current and forecast earnings capacity of the bank and how its improvement or deterioration could affect liquidity
5. the current and forecast asset quality of the bank and how its improvement or deterioration could affect liquidity.

If after reviewing the liquidity funding report it was decided that liquidity funding was needed, ALCO and senior management had to decide how to meet those needs. Methods of meeting the liquidity needs require liability management, as well as asset management. Consideration must be given to the type, cost, and maturity/matching on both sides of the balance sheet. Absolute amounts of liquidity may remain constant; however, the adequacy of these levels may change, depending on the changing economic environment in which the bank operates.

CONTINGENCY PLANNING

ALCO was again responsible for managing Citizens through a contingency/unexpected drain in liquidity and funding, were such a situation to arise. Contingency plans need to be made well in advance because early action can limit losses. An outline of steps should be in place and included in the formalized liquidity policy, including what events or early warnings should trigger the contingency funding process. Examples of these early warning signals are deterioration in net loans to assets, non-performing assets to loans, leverage, profitability compared to peer groups, profitability compared to recent performance, short- and long-term debt ratings, bank line coverage, and net funding requirements over the next seven, 30, and 90 days. The liquidity report was the tool to be used to monitor and to provide an early warning to management. Survival of a liquidity crisis requires more than anything else, depositor's confidence in the bank. Citizens had been very fortunate to have its origins as a local community bank with a strong branch network and strong depositor relationships. The hallmark of a good liquidity contingency plan is the clear delineation of responsibilities and decision-making authority. If a funding drain or liquidity shortfall does arise, or is anticipated as a result of deterioration in the bank's economic or financial situation, the following duties would be performed:

1. ALCO would hold regular or special meetings as the need may arise to maintain and monitor the components of liquidity (as monitored on the liquidity funding report) at Citizens.
2. A contingency plan would be adopted by ALCO based on the changes projected in cash flow and funding as presented in the liquidity funding report. ALCO would decide on the amounts, costs and timing of the liquidity needed. All reporting and monitoring would be channeled through the CFO.
3. The CFO would coordinate the contingency funding plan, and monitor and report weekly all inflows and outflows of funds to the president and ALCO. Through this coordination the goal would be to provide sufficient funding necessary for loan growth or growth in other asset categories, as well as providing necessary funds for actual or projected deposit runoffs. The CFO would handle investor, rating agency, analyst, auditor and regulator relations.
4. The investment division head would monitor and report weekly on:
   - maintaining the Jumbo CD and repurchase agreement pool at reasonable costs, as recommended by the contingency plan
   - monitoring and reporting on the competitive Jumbo CD and repurchase agreement pricing. Forward a report, including competitive bidding and customer reaction/sentiment toward the bank, weekly to the president and the CFO
   - providing information about readily salable investments if this becomes a need, including maturity, yield, pledging, and if securities are held at a profit or loss
   - keeping Federal Funds lines tested and open during contingency liquidity management
   - reporting any closure of Federal Funds or correspondent lines of credit immediately to the president and the CFO
   - reporting current and projected pledging requirements.
5. Branch administration shall monitor and report weekly on:
   - customer reaction to the bank's pricing of retail deposits by sending a weekly report of money outflow to the president and the CFO detailing amounts and reasons for leaving the bank
   - which CD and savings categories customers are investing in
   - the early redemption of deposits

- the overall condition/image that was perceived by the customer base
- the branch system, which would be supplied with current information about the condition of the bank to control rumors and to spread factual news.

6. The loan division head would monitor and report weekly on:
    - changes in customer relationships and borrowing
    - changes in loan quality
    - information about readily salable loan categories
    - changes in loan demand and mix.

As a result of the contingency planning and reporting, ALCO would take steps to:

1. maintain, strengthen or replace funds at acceptable premiums that are projected to runoff
2. look for alternative funding sources, both retail and wholesale
3. sell any liquid securities or loans if needed
4. sell or decrease holdings of non-liquid assets if needed
5. increase capital funds if possible
6. communicate immediately to the president and the CFO any customer resistance to dealing with Citizens
7. borrow against assets that are non-liquid or too profitable to sell.

The liquidity position was measured by comparing the actual dollar amounts of the sources and uses of the funds that made up the balance sheet. This comparison was presented both on a historical basis as well as on a projected basis. This approach shows trends that are developing or continuing.

Exhibit 12.10 Description

The measurement and analysis of Citizens' past and future liquidity position was accomplished by following the guidelines in the following exhibit:

Rows (1–6) Projected Deposit Growth (Net)

Citizens has always been able to attract retail CDs through its branch network. These projected deposits have grown or contracted at a rate with a high degree of predictability, based on the level of prices compared with our competitor's rates. The customer deposit base has in the past shown a high degree of loyalty because of the relationships built up over the years. The average age of the different deposit categories was calculated and included in the discussions below. Price competition and sensitivity was measured on a weekly basis. Peer competitors' deposit rates are prioritized, showing highest rates on top of the list. An average of all peer

EXHIBIT 12.10 Measurement and analysis of Citizens' liquidity position

		Actual						Forecast			
	Sep-91	Oct-91	Nov-91	Dec-91	Jan-92	Feb-92	Mar-92	Apr-92	May-92	Jun-92	Jul-92
A) Fed Funds sold (Beg. of Month)	165.0	90.0	60.0	135.0	90.0	90.0	105.0	115.0	75.0	90.0	80.0
Funding sources:											
1. Sav/MMkt growth	0.0	10.0	0.0	0.0	14.0	5.0	5.0	5.0	5.0	0.0	0.0
2. Time growth	0.0	0.0	0.0	0.0	0.0	0.0	0.0	0.0	0.0	0.0	0.0
3. DDA growth	0.0	4.0	0.0	40.0	0.0	0.0	20.0	0.0	10.0	0.0	0.0
4. NOW growth	0.0	19.0	0.0	25.0	1.1	0.0	20.0	0.0	10.0	0.0	0.0
5. CD>$100m growth	0.0	0.0	23.0	0.0	0.0	0.0	0.0	0.0	0.0	0.0	0.0
6. Repo & advance growth	0.0	0.0	0.0	2.0	0.0	0.0	0.0	0.0	0.0	0.0	0.0
7. Investment reduction	7.0	25.0	1.0	0.0	16.9	50.0	20.0	20.0	15.0	0.0	0.0
8. Asset sales	150.0	0.0	110.0	90.0	0.0	50.0	0.0	0.0	0.0	0.0	0.0
9. Loan (reduction)	21.0	9.0	20.0	9.0	19.0	10.0	5.0	0.0	0.0	0.0	0.0
10. Reduction in other asset categories	31.0	0.0	41.0	0.0	10.0	2.0	0.0	0.0	0.0	0.0	0.0
11. Increase in other liability categories	2.0	0.0	1.0	4.0	0.0	11.0	0.0	0.0	0.0	0.0	0.0
B) Total sources of funds	211.0	67.0	196.0	170.0	61.0	128.0	70.0	25.0	40.0	0.0	0.0
Funding uses:											
1. Net loan production	0.0	0.0	0.0	0.0	0.0	0.0	0.0	5.0	5.0	5.0	5.0
2. Investment increases	246.0	39.0	65.0	125.0	0.0	50.0	45.0	20.0	15.0	0.0	0.0
3. Sav/MMkt reduction	4.0	0.0	0.0	2.0	0.0	5.0	0.0	0.0	0.0	0.0	0.0
4. Time reduction	3.0	22.0	22.0	19.0	26.0	15.0	15.0	10.0	5.0	5.0	5.0
5. DDA reduction	1.0	0.0	23.0	0.0	26.0	29.0	0.0	10.0	0.0	0.0	0.0
6. NOW reduction	4.0	0.0	10.0	0.0	0.0	13.0	0.0	20.0	0.0	0.0	0.0
7. CD>$100m reduction	24.0	19.0	0.0	37.0	0.0	1.0	0.0	0.0	0.0	0.0	0.0
8. Repo & advance reduction	4.0	1.0	1.0	0.0	2.0	0.0	0.0	0.0	0.0	0.0	0.0
9. Asset purchase	0.0	0.0	0.0	0.0	0.0	0.0	0.0	0.0	0.0	0.0	0.0
10. Increase in other asset categories	0.0	12.0	0.0	32.0	0.0	0.0	0.0	0.0	0.0	0.0	0.0
11. Decrease in other liability categories	0.0	4.0	0.0	0.0	7.0	0.0	0.0	0.0	0.0	0.0	0.0
C) Total uses of funds	286.0	97.0	121.0	215.0	61.0	113.0	60.0	65.0	25.0	10.0	10.0
D) Fed Funds sold (end of month) (A+B-C)	90.0	60.0	135.0	90.0	90.0	105.0	115.0	75.0	90.0	80.0	70.0

rates has been tabulated over the last couple of years. Price sensitivity can be measured by how much deposit production was generated as compared to how the rate paid varied from peer banks.

Row 1, Savings MMKt growth:

This area has experienced strong growth in the last two years, both nationally as well as on our balance sheet. Customer preference has been shifting from the time deposit products to savings products in greater numbers. The most probable reason for this is that bank customers can improve the liquidity of their money, since it can be withdrawn at any time without waiting for a maturity date to arrive. This increased liquidity can be explained by the lack of opportunity cost of interest rates. The rate differential between time deposits and savings deposits has come down dramatically. The current profile of the bank's average savings customer reveals that out of 98,000 accounts, 84,000 accounts are under $10,000 and 52,000 of those are under $1,000. At the upper end of savings account profile are those with accounts in excess of $100,000. There are currently 356 accounts with $75 million in deposits or 13% of the entire savings category. The average time that these savings accounts have been open was 4.7 years.

Row 2, Time growth:

Growth over the last two years has been on a downward trend both nationally and locally in small time (under $100,000), as well as in large time deposits (over $100,000). The over $100,000 time deposit category was now tracked on a monthly basis. Branches have become more proactive toward these deposits as the competition for these accounts has heated up. Depositors were notified and offered assistance in what to do with maturing time certificates to build goodwill and confidence in the bank. This downward trend has been caused by falling interest rates, and lower reinvestment rates than has been seen in the past 15 years. There also has been a movement toward higher liquidity products such as savings accounts. The other easily identifiable trend was deposits reaching for higher yields in mutual bond and equity funds. However, growth still continued to exist in the shorter maturity categories like bank savings accounts, especially when these products had pricing that was favorable to competitors.

Row 3, DDA growth:

This deposit category displays a very regular and seasonal type of fluctuation, which was very similar to national trends. The weighted average age of all checking accounts has been calculated to be 6.7 years. The 1992 levels of DDA are similar to levels experienced in 1991 and 1990; however, the percentage of DDA to total deposits has risen.

Row 4, NOW growth:

NOW accounts again show fluctuations on a regular and seasonal pattern. There has been an influx of funds into these accounts, both nationally as well as on our balance sheet. Deposit levels in this category have been caused by the relatively low level of interest rates and very small yield give-up when comparing interest-bearing checking to other interest-bearing options. Most new checking accounts are opened as interest-bearing accounts. The weighted average age of these accounts has been calculated to be 6.7 years.

Row 5, CD>$100m growth:

Jumbo CD growth was drawn from our local community and county governments. Ninety percent of these deposits are from governmental depositors with 90% of the maturities 30 days or under. These deposits are very seasonal with large amounts of municipal money shown to the bank to quote a competitive rate. The large influx of municipal money coincides with real estate taxes being paid by local homeowners. The majority of the municipal deposits are protected from loss by the Governmental Unit Deposit Protection Act of New Jersey.

Row 6, Repo & advance growth:

Repurchase agreements show little growth or contraction. This category was technically not a deposit, but it does provide customers with market rates and short maturities. This account's average maturity was usually under 30 days. Borrowing was another potential source that was available when Citizens' credit ratings and earnings were good. Citizens was a net seller of Federal Funds, and only offers to purchase funds from some small correspondent banks as a convenience and does not use this funding source in a meaningful way.

Row 7, Investment reduction:

These securities are US Treasuries, US Agencies, short-term money market instruments, tax-exempt securities and corporate securities that are maturing each month. The securities held in the portfolio by policy are kept under the five-year maturity horizon, with most securities to be purchased in the two-year or under horizon. This strategy provides for a regular ladder of investment maturities that can supply liquidity at any time.

Rows 8, Asset sales:

This category represents assets that have been sold or are planned to be sold. This category usually would consist of securities or mortgage-backed securities, or other asset accounts that have been originated in-house. The bank frequently retains the servicing rights to the mortgages it sells, thereby retaining the customer relationship.

Row 9, Loan (reduction):

This category represents the pay-down of loans net of new loans made, which was generally the result of slow economic growth.

Row 10, Reduction in other asset categories:

This category represents decreases in items such as currency and coin, other cash and correspondent bank balances, fixed assets, accrued income receivable, and other assets.

Row 11, Increase in other liability categories:

This category represents increases in items such as unearned income, accrued expenses and other miscellaneous liabilities.

Primary Liquidity Funding Uses

Uses of Liquidity: (C)

Row 1, Net loan production (net new loans):

Total new loan production less maturities and pay-downs would vary, depending upon the current economic environment. The primary purpose of deposits is to fund loan growth, which is the business Citizens is in.

Row 2, Investment increases:

This represents the purchase of new investment securities. The level at which these purchases are made is based on asset/liability decisions that factor in maturity, quality, pledging requirements, and liquidity and its impact on the entire investment portfolio.

Rows (3–8) Deposit reductions:

Expected deposit reductions may occur due to seasonal trends, asset/liability management decisions, capital planning strategies, as well as the level of interest rates in the marketplace.

Row 3, Savings, MMKt reduction:

This occurs because of price sensitivity or because alternative investment choices have been made by customers. As noted earlier, 356
accounts have $75 million in deposits. Only $35.6 million of these
accounts are covered under FDIC insurance.

Row 4, Time reduction:

This occurs because of price sensitivity, trends and levels of interest
rates. There was also a continuing trend, both national and local,
to move deposits to be covered by FDIC insurance. Time deposits
over $100,000 are tracked at the account level each month. There
continues to be a shrinking on a steady basis.

Row 5, DDA reduction:

DDA continues to display a seasonal pattern, and reductions in these
accounts appear on a predictable basis.

Row 6, NOW reduction:

NOW accounts also continue to show seasonal patterns. Reductions
in these accounts appear on a predictable basis.

Row 7, CD>$100m reduction:

Reduction in these deposits are both seasonal and competition
driven. The deterioration in the financial condition of an institution
can be a reason for the reduction in these funds.

Row 8, Repo & advance reduction:

Reduction in these funds are both seasonal and competition driven.
The deterioration in the financial condition of an institution also can
be a reason for the reduction in these funds.

Row 9, Asset purchase:

The purchase of additional loans or other assets.

Row 10, Increase in other asset categories:

This category represents increases in items such as currency and
coin, other cash and due from banks, net fixed assets, accrued
income receivable, and other assets.

Row 11, Decrease in other liability categories:

This category represents decreases in items such as unearned income,
accrued expenses, and other miscellaneous liabilities.

The result of these projections (A) + (B) less (C) is referred to the in the
report as Net liquidity (Fed Funds Sold at end of month) CD. Net liquidity
(0) in this report refers to expected changes in cash flow.

Contingency liquidity sources (E) are those additional sources the
bank may use if there is a deterioration in its primary liquidity posi-
tion/adequacy. These contingent liquidity sources are listed with the
corresponding time needed to convert them. If no time frame is listed the
contingent liquidity source can be converted within a few days.

EXHIBIT 12.11   Contingency liquidity sources

D) Fed Funds sold(end of month) (A+B-C)	90.0	60.0	135.0	90.0	90.0	105.0	115.0	75.0	90.0	80.0	70.0
Contingency liquidity sources:											
1. Securities-non pledged	240.0	222.0	251.0	303.0	303.0	303.0	296.0	296.0	296.0	296.0	296.0
2. Borrowing potential & FFP lines	10.0	10.0	10.0	10.0	10.0	0.0	0.0	0.0	0.0	0.0	0.0
3. Loan portfolio(within 30 days)	34.0	34.0	35.0	21.0	21.0	21.0	21.0	21.0	21.0	21.0	21.0
4. Loan portfolio(within 60 days)	135.0	134.0	133.0	133.0	132.0	132.0	131.0	131.0	131.0	131.0	131.0
5. Loan portfolio(within 90 days)	0.0	0.0	0.0	0.0	0.0	0.0	0.0	0.0	0.0	0.0	0.0
E) Total contingency liquidity sources:	419	400.0	429.0	467.0	466.0	456.0	448.0	448.0	448.0	448.0	448.0
Contingency liquidity uses:											
1. 10% DDA & NOW	55.0	56.0	55.0	62.0	60.0	54.0	36.8	37.3	37.7	38.0	38.6
2. 10% Savings (money market savings)	51.0	51.0	52.0	51.0	53.0	53.0	53.9	54.5	55.1	55.6	56.2
3. 10% Time	75.0	75.0	72.0	71.0	69.0	69.0	52.1	45.5	45.5	45.1	44.5
4. 20% Repo, CD>$100m	66.0	66.0	65.0	54.0	58.0	58.0	46.0	46.0	46.0	46.0	46.0
5. 100% Borrowing potential & addl pledg.	10.0	10.0	10.0	10.0	10.0	0.0	0.0	0.0	0.0	0.0	0.0
6. 100% Increase in LOC usage	0.0	0.0	0.0	0.0	0.0	0.0	0.0	0.0	0.0	0.0	0.0
F) Total contingency liquidity uses:	257.0	258.0	254.0	248.0	250.0	234.0	188.8	183.4	184.3	184.7	185.3
(G)Total liquidity before FRB borrowing(D+E+F)	252.0	202.0	310.0	309.0	306.0	327.0	374.2	339.6	353.7	343.3	332.7

The measurement of the Bank's contingent liquidity position is critical in showing management and regulators that a liquidity crisis can be averted. This was accomplished by following the guidelines in Exhibit 12.11.

Row 1, Non-Pledged Securities: Shorter-term securities could be sold at or close to market value since they mature in one year or less. The shorter an investment's maturity the less likely it would be sold at a loss. Longer-term securities could be sold close to market value because they mature in one to two years. The decision to increase liquidity by selling securities that were held at a loss becomes a more difficult one. The decision to sell these securities to provide contingency liquidity would be greatly influenced by what the market value is compared to the book value.

Row 2, Borrowing potential: This category includes tested lines of credit with the FHLB, as well as local and money center banks.

Row 3, Loan Portfolio (within 30 days):   The bank was the originator of the Freddie Mac qualified mortgage loans and could prepare documentation and deliver these loans for sale within 10 days. Student Loan Portfolio had a liquid secondary market and these loans could be sold within 30 days – The 30 day time period reflects the amount of time it would take to prepare the documentation for delivery.

Row 4, Loan Portfolio (within 60 days):   Home Equity Portfolio could be sold within 60 days – The 60 day time period reflects the amount of time it would take to prepare the documentation for delivery.

Row 5, Loan Portfolio (within 90 days):   This category represents Commercial Mortgage, Account Receivable financing loans, credit card and consumer loans portfolios which can be sold. The 90 day time period reflects the amount of time it would take to find a buyer and prepare the documentation for delivery.

Row 6, Salable loans (within 90 days):   This category represents salable Freddie Mac qualified loans. The bank was the originator of the underlying mortgage and can prepare documentation and deliver these loans within 10 days.

Contingency Liquidity Uses

Net contingency uses (F) are calculated at the percentage of runoff each funding category might incur during a liquidity crisis. The percentage of possible runoff was a subjective number, but it does reflect the maturity, liquidity and size characteristics of the bank's funding. IRA and Keogh deposits make up 36% of non-checking deposits. These tax-deferred savings deposits have shown a downtrend; however, these deposits have shown a much higher retention rate than regular deposits. This has added extra stability to the core deposit base.

Those contingency numbers are as follows:

Row 1, 10% of the total of DDA and NOW checking accounts: These funds are considered core deposits that fluctuate on a seasonal basis, and levels have been very predictable. The average amount of time these accounts have been open was 6.7 years. These deposit categories have shown solid growth over the last 10 years. A 10% runoff factor was considered adequate.

Row 2, 10% of the total of SIA and Passbook savings accounts: 10% coverage was considered adequate protection since there was a very broad customer base. Passbook, SIA, and MMDA savings balances have fluctuated very little in the last few years. The average amount of time these accounts have been open was 4.7 years. These sources of funds have become a larger percentage of Citizens' overall funding. IRA savings deposits make up 17% of this category.

Row 3, (10% Time) category represents the amount of term CDs (three month through 60 month maturities):   10% coverage would be needed for these accounts as maturities are subject to prepayment options and non-renewal by customers in a contingent situation.

Row 4, (20% Repo, CD>$100):   Total Public Funds account for about 50% of the total *Repo CD* position. A factor of 20% was allowed for protection against an extraordinary drain that might be caused by large withdrawals by municipalities, county funds or other corporate customers. High Performance Fund accounts have remained very stable and have declined only marginally.

Row 5, 100% Borrowing Potential & Additional Pledging: Includes reductions in contingency liquidity for additional pledging that may be required as capital ratios or earning levels fall below levels of state and local municipality guidelines. Lines of credit with the Federal Home Loan Bank (FHLB), local banks and money center banks may also disappear as earnings and bank ratings remain below credit standards.

Row 6:   10% LOC usage category represents additional drawdown of lines of credit by companies experiencing increased credit needs. This may come at a time when the Bank is trying to found its own liquidity needs.

Total liquidity before FRB borrowing (net contingency liquidity) (G) is calculated as Federal Funds sold at the end of month (net liquidity) (D) plus Total contingency sources (E) less Total contingency uses (F).

Federal Funds sold at end of month and Total liquidity before FRB borrowing (total contingency liquidity) must be determined as adequate by ALCO for the current and projected economic environment that the bank was operating in. If it were found that Federal Funds sold at the end of the month or Total liquidity before PRB borrowing (total contingency liquidity) was not adequate, then steps (as mentioned in the above liquidity plan) would be taken to improve and bring the bank's liquidity to a satisfactory level.

The liquidity forecast and monitoring report has been designed to measure normal/most likely bank liquidity sources and uses. This is measured in sections $A + B - C = D$. The report also measures the contingent (backup) sources and uses of liquidity if a need for them arises. These contingent sources and uses are then added to the Federal Funds sold at end of month; $D + E - F = G$. Total liquidity before FRB borrowing has been placed at the bottom of the report because according to the guidelines, banks must have an appropriate reason for borrowing and must have sought alternative sources of funding first. Appropriate reasons for borrowing include: (1) liquidity needs arising from unanticipated deposit or loan activity; (2) the avoidance of overdrafts in reserve accounts; and (3) liquidity needs arising from outside sources, such as wire transfer failures. Citizens had a ready portfolio of one to four family mortgages to be used as collateral in case borrowing from the discount window becomes necessary. These one to four family mortgages are not included in any other contingent liability sources previously discussed. The Federal Reserve Bank does hold to this policy as borrowings are held to a minimum.

QUANTITATIVE LIQUIDITY RATIOS AND GUIDELINES

Liquidity must be measured and compared by Citizens to itself and to its peers. By measuring liquidity against historical information, trends can be discovered. Measuring liquidity against peer ratios helps form comparisons showing how similar or dissimilar the bank is. The Uniform

Bank Performance Report (UBPR) for December 31, 1991, used by management and by the OCC covers some of the most important measures of liquidity.

Core deposits (see Exhibit 12.12) were a measure of the most stable deposit customer. This category includes demand deposits, NOW, MMDA, other savings and time deposits under $100,000. Citizens ranks in the 99th percentile in both 1990 and 1991, confirming a strong core deposit base.

EXHIBIT 12.12   Core deposits ratio

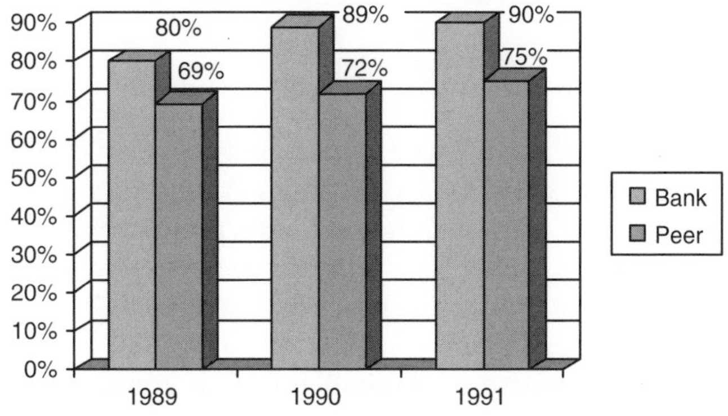

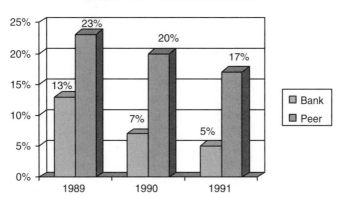

Volatile liabilities (see Exhibit 12.13) include time deposits over $100,000, deposits in foreign offices, Federal Funds purchased, and other borrowing. Citizens ranked in the third percentile in terms of the level of volatile liabilities. Citizens ranked very low compared to its peers because it has always raised funds through its branch network, drawing mainly on its core time depositor.

Temporary investments (see Exhibit 12.14 on page 290) include interest-bearing bank deposits, Federal Funds sold, trading accounts, and securities with maturities greater than one year. Citizens ranks in the 85th percentile, showing that it was indeed a net seller of Federal Funds.

EXHIBIT 12.13   Volatile liabilities ratio

EXHIBIT 12.14   Temporary investments ratio

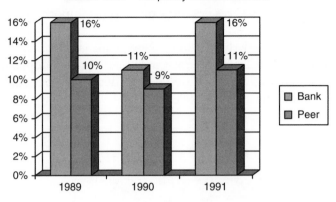

Volatility liability dependence is calculated as volatile liabilities less temporary investments divided by earning assets less temporary investments. This ratio shows how dependent a bank is on the volatile liabilities and compares it to peer banks. This ratio has declined to where Citizens is in the third percentile. This again shows that relative to its peers its level of volatile deposits is not a factor.

Temporary investments to volatile liabilities is a measure that shows how much short-term investments are compared to the volatile liability. Citizens ranks in the 91st percentile, exemplifying its lack of volatile liabilities.

Other ratios that are necessary to observe are the net loans to deposit ratio, equity to total assets, and total securities and Federal Funds sold to total assets. Ratio minimum and maximum levels is an added measure useful in keeping liquidity from becoming excessive or inadequate. The following ratio minimum/maximum guidelines had been developed with past levels being observed as well as where current policy had been set. The policy limit for the net loans to deposit ratio was set by the Board of Directors at a minimum of 65% to a maximum of 85% (see Exhibit 12.15 on page 291). If the loan to deposit ratio trends toward the minimum or maximum levels, mention would be made as to balance sheet restructuring that should be enacted to maintain the ratio within current limits.

Equity to total assets ratio (minimum of 5%): If the equity to total asset ratio falls, steps would be taken to establish a clear plan/projection of the profitability of the bank's earning stream. A strategic plan would be put in place to provide for capital adequacy of the bank.

Total securities and Federal Funds sold to total assets ratio (minimum 16% to a maximum of 30%): This total represents salable securities and Federal Funds sold that are readily convertible to cash. The entire bank's investment portfolio is saleable at current market prices. These funds can therefore contribute to any liquidity situation that may occur.

EXHIBIT 12.15 Loan to deposit ratio

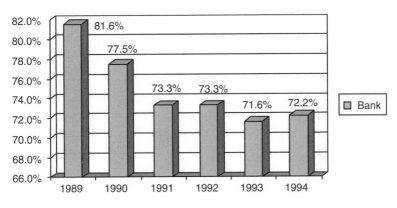

CONCLUSION

Liquidity funding and monitoring had become a topic of increased importance and awareness. Events of the period 1989–1994 warranted the need for improved reporting methods. The liquidity committee was formed to improve the level of detail; this was monitoring and forecasting ability not present in past liquidity reports. After polling local peer banks, reading literature specializing in liquidity reporting and through meetings and interviews with examiners from the OCC, the redesigned liquidity funding report was adopted. The committee also recommended that the liquidity management is an evolving report and warrants continued study. I acknowledged the importance of maintaining the confidence of the customers, maintaining relationships with the regulators, avoiding "fire sales" of assets to raise liquidity when price may be adverse, and avoiding the use of the Fed's discount window.

This liquidity report has become a very useful report to management because it points out trends that are developing in the sources and uses of liquidity. The BoD was presented with the new liquidity report at a regularly scheduled meeting. After a discussion and education period the liquidity report was adopted. The liquidity report is now included in the monthly management information package that is presented to the BoD, and gives a much improved understanding of liquidity levels and their adequacy.

Following the adoption of the liquidity report a whole new level of monitoring and reporting liquidity has now been implemented. The report is also used as a discussion piece at ALCO to talk about possible balance sheet decisions, as well as to discuss the development of trends or seasonal fluctuations that may occur. The report format is set to report and project liquidity on a monthly basis. Contingency plans exist for situations when projections made on the liquidity funding report turn out to be wrong. Effective contingency planning involves identifying minimum and maximum liquidity needs and weighing alternative courses of action designed to meet them. The liquidity funding report is again the tool that helps detail what management decisions would be needed during contingency liquidity planning. Success in monitoring and forecasting liquidity in the future would depend on management's ability to change with the times. As mentioned before, banking and its liquidity are forever changing. Banks must keep pace with the rapid changes. The bank's ability to cross-sell bank products and services to our existing core deposit customers and to forge new customer relationships would be one of the main ingredients for success. Banks would have to be innovative and offer additional products that would fill the needs of its customers adequately. These products would be both on and off the balance sheet. National trends are already pointing to shifts in depositor behavior. Citizens must offer a full range of financial products to its customers or lose fee income, deposits, and most likely the solid relationships that it has built up over the years. Refusal to keep pace with the times would negatively impact liquidity levels, as well as the profitability of the organization.

In 1992 Citizens went on to raise an additional $75 million of capital. By successfully addressing the mandates in the cease and desist order regulatory sanctions were lifted. In 1993 and 1994 the bank returned to levels of profitability on par with 1989. The bank had successfully raised capital, put policies and procedures in place, and reduced the overhang of non-performing loans. The successful outcome and return to financial stability was only possible through the confidence of the bank's customers and the diversified nature of Citizens core deposit structure.

NOTE

[1] Editors' note: Every year some five to 10 US banks fail. These are small banks. Nevertheless, many insights, useful to banks of all sizes, can be gleaned from their experiences. In this chapter the author provides an illuminating case study of a small bank liquidity funding crisis.

CHAPTER 13

Liquidity Management at UBS

Bruce McLean Forrest

UBS'S GENERAL APPROACH TO LIQUIDITY MANAGEMENT

In line with its business model as a globally integrated financial services firm, UBS adopts a fully integrated approach to its liquidity and funding management. UBS's dependency on any individual source of funding or on any particular type of asset for its investments tends to be reduced by the highly diversified nature of its various global business activities, which span a wide variety of product lines, thereby leading naturally to a diversification across market, product and currency on both sides of the balance sheet.

UBS's business activities are performed through its three main business groups. These are:

- Global Wealth Management & Business Banking, which provides financial services to wealthy clients throughout the globe as well as to individual and corporate clients in Switzerland.
- Global Asset Management, which provides a variety of investment solutions to financial intermediaries and institutional investors.
- Investment Bank, which provides investment banking and securities business products and services to institutional and corporate clients, hedge funds, banks, brokers and financial intermediaries.

At the overall group level, the Corporate Center is responsible for ensuring that an appropriate balance is maintained between risk and reward, and for managing UBS's corporate governance processes, including regulatory compliance. It also houses the functional heads for UBS's financial, tax and capital management; and its risk control, legal and compliance activities exercise authority across UBS's businesses for their functional expertise.

Of course, this natural diversification of business activities in no way warrants a mere passive approach to our liquidity and funding risk profile, since particular dependencies could nevertheless be built up – whether consciously or not – and might only become apparent when viewed on a consolidated basis. They, moreover, might only crystallize under adverse circumstances. Rather, we are of the firm belief that our actively managed, centralized liquidity and funding process, which covers all branches and subsidiaries, allows us to reap the benefits of our overall business model, while maintaining tight control on both our global cash position and our stock of highly liquid securities. We view this as a crucial prerequisite for ensuring that we will always have sufficient liquidity available to meet our obligations in a timely manner, under both normal and stressed conditions, without incurring unacceptable losses or risking sustained damage to our various business franchises.

Being a globally active firm, we consider that our liquidity and funding capacity can be safeguarded best by employing a global framework, as liquidity problems that might begin as a local phenomenon could rapidly develop into a widespread issue. Nonetheless, we do, of course, give due consideration in our approach to local aspects of liquidity management; for example, formal transfer risk between jurisdictions, or the feasibility of employing liquidity in the form of cash or collateral arising in one currency and time zone in other currencies and time zones. We fully recognize the jurisdiction of local regulators over their own currency; that is, payment obligations in a given local currency must generally be met in that currency. Similarly, local regulatory liquidity reporting is delegated to the respective entities in each jurisdiction.

DEFINITION OF LIQUIDITY AND FUNDING RISK

It has become common wisdom that, despite the increasing importance that is being attributed to liquidity risk management, there is still no general consensus on how to uniquely identify and measure "liquidity risk," and, as a result, various definitions and similes are used to describe equivalent components of what is essentially the same core concept. For this reason, we find it appropriate to define at the outset precisely what we mean by "liquidity" and "funding" risk within the context of the following discussions.

We define "funding risk" as the risk to UBS's ongoing ability to raise sufficient funds to finance actual or proposed business activities on an unsecured or even secured basis at an acceptable price. The main focus is therefore primarily one of P&L. In stress situations (which could be exacerbated due to inadequate funding risk management) this could, however, *in extremis* turn into a "liquidity risk" issue; that is, the risk of UBS being unable to meet its payment obligations when due – at any price.

Funding and liquidity risks are obviously interrelated, as failure to properly manage funding risk may suddenly produce or exacerbate a liquidity problem, while inadequate liquidity risk management may give rise to or increase longer term funding risk. However, we place a shorter term focus on our liquidity risk management; in essence, from intra-day up to one month. Under assumed stress, it is also more of a "binary" measure in the sense that the bank either has enough liquidity (or can create it quickly enough) in a given situation or it does not. In a liquidity crisis, the primary focus is on survival and any P&L effects that may manifest in the aftermath of a crisis (assuming survival!), though of importance, are much more difficult to quantify. They are effectively a subjective function of the estimated funding shortfall that must be covered by contingent liquidity sources, which is itself a subjective measure.

In summary, we largely view funding risk under the assumption of a going-concern scenario or less-severe stress situations where assets are generally not actively unwound and maturing assets are rolled over. Its primary concern is the costs at which the going concern can be funded and the bank's residual funding capacity. The time horizon for funding risk considerations is longer; it is sometimes elsewhere referred to as "structural liquidity." The shorter term time bands are coarser than in our liquidity risk views, but the set of funding risk time bands span a longer time horizon – of many years. So, while the level of stress that we consider for funding risk is less severe than for liquidity risk, the duration of the stress is generally much longer; for example, that the unsecured funding markets are inaccessible for up to one year. Liquidity risk focuses on being able to survive; that is, meet all potential obligations, should a crisis situation arise. In extreme cases it assumes that (trading) assets will have to be unwound and that certain maturing asset positions will not be renewed.

In short, our liquidity risk management can be viewed as providing a "cost-efficient life insurance" for UBS and the overriding principle is that UBS's going-concern liquidity profile should always be structured such as to keep the bank in a position out of which it could survive a UBS-specific liquidity crisis. This is complemented by our funding risk management, which aims at an optimal liability structure, given our asset mix, so that our businesses may be refinanced in a cost-efficient and reliable manner.

ORGANIZATION AND RESPONSIBILITIES

UBS has implemented a central treasury process, which enables group-level governance of treasury processes and transactions and of the corresponding risk management. It restricts the bank's general access to wholesale cash markets to the Investment Bank's Cash & Collateral Trading (IB FXCCT) unit. As a rule, all funds that are externally raised are channeled into IB FXCCT, who are responsible for satisfying internal demand for funding. External funds may be actively raised from various sources: in the form of issued securities, actively raised through wholesale deposit taking or generated through the collection of deposits and accounts. In general, only IB FXCCT has the right to actively raise unsecured funding to satisfy the group's funding needs. Businesses with business models having intrinsic self-funding capabilities are exempted from this rule. The issuance of debt securities lies solely within the responsibility of Group Treasury, which resides in the Corporate Center. The proceeds from these issuances are likewise channeled to IB FXCCT in accordance with the central treasury process. We think that only such a centralized funding approach allows the full netting benefits to be captured and a uniform market appearance to be guaranteed.

Within UBS's centralized liquidity and funding process, Group Treasury is responsible for establishing the framework of policies and risk limits within the parameters of which IB FXCCT performs the necessary cash and collateral management on behalf of the whole group. The group's liquidity and funding policies and liquidity contingency plan are reviewed and approved by the Group Executive Board (GEB) and the Board of Directors (BoD). The GEB and the BoD are also responsible for setting the various exposure limits incorporated within the overall liquidity and funding framework. Group Treasury undertakes the liquidity and funding risk governance role by regularly monitoring the bank's overall liquidity and funding status and reporting its findings to the GEB. This includes controlling the bank's daily liquidity exposures, conducting regular "what-if" liquidity stress scenarios, and assessing the bank's overall funding risk profile, as described in the following.

LIQUIDITY RISK MEASUREMENT AND MONITORING

UBS's tool set for measuring and controlling its liquidity and funding risk profile can be divided into three main categories, which are summarized in Exhibit 13.1 and are described in more detail below:

- In the immediate to short term – ranging from intra-day to one month – we restrict the bank's net unsecured overnight funding in all entities/areas that access external markets. This limits the exposure with which we would enter into any stress or crisis situation, should it arise.

EXHIBIT 13.1 Summary of UBS's main liquidity risk control measures

Time horizon	Liquidity risk measurement
Intra-day, overnight	Projected net overnight unsecured funding requirement vs Liquidity-generation capacity
One day to one month	Cumulative net unsecured funding requirement vs Liquidity-generation capacity
≤ 1 month	Liquidity crisis shortfall vs Secured contingency funding
≤ 1 year	Secured funding capacity (unencumbered assets vs short-term wholesale unsecured funding)
> 1 year	Cash capital (long-term funding sources vs Illiquid assets)

- We conduct monthly liquidity stress scenario analyses to assess our capacity to withstand a severe UBS-specific crisis with an assumed duration of one month.
- We perform, also on a monthly basis, "cash capital" and "secured funding capacity" analyses to ensure that (1) we have a surplus of long-term funding sources compared to illiquid assets and (2) that we can continue to fund our businesses for an extended period assuming we have no access to the wholesale unsecured funding markets. Both of these analyses have a one-year time horizon.

DAILY LIQUIDITY MANAGEMENT

In addition to managing the group's liquidity on a daily basis within the parameters of the short-term liquidity framework and monitored by Group Treasury, IB FXCCT is part of the Investment Bank's Foreign Exchange and Cash and Collateral Trading (FXCCT) business line. This also plays the key role of acting as a market-maker for foreign exchange, money market, collateral products, and related services. IB FXCCT's business model is characterized by:

- centralized booking – thereby maximizing netting on a group-wide basis
- use of multiple products such as FX, interest rates and collateral – allowing cash-flow netting to be maximized across products
- risk management – including, in particular, daily liquidity and funding management – is conducted using globally centralized books, which are passed around the various locations on a "follow-the-sun" basis.

IB FXCCT therefore operates on a "one global book" principle that is cross-currency, cross-product and cross-location. Within IB FXCCT, the Relative Value Trading (RVT) unit is responsible for coordinating and optimizing the implementation of this principle on a multidimensional basis, which therefore spans currency, product and location. It is also mandated to ensure consistent/no-arbitrage conditions across all IB FXCCT price curves. RVT's decision making and risk management processes take account of the various underlying risk parameters where a range of relevant factors is balanced and run within tightly set liquidity, market and credit risk parameters. While executing their strategies they are free to shift liquidity between currencies and products. This might entail, for instance, meeting a short-term funding need in the Japanese yen (JPY) cash book early in the global trading day by swapping US dollars (US$) into the required amount of JPY. This would have the effect of creating an additional funding need in US$, which is then managed in the global US$ cash book.

The daily liquidity management process also includes deciding on the extent of participation in central bank open market operations where UBS has direct access to central bank money. RVT also maintains a diverse portfolio of high-quality liquid assets that can serve as a liquid cushion that can be drawn down quickly to fund unexpected cash needs. This includes securities that are eligible for repo transactions or pledging at major central banks. This would be the bank's first line of defense should it suddenly experience difficulties in raising sufficient unsecured funding.

The centralized nature of the IB FXCCT trading books eliminates any arbitrage or discrepancies between regions, products or the treasury function. The routing of all flows through a single centralized process allows the diverse funding flows across UBS's businesses lines and main business groups to be efficiently exploited, and all long and short positions to be systematically netted. The need to enter the external market on a local or product basis is thereby minimized, which also naturally leads to an optimal use of credit risk as IB FXCCT only need to invest excess funds externally on a netted basis. Moreover, in terms of liquidity and funding management, this set-up facilitates the global coordination and planning of the group's overall cash requirements. And, crucially, in times of stress or during crisis situations, efficient centralized liquidity management with around-the-clock coverage is automatically guaranteed, since the organization is no different from the business-as-usual situation. There is no need to radically overhaul organizational structures to implement ad-hoc contingency management changes as the general *modus operandi* can remain intact.

SHORT-TERM FRAMEWORK

Our integrated liquidity framework incorporates an assessment of all known material cash flows within the group and the availability of high-grade collateral that could be used to generate additional liquidity if required. It is Group Treasury's aim to propose a set of exposure parameters such that the bank will at all times be able to meet its payment obligations when due – whether under normal conditions or during times of stress. While the starting point of such considerations will always be based on a cash ladder comprising future known and expected cash flows under the assumption of business-as-usual conditions, prudent liquidity management demands that due account must also be taken of the uncertain nature of liquidity.

The group's liquidity management is complemented by its funding management, which concentrates on the medium to long term and ensures that the bank's funding capacity is not over-stretched, thereby helping to reduce the risk of liquidity problems arising that are specific to UBS. The focus of our liquidity management has a shorter term horizon (overnight to one month) and strives to ensure that the bank can survive any severe liquidity problems that might suddenly arise, however unlikely they may appear, and, that in doing so, the risk to its ongoing funding capacity will not be unduly damaged. In seeking to ensure that the group's capacity to generate liquidity will always be sufficient to cover our payment obligations, our liquidity framework takes into account basic factors such as currency and time zone, and the assessment of our liquidity capacity under potential stressed or crisis situations in addition to going-concern conditions.

The main tool used for implementing this liquidity management and control framework is the global liquidity sheet (GLS), which is used by IB FXCCT for their daily liquidity management and by Group Treasury for monitoring the group's overall net funding requirements and for controlling that they are always kept within the imposed capacity limits. The liquidity situation as shown by the various individual currency cash ladders in the GLS represent a conservative scenario of potential net funding needs. The general underlying assumption is that maturing asset positions will have to be renewed and that any net funding requirement can only be met on an overnight basis (which therefore tends to lead to a rapidly accumulating assumed net funding requirement along the cash ladder). The immediate liquidity exposure is limited by restricting the cumulative projected net overnight funding requirement. The imposed limit structure on this cumulative funding requirement (projected for overnight and each day out to one month under the aforementioned conservative assumptions) is derived from the bank's estimated capacity to generate liquidity when required. While this will, of course, vary in general, an overall constant limit structure is imposed, acting as a ceiling on the projected net funding requirement along the cash ladder. This set of absolute limits is based on a firm-specific crisis assumption, which we regard as a worst case scenario – since in general the lenders of last resort will in all probability be less forthcoming than they would be during a more general market-wide crisis, and since we assume that unsecured funding sources will become inaccessible. Within this limit structure of constant ceilings (which can only be changed upon obtaining GEB and BoD approval), going-concern limits are set based on our estimated capacity under business-as-usual conditions, which are reviewed regularly to reflect, for example, changes in perceived market conditions. It is always the most-severe restrictions that apply, so if the going-concern capacity is deemed to drop below the overall crisis capacity assumptions, the working limits will be reduced accordingly. (It is conceivable that this may occur since the going-concern assumptions only include assumed access to collateralized liquidity facilities from our major central banks up to an extent that is deemed to be within a "no questions asked" basis.)

The limits imposed on the projected overnight funding requirement is time-zone-dependent, since access to liquidity will depend on the time of day. At the beginning of the global trading day, the limits are less severe, since more time is available to mobilize funding sources or, if necessary, to initiate asset sales to generate additional liquidity. As the day proceeds and currency zones begin to close, the limits become tighter, with the strictest limits placed later in the day when only the US markets are available.

The limit structure is illustrated schematically in Exhibit 13.2, including the time-zone-dependent limits applied on the same-day (T + 0) position, split into Asian, European and US time zones.

The going-concern liquidity capacity assumptions are based on:

- untapped market capacity from additional unsecured funding sources (derived from historically observed volumes)
- the availability of assets for liquidation via repo with third parties or sale: sell-down assumptions are subject to the limitation that they must not endanger UBS's franchises and not lead to unwanted market attention
- access to collateralized liquidity from major central banks on a "no questions asked" basis (with only assets already pledged being recognized as having same-day liquidity value)
- the assumed capacity is then reduced by a safety buffer to account for potential outflows due to natural fluctuations arising from, for example, unexpectedly large account withdrawals (but still within

EXHIBIT 13.2   Schematic illustration of the short-term liquidity limit structure

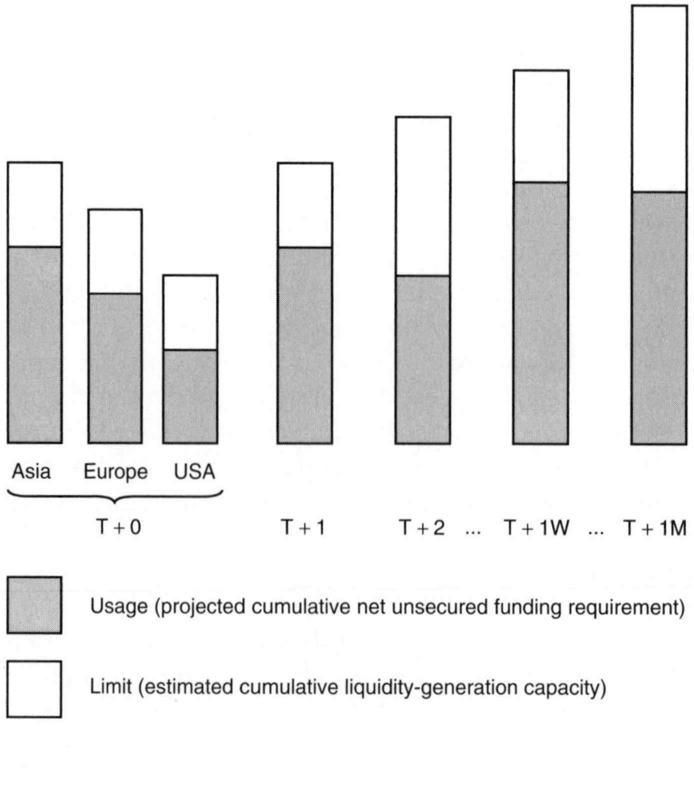

Usage (projected cumulative net unsecured funding requirement)

Limit (estimated cumulative liquidity-generation capacity)

a business-as-usual context; that is, without being due to specific concerns about UBS).

This then yields an estimate for our maximum net liquidity capacity. The above assumptions are broken down along the time axis, starting with liquidity capacity on a same-day basis and then extending out with daily granularity (tomorrow/next, spot/next, and so on) to infer our maximum net liquidity capacity at each tenor out to a one-month time horizon.

To determine our liquidity capacity under a firm-specific crisis, we modify the above going-concern assumptions as follows:

- very restricted, if any, access to unsecured funding markets
- the potential outflows are increased to cover, for example, large amounts of undrawn committed credit facilities, generally increased crisis volatility impacting collateral haircuts and margins, additional firm-specific client withdrawals, and so on.
- generally full access to collateralized facilities from major central banks.

The above-mentioned safety buffer for unexpectedly large net outflows is regularly assessed by monitoring the daily fluctuations in the actual position per major currency compared to the expected position as represented by the respective GLS cash ladder. From the history of daily observations, a distribution of these fluctuations – both positive and negative – is constructed and a "Liquidity-at-Risk" (LaR) figure is derived for each major currency, as well as for the consolidated cash position over all currencies. This is determined by analyzing the left-hand tail of the observed distribution to estimate the largest negative fluctuation (and hence net additional outflow) with a 99% confidence level. In this way, we can assess whether the safety buffer in the GLS is sufficiently large to account for unexpectedly large net outflows. An example calculation is shown in Exhibit 13.3 on page 302, which is based on the daily fluctuations consolidated over all major currencies as observed during 500 business days. This implies that, with a 99% confidence level, the largest negative fluctuations did not exceed about 65% of the safety buffer.

THE GLOBAL LIQUIDITY SHEET

The GLS was developed in-house by IB FXCCT as a centralized tool, accessible across all main locations, to manage the bank's short-term funding requirement. As mentioned above, it is also Group Treasury's primary tool for its daily monitoring of the immediate group-wide UBS funding requirement and its compliance with the imposed limit structure. The GLS cash ladders show a balance for dates starting today out to six months including:

EXHIBIT 13.3   Checking the suitability of safety buffer by means of an LaR measure

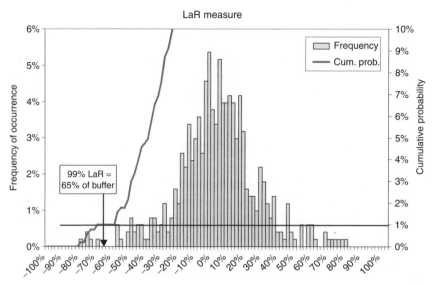

Net unexpected cash flow as percentage of safety buffer

- maturities of loans and deposits
- securities positions that are not funded by repos or securities borrowing
- FX swap cash flows
- cash management balances.

The GLS is a dynamic application in which the cash ladders can be displayed by individual currency and by individual location, or in which cash ladders can be aggregated across currencies and/or locations.

The cash ladders contained in the GLS comprise a "system" cash ladder and an "adjusted" cash ladder. The system cash ladder displays the cash positions stemming from transactions entered in IB FXCCT's risk management systems. It therefore shows a "contractual cash flow snapshot"; that is, the net daily cash flow assuming no new transactions or renewals (and assuming perfect settlement and the absence of credit risk). This, of course, does not generally represent the *expected* set of cash flows, which is needed for proper and prudent liquidity management. The transition from the "contractual" cash ladder to the expected cash ladder is achieved by augmenting the system cash ladder with the so-called "adjusted" cash flows. This then yields the adjusted cash ladder, which contains expected cash flows that have not yet been booked into any system yet, including, in particular, probable rollover transactions. Each such adjustment flow is assigned a percentage probability in the GLS. Once an expected transaction is actually executed and booked, the respective adjustment trade in the GLS is deleted and therefore replaced by the new contractual cash flows. As part of its overall liquidity governance role, Group Treasury regularly reviews the methodology employed by the IB FXCCT traders for entering such adjustment trades into the GLS.

Since the GLS is a predictive liquidity management tool, it is important that its reliability is regularly controlled. A core component of this reliability check is the daily crosschecks that are performed between the expected end-of-day position per major currency and the actual liquidity position; that is, as shown by the respective nostro account. As described above these observations are used to determine an appropriate size for the safety buffers that are incorporated as potential unexpected outflows into the imposed limit structure.

LIQUIDITY STRESS TESTING

The short-term liquidity framework described above restricts the bank's liquidity exposure within a going-concern environment. While it limits the immediate exposure with which the bank would enter into any stress or crisis situation by restricting the maximum projected cumulative funding requirement at the shortest tenors, it is also important to ensure that the bank's short-term structural liquidity position is always such that it could survive a crisis situation that might persist longer than for a few days to a week. To this end, Group Treasury conducts monthly "what-if" stress scenarios under an assumed severe UBS-specific crisis, with a time horizon of one month.

Since a liquidity crisis could have a myriad of causes, we focus on a worst case scenario that should encompass all potential stress effects. We regard a firm-specific crisis as a worst case since in such a situation it would be unwise to assume that the major central banks would be as forthcoming as during a widespread market crisis. The rationale behind our choice of a one-month time horizon is twofold. First, we expect that the most intense – and critically decisive – period of a worst case liquidity crisis would probably be concentrated into at most a few weeks. Second, high-quality group-wide consolidated financial data are available at each month-end for financial reporting purposes and serve as one of the major data sources for our simulations.

In a first step, we construct a cash ladder derived from the cash flows from contractually maturing (and callable) transactions and then make an assessment of the likelihood of asset and liability rollovers in a firm-specific crisis scenario, as well as the liquidity value of assets available for sale or repo transactions. The various impairments we consider include large withdrawals on otherwise stable sight deposits and retail savings accounts, and an inability to renew or replace maturing unsecured funding positions. We ensure that the assumed sight, saving and deposit account withdrawal rates are conservative compared to the historically observed fluctuations. In the crisis scenario analysis we effectively simulate a simultaneous combination of severe impairments to UBS's overall liquidity situation across all markets, currencies and products. We also take due account of additional liquidity outflows stemming from potentially large drawdowns due to contingent liabilities; in particular, from the undrawn portion of committed credit lines that we have sold.

We then assess the extent to which the potential crisis-induced shortfall could be covered by generating contingent funding that is raised purely on a secured basis or by unwinding liquid inventory. These assumptions are all subject to crisis-level collateral haircuts. We assume that no contingent funding could be raised on an unsecured basis and in particular do not rely on buying third-party committed credit lines for such purposes. Instead, we aim to retain strong relationships through regular close dialogues with our major central banks, where, as part of our general contingency plans, we maintain pledges of high-quality collateral, so that we can access central bank funds on a secured basis if needed.

As part of our overall assessment, we regularly monitor latent liquidity risks that could suddenly materialize during a crisis situation. Apart from those stemming from unutilized credit facilities, we regularly examine our exposure to "rating trigger" clauses, especially in derivative contracts with net negative replacement value, since these could result in immediate cash outflows due to the forced unwinding of derivatives or the need to post additional margin. Furthermore, we analyze the potential net liquidity outflow that could be induced due to adverse fluctuations in market value in our portfolio of collateralized derivative transactions. While this in general may not be highly correlated with a firm-specific crisis scenario, it is nonetheless conceivable that market volatility could substantially increase under such circumstances and exacerbate the situation. It is therefore important to estimate the potential order of magnitude of net collateral margin moves that could thereby be induced.

Although it is important to pay attention to the absolute results from our crisis scenario analyses, we recognize that they inevitably contain a certain degree of subjectivity. For this reason we also pay particular attention to any observed trend in the monthly results, whereby the underlying assumptions are kept as constant as possible, so that any material developments can be understood and explained – as they might be early warning indicators for unfavorable shifts in our overall liquidity profile and robustness.

CONTINGENCY PLANNING AND CRISIS MANAGEMENT

If the "theory" described in the previous section should become practice – that is, if a significant liquidity stress or even crisis were indeed to arise – then our group-wide liquidity management and contingency planning would be activated. This consists of a core (global) liquidity crisis team comprising key members from IB FXCCT – as the group's daily liquidity managers – and related areas such as Payments/Settlements,

IT/infrastructure, Credit Risk, Margin Management, and Group Treasury, as the group's liquidity controllers.

As described above, the bank's day-to-day liquidity management that is performed by IB FXCCT is already implemented using globally centralized books that ensure 24-hour coverage. This structure lends itself naturally to ensure efficient liquidity crisis management.

The liquidity crisis management is embedded within the group-wide global crisis management concept, which is dedicated to covering all types of crises. While this is organized locally, based on regional task forces (with the head of the regional task force where the crisis arises becoming the "crisis management owner" and assuming overall lead across the locations), the liquidity management is a global team since major liquidity problems will inevitably develop into a global issue and need tight coordination across all locations. Should the possibility of a liquidity crisis occur, the global liquidity crisis management team is called together. This team links into the regional task force in charge of the overall crisis management within the global crisis management organization.

In line with our crisis analysis assumptions, a cornerstone of our contingency actions during severe liquidity problems would be our access to secured funding, either from the market or from our major central banks, coupled with the ability to turn sufficient liquid assets into cash within a short time frame. We are convinced that it is better to rely on a common group-wide pool of contingent liquidity that is managed centrally and can be readily deployed where needed, instead of having a collection of disparate regional cushions of liquidity buffers that are managed locally.

The efficiency and reliability of such an approach would, of course, be further enhanced should cross-border central bank facilities be made available as liquidity could be more readily transformed on a secured basis from one currency and location to another as required.

GROUP FUNDING MANAGEMENT

UBS's Group Funding Management looks beyond the detailed shorter term focus of its Group Liquidity Management described in the foregoing sections, albeit with a necessarily less granular cash ladder. It aims to structure its medium- and long-term funding so as to strike an optimal balance with the bank's asset base: both in respect of the effective maturity of its assets, as well as regarding their liquidity quality. This includes considering the amount of maturing debt that will be due for renewal, as well as taking into account UBS's ability to continue to finance its ongoing business activities throughout turbulent market conditions that could potentially persist for periods of up to one year.

In short, our approach to funding management is to implement a framework that will allow sustainable and cost-efficient funding for the group's business activities using a well-diversified portfolio of funding sources. As a means to this end, we seek to adhere to the following main principles:

- client deposit-taking and secured funding are the two favored funding sources
- Group Treasury has the sole responsibility for approving all issuances of debt securities, either by UBS AG or by a group company
- Group Treasury sets the minimum pricing levels at which funds can be raised through medium- to long-term wholesale deposit-taking or through the issuance of bonds and notes
- the funds that are raised must be transferred internally in accordance with the Central Treasury Principle (that is, either with IB FXCCT or Group Treasury)
- all funding needs must be met internally from IB FXCCT or, in some specific cases, Group Treasury (As mentioned previously, IB FXCCT acts as the sole interface into the short-term wholesale funding markets.)
- pre-netting of funding is not allowed without prior approval from Group Treasury.

The above principles guarantee that UBS will always have a uniform market appearance when raising funds from the wholesale markets.

This approach allows UBS to employ a price-driven approach to its medium- to long-term debt management in which a large portion can be generated through structured debt, whereby the debt portion of the issuances is stripped out and subject to the same aforementioned conditions as straight debt.

To ensure that we preserve a well-balanced and diversified liability structure, Group Treasury regularly monitors the overall funding status of the group. In so doing it employs two main analysis tools on a monthly basis, assessing the group's:

- cash capital
- secured funding capacity.

Additionally, we complement this with regular concentration risk assessments of our main funding portfolios.

Both the cash capital and secured funding capacity analyses are concepts that have their origin in the assessment of the funding status of US securities firms, but have since been adapted and extended to gauge the funding profile of banks in general.

Cash Capital

With the cash capital analysis we seek to ensure that we have enough long-term funding to cover the amount of illiquid assets on our balance sheet.

"Long-term" and "illiquid" both refer to a time horizon of one year. We demand that a minimum surplus of long-term funds over illiquid assets is constantly met. We regard the following assets as being illiquid within a one-year time horizon for the purposes of this analysis, which assumes a business-as-usual scenario: property, equipment, investments in associates, private equity investments, goodwill, intangibles, and a large part of the loan portfolio. Additionally, we apply safety buffers ("haircuts") to the assets in our trading portfolio to reflect the discount on the otherwise liquid asset that could be pledged against cash in repo or securities lending transactions, or that could be sold within the given time horizon. This haircut is regarded as illiquid and hence must also be funded by cash capital. On the other side of the equation, the long-term funding sources that comprise cash capital consist of shareholders' equity, hybrid capital securities, long-term debt with a remaining maturity of over one year (and non-callable within one year), and the portion of core deposits that, despite being contractually short term, we safely consider to be behaviorally long term under business-as-usual conditions.

Secured Funding Capacity

The secured funding capacity analysis is designed to reveal whether short-term unsecured (wholesale) funding is effectively being invested in unencumbered (freely marketable) assets. If this is not the case, then the bank could be exposed to the situation where it suddenly has restricted access to the capital markets during a possibly extended period of time. In such a situation the bank could experience difficulties covering its maturing wholesale unsecured funding as it might not have sufficient capacity to raise secured funding (or sell sufficient assets quickly enough) to cover these obligations. As a precautionary measure, we therefore seek to maintain at all times a minimum stock of unencumbered assets and cash that exceed our outstanding short-term unsecured wholesale borrowings. We therefore perform a secured funding analysis on a monthly basis to assess whether we still have at our disposal sufficient cash and unencumbered assets that could be sold or pledged in repo or securities lending transactions to repay all of our unsecured wholesale debt that will mature within one year.

The haircut assumptions that we apply are more severe than those for the cash capital analysis, since the secured funding capacity represents a stressed scenario (as we assume we have no access to wholesale unsecured funding markets for an entire year).

THE ROLE OF COLLATERAL

The availability and regular usage of high-quality collateral is one of the main pillars of our liquidity and funding framework. Especially in times of stress – be it firm-specific or of a more market-wide nature – it can be crucial to have access to additional sources of secured funding in case the ability to renew maturing unsecured funding sources should suddenly become impaired. We therefore regularly assess the pool of collateral that we can tap to generate additional funding on a secured basis if the need arises. During the normal course of business, UBS typically lends out more funds on a collateralized basis (via reverse repos and securities borrowing against cash) than it raises against collateral (via repos and securities lending against cash), due to our ability to generate unsecured funding at favorable rates. This naturally generates an additional cushion of securities that are eligible for repos.

Our assessment of the pool of available collateral also includes monitoring the potential drains it is exposed to; for example, from net margin outflows driven by adverse market-value fluctuations or automatic outflows that could be induced from UBS's credit rating being downgraded.

In the considerations outlined above – whether for assumptions inherent in our liquidity framework or for the secured funding capacity analysis – there is a tacit assumption that, given that we have enough unencumbered eligible assets at our disposal, we could use these to raise additional liquidity on a secured basis via repo or securities lending transactions. This, however, only holds assuming we have sufficient access to the markets for those respective instruments. We therefore regularly assess this by ensuring that a minimum amount of these assumed liquid assets are indeed being funded via the repo markets so that we could, if need be, ramp up the amount of secured funding via these channels without raising undue market attention. This addresses the practical dimension of the effective liquidity value of our pool of available securities that could serve as an additional source of funding. Without having proven access to the necessary market channels, the mere availability of reserve collateral, even if it is of high quality, is no guarantee that it could indeed be used to generate cash if required.

Just as for cash management, IB FXCCT is also responsible for managing collateral flows that are material for the bank's liquidity management. Once again, our centralized approach to liquidity management is a further important ingredient in our ability to mobilize additional collateral when required.

CONCLUSION

While the statement "only liquid is solid" might appear paradoxical to a physicist, we would agree that it certainly applies to the state of health of financial institutions and of banks in particular as liquidity providers. Determining whether a bank is liquid enough is, however, not an exact science and there is no unique scale to assess an institution's "liquidity." On the contrary, the set of methods that should be applied inevitably contain a certain portion of subjectivity and, moreover, tend to be particular to each bank's business mix. But such methods do have in common the general tenet that prudence should receive due consideration.

We are convinced that our fully integrated and centralized approach to liquidity and funding management optimally befits our business model as a globally integrated financial services firm. Moreover, it facilitates tight control on both our liquidity exposure and on our stock of highly liquid securities, which would serve as a crucial contingency buffer should liquidity problems arise. The overall liquidity and funding framework, which entails both careful monitoring and control of our daily liquidity position, as well as regular stress testing, is designed to ensure that we will always have sufficient liquidity available to meet our obligations in a timely manner, under both normal and stressed conditions, without incurring unacceptable losses or risking sustained damage to our various business franchises.

CHAPTER 14

Sound Liquidity Management as an Investment Criterion

Dierk Brandenburg

N ext to the banking system, fund managers play an increasing role as providers of liquidity as the process of disintermediation feeds through the financial system. While the fund management industry is largely associated with long-term investments into equities, real estate and bonds, short-term investment funds play an increasing role as well as an alternative to traditional bank deposits. Triggered by heavy regulation in the United States, the market developed there from the mid-1970s, and has seen strong growth throughout the 1990s and the aftermath of the equity bubble. Development in Europe only took off after the introduction of the euro created sufficiently large capital markets that allowed investors to diversify outside their home currencies and bank deposits into credit markets. This chapter looks into the functioning of money market funds and their interaction with the financial markets. It highlights that liquidity assessment is a key parameter for money funds and explains the approach to liquidity analysis, as well as the capital markets instruments that are available to money funds to achieve their objectives.

A STABLE NET ASSET VALUE (NAV) CONCEPT IN FUND MANAGEMENT

Assessment of liquidity, both at the instrument level as well as the issuer level, is a key part of fixed income fund management. Equity funds typically deal with one liquid share class of a given company that is usually also traded on a public exchange. Fixed-income funds on the contrary can take exposure to a variety of debt instruments from a given issuer, most of which trade on the OTC market. Market liquidity for these instruments can vary significantly across different parts of the capital structure of the same issuer and is also subject to fluctuation across time.

Within the universe of fixed-income funds a broad-based distinction can be made on the basis of the "relative value" concept and products that use cash as a benchmark ("stable value"). The relative value concept focuses on fund performance relative to a given benchmark with the aim to outperform a peer group and managing tracking error. Liquidity analysis mainly focuses on demand and supply "technicals" of the bonds in a given index, as well as the interaction between the cash and the derivative markets for these assets.

The benchmark of the stable value fund is simply cash with a high focus on principal preservation and a minimal deviation between market value (NAV) and book value of the fund. While technicals also play a role in liquidity analysis, the main focus is on debt issuers being able to either repay or roll over their short-term obligations in a timely fashion. Thus, focus is on the issuer's ability to access external liquidity or generate liquidity internally from its balance sheet.

The stable NAV concept is synonymous to US money market funds, though not all money funds, particularly those in Europe, are necessarily based on the stable NAV concept. The latter is, however, a regulatory requirement for most US money funds and an important factor for many institutional investors in cash funds in general.

US REGULATIONS: RULE 2A-7

"Rule 2a-7" forms part of the Investment Company Act of 1940. It regulates US money market funds. These are subject to supervision by the SEC. The SEC periodically amends the rules and also carries out controls and enforcement.

The core of rule 2a-7 established the restrictions that preserve a *stable "$1" NAV* by limiting price volatility of investments by money market funds through:

- issuer credit quality
- type of debt/maturities (<13 months)
- portfolio duration (<90 days weighted asset maturity, WAM)
- portfolio diversification.

Within this framework, public ratings agencies are assigned a key role in assisting the SEC to define suitable issuers and monitor issuer credit quality in money market funds. The backbone of this process is the accreditation of a public rating agency as an "NRSRO." Under this concept, the SEC has designated a list of Nationally Recognized Statistical Ratings Organizations (for example, Moody's, Standard & Poor's, Fitch, AM Best), whose ratings scales and annotations are being used to assess credit quality in money market funds. As no security without a rating can be purchased by a 2a-7 fund, the NRSROs are effectively the gatekeepers for assets that can be purchased by US money funds.

EXHIBIT 14.1   Rule 2a-7 eligibility

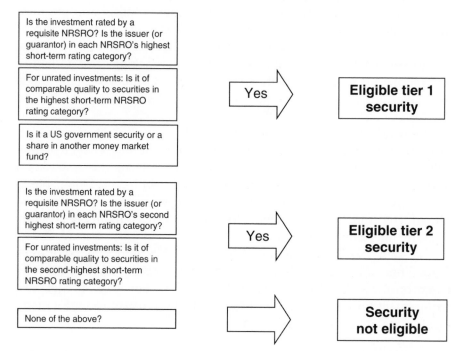

Requisite NRSRO: any two NRSROs that have issued a rating or one NRSRO if only rated by one agency

Within their NRSRO approach, the SEC has divided the investable universe into credit quality tiers that further differentiate the eligible asset base for money market funds. These tiers are applied at purchase and throughout the life of the assets:

- First tier assets: Security (issuer, guarantor) rated in each ratings agency's highest category for short-term ratings – except for US government securities, shares in other money market funds, securities that are deemed of comparable quality to the highest category of short-term rating.
- Second tier assets: Security (issuer, guarantor) rated in each ratings agency's second-highest rating category for short-term ratings. Unrated securities have to be of comparable quality.

Based on the above tiering in Exhibit 14.1, the 2a-7 framework also specifies investment limits for money fund holdings that determine the asset allocation of these funds. These include a:

- 5% maximum per tier 1 issuer
- 1% maximum per tier 2 issuer, 5% overall limit for tier 2 issuers.

The above set of rules has implications for both issuers and investors in short-dated paper:

- From an issuer perspective, tier 1 status implies significantly better access to short-term funding than a tier 2 status. Loss of tier 1 status caused by a downgrading of external credit ratings by an NRSRO will have a severe impact on market access and thus the liquidity profile of the company. Ratings agency arbitrage is possible as there are more than two NRSROs and only the two ratings are taken into account.
- From an investor's perspective, high sensitivity to downgrades as loss of tier 1 status by an issuer implies a severe reduction of the fund's capacity to hold an asset. Investors need to anticipate potential downgrades well ahead of time. The loss of tier 1 (or tier 2) status is likely to result in a severe deterioration of the liquidity position of an issuer, affecting his or her ability to repay short-term obligations.

US REGULATIONS: MINIMAL CREDIT RISK

Despite the above reliance on public credit ratings by the regulator there is an additional fiduciary requirement for a fund's manager to apply an internal judgement on whether a particular asset is suitable for a stable NAV fund. This so-called "minimal credit risk determination" lays out the duty to determine, independently of an external ratings agency, that the asset poses only a minimal threat to the stable NAV. Ultimately, it is this assessment that drives money fund investment and not the public credit ratings cited above.

Again, the SEC has given specific guidance, noting in particular that the Oversight Board of a money fund cannot merely conclude that, because a security is rated high quality by an NRSRO, it represents minimal credit risk. In view of the SEC, the BoD can only make this determination upon an analysis of the issuer's capacity to repay its short-term debt in a timely manner. The SEC lists examples of such analyses:

- cash flow analysis
- analysis of competitive position, cost structure and capital requirements
- including backup credit lines from banks and other sources of liquidity that are available to repay short-term liabilities
- scenario analysis that looks at the issuer's ability to repay its debt from cash or by liquidating assets where backup facilities are unavailable.

EUROPEAN GUIDELINES

The framework for funds domiciled in Europe (UCIT, for example, SICAV, Dublin reg., or German KAG) are generally much wider and do not prescribe a dedicated stable NAV framework for money funds. While there is the perception that these funds invest in shorter dated assets, the leeway in generally much larger and principal protection is not necessarily equal to a matching of NAV to book value at any point in time. There are, however, some basic rules on diversification (for example, the 5/40 rule under UCIT) and with regard to eligible products (for example, derivatives). Unlike in the United States there is no explicit role for public ratings agencies in the regulation of funds.

RATED MONEY FUNDS

The element that links institutional money funds globally is the framework that fund ratings companies have developed for assessing short-term funds. These ratings address the ability of a fund to maintain principal value and limit losses. Essentially, they are derived from the US "2a-7" framework with additional restrictions.

These fund ratings do not assess the track record of a fund or its performance after fees, but are solely focused on its ability to preserve stability of principal. Next to credit risk (quality and diversification) they cover market risk (duration and liquidity) and operating risk (quality of manager) of the fund. Not surprisingly, the main players in money fund ratings are found among the NRSROs that are the gatekeepers of the US money fund industry (for example, Moody's and Standard & Poor's).

The global benchmark of the industry are the "triple A"-rated money funds where investments are limited to the highest short-term ratings category (tier 1 under 2a-7) and interest rate risk to a weighted average maturity (WAM) of only 60 days, leaving the manager even less leeway than the US-style "2a-7" framework. Under the ratings agencies' approach, a fund that experiences realized or unrealized losses greater than 50 bps of its NAV is considered to be in default. Such default can be brought about by credit events.

INVESTMENT PROCESS

The above constraints require a dedicated investment management process for money market funds with research that addresses the specific needs of short-term funds. As many high grade companies, banks in particular are active globally, both in their business activities, as well as their funding strategies. This process requires a research network with global coverage of issuers and their activities in different markets.

The credit research process for these funds is invariably "bottom-up" and built out as a separate function, often with a high degree of independence from portfolio management to ensure an unbiased credit assessment. Detailed bottom-up analysis of each issuer to determine minimal credit risk is at the core of this process, relying on financial modeling, detailed discussions with the management of an issuer, as well as a review of external credit ratings. These factors determine the suitability of an investment.

To ensure efficient asset allocation from a credit risk perspective, individual issuers are ranked by absolute financial strength, both within a given sector (for example, financials) as well as across sectors (for example, financials versus corporates versus structured finance). Regular, at least annual monitoring of the credit profile is required, as is background research on issues affecting an industry sector or a particular group of issuers.

An internal ratings scale for short-term issuers is one way of further expressing differing degrees of creditworthiness within the universe of issuers that qualify for "minimal credit risk" status and money fund eligibility. Such an analysis focuses on the balance of the factors that make up a credit profile. These factors include hard facts, such as earnings and leverage (asset quality in the case of financial institutions), and soft facts, such as management and franchise.

Liquidity plays a central role here. The same goes for the short-term investor, where increasing availability of on- and off-balance sheet liquidity can be used to offset weaknesses elsewhere in the credit profile. Available liquidity also determines the ability of an issuer to withstand one or more external shocks without losing its minimal credit risk status. Thus, the analysis of the liquidity profile of an issuer will be one of the key determinants for assessing and ranking the credit profile.

QUANTITATIVE MODELING

The use of quantitative techniques plays an increasing role in assessing the risk of portfolios and the default risk of individual issuers. Most quantitative credit models tend to focus on relative value analysis, such as rich/cheap analysis across the curve or capital structure arbitrage between debt and equity. The perspective for a short-term fund is again different, as the focus here is on the actual likelihood of default, rather than arbitrage opportunities arising from the mispricing of a particular part of the capital structure.

The perspective of the short-term fund is therefore more akin to that of a bank that seeks to assess the economic risk capital requirement for a lending book through estimating the expected and unexpected loss. The main complication for a money fund is the fact that by definition issuers who make up the "minimal credit risk" universe default very rarely in general, even more so over the short investment horizon of these funds. Nevertheless, even minute credit quality changes need to be picked up by the model quickly to give an early warning of credit deterioration.

Structural credit models relying on Black/Cox-style contingent claims analysis have the advantage that they can exploit pricing information from highly liquid equity markets to estimate changes in credit quality, as well as rank issuers' default risk based on linking underlying asset risk with debt leverage. Equity price information is used to determine the market value and volatility of a firm's assets, and defaults occur when a firm's assets hit a critical value, the default point. Combined with an assessment of recovery values and collateral, this provides an expected loss estimate. At the portfolio level, such models can also be used as an input to derive unexpected loss by assessing default correlations and issuer concentrations.

While useful at the portfolio level, these models do not yet give the precision that is required for short-term credit analysis of very high quality issuers. Their output is also highly sensitive to equity movements, and thus at times changes appear volatile and overstated. However, they are a useful complement in assessing cyclical factors and the impact of volatility and leverage through the credit cycle.

LIQUIDITY ANALYSIS: BASIC CASH CAPITAL FRAMEWORK

Financial institutions (commercial banks, investment banks, insurers) play a key role among issuers at the short end of the market, and are also the main source of liquidity for non-bank issuers through backup facilities, and by providing secondary markets for a variety of assets and receivables. Thus, the assessment of financial institutions' liquidity profile is one of the core determinants for asset allocation decisions of short-term investors.

Traditionally, many players in the financial sector have benefited from an either explicit or implicit "too large to fail" guarantee derived from the role as (retail) deposit-takers and their importance for monetary policy. The scope of this protection has however declined as authorities have made the likelihood of intervention more ambiguous to reduce moral hazard. Increasing specialization and differentiation within the financial sector has also resulted in a wide variety of sizable short-term issuers outside the traditional "too large to fail" universe.

Accounting and financial statement information only gives a limited amount of information on the liquidity profile of an issuer, as do regulatory ratios. Only few banking regulatory frameworks (for example, Germany) demand formal reporting of the liquidity position against mandatory minimum requirements. The most common framework for assessing liquidity from an outside perspective is the cash capital framework (see Exhibit 14.2) developed by investment banking operations and ratings agencies. It effectively expands the classic loans/deposit ratio into a broader view of the funding requirement for illiquid assets.

UNSECURED VS SECURED FUNDING

From the perspective of the short-term investor, this basic framework today falls short in crucial aspects, such as the use of derivatives and the increasing use of off-balance sheet vehicles to house assets and raise

EXHIBIT 14.2   Basic cash capital framework

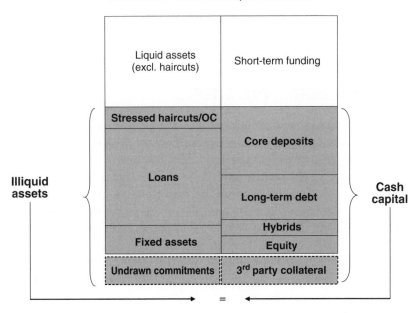

funds. Thus, an expanded view of cash capital should take into account illiquid derivatives claims, as well as collateral and commitments that are available off-balance sheet (see Exhibit 14.3). Secured funding sources (repos and covered bonds) and their over-collateralization requirements also play an increasingly important role. These developments are driven

EXHIBIT 14.3   Secured vs unsecured funding

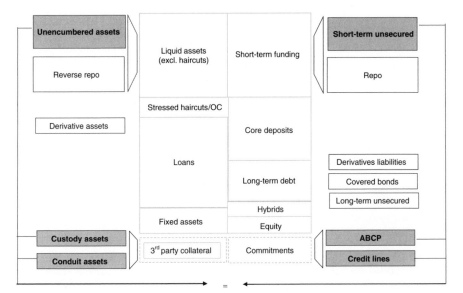

by issuers' increasing funding diversification and more sophisticated arbitrage strategies in raising funds. While this poses additional complexity to the analysis of the funding profile, the flip-side is that it also poses a wider set of investment opportunities at the short-end.

EUROPEAN COMMERCIAL PAPER (ECP)

The development of the ECP market highlights the above trends. This market has enjoyed strong growth since the introduction of the euro, reaching the equivalent of US$500 billion by 2005. This outpaced the growth of domestic CP markets (for example, French BT) and provides the short-term investor with an alternative to traditional CDs and short-term deposits with banks. One of the main drivers of the ECP market has been the growth of asset-backed commercial paper that accounts for roughly one-third of outstanding ECP. With that development, the ECP market has followed the mature US domestic market.

ABCP is sponsored mainly by commercial banks that use it to manage their regulatory capital ratios and to diversify their funding away from unsecured on-balance sheet funding to secured off-balance sheet instruments. Investors are attracted to ABCP as it pays a slightly higher yield than bank paper, while being perceived as less risky than many corporate CP programs.

The credit quality of ABCP relies on the presence of a strong sponsor, usually a highly rated bank and the structural protection offered to CP investors. The latter rests on a bankruptcy-remote special purpose vehicle (SPV) that holds the assets that are used as collateral. The CP issued by the SPV is supported by liquidity facilities from highly rated banks and various forms of credit enhancement designed to meet potential collateral shortfalls.

Ratings agencies are the gatekeepers to the ABCP market, as this type of CP has to have at least two short-term ratings in the highest category (A-1/P-1, corresponding to long-term ratings of A2/A and above) to meet investor demand. As part of their analysis, the agencies review the structure (bankruptcy remoteness, liquidity facilities, LOCs, and so on), the capability of the administrator (structuring, servicing) and the quality of the assets, and the required credit enhancement before they are included in a program.

The ABCP sector can be broken down into four generic classes of issuers:

- *Single-seller programs* are used by commercial banks to refinance pools of short-term receivables; for example, trade bills. The term "single-seller" refers to a single company (that is, the bank) selling receivables to a bankruptcy-remote SPV, which then issues commercial paper that is secured by these receivables. This structure, with variations, is found in most types of ABCP. To ensure timely payment of the CP the bank provides a liquidity facility that covers all interest and principal payments on outstanding CP, provided that none of the assets have defaulted. The bank also maintains a first loss piece to cover defaults in the form of a letter of credit (LOC) or cash. The first loss piece is sized on the basis of historical loss experience of the receivables and has to be agreed to by the ratings agencies (usually at least two, if not three).

- *Multi-seller programs*: Exhibit 14.4 provides a schematic overview of a multi-seller ABCP program. Broadly similar to single sellers, these are used by commercial banks and investment banks to fund working capital requirements of their corporate and financial institutions clients. The bank arranges for a number ("multi-". . .) of clients (. . . "sellers") to transfer their receivables into the SPV. Each seller maintains a first loss piece of its assets and the bank refinances the remaining pool through CP issued by the SPV, providing full liquidity support and additional program-wide credit support in the form of a LOC. Both the first loss piece by the seller and the program-wide credit support are sized to the requirements of the ratings agencies based on historical loss experience.

- *Credit arbitrage programs*: The basic structure of a credit arbitrage program is described in Exhibit 14.5 on page 320. These are used by commercial banks to fund portfolios of highly rated assets, usually AAA-rated tranches of asset-backed securities (ABS). Like other investors, banks buy these ABS securities in the primary market for their own account, and they generate spread-income by

EXHIBIT 14.4   Structured products: multi-seller ABCP program

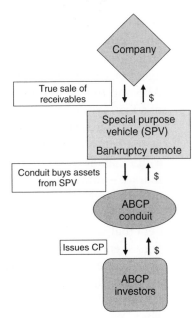

- Used by banks to finance trade and term receivables:
  - cost of regulatory capital
  - funding diversification
- Credit enhancement:
  - first loss piece with seller
  - bank provides program-wide second loss piece
- 100% liquidity support from bank lines:
  - covers all CP outstanding including interest
  - covers only non-defaulted assets
- Ratings agencies play key role:
  - rate the structure
  - review the assets that go into the conduits
  - only limited disclosure to CP investors

EXHIBIT 14.5   Structured products: securities arbitrage

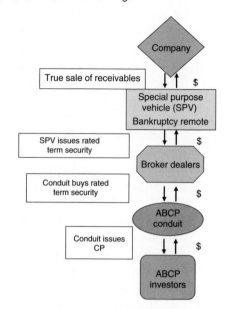

* Effectively CDOs of ABS that are financed through issuance of CP

* Invest mainly in senior tranches of ABS deals

* Credit enhancement:

  –sub-ordination on senior ABS

  –program-wide support for lower rated assets

* Roll-over risk 100% covered by liquidity facilities:

  –fund performing assets at par

  –do not fund at all if downgraded below a certain level (CCC)

* Ratings agencies play a key role. They:

  –rate the conduits

  –rate the assets that go into the conduit

  –limited disclosure to CP investors

refinancing them through short-dated ABCP, using the securities as collateral. The securities are kept off-balance sheet to avoid onerous regulatory capital charges. A liquidity facility covers interest and principal on all outstanding CP, provided that the assets are rated at least CCC (three grades below investment grade). As highly rated ABS tranches are already protected by subordination within their structure, these programs have little, sometimes no additional credit enhancement.

* *Structured investment vehicles (SIVs)*: These are finance companies, structured as bankruptcy remote SPVs, that are set up by asset managers or banks to invest in investment grade assets (mainly AAA ABS and highly rated financials). Exhibit 14.6 shows the structure of a SIV. While broadly similar to market value collateralized debt obligations (CDOs), SIVs are designed as a going concern with managers focused on building out franchise value of the asset, as well as the liability side. Partly refinancing high rated assets in the CP market – among other funding sources such as MTNs – provides positive carry that accrues within the SPV. To attain a high credit rating (AAA by at least two agencies) the SPV issues subordinated debt that is sized according to a capital model (approved by the ratings agencies) which ensures that subordination is sufficient, even under severe stress, to repay all senior note-holders, if necessary by liquidating the entire portfolio. Unlike other ABCP programs, CP issued by SIVs does not benefit from full liquidity cover, which sets SIV paper apart from other ABCP. The capital test is monitored

EXHIBIT 14.6   Structured products: SIVs

- Asset management product broadly similar to CDOs
- More complex capital structure than conduits:
  - –issue sub-debt as "capital"
  - –issue MTNs and CP
- Have ALM-mismatch with limited liquidity back-stops
- Investors exposed to liquidity risk and credit risk:
  - –operating limits
  - –capital model
  - –manager quality
- Ratings agencies play key role:
  - –approve capital model & limits
  - –rate all assets

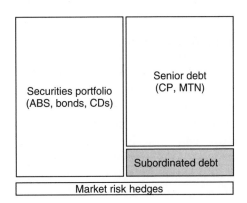

weekly with all assets marked to market. Provided that this capital test is met, excess spread is distributed to the subordinated note investors and the manager.

ABCP growth in recent years has been dominated by the credit arbitrage programs and the SIV sector, while the single and multi-seller structures have lagged with many multi-sellers moving into credit arbitrage. This is a reflection of low margins and low corporate demand for working capital and bridge financing. Arbitrage programs have benefited from the growth in the ABS market, particularly from UK and US consumer assets (mortgages and credit cards).

The SIV sector has seen significant growth fueled by rising demand for their levered subordinated notes as spreads tightened. For most programs, ECP provides only part of the funding, as they also tap the much deeper US CP market and SIVs also increasingly use longer dated MTNs as part of their funding. Funding requirements tend to be dominated by US dollar-denominated assets, especially in credit arbitrage and SIVs. ECP issuance has suffered from the EUR/US$ swap, while the increasing holdings of RMBS GBP-denominated mortgage ABS have led to increased GBP issuance.

Going forward, the ABCP market is likely to be influenced by a number of trends that will change issuing patterns. A relative scarcity of available liquidity facilities from highly rated banks has emerged as the market continues to grow. Increasingly, programs are looking to alternative forms of liquidity backup that moves away from the full support currently offered on most programs. International Financial Reporting Standards (IFRS) (consolidation of SPVs) and Basel II (regulatory capital treatment of liquidity facilities) are likely to exacerbate that pressure. From 2007,

Basel II will also fundamentally change the way banks are charged for regulatory capital, which removes part of the regulatory arbitrage.

RESEARCH APPROACH

Despite the strong involvement of the ratings agencies in the structuring and ongoing monitoring of ABCP conduits, internal reviews are required for each program. Like with all other entities, the research process is bottom-up and focuses on identifying those programs that pose minimal credit risk to the funds. In most cases the sponsoring bank will play a key role in the investment rationale. This is, however, not sufficient and needs to be complemented by an operational review of the administrator, the assets, and the structural protection available to CP investors. This includes detailed discussions with management and on-site visits, as well as discussions with the ratings agencies. Once approved, programs are monitored in regular intervals to ensure that the risk profile stays within expectations. As ongoing disclosure varies widely within the industry and is so far poor on average, regular bilateral contact with administrators is required to keep up to date on developments.

STRUCTURED LIQUIDITY NOTES

Within the ABCP market the structured liquidity note (SLN) segment has seen the fastest growth recently, now accounting for more than 10% of outstandings in the United States. Growth in this market has been driven by issuers looking to fund large highly granular portfolios of consumer and mortgage assets without resorting to expensive full liquidity support from a bank. The main target for these notes is US-style 2a-7 funds with their 13-month restriction on maturity. Correspondingly, the legal final maturity of SLNs is usually set at 13 months (or 270 days to qualify as CP under US regulations). Exhibit 14.7 provides the detailed time-line for a structured liquidity note from an investor's perspective. Within this framework, the issuer has the ability to specify expected maturity dates for each issue, depending on the type of asset financed through the program. During the expected maturity period the SLN operates like standard ABCP. If the issuer cannot roll the paper at expected maturity, the note extends (subject to a 25-bps coupon step-up) and the underlying assets are sold or amortized. Further support may be available during that process in the form of market value swaps or liquidity facilities. The main attraction in most instances is, however, that the ratings agencies will base their ratings assessment on the cash flows available from the assets to repay obligations at their legal final maturity. Thus, only minimal or no bank liquidity facilities are required to achieve the ratings level required for money fund investors.

From an investor's perspective these structures offer higher spreads than traditional ABCP with similar ratings. The analysis of the structure

EXHIBIT 14.7   Structured products: SLNs

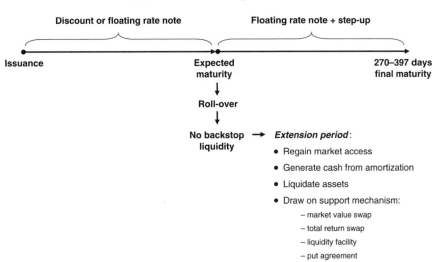

will focus on the likelihood of extension in the structure; that is, minimizing the option value for the issuer to exercise up-front. While a step-up would look attractive under certain market conditions, any extension would be considered a negative event, as it would point to liquidity issues with the issuer or the asset class. In addition, the stable value fund investor will also have to determine that, upon extension, the market value of an SLN can reasonably be expected to approximate its amortized cost value.

CONCLUSION

Regulatory and investor requirements put tight constraints around the management of short-term investment funds, particularly those that target a stable net asset value. Credit ratings agencies play a key role not only for issuers of short-term debt, but also for investors as the same agencies rate both the issuers and many of the funds that invest in short-term debt. Investment managers need to assess the short-term liquidity position of issuers anticipating potential ratings downgrades well ahead of time to allow for the timely re-positioning of investments. Issuers also need to anticipate these movements and to provide timely and sufficient information to their investor base to allow for an assessment of their liquidity position. Next to unsecured CP, issuers and investors can today chose from a variety of secured assets that have been specifically structured for short-term funds. These allow for better diversification of funding sources on the issuing side and more efficient asset allocation for investors.

Part 4

Cutting Edge

CHAPTER 15

Dynamic Modeling and Optimization of Non-maturing Accounts

Karl Frauendorfer and Michael Schürle

T he risk management of non-maturing account positions in a bank's balance-like savings deposits or certain types of loans is complicated by the embedded options that clients may exercise. In addition to the usual interest rate risk, there is also uncertainty in the timing and amount of future cash flows. Since the corresponding volume risk cannot directly be hedged, the account must be replicated by a portfolio of instruments with explicit maturities. This chapter introduces a multistage stochastic programming model that determines an optimal replicating portfolio from scenarios for future outcomes of the relevant risk factors: market rates, client rates, and volume of the non-maturing account. The weights for the allocation of new tranches are frequently adjusted to the latest observations of the latter. A case study based on data of a real deposit position demonstrates that the resulting dynamic portfolio provides a significantly higher margin at lower risk compared to a static benchmark.

INTRODUCTION

A significant portion of a typical bank's balance are so-called non-maturing accounts (NMAs). Their characteristic feature is that they have no specific contractual maturity, and individual clients can always add or withdraw investments or credits at no (or a negligible) penalty. On the other hand, the bank is allowed to adjust the customer rate any time as a matter of policy. Typical examples of NMAs include savings and sight deposits on the liability side of the balance, as well as credit card loans or variable-rate mortgages as they are common in some European countries on the asset side.

Although the client rate is mostly adjusted in sympathy with the direction of changes in money and capital market yields, it does not completely depend on the latter. In practice, an adaption (often in discrete increments) follows only after larger variations in open-market rates and with some delay due to administrative and other costs involved. There might also be a (political) cap like in the case of variable-rate mortgages in Switzerland where housing rents are indexed to an "official" mortgages rate.

Specific Problems of Non-maturing Accounts

One can often observe that the volume of a NMA position fluctuates heavily as clients react to changes in the customer rate and the relative attractiveness of alternative investment or financing opportunities and so on. For example, in the past a typical Swiss bank faced a significant increase in homeowners' demand for variable-rate mortgages during a period of high interest rates (see Exhibit 15.1) while refinancing them on the inter-bank market is particularly unfavorable. At the same time, depositors tend to substitute their savings by long-term investments to "lock up" the high level of yields (withdrawal).

When interest rates are low, clients switch to fix-rate mortgages in order to hedge themselves against a future rise (prepayment), while the deposit rate becomes more profitable compared to alternative short-term investments which attracts additional savings volume. Since the volume of the variable positions on both sides of the balance fluctuates "phase-delayed", mortgages (or other non-maturing loans) cannot be funded completely by deposits. Therefore, numerous Swiss banks suffered significant losses on their variable mortgage positions during the early 1990s when they had to refinance them at market rates around 10%, while the corresponding client rate never climbed over 7% due to the cap.

In general, the incomplete adaption of the client rate to money and capital market rates may have a significant impact on the profitability and often result in unstable margins. Moreover, the embedded prepayment and withdrawal options induce a *volume risk*. Unlike the interest rate risk associated with fixed income instruments, the latter cannot be hedged

EXHIBIT 15.1 Correlation between client rate and volume during the early 1990s

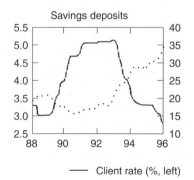 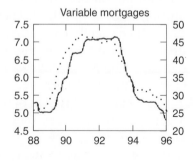

—— Client rate (%, left)   ····· Volume (bio. CHF, right)

directly since the volume is not traded in the market. Hence, conventional hedging techniques like duration matching can only be applied with additional assumptions about the amount and timing of (future) cash flows. A fixed maturity profile must therefore be assigned to the NMA in order to transform the uncertain cash flows into (apparently) certain ones.

Implications for Risk Management

To obtain such a transformation, a *replicating portfolio* that mimics the payments of the variable position is constructed using traded standard instruments. Then, one is able to immunize (at least theoretically) the position against the risk of changes in interest rates. The replicating portfolio also defines the transfer price at which the margin is split between the business unit retail that "acquires" the account and the Treasury as the bank's central unit where interest rate risk is managed. Obviously, an accurate determination of the replicating portfolio composition is of utmost importance for the risk exposure, since an incorrect transformation may result in inefficient hedging decisions.

Given the significant amounts of NMAs in the balances of most retail banks, a proper management of the associated interest rate and volume risk therefore becomes a critical issue. Its importance has increased since the regulation of interest rate risk in the banking book plays a central role in the second pillar of Basel II (see Fiedler et al. 2004). For example, a number of banks regard savings accounts as short-term liabilities (according to their legal maturity) and, thus, have assigned a short maturity to them in their interest obligation balance. When the term transformation is carried out by the Treasury and variable positions are invested at longer terms to take advantage of higher rates in a normal yield curve, a term mismatch results. Although the latter will not directly be charged with capital, it leads to a "quasi capital adequacy," since the corresponding risk must not exceed 20% of the bank's Tier 1 and Tier 2 capital – otherwise the bank is disqualified as an "outlier" (Basel Committee on Banking Supervision 2004).

Similar problems are currently arising in the context of hedge accounting under International Financial Reporting Standards (IFRS). For example, a bank with large savings positions can hardly find "natural hedges" in its balance for the credit business due to the provisional non-approval of deposit accounts. Qualification for hedge accounting would require that the hedge effectiveness of non-maturing deposits could precisely be estimated.

Last but not least, pressure on the profit side has also increased after the introduction of alternative products such as money market funds or the appearance of direct banks in different countries that have achieved a large share in the savings market by aggressively offering attractive deposit rates. As a consequence, a number of traditional institutions have experienced a substantial contraction in their deposit volumes, which had been an inexpensive funding opportunity so far. Even banks with stable volumes had to face smaller margins in the recent past due to historically low credit rates while the client could not be charged a negative deposit rate (see Fiedler et al. 2004).

Therefore, any methodology for the determination of the replicating portfolio not only has to hedge the inherent risk adequately but must also provide a sufficient margin that allows a bank to remain in the competition for "cheap" funding sources. In this sense, it is required to manage the "tradeoff" between risk and return successfully. The fact that non-maturity products typically exhibit a complex dependency of the cash flows on the evolution of the yield curve demands for sophisticated modeling and decision-making techniques.

At present, the banking industry uses mostly static portfolios (that is, with constant weights) whose composition is fitted to historical data. We illustrate in the next section that this approach is inefficient and holds a significant model risk. Based on an analysis of its shortcomings, we motivate why the replicating portfolio should be frequently readjusted to scenarios for the future risk factors: market rates, client rate and volume. The problem of the determination of a *dynamic replicating portfolio* is formulated below as a multistage stochastic program that can be solved with standard optimization algorithms. Models for the stochastic evolution of the risk factors are described in the section on risk factors considering Swiss savings deposits as an example. As discussed in the scenario generation section, specific attention must be paid to the generation of scenarios that serve as input to the optimization problem to ensure consistence and robustness of the solution. The savings deposits section presents results of a case study for real Swiss savings deposit data that show the advantage of dynamic replication over the conventional static approach. The chapter concludes with some remarks on the application to different products and future directions of research

MODELING NON-MATURING ACCOUNTS

Shortcomings of Static Replication

A widely used method in many European countries is the construction of the replicating portfolio by an analysis of the past evolution of the NMA position. This requires a set of historical data of client rates, volumes, and market rates that may be used for reinvesting or financing. The portfolio composition is then determined under the condition that the cash flows of the (fixed income) instruments used for replication match those of the NMA (except for the margin) as close as possible; that is, the average yield on the portfolio moves parallel to the client rate, and a drop in volume is compensated by maturing instruments. By minimization of the tracking error between the payments of the portfolio and the underlying NMA position, one aims at the minimization of the margin's volatility, and an estimate for its expectation may be obtained from the average of the sample period.

For the practical implementation, the resulting portfolio weights remain constant over time. Therefore, this method can be categorized as a *static* approach. Maturing instruments are always renewed at the same maturity except for volume changes that are compensated by buying additional or selling existing tranches of the specified instruments. Another possibility is the segmentation of the portfolio into a constant core volume and a volatile component. The core is itself subdivided into portions that are invested (or funded) in different time bands using medium- and long-term maturities, and maturing tranches are always reinvested in the same time band. The volatile part consists of overnight money and serves as a "buffer" for volume fluctuations. Since in both cases only a small portion of the replicating portfolio is renewed at a certain point in time, the portfolio return as an average of several market rates exhibits a low volatility and changes only slowly over time, similar to the client rate of a typical NMA.

An example for the former variant can be found in Exhibit 15.2 for an asset (variable mortgages) and a liability product (deposit account, see Bühler 2000). The "optimal" portfolio composition in the static framework was determined by minimization of the tracking error for a period of approximately 6.5 years (December 1992 to June 1999). For instance, if savings deposits had been replicated by a constant mix of 17% six-month and 83% five-year instruments, then – in this *ex post* analysis – a least volatile margin of 383 basis points (bps) would have been achieved during the sample period. Applying the same calculation for variable mortgages would have provided a rather small margin of 31 bps only, which might not be sufficient to cover the administrative and other non-interest costs for holding the account.

In a second step, the authors of this study divided the entire sample period into two subperiods (December 1992 to March 1996 and April 1996 to June 1999) and applied the same analysis to each of them. According to Exhibit 15.2, this results in completely different portfolio compositions for both products. The observation that the weights depend heavily on

EXHIBIT 15.2 Characteristics of static replicating portfolios for two non-maturing accounts over a historical sample period and two subperiods (Bühler 2000)

	Deposit account			Variable mortgages		
Begin	**Dec 92**	**Dec 92**	**Apr 96**	**Dec 92**	**Dec 92**	**Apr 96**
End	**Jun 99**	**Mar 96**	**Jun 99**	**Jun 99**	**Mar 96**	**Jun 99**
6M	0.17		0.19			
1Y		0.11	0.81	0.22	0.07	0.51
2Y					0.48	
3Y						0.36
4Y		0.31				
5Y	0.83	0.58		0.78	0.45	0.13
margin [%]	3.83	4.25	1.50	0.31	2.71	1.68

the sample period and the corresponding margins are unstable implies a substantial *model risk* and this has a direct impact on risk management and transfer pricing. The significant fluctuations in the portfolios would make hedging strategies inefficient, and the apparently low margin of mortgages from December 1992 to June 1999 might have led the bank management to the conclusion that the product is not profitable, although an analysis for a different period could provide a completely different result.

In practice, one would determine the (static) replicating portfolio once and adjust the weights and transfer prices only in longer intervals (for example, yearly). If this results in a new portfolio composition, then instruments of the existing portfolio must be squared, and it is not clear which unit in the bank has to bear the losses that result more or less from the pure adjustment of a "calculation rule" only, and not from a fundamental change in the market or client behavior. Moreover, the observation that the least volatile margin may (apparently) be not sufficient to cover the (non-interest) costs questions the usefulness of the (lowest) variance as an appropriate risk measure.

To overcome these obvious deficiencies of the conventional static replication approach, we suggest the abandonment of two basic assumptions made so far:

1. Instead of a constant portfolio composition and identical maturities (up to the next readjustment), the weights and also relevant maturities at which maturing instruments and a volume change are (re-) invested or financed have to be recalculated frequently.
2. The replicating portfolio is not derived from a *single historical* scenario, but from a *large number* of scenarios for the possible *future* outcomes of the relevant risk factors; that is, market rates, client rate and volume.

The motivation of the first point is to exploit the latest information from the markets and client behavior whenever instruments must be allocated. The second point requires a quantitative model that describes the (joint) stochastic dynamics of market rates, client rates, and volume over time, as well as the dependencies between them for specific retail products.

Stochastic Models

Given the practical relevance of NMAs, there has been a relatively small number of papers on their stochastic analysis. Selvaggio (1996) analyzes the premiums that banks pay for the acquisition of demand deposit accounts (DDAs) and explains the volume as a function of interests and nominal income with some time lag plus a seasonal correction. This volume model is then combined with the short rate process of Cox, Ingersoll, and Ross (1985) (CIR) to calculate an option-adjusted spread and the net present value (NPV) of future payments associated with deposit liabilities. Risk can be quantified by a recalculation of the NPV after shifts in the underlying term structure that, in principle, allows the determination of a hedging policy. Unfortunately, data for DDA premiums required for calibration are not available for European markets, and the significance of nominal income as an explanatory variable for the volume of individual banks is not fully plausible.

Hutchison and Pennacchi (1996) employ a general contingent claims framework for valuation and calculate duration measures for demand deposits analytically. In contrast to these equilibrium-based models, Jarrow and van Deventer (1998) (JvD) introduce an arbitrage-free modeling approach to obtain the value of NMAs, which allows for consistence with the pricing and risk management of traded products. They also show how the risky position may be hedged by a replicating portfolio that results from investing and financing in fixed income securities.

These first arbitrage-free and equilibrium-based models are often based on simplifying assumptions for the number and type of underlying risk factor processes and, in particular, the dependencies between client rate, volume, and market rates to derive closed form solutions of the corresponding pricing equations. For example, the client rate in the original JvD model is a deterministic function of the short rate as the only source of uncertainty, and the aggregated volume depends only on the evolution of the term structure. To reflect the typical stickiness of client rates, O'Brien (2000) models balances and deposit rates as autoregressive processes and also studies alternative specifications with asymmetric adjustments. Here, the CIR one-factor interest rate model is used again to describe the dynamics of market rates.

While these papers provide empirical evidence for the US market (see also Janosi et al. 1999 for an investigation of the JvD approach), an application on European market calls for some modifications due to the different characteristics of retail products. For example, Laurent (2004) extends the JvD model to the case that, as in the Benelux, fidelity premium rates are rewarded for deposits that have remained in the account for a certain period. Kalkbrener and Willing (2004) propose a very general modeling approach with two factors for market rates that allow for more complex movements of the yield curve. A two-factor Vasicek-type model in the Heath, Jarrow, and Morton (1992) (HJM) framework is used for this purpose. The latter turned out to be superior to alternative specifications in an empirical analysis (Heitmann and Trautmann 1995).

Because the main focus is a realistic development of interest rates over a long period of time, historical time series are used for calibration instead of fitting the model parameters to the current market prices of plain vanilla instruments as in derivative pricing. The client rate is described as a piecewise linear function with the short rate as stochastic argument only, and a (log-) normally distributed diffusion model is used for the volume with a third stochastic factor that may be correlated with the two factors of the market rate model. In this way, correlations between market rates and volume observed in the German market are taken into account. Monte Carlo simulation is then applied to compute the value and sensitivities of an NMA; the delta profile obtained from shifting (parts of) the yield curve is used for the construction of a replicating portfolio. Certainly, this numerical approach requires some more computation time than analytically solvable models, but this slight drawback is offset by a more realistic description of risk factor dynamics. Due to its generality, any of its components – term structure, deposit rate and volume model – may be replaced by some alternative specification that reflects the characteristics of the relevant market and/or retail product more appropriately.

All of the latter models are motivated by the trend to MTM risk management in banking and have been derived by extending some "classical" term structure models (that have originally been developed for the pricing of interest rate derivatives) by client rates and volume as additional risk factors. In principle, a replicating portfolio would be defined as the combination of fixed income securities that exhibits the same delta profile. Caps and floors may additionally be integrated if there is a significant vega risk. However, Monte Carlo-based approaches become computationally more complex when the sensitivity is calculated with respect to shifts of *several* key interest rates. The existence of volume risk would also require the consideration of liquidity constraints. Unfortunately, little is reported about the practicability and efficiency of such replicating strategies in the long run.

Dynamic Replication

Immunizing the actual NMA position against movements of the present term structure only is in some sense a myopic policy. Positions of today's "perfect hedge" possibly have to be squared at a later point in time and, thus, large transaction volumes might be cumulated. To overcome any potential inefficiencies arising from this "lack of foresight," future responses to changes in the risk factors should also be taken into account in the determination of the current decision that can be achieved by *multistage stochastic programming* techniques. Given the (conditional) probability distributions of the future risk factors, those policies are determined that satisfy some optimality criterion and are feasible for all possible instances of the random data. For practical reasons that will be motivated later, the probability distributions are typically expressed by a set of scenarios.

In the context of NMA replication, this allows us to address the two aspects motivated at the end of the previous section. Instead of fitting the weights of the replicating portfolio to a single historic scenario only, the optimal allocation of new tranches for a given planning horizon is calculated at all points in time along each scenario for future market rates, client rate and volume. "Optimal" can be specified in a number of ways; for example, minimization of the tracking error and maximization of the margin subject to risk limits. Relevant constraints include liquidity; that is, a drop in volume must be compensated by maturing tranches (or existing instruments must be sold that may affect the P&L and/or margin). Additional restrictions, for example, for minimum margin, loss, portfolio composition and implementable strategies, may easily be integrated if desired.

Note that, in contrast to static replication, the weights at which new tranches are allocated will be readjusted from stage to stage along each scenario. There are numerous examples from portfolio management that dynamic strategies derived in this way are superior to static ones with respect to risk and return (for example, see Carino et al. (1994) for a comparison of multistage stochastic programming with single-period mean variance optimization, Consiglio and Zenios (2001) for tracking fixed-income indices, or Fleten et al. (2002) for an analysis of dynamic and fixed mix portfolio models, to mention just a few).

Multistage stochastic programming was also used in our earlier models for the determination of profit-maximizing investment or cost-minimizing funding strategies, respectively, for positions with uncertain maturities. These are based on scenarios for the future evolution of interest rates and volume; client rates were explicitly not taken into account because they do not affect the optimal policy under this objective.

The motivations for this specification are the often insufficient profits for many retail products in the banking industry. There is evidence from various applications like savings deposits (Forrest et al. 1998, Frauendorfer and Schürle 2003) or variable mortgages (Frauendorfer and Schürle 2005) that dynamic policies obtained from these stochastic programming models provide higher and simultaneously less volatile margins than the static replicating portfolio approach, although they were not constructed to "track" the non-maturing asset or liability exactly. The next section describes the formulation of a multistage stochastic program for the *dynamic replication* of NMAs. To this end, the client rate will also be included in the model, and investment or financing strategies are optimized relative to the latter as a benchmark.

FORMULATION AS A MULTISTAGE STOCHASTIC PROGRAM

For simplicity, we restrict ourselves to a description of the model for the management of liability positions like deposit accounts. The formulation for asset products is equivalent and can easily be derived from this specification when investing is replaced by borrowing and vice versa. At this time, we do not make any assumptions on the stochastic evolution of the risk factors except that – in addition to the factors that drive the evolution of the term structure – there is at least one additional stochastic variable that affects solely the total volume of the relevant NMA position. This is motivated by the fact that – despite the high correlations between interest rates and volume that are observed for many retail products – the volume dynamics cannot be explained fully by interest rates. Potential candidates of such additional factors may be the return on stocks as investment opportunities competing with savings deposits, or simply a residual variable for non-systematic variations in volume.

Notation

Let D be the longest maturity used for the construction of the replicating portfolio. $\mathcal{D} = \{1, \dots, D\}$ denotes the set of dates where fixed-income securities held in the portfolio mature. Maturities of standard instruments that can be used for investing are given by the set $\mathcal{D}^S \subseteq \mathcal{D}$. The model also has the option to square existing instruments prior to maturity, which would be required if a decline in volume cannot be compensated by maturing tranches. This is modeled as borrowing funds of the corresponding maturities.

Due to liquidity restrictions that apply for some markets, for example the inter-bank market for the Swiss franc, the bid-ask spreads may increase if a certain transaction volume is exceeded. This might occur when a major bank places larger amounts particularly in longer maturities. Therefore, the transaction volume in each maturity is split into *several tranches* that are priced at different spreads. The number of possible tranches is given by I^d for maturity d, $\mathcal{I}^d := \{1, \dots, I^d\}$ is a corresponding index set and ℓ_i^d the maximum amount that can be traded in the i-tranche.

The joint evolution of random data (market rates, client rate and volume of the relevant position) is driven by a stochastic process $\omega := (\omega_t; t = 1, \dots, T)$ in discrete time. The latter is formally defined on a probability space $(\Omega, \mathcal{F}, P)$ where $\Omega = \Omega_1 \times \dots \times \Omega_T$ is the sample space, $\mathcal{F}$ the σ-field of subsets on Ω and P a probability measure. The filtration $\mathcal{F}_t := \sigma\{\omega^t\}$ generated in Ω by the history $\omega^t := (\omega_1, \dots, \omega_t)$ of the stochastic process ω defines the information set available at time t and satisfies $\{\emptyset, \Omega\} \subset \mathcal{F}_1 \subset \dots \subset \mathcal{F}_T$. The random vector $\omega_t := (\eta_t, \xi_t) \in \Omega_t^\eta \times \Omega_t^\xi =: \Omega_t \subseteq \mathbb{R}^{K+L}$ can be decomposed into two components: $\eta_t \in \Omega_t^\eta \subseteq \mathbb{R}^K$ is equivalent to the state variables of a K-factor term structure model and controls market rates, client rate, and volume. $\xi_t \in \Omega_t^\xi \subseteq \mathbb{R}^L$ represents L additional (economic) factors that influence only the volume.

The relevant stochastic coefficients in the optimization model derived from outcomes of ω^t at time $t = 1, \dots, T$ are:

$r_{i,t}^{d,+}(\eta^t)$ bid rate per period for investing in the i-th tranche ($i \in \mathcal{I}^d$) of maturity $d \in \mathcal{D}^S$

$r_{i,t}^{d,-}(\eta^t)$ ask rate per period for borrowing in the i-th tranche ($i \in \mathcal{I}^d$) of maturity $d \in \mathcal{D}^S$

$c_t(\eta^t)$ client rate paid per period for holding the deposit account

$v_t(\omega^t)$ volume of the relevant position.

The initial bid and ask rates $r_{i,0}^{d,+}$ and $r_{i,0}^{d,-}$ for $i \in \mathcal{I}^d$, $d \in \mathcal{D}^S$, as well as the client rate c_0 and volume v_0 at time $t = 0$, can be observed in the market and, hence, are deterministic. In the sequel, the dependency of the stochastic coefficients on ω^t or η^t will not be stressed in the notation for simplicity.

At each point in time $t = 0, \ldots, T$, where T denotes the planning horizon, decisions are made on the transactions in each maturity for the allocation of maturing tranches (which are in general *not* renewed in the same maturity) plus the change in volume. This requires the following decision and state variables:

$x_{i,t}^{d,+}$ amount invested in the i-th tranche ($i \in \mathcal{I}^d$) of maturity $d \in \mathcal{D}^S$

$x_{i,t}^{d,-}$ amount financed in the i-th tranche ($i \in \mathcal{I}^d$) of maturity $d \in \mathcal{D}^S$

x_t^d nominal amount maturing after $d \in \mathcal{D}$ periods

x_t^S surplus in absolute terms (income from the replicating portfolio

       minus costs for holding the account).

A variable x_{-1}^d with negative time index represents the nominal volume in the initial portfolio with maturity $d \in \mathcal{D}$ that results from decisions in the past. The corresponding cash flow cf_{-1}^d received from these positions at date d are also known.

Specification of Constraints

To ensure feasibility of investment and borrowing decisions, budget constraints must hold at each stage t that correct the nominal volume with maturity date $d \in \mathcal{D}$ by the corresponding transaction amounts:

$$
\begin{aligned}
x_t^d &= x_{t-1}^{d+1} + \sum_{i \in \mathcal{I}^d} x_{i,t}^{d,+} - \sum_{i \in \mathcal{I}^d} x_{i,t}^{d,-} \quad \forall\, d \in \mathcal{D}^S \\
x_t^d &= x_{t-1}^{d+1} \qquad\qquad\qquad\qquad\quad \forall\, d \in \mathcal{D} \backslash \mathcal{D}^S
\end{aligned}
\tag{15.1}
$$

The next restriction controls that the sum of all positions in the portfolio matches the volume of the managed NMA at time t:

$$
\sum_{d \in \mathcal{D}} x_t^d = v_t.
\tag{15.2}
$$

Limits for the portion of the nominal volume in certain time buckets may optionally be defined. Let w_i^l and w_i^u be the lower and upper bound for the percentage of the i-th bucket defined by the subset of maturity dates $\mathcal{D}_i^\omega \subseteq \mathcal{D}$, $i = 1, \ldots, n$, where n is the number of time buckets for which such restrictions apply:

$$
w_i^l \cdot v_t \leq \sum_{d \in \mathcal{D}_i^\omega} x_t^d \leq w_i^u \cdot v_t \quad i = 1, \ldots, n
\tag{15.3}
$$

Generally, the decision-maker should not constrain the structure of the replicating portfolio too much since it should be a result of the optimization and not an input. However, these limits may be useful to ensure that a certain percentage of the portfolio matures in the short term for liquidity reasons. A lower bound of zero for all positions enforces that all netted exposures per maturity date have a positive sign; that is, leverage using term transformation is not allowed. Corresponding bounds for absolute limits instead of percentages of the total volume can be defined analogously.

Without any further constraints, the model may decide to reduce the exposure in existing instruments and reinvest the money from squared positions in different maturities. Such activities can be restricted at time t to an amount equal to the sum of tranches maturing in $t, \ldots, t + m - 1$:

$$\sum_{d \in \mathcal{D}^S} \sum_{i \in \mathcal{I}^d} x_{i,t}^{d,+} - \sum_{d=1}^{m} x_{t-1}^d \leq v_t - v_{t-1}. \tag{15.4}$$

As a stronger limitation, short positions may be used only when a volume decline in t cannot be compensated by maturing tranches:

$$\sum_{d \in \mathcal{D}^S} \sum_{i \in \mathcal{I}^d} x_{i,t}^{d,-} \leq \max\{0, -v_t + v_{t-1}\}. \tag{15.5}$$

Because the income from the replicating portfolio must be sufficient to cover the payments to clients and non-interest expenses α_0 for holding the deposit, we define the earnings surplus that results from transactions up to time t as:

$$x_t^S = \sum_{\tau=0}^{\min\{t,D-1\}} \sum_{\substack{d \in \mathcal{D}^S \ i \in \mathcal{I}^d \\ d > \tau}} \left(r_{i,t-\tau}^{d,+} \cdot x_{i,t-\tau}^{d,+} - r_{i,t-\tau}^{d,-} \cdot x_{i,t-\tau}^{d,-} \right) + cf_{-1}^{t+2} \tag{15.6}$$

$$- (c_t + \alpha_0) \cdot v_t.$$

The first line contains the interest cash flows from positions in the replicating portfolio that have not yet matured in time t. Here, it is assumed that a corresponding fraction of the (yearly) coupon is paid at each point in time; that is, the first line divided by the volume represents the average yield of the replicating portfolio. Note that the first cash flow resulting from a transaction in t is already taken into account in the constraint of the same stage, although it actually accrues one period later. Because D is the longest available maturity, only instruments from transactions after stage $t - D$ contribute to the earnings in the first term of (15.6) according to this definition. The formulation of the optimization model can be extended by a large number of additional constraints for feasible portfolio compositions, implementable transactions, minimum margin (surplus divided by volume), and so on. Since these are not relevant for an understanding of the model, we do not continue the discussion here.

Complete Optimization Model

There is a large controversy among theorists as well as practitioners about appropriate risk measures (for example, see the recent compilation by Szegö 2004). Volatility measured by the variance has often been criticized in this respect since it "penalizes" also above-average returns. As referred to in the section on shortcomings of static replication, the replicating portfolio with the lowest variance might generate a margin that is insufficient to cover the total costs (including non-interest expenses). Therefore, it cannot be seen as the "risk-minimal" portfolio if its implementation leads to a sure loss. Based on these considerations, the suggested objective of the multistage stochastic program for dynamic replication of an NMA is to minimize the expected downside deviation of not meeting the overall costs $(c_t + \alpha_0)$ for all stages $t = 0, \ldots, T$, as a "benchmark" for the earnings:

$$
\min \quad \int_\Omega \sum_{t=0}^{T} x_t^M \, dP(\omega)
$$

$$
\begin{array}{llll}
\text{s.t.} & \text{mandatory constr.} & (1), (2), (6) & t = 0, \ldots, T; \text{a.s.} \\
& \text{optional constr.} & (3), (4), (5) & t = 0, \ldots, T; \text{a.s.} \\
& x_t^M \geq -x_t^S & & t = 0, \ldots, T; \text{a.s.} \\
& 0 \leq x_{i,t}^{d,+} \leq \ell_i^{d,+} & \mathcal{F}_t\text{-meas.} & t = 0, \ldots, T; \forall i \in \mathcal{I}^d; \forall d \in \mathcal{D}^S; \text{a.s.} \\
& 0 \leq x_{i,t}^{d,-} \leq \ell_i^{d,-} & \mathcal{F}_t\text{-meas.} & t = 0, \ldots, T; \forall i \in \mathcal{I}^d; \forall d \in \mathcal{D}^S; \text{a.s.} \\
& x_t^d \in \mathbb{R}; & \mathcal{F}_t\text{-meas.} & t = 0, \ldots, T; \forall d \in \mathcal{D}; \text{a.s.} \\
& x_t^S \in \mathbb{R}; x_t^M \geq 0 & \mathcal{F}_t\text{-meas.} & t = 0, \ldots, T; \text{a.s.}
\end{array}
$$

$$(15.7)$$

The (non-negative) auxiliary variable x_t^M ensures that only a negative surplus at stage t enters the objective and, hence, earnings with a positive sign will not be minimized. All decisions and state variables in the multistage stochastic program (15.7) for $t > 0$ are stochastic since they depend on observations of the random data process ω^t up to time t. Therefore, they are adapted to the filtration $\mathcal{F}_t$ that specifies the information structure; that is, they are taken only with respect to the information available at this time *(nonanticipativity)*. All constraints must hold *almost surely (a.s.)*; that is, for all $\omega \in \Omega$ except for sets with zero probability.

The numerical difficulty in the solution of the optimization problem above lies in the integration of the objective function with respect to the probability measure P. The costs in the objective at each stage $t > 0$ depend on a decision that results from the solution of a multistage stochastic program for the remaining stages $t + 1, \ldots, T$. Because the objective function is not given explicitly, the integration in (15.7) cannot be performed analytically, and numerical methods are required.

EXHIBIT 15.3   Scenario tree (a) and nonanticipativity constraints (b)

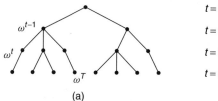

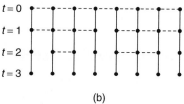

(a)   (b)

A common approach to make a stochastic program computationally tractable is the substitution of the original (continuous) distributions by discrete ones. To this end, the vector stochastic process ω in (Ω, F, P) is approximated by a finite sample of its paths that may be represented conveniently as a *scenario tree* (see Exhibit 15.3 (a)), and each scenario corresponds to a trajectory of the process $\omega^T = (\omega_1, \ldots, \omega_T)$ at the horizon T. The generation of the sample data paths is a crucial step for the solution of the problem and will be discussed separately in a later section. As a result of the approximation, the integration in the objective is replaced by probability weighted summations over the finite number of scenarios, and the constraints are duplicated for each single path. To ensure *nonanticipativity* of decisions, additional constraints link those decision and state variables that share a common history up to a certain node of the scenario tree (see Exhibit 15.3 (b)).

The resulting deterministic equivalent problem (DEQ) is a large-scale linear program that can be solved efficiently with the simplex or interior point methods. Alternatively, structural properties of the DEQ can be exploited by specialized decomposition methods (Birge et al. 1996; Rosa and Ruszczyński 1996; Ruszczyński 1993 and 1997), but a detailed discussion of solution algorithms is beyond the scope of this chapter (see the textbook by Birge and Louveaux (1997) or the compilation by Wallace and Ziemba (2005) for an introduction to currently available algorithms). The fact that the scenario tree grows exponentially with the number of stages leads to a corresponding growth in the size of the optimization problem, which imposes some practical restrictions on the planning horizon T due to the available computational capacities. However, the significant improvement in hardware and algorithmic research in recent years has made stochastic programming problems now solvable within reasonable time on an ordinary personal computer.

MODELS FOR THE EVOLUTION OF RISK FACTORS

In this section, we give some examples of models for the stochastic evolution of the relevant risk factors. The latter are used in combination with the stochastic programming model (15.7) for the management of savings deposits in Switzerland. Note that the methodology itself is not restricted to certain specifications or modeling frameworks. For instance, while we use a term structure model to describe the dynamics of the yield curve, other approaches like econometric models or random fields may also serve well (for example, see James and Webber (2000) for a good introduction to traditional and latest term structure modeling approaches). The deposit rate and volume model can also be replaced easily for retail products with different characteristics.

The Market Rate Model and its Calibration

The market rate model describes the evolution of those interest rates that are relevant for the reinvestment of the deposit position. In an earlier work (Frauendorfer and Schürle 2001), we compared one- and multi-factor versions of the classical term structure models of Vasicek (1977); and Cox, Ingersoll, and Ross (1985) (CIR) where different types of diffusion processes are used to model the state variables. A specific diffusion implies a certain (conditional) distribution of the factors, their number also determines the possible shapes of the yield curve and if interest rates of different maturities can change independently from each other. One-factor models imply a perfect correlation between rates of all maturities, which clearly contradicts empirical observations. Moreover, the set of possible term structures is restricted to uniformly rising, falling or unimodally humped yield curves, while a U-shaped curve can only be represented by multi-factor models.

According to our study, an extension of the Vasicek model with $K = 2$ factors provides the best description for the evolution of Swiss market rates. The dynamics of these two factors are described by the stochastic differential equations:

$$d\eta_{1t} = \kappa_1(\theta - \eta_{1t})\,dt + \sigma_1 dz_{1t} \tag{15.8}$$

$$d\eta_{2t} = -\kappa_2\eta_{2t}\,dt + \sigma_2 dz_{2t}.$$

Both state variables exhibit mean reversion around long-term means of θ and zero, respectively. The parameters $\kappa_i, i = 1, 2$, control the speed at which the factors revert to these levels, while σ_i quantifies the instantaneous volatility of the i-th process. Under the assumption that the two Wiener processes z_1 and z_2 are uncorrelated, and the factors sum up to the instantaneous short rate, the fundamental equation for the price B of a pure discount bond with maturity d at time t has some affine structure:

$$-\ln B(d; \eta_{1t}, \eta_{2t}) = \sum_{i=1}^{2}[-a_i(d) + b_i(d) \cdot \eta_{it}] \tag{15.9}$$

where

$$a_i(d) = \frac{(b_i(d) - d)(\kappa_i\phi_i - \sigma_i/2)}{\kappa_i^2} - \frac{\sigma_i^2 b_i^2(d)}{4\kappa_i}$$

$$b_i(d) = (1 - e^{-\kappa_i\, d})/\kappa_i$$

and $\phi_1 = \kappa_1\theta_1 + \lambda_1\sigma_1, \phi_2 = \lambda_2\sigma_2$. The parameters λ_1 and λ_2 are called the "market prices of risk" with respect to both factors, and control the shape of the term structure. Exhibit 15.4 illustrates that the first factor closely tracks the five-year rate and the second factor the difference between the three-month and the five-year rate. This motivates their interpretation as "level" and "spread" factors.

If the values η_{1t}, η_{2t} at time t are known, then the factors at time $s > t$ are normally distributed with expectations and variances:

$$E(\eta_{1s}|\eta_{1t}) = \theta + (\eta_{1t} - \theta)e^{-\kappa_1(s-t)}, \quad E(\eta_{2s}|\eta_{2t}) = \eta_{2t}e^{-\kappa_2(s-t)} \tag{15.10}$$

$$\text{Var}(\eta_{is}|\eta_{it}) = \frac{\sigma_i^2}{2\kappa_i}(1 - e^{-2\kappa_i(s-t)}), \qquad i = 1, 2. \tag{15.11}$$

Since our intention is a realistic description of the interest rate evolution for a planning horizon of several years, historical data are used for the calibration where the sample period covers a complete cycle; that is, includes a high and low level of rates, normal, and inverse yield curves, and so on. We do not explicitly fit the model to currently observed option prices only as common in derivative valuation because this may result in unstable parameter estimates over time. Obviously, this would not be suitable for scenario generation with a long planning horizon.

The specific estimation method is a modification of the maximum likelihood approach used by Chen and Scott (1993) for the calibration of one- and multi-factor CIR models. Given N observations of each state variable, the sum of logarithms of its conditional density that will enter the log likelihood function is:

$$\mathcal{L}(\eta_{i1},\dots,\eta_{iN}) = \sum_{t=1}^{N} \ln\left[\frac{1}{\sqrt{2\pi V_{it}}} \exp\left(-\frac{(\eta_{it} - E_{it})^2}{2V_{it}}\right)\right], \quad i = 1, 2,$$
$$\tag{15.12}$$

with the expectations and variances

$$E_{it} := E(\eta_{it}|\eta_{i,t-1}), \quad V_{it} := \text{Var}(\eta_{it}|\eta_{i,t-1}), \quad t = 2,\dots,N$$

according to (15.10) and (15.11). The first observation cannot be conditioned on a previous one, therefore the expectations $E_{11} := \theta$, $E_{21} := 0$ and variances $V_{i1} := \sigma_i^2/(2\kappa_i)$, $i = 1, 2$, of the unconditional distribution are used for $t = 1$.

EXHIBIT 15.4   Interpretation of the state variables of the 2F-Vasicek model: The first factor moves parallel to the 5Y rate (top), the second factor is highly correlated with the spread between short and long rates (middle). Therefore, η_1 and η_2 may be seen as "level" and "spread" factors. By construction, their sum $\eta_1 + \eta_2$ is equivalent to the instantaneous short rate of a single-factor model (below)

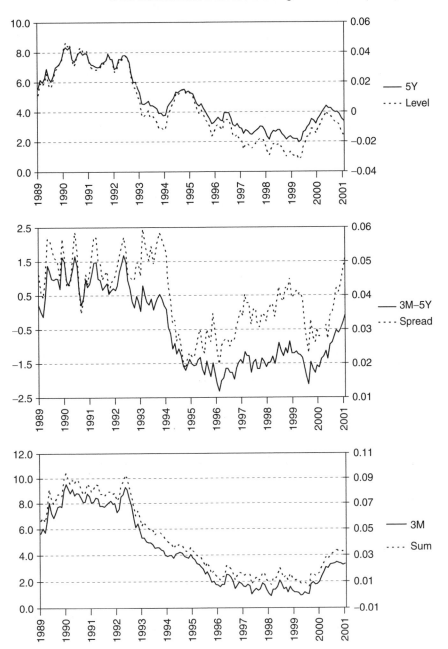

Because the factors η_1 and η_2 are not directly observable, a change of variables is applied to construct the likelihood function from the joint density of logarithms of discount bond prices that are linear functions of the state variables. If there is no market for discount bonds, their (hypothetical) prices can easily be derived from observed par rate curves (Deacon and Derry 1994). To exploit information from different segments of the term structure, discount bonds of four different maturities $d_1, \dots, d_4$ are included in the estimation (for example, the use of two bonds only would make the calibration sensitive to the choice of maturities, see also Pearson and Sun 1994). Since this exceeds the original number of factors, additional stochastic variables φ_1 and φ_2 are introduced that control the measurement errors; that is, the differences between observed discount bond prices and those obtained from the model. Given a historical time series of N observations of the four discount bonds, the model factors and measurement errors at time $t = 1, \dots, N$ can be obtained from the linear system of equations:

$$- \ln B(d_j; \eta_{1t}, \eta_{2t}) = \sum_{i=1}^{2} [-a_i(d_j) + b_i(d_j) \cdot \eta_{it}] + u_{jt}, \quad j = 1, \dots, 4, \quad (15.13)$$

with

$$u_{1t} := 0, \quad u_{2t} := \varphi_{1t}, \quad u_{3t} := -(\varphi_{1t} + \varphi_{2t}), \quad u_{4t} := \varphi_{2t};$$

that is, the price for the shortest maturity is observed without bias and the errors for the remaining maturities sum up to zero. This structure is motivated primarily by tractability in deriving the likelihood function. The evolution of the error variables is modeled by two first-order autoregressive processes:

$$\varphi_{jt} = \rho_j \cdot \varphi_{j,t-1} + \varepsilon_{jt}, \quad t = 1, \dots, N; j = 1, 2,$$

with $\varphi_{10} = \varphi_{20} := 0$. Because all stochastic variables are normally distributed, the log likelihood function for the calibration with discount bond prices becomes:

$$\sum_{i=1}^{2} \mathcal{L}(\eta_{i1}, \dots, \eta_{iN}) - N \ln |J| - N \ln(2\pi) - \frac{N}{2} \ln |\Sigma| - \frac{1}{2} \sum_{t=1}^{N} \varepsilon_t' \Sigma^{-1} \varepsilon_t,$$

$$(15.14)$$

where Σ is the covariance matrix of $\varepsilon_t := (\varepsilon_{1t}, \varepsilon_{2t})'$. The matrix J is the Jacobian of the linear transformation from latent factors η_{1t}, η_{2t} to observed price logarithms $[-\ln P(d_j; \eta_{1t}, \eta_{2t})]$ due to the change of variables (Intriligator et al. 1996, p. 85), and the elements of J are functions of $b_i(d_j)$.

The maximum of function (15.14) can be found using standard algorithms for non-linear optimization. Because the likelihood function is extremely flat, analytical derivatives must be exploited. We use the BFGS-algorithm in the implementation of Press et al. (1992), combined with an extensive grid search over the parameter space for promising starting values. Typically, this requires some minutes on a personal computer for sample periods of 120 months and more. Note that other specifications of the stochastic processes than (15.8) may increase the numerical efforts significantly. For example, the densities in a CIR-type model are non-central χ^2, which would require complex calculations of modified Bessel functions of the first kind and their derivatives with respect to the (non-integer) order.

Evolution of Deposit Rate and Volume

The client rate represents the "benchmark" for the surplus constraint (15.6) in the optimization model and has direct impact on the composition of the replicating portfolio. Therefore, particular attention must be paid to the specification of its evolution and dependency on interest rates. In the case of Swiss savings accounts, one can observe that the deposit rate remains constant for longer time periods. After larger changes in the level of market rates, it is then adjusted by the bank with some delay at discrete increments of 25 or 50 bps. The reason for these "frictions" are the associated costs (marketing, operational, and so on) for such corrections.

Often an asymmetric response to market rate changes can be observed; that is, deposit rates move more rapidly when market rates drop than when they rise (see Exhibit 15.5 on page 346). Moreover, the deposit rate does not exceed a certain level even if market rates are still increasing. This results from the political cap on variable mortgage rates in Switzerland, since both are typically adjusted at the same pace. As a consequence, ordinary least square regression cannot be used for the estimation. The fact that the dependent variable remains unchanged while market rates fluctuate without restriction contradicts the assumption of a normally distributed error term and will lead to biased and inconsistent estimators (see Judge et al. 1987, p. 770).

We propose to use the previous value of the deposit rate as well as the current and past observations of the level factor as explanatory variables for the model. Assume that the possible values for the (discrete) deposit rate increments are given by $\delta_0 < \ldots < \delta_n$ (including the value 0 for an unchanged rate). The *actual* change at time t depends on the outcome of a (latent) control variable:

$$c_t^* = \beta_0 c_{t-1} + \beta_1 \eta_{1t} + \ldots + \beta_{m+1} \eta_{1,t-m} \tag{15.15}$$

and follows the rule:

$$
\Delta c_t = \begin{cases}
\delta_0 & \text{if } c_t^* \leq \gamma_1 \\
\delta_1 & \text{if } \gamma_1 < c_t^* \leq \gamma_2 \\
\vdots & \\
\delta_{1-1} & \text{if } \gamma_{n-1} < c_t^* \leq \gamma_n \\
\delta_n & \text{if } \gamma_n < c_t^*,
\end{cases}
\tag{15.16}
$$

where $\gamma_1 < \ldots < \gamma_n$ represent some threshold values. Note that an asymmetric adjustment of the deposit rate is reflected by different thresholds for positive and negative increments of the same size.

The deposit rate model given by (15.15) and (15.16) can be calibrated as follows. For simplicity, define the vectors:

$$
\beta := (\beta_0, \ldots, \beta_{m+1})' \quad \text{and} \quad \psi_t := (c_{t-1}, \eta_{1t}, \ldots, \eta_{1,t-m})'.
$$

Let $\epsilon_t := c_t^* - \beta' \psi_t$ be the residuum for the control variable with standard deviation σ_ϵ. Then, parameter estimates are obtained by maximizing the likelihood function:

$$
\sum_{t=1}^{N} \left\{ I_0(\Delta c_t) \cdot \ln \Phi \left(\frac{\gamma_1 - \beta' \psi_t}{\sigma_\epsilon} \right) + \right.
$$

$$
I_1(\Delta c_t) \cdot \ln \left[\Phi \left(\frac{\gamma_2 - \beta' \psi_t}{\sigma_\epsilon} \right) - \Phi \left(\frac{\gamma_1 - \beta' \psi_t}{\sigma_\epsilon} \right) \right] + \ldots +
$$

$$
I_{n-1}(\Delta c_t) \cdot \ln \left[\Phi \left(\frac{\gamma_n - \beta' \psi_t}{\sigma_\epsilon} \right) - \Phi \left(\frac{\gamma_{n-1} - \beta' \psi_t}{\sigma_\epsilon} \right) \right] +
$$

$$
\left. I_n(\Delta c_t) \cdot \ln \left[1 - \Phi \left(\frac{\gamma_n - \beta' \psi_t}{\sigma_\epsilon} \right) \right] \right\}
\tag{15.17}
$$

EXHIBIT 15.5   The deposit rate often exhibits a cap or asymmetric adjustments

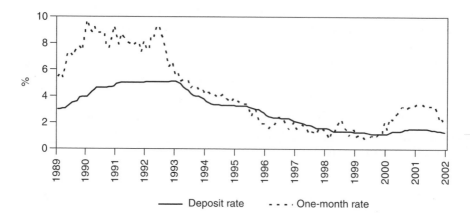

EXHIBIT 15.6 Aggregated savings volume (mio CHF or million swiss francs) of all banks in Switzerland compared to the one-month rate

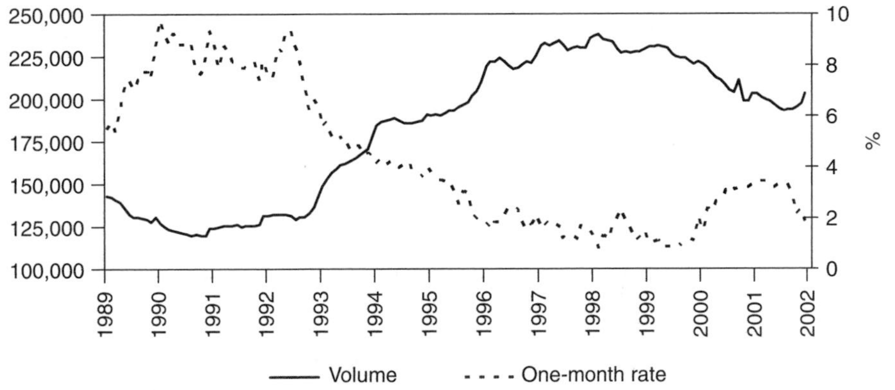

—— Volume   · · · · One-month rate

Source: reports of the Swiss National Bank

where Φ is the standard normal cumulative distribution function and the indicator function $I_i(\Delta c_t)$ takes on value 1 if $\Delta c_t = \delta_i$ and 0 otherwise. The optimum of the likelihood function (15.17) can be found; for example, by Newton's method.

A dependency on interest rates (or the relevant stochastic factors that drive the evolution of the term structure, respectively) must also be taken into account in a volume model. Exhibit 15.6 illustrates that the volume of savings deposits is low when market rates are above average and vice versa as clients transfer money from or to other investment opportunities. Therefore, we model relative changes in the deposit volume v_t over time by:

$$\ln v_t = \ln v_{t-1} + e_0 + e_1 t + e_2 \eta_{1t} + e_3 \eta_{2t} + \xi_t. \qquad (15.18)$$

The constant e_0 and the time component $e_1 t$ reflect that the total deposit volume exhibits a positive trend. The factors η_1 and η_2 of the term structure model are included as explanatory variables to reflect the discussed dependency on market rates. An additional stochastic factor, ξ, which is uncorrelated with the market rate model factors takes into account that the latter do not fully explain the observed evolution of the balance. Given a time series of η_1 and η_2 from the calibration of the term structure model factors, equation 15.18 can easily be estimated by ordinary least squares regression. The volatility σ_ξ of the residuum factor ξ is then derived from the standard error.

SCENARIO GENERATION

The models introduced in the previous section imply that the stochastic factors $\omega_t := (\eta_{1t}, \eta_{2t}, \xi_t)$ at $t = 1, \ldots, T$ are multivariate normally distributed with conditional expectation:

$$
\mu(\omega_t | \omega^{t-1}) = \begin{pmatrix} \theta + (\eta_{1,t-1} - \theta) \cdot e^{-\kappa_1 \cdot h} \\ \eta_{2,t-1} \cdot e^{-\kappa_2 \cdot h} \\ 0 \end{pmatrix} \tag{15.19}
$$

and covariance matrix

$$
\Sigma(\omega_t | \omega^{t-1}) = \begin{pmatrix} \frac{\sigma_1^2}{2\kappa_1}(1 - e^{-2\kappa_1 \cdot h}) & 0 & 0 \\ 0 & \frac{\sigma_2^2}{2\kappa_2}(1 - e^{-2\kappa_2 \cdot h}) & 0 \\ 0 & 0 & \sigma_\xi^2 \end{pmatrix}. \tag{15.20}
$$

The parameter h is the period length between two successive stages of the multiperiod optimization problem (15.7). We have already motivated at the end of the section on the complete optimization model that these continuous distributions must be approximated by discrete ones to make the multistage program computationally tractable. Moreover, the approximation is a critical element for the solution with respect to accuracy and robustness. Loosely speaking, the substitution of the complete universe of possible outcomes by a relatively small sample should lead to the same solution as it would be in the (non-tractable) case of the original distributions. Therefore, an adequate representation of the underlying random data is of utmost importance.

At first glance, Monte Carlo simulation might be an obvious approach to generate finite sets of samples of the given distributions. Unfortunately, we must inevitably draw large numbers of points to obtain a reasonable accuracy (in the sense of small confidence intervals and robustness of the solution with respect to a "contamination" of the sample; for example, by using a different initial value for the random number generator). While a large set of samples can be acceptable for two-stage problems, the number of required scenarios would become too large for a multistage stochastic program due to the exponential growth in problem size with the number of stages. Therefore, any Monte Carlo-based sampling procedure must be combined with a variance reduction technique like importance sampling (Dantzig and Infanger 1993) for example.

A special variant of the latter that appears promising for multistage stochastic programming problems uses the *expected value of perfect information* (EVPI) (Dempster 1981) to identify scenarios with higher impact on the solution. The EVPI describes the loss in the objective value due to uncertainty and thus measures the amount a decision-maker would pay in return for complete information. Local EVPIs are calculated for each node of the scenario tree from the difference in the objective values of the original solution and a corresponding problem where the nonanticipativity constraints for this node and all of its successors are relaxed. Starting with a tree generated by Monte Carlo, scenarios are then added at nodes with a large EVPI or possibly removed where the value is close to zero. By this means, a sequence of scenario trees is generated and corresponding (large-scale) optimization problems are solved until a stopping criterion is fulfilled.

An alternative to sampling procedures, which provide probabilistic error bounds only, are bound-based approximations. As an example, the *barycentric approximation* proposed by Frauendorfer (1994 and 1996) deliberately constructs the scenario trees so that exact upper and lower bounds to the stochastic program with the original distributions are derived. The analysis of the discretization error – defined as the difference between the two bounds – identifies those nodes where the approximation must be improved by generating additional scenarios until the accuracy is sufficient. Again, this might require the solution of a sequence of increasingly larger optimization problems, although experience from our earlier model for income maximization of variable products (Frauendorfer and Schürle 2003 and 2005) where we used this technique implies that the iteration can already be stopped after calculation of the first lower and upper bound. A drawback is that the method requires certain structural properties of the stochastic processes and the formulation of the optimization problem such as deterministic left-hand-sides of the constraints, which are not given for the dynamic replication model (15.7).

For practical reasons, a robust solution should preferably already be available after the solution of a single optimization problem to reduce the overall computation time. Thus the initial scenario tree must be "accurate enough" to provide such a result. Another approach first suggested by Høyland and Wallace (2001) and Dupacová et al. (2000) builds the tree in a way so that some statistical properties of the data process are preserved; for example, expectations, variances, correlations (also over time), and so on. This is achieved by matching the moments of the discrete approximated distributions to those of the original (continuous) ones.

As an illustration, consider a random variable ω for which values of certain moments or expectations of continuous functions $\mu_k = \int_\Omega u_k(\omega)dP, k = 1, \ldots, m$, are given. Then, a modest number of sample points ω^s with nonnegative probabilities $p_s, s = 1, \ldots, S$, is determined so that the probabilities sum up to one and the moment values are matched as well as possible. To this end, a measure of distance, for example the square norm, is minimized with the outcomes and probabilities as decision variables where different weights, $\gamma_k, k = 1, \ldots, m$, may be used to account for the relevance of the k-th moment:

$$\min \sum_{k=1}^{m} \gamma_k \left(\sum_{s=1}^{S} p_s u_k(\omega^s) - \mu_k \right)^2 \qquad (15.21)$$

subject to

$$\sum_{s=1}^{S} p_s = 1,$$

$$p_s \geq 0, \qquad s = 1, \ldots, S.$$

Kouwenberg (2001) presents a case study where this type of approach is compared with Monte Carlo sampling: His stochastic programming model with randomly sampled scenario trees performs poorly, and the solutions exhibit extremely large buying and selling amounts. Fitting the tree to the expectations and covariances of the original distributions stabilizes the optimal decisions and greatly improves the performance that underlines the importance of choosing an appropriate scenario generation method.

However, the optimization problem (15.21) is highly non-linear, and its solution in each node of the scenario tree can make the generation of the latter extremely time-consuming. Some authors try to overcome this obstacle by restricting themselves to the first two moments only (Kouwenberg 2001), or by using heuristics to identify a local optimum as a "sufficiently good" solution of the moment matching problem (Høyland and Wallace 2001; Høyland et al. 2001).

As an alternative, a representative selection of scenarios may be derived by a discrete distribution that converges to the desired one by refinements. Siede (2000) approximates the multivariate normal distributions defined by (15.19) and (15.20) by a multinomial distribution that reveals the same expectations and covariance matrix after a transformation. This procedure can roughly be outlined as follows (for a k-dimensional normal distribution). Consider a multinomial distribution $\mathcal{N}$ with parameters:

$$(l; \underbrace{\frac{1}{k+1}, \ldots, \frac{1}{k+1}}_{k+1}),$$

that is, the probability distribution of a $(k + 1)$-dimensional random vector $(X_0, \ldots, X_k)$ with nonnegative integer elements that satisfies $X_0 + \ldots + X_k = l$. In the first step, an orthogonal transformation $\mathcal{T}$ is applied to the support of $\mathcal{N}$, which will remove the correlations between the components and sets the expectations $\mathrm{E}(\mathcal{T} \cdot n_i), n_i \in \mathcal{N}$, for $i = 1, \ldots, k$ to zero. A second transformation "stretches" the variances to one. The first two moments are now equivalent to those of a standard normal distribution. Denote the resulting random vector by $y \in \mathbb{R}^k$. The distribution of y converges to the k-dimensional standard normal distribution for $l \to \infty$. Thus by the transformation

$$\hat{y} := \mu + Ly$$

EXHIBIT 15.7 Impact of the parameter *l* on the sample size

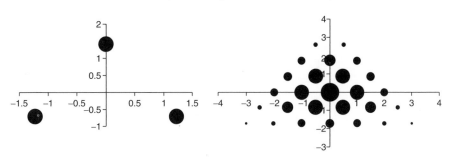

a random variable $\hat{y}$ can be constructed with expectation μ and covariance matrix $\Sigma = LL'$ (that is, L is the Cholesky decomposition of Σ). It converges for $l \to \infty$ to the k-dimensional multivariate normal distribution with expectation μ and covariance matrix Σ.

As a consequence, for a given multivariate normal distribution a discrete approximation $y(n)$ can be constructed that is based on the multinomial distribution and has $(l+1) \cdot \ldots \cdot (l+k)/k!$ sample points. The influence of l on sample size is illustrated in Exhibit 15.7 for the approximation of a two-dimensional standard normal distribution. Note the different scaling of the left ($l = 1$) and right ($l = 6$) diagram: the larger the parameter, the more extreme (but less likely) scenarios are generated. The probability of a point is represented by its diameter.

The advantage of this approach is that the time required for the generation of the scenario tree becomes negligibly short. We also compared discretizations by multinomial distributions with approximations from exact bounds for benchmark problems that satisfy the properties required for the latter. The obtained solution was practically identical to those derived from the bounded problems with low discretization error after some refinement iterations. Thus we can be confident that the approximation is sufficiently accurate.

APPLICATION TO SAVINGS DEPOSITS

The ability of the multistage stochastic programming model (15.7) to replicate a NMA position was tested in a case study and compared to the "conventional" static approach. Client rate and volume data of a real Swiss savings deposit account were provided by a bank, the investigation started in January 1989 and ended in December 2001. This case study period is characterized by an increase in interest rates shortly after the beginning. The yield curve was inverse on a high level during the first half of the 1990s, then interest rates dropped sharply while the volume increased for most of the remaining time. The evolution of the relevant interest rates, deposit rate, and volume for the case study period is shown in Exhibit 15.8 on page 352.

EXHIBIT 15.8   Market rates, client rate and volume used as input for the case study

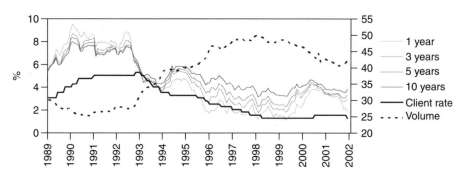

Money market instruments and swaps with maturities of one, two, three, four, five, seven and 10 years were allowed for the composition of the replicating portfolio. Because the Swiss inter-bank market exhibits a limited liquidity in particular at the long end of the yield curve, the spreads in each maturity increase with the transaction volume. The bid/ask spreads for maturities up to five years were set to 10 bps for initial tranches of 200 million Francs (except five bps for the maturity one year) and increased by one bp for each additional tranche of 100 million. In addition, absolute upper limits of 200 million were applied to the amounts in seven and ten years. Short sales (squaring positions) were only permitted if a drop in volume could not be compensated by maturing tranches. The objective of the optimization model was to minimize the downside of not achieving a margin of 200 bps that is considered as a reasonable target for the income. The planning horizon was set to seven years (one stage equals one year).

The static benchmark strategy was also calculated by the bank using a tracking error minimization over historical data and was frequently readjusted. The rule applied to the allocation of new positions worked as follows: maturing tranches were always reinvested at their original maturity. Any change in volume is invested or financed at fixed weights, where negative amounts in case of a volume drop are set against maturing tranches. The initial portfolio for the investigation of both approaches was constructed under the assumption that a static mix of two-year and five-year tranches had been applied before; that is, for a total volume of 30 billion an amount of 875 million matures in each of the first 24 months and 250 million in each of the following 36 months.

Starting with the first observations of market rates, deposit rate and volume in January 1989, an optimal investment policy for the maturing 875 million was obtained from the optimization model and implemented by an update of the positions in the existing portfolio. This new portfolio was then used for the next optimization in February, together with the new interest rate curve, a new deposit rate and volume, and so on. After processing the complete 13-year period, the resulting margins defined

EXHIBIT 15.9 Margin evolution: Dynamic (solid) vs static replication (dashed)

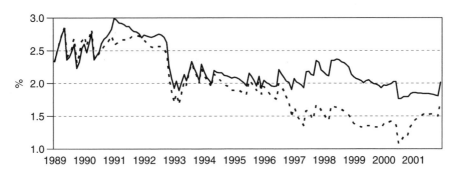

as the income from the replicating portfolio minus the client rate were calculated for each month.

The corresponding evolutions for both approaches are shown in Exhibit 15.9. It can be seen that the dynamically managed portfolio mostly outperforms the static one. The fact that there is only a small difference between both methods at the beginning of the study can be attributed to the following reasons. First, it took five years until the last tranche from the initial portfolio matured; that is, a large portion of the replicating portfolio stems from old positions during the first years. Second, the market environment at the beginning was also "comfortable" for the static approach because the cap on the deposit rate allowed for large margins with any possible strategy. After the drop in market rates, the margin of the static portfolio reduces continually. On the other hand, the stochastic programming model achieves the specified target well for the remaining time.

Exhibit 15.10 on page 354 summarizes the relevant key data. Over the entire 13-year period, the average margin could be improved by 30 bps at a lower standard deviation using the dynamic replication. This shows that the latter can manage the tradeoff between risk and return more efficiently. Since the volatility of the margin is reduced, the portfolio obtained from the stochastic optimization model may be viewed as the better replication of the uncertain position. For a better assessment of the given performance numbers, "difference to 3M portfolio" relates to the additional income in comparison with a portfolio of three continuously renewed three-month tranches.

Exhibit 15.11 on page 354 displays the composition of both portfolios over time. The stochastic programming model also uses to some extent longer maturities that are not considered by the static replication. However, a "dynamic management" does not result in larger fluctuations of the time buckets than a static rule as one might suspect. The dynamic portfolio exhibits a higher duration, indicating that the "true" maturity of the savings deposit position is approximately 0.5 years longer than implied by the static replication. One might argue that the higher margin results from an extension of the duration only. An analysis of potential static portfolios (with constant weights), where the average maturity was

EXHIBIT 15.10   Case study results (including transaction costs)

	Dynamic	Static
Mean margin	2.23%	1.93%
Standard deviation	0.32%	0.49%
Difference to 3M portfolio	92 bps	62 bps
Avg. portfolio maturity	2.37 yrs	1.81 yrs
No. financing activities	14	26

EXHIBIT 15.11   Portfolio compositions over time: Static (top) vs dynamic (below)

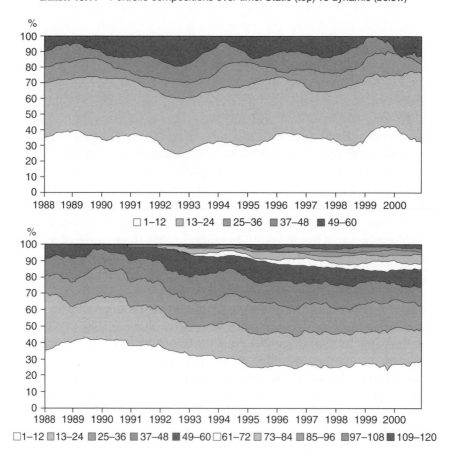

extended by half a year reveals that this would provide at most a gain of 10 bps at a larger volatility. Therefore, we can conclude that the extended margin here can mainly be attributed to the added value of dynamic management.

Finally, the number of financing activities refers to cases where a drop in volume could not be compensated by maturing tranches and, thus, existing positions had to be squared. Despite the longer duration, this occurs less frequently with the dynamic model than in the static approach. This can be explained by the fact that the volume risk is reflected more

EXHIBIT 15.12   Impact of the margin target on the optimal solution. The expected margins (*y*-axis) and their standard deviation (*x*-axis) are calculated from the replicating portfolios along the paths of the scenario tree

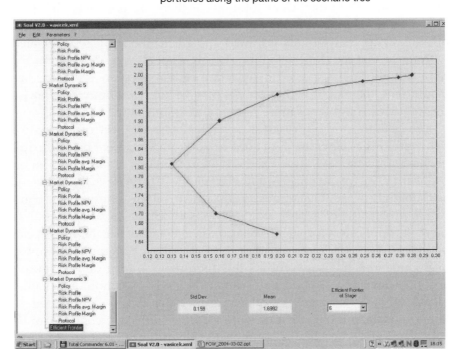

appropriately because the corresponding stochastic model also takes the correlations with interest rates into account.

CONCLUSION

The problem of calculating a replicating portfolio for non-maturing account (NMA) positions was formulated as a multistage stochastic program that can be solved by standard optimization algorithms. As opposed to the conventional approach where the portfolio weights are adjusted once by minimizing the tracking error over a historical sample period, the model is applied anytime when positions must be reinvested or financed due to maturing tranches or a change in volume. Instead of a single historical scenario, the decision about the allocation of new tranches is made with respect to a large set of scenarios for the relevant risk factors. Furthermore, future transactions subject to various constraints and their impact on today's portfolio are also taken into account.

Compared to the static approach, the dynamic replicating portfolio turned out to be more efficient since it provides a higher margin at reduced volatility. The selection of a different margin target in the downside minimization certainly has some impact on the realized earnings and volatility. In this sense, the model also allows for an analysis and optimization of the tradeoff between risk and return. Exhibit 15.12 shows the impact of different targets on the expected margins that are calculated from the portfolios along each path of the scenario tree. Targets that are too low can lead to inefficient solutions as there are portfolios that provide a higher margin at lower volatility. A decision-maker with the goal of minimizing margin volatility will implement the strategy associated with the lowest standard deviation (which is not always obtained for the same target). If the expected margin of a certain decision is regarded as insufficient, the risk of higher targets may be analyzed *ex ante*. Likewise the influence of tighter or more relaxed constraints may be assessed.

The optimization approach is very flexible in respect of alternative risk measures as objective functions or additional restrictions. Although we have implemented some alternative formulations of the optimization problem (15.7), we did not give any examples here because such extensions are straightforward. Due to the fact that the resulting deterministic equivalent problem is of a large size (all decision variables and constraints must be duplicated for each scenario), it is beneficial if the model can be formulated as a *linear* or other type of convex program. A number of popular risk measures fulfills this requirement; for example, mean-absolute deviation (Konno and Yamazaki 1991) or conditional value-at-risk (CVaR) (Rockafellar and Uryasev 2002) can be formulated as linear models, minimization of variance in a multistage context can be solved efficiently by suitable optimization algorithms (Steinbach 2001), or approximated by piecewise linear functions (Konno and Suzuki 1992). On the other hand, using VaR as an objective leads to nonconvex optimization problems (Gaivoronski and Pflug 2005) that are extremely hard to solve.

Analogously, the multistage stochastic programming approach is not restricted to certain models for the evolution of risk factors. Arbitrary specifications can be chosen to describe the adjustment of client rates or dependency of the volume on interest rates to take certain characteristics of the relevant product into account. The models for interest rates, client rate, and volume are estimated individually and, hence, different sample periods can be used for each of them. This can be useful for products where only short time series of the bank-specific client rate and/or volume are available, while long interest rate histories for the calibration of the term structure model can be easily obtained from public sources. According to our experience with the factor model described in the market rate model section, the data should cover at least one interest cycle to ensure that the parameter for the mean reversion level is not biased by the selection of a specific sample period.

The dynamic optimization framework represents also a substantial difference to the stochastic models reviewed in the relevant section above. The latter primarily calculate the value of an NMA position, a replicating portfolio can then be derived as the combination of instruments with known prices that have similar characteristics; that is, sensitivity with respect to changes in the *current* yield curve. Through a consideration of *future* transactions, the multistage stochastic programming model takes possible corrections of the initial hedge into account. One can expect that this helps reduce (costly) transactions at later points in time and might also lead to a more efficient replication of the NMA. However, a comparison of our stochastic programming model with the contributions from the financial literature remains subject to further research.

BIBLIOGRAPHY

Basel Committee on Banking Supervision (2004). *Principles for the Management and Supervision of Interest Rate Risk*. Bank for International Settlements, Basel.

Birge, J.R., Donohue, C.J., Holmes, D.F., and Svintsitski, O.G. (1996). "A Parallel Implementation of the Nested Decomposition Algorithm for Multistage Stochastic Linear Programs," *Mathematical Programming*, 75, pp. 327–52.

Birge, J.R. and Louveaux, F. (1997), *Introduction to Stochastic Programming*, Springer, New York.

Bühler, A. (2000). "Modellierung von Bodensatzprodukten," *Schweizer Bank* 15, pp. 44–5.

Cox, J.C., Ingersoll, J.E., and Ross, S.A. (1985). "A Theory of the Term Structure of Interest Rates," *Econometrica*, 53, pp. 385–407.

Carino, D.R., Kent, T., Myers, D.H., Stacy, C., Sylvanus, M., Turner, A.L., Watanabe, K., and Ziemba, W.T. (1994). "The Russell–Yasuda Kasai Model: An Asset/Liability Model for a Japanese Insurance Company Using Multistage Stochastic Programming," *Interfaces*, 24, pp. 29–49.

Chen, R.-R. and Scott, L. (1993). "Maximum Likelihood Estimation for a Multifactor Equilibrium Model of the Term Structure of Interest Rates," *Journal of Fixed Income*, 3, pp. 14–31.

Consiglio, A. and Zenios, S.A. (2001). "Integrated Simulation and Optimization Models for Tracking International Fixed Income Indices," *Mathematical Programming (Ser. B)*, 89, pp. 311–39.

Dantzig, G.B. and Infanger, G. (1993). "Multi-stage Stochastic Linear Programs for Portfolio Optimization," *Annals of Operations Research*, 45, pp. 59–76.

Deacon, M. and Derry, A. (1994). *Estimating the Term Structure of Interest Rates*, Working paper, Bank of England, London.

Dempster, M.A.H. (1981). "The Expected Value of Perfect Information in the Optimal Evolution of Stochastic Problems," in M. Arato, D. Vermes, and A.V. Balakrishnan, eds: *Stochastic Differential Systems*, Springer (Lecture Notes in Information and Control Vol. 36), Berlin, pp. 25–40.

Dupacová, J., Consigli, G., and Wallace, S.W. (2000). "Scenarios for Multistage Stochastic Programs," *Annals of Operations Research*, 100, pp. 25–53.

Fiedler, R., Frauendorfer, K., and Schürle, M. (2004). "Dynamic Management of Core Deposits," *Banking and Finance*, 3, pp. 19–23.

Fleten, S.-E., Høyland, K., and Wallace, S.W. (2002). "The Performance of Stochastic Dynamic and Fixed Mix Portfolio Models," *European Journal of Operational Research*, 140, pp. 37–49.

Forrest, B., Frauendorfer, K., and Schürle, M. (1998). "A Stochastic Optimization Model for the Investment of Savings Account Deposits," in P. Kischka,

H.-W. Lorenz, U. Derigs, W. Domschke, P. Kleinschmidt, and R. Möhring, eds: *Operations Research Proceedings 1997*, Springer, Berlin, pp. 382–7.

Frauendorfer, K. (1994). "Multistage Stochastic Programming: Error Analysis for the Convex Case," *Mathematical Methods of Operations Research*, 39, pp. 93–122.

Frauendorfer, K. (1996). "Barycentric Scenario Trees in Convex Multistage Stochastic Programming. *Mathematical Programming (Ser. B)*, 75, pp. 277–93.

Frauendorfer, K. and Schürle, M. (2001). "Term Structure Models in Multistage Stochastic Programming: Estimation and Approximation," *Annals of Operations Research*, 100, pp. 189–209.

Frauendorfer, K. and Schürle, M. (2003). "Management of Non-maturing Deposits by Multistage Stochastic Programming," *European Journal of Operational Research*, 151, pp. 602–16.

Frauendorfer, K. and Schürle, M. (2005). "Refinancing Mortgages in Switzerland," in S.W. Wallace and W.T. Ziemba, eds: *Applications of Stochastic Programming*, MPS-SIAM Series in Optimization, Philadelphia, pp. 445–69.

Gaivoronski, A.A. and Pflug, G. (2005). "Value at Risk in Portfolio Optimization: Properties and Computational Approach," *Journal of Risk*, 7, pp. 1–31.

Heath, D., Jarrow, R., and Morton, A. (1992). "Bond Pricing and the Term Structure of Interest Rates: A New Methodology for Contingent Claims Valuation," *Econometrica*, 60, pp. 77–105.

Heitmann, F. and Trautmann, S. (1995). *Gaussian Multi-factor Interest Rate Models: Theory, Estimation, and Implications for Option Pricing*, Working paper, Johannes Gutenberg University Mainz.

Høyland, K., Kaut, M., and Wallace, S.W. (2001). "A Heuristic for Moment-matching Scenario Generation," *Computational Optimization and Applications*, 24, pp. 169–85.

Høyland, K. and Wallace, S.W. (2001). "Generating Scenario Trees for Multistage Decision Problems," *Management Science*, 47, pp. 295–307.

Hutchison, D.E. and Pennacchi, G.G. (1996). "Measuring Rents and Interest Rate Risk in Imperfect Financial Markets: The Case of Retail Bank Deposits," *Journal of Financial and Quantitative Analysis*, 31, pp. 399–417.

Intriligator, M.D., Bodkin, R.G., and Hsiao, C. (1996). *Econometric Models, Techniques, and Applications*, Prentice-Hall, Upper Saddle River, NJ.

James, J. and Webber, N. (2000). *Interest Rate Modelling*, Wiley, Chichester.

Janosi, T., Jarrow ,R., and Zullo, F. (1999). "An Empirical Analysis of the Jarrow–van Deventer Model for Valuing Non-maturity Demand Deposits," *Journal of Derivatives*, 7, pp. 8–31.

Jarrow, R.A. and van Deventer, D.R. (1998). "The Arbitrage-free Valuation and Hedging of Demand Deposits and Credit Card Loans," *Journal of Banking and Finance*, 22, pp. 249–72.

Judge, G.G., Hill, R.C., Griffiths, W., Lütkepohl, H., and Lee, T.-C. (1987). *Introduction to the Theory and Practice of Econometrics*, Wiley, New York.

Kalkbrener, M. and Willing, J. (2004). "Risk Management of Non-maturing Liabilities," *Journal of Banking and Finance*, 28, pp. 1547–68.

Konno, H. and Suzuki, K. (1992). "A Fast Algorithm for Solving Large Scale Mean-variance Models by Compact Factorization of Covariance Matrices," *Journal of the Operations Research Society of Japan*, 35, pp. 93–104.

Konno, H. and Yamazaki, H. (1991). "Mean-absolute Deviation Portfolio Optimization Model and its Application to Tokyo Stock Market," *Management Science*, 37, pp. 519–31.

Kouwenberg, R. (2001). "Scenario Generation and Stochastic Programming Models for Asset and Liability Management," *European Journal of Operational Research*, 134, pp. 279–92.

Laurent, M.-P. (2004). *Non-maturity Deposits with a Fidelity Premium*, Working paper, Solvay Business School, Université Libre de Bruxelles.

O'Brien, J.M. (2000). *Estimating the Value and Interest Rate Risk of Interest-bearing Transactions Deposits*, Board of Governors of the Federal Reserve System, Washington D.C.

Pearson ,N.D. and Sun, T.-S. (1994). "Exploiting the Conditional Density in Estimating the Term Structure: An Application of the Cox, Ingersoll, and Ross Model, *Journal of Finance*, 49, pp. 1279–304.

Press, W.H., Teukolsky, S.A., Vetterling, W.T., and Flannery, B.P. (1992). *Numerical Recipes in C* (2nd ed.), Cambridge University Press, Cambridge.

Rockafellar, R.T. and Uryasev, S., (2002). "Conditional Value-at-Risk for General Loss Distributions," *Journal of Banking and Finance*, 26, pp. 1443–71.

Rosa, C.H. and Ruszczyński, A. (1996). "On Augmented Lagrangian Decomposition Methods for Multistage Stochastic Programs," *Annals of Operations Research*, 64, pp. 289–309.

Ruszczyński, A. (1993). "Parallel Decomposition of Multistage Stochastic Programming Problems," *Mathematical Programming*, 58, pp. 201–28.

Ruszczyński, A. (1997). "Decomposition Methods in Stochastic Programming," *Mathematical Programming*, 79, pp. 333–53.

Selvaggio, R. (1996). "Using the OAS Methodology to Value and Hedge Commercial Bank Retail Demand Deposit Premiums," in F. Fabozzi and A. Konishi, eds: *The Handbook of Asset/Liability Management*, Irwin, Boston, pp. 363–73.

Siede, H. (2000). *Multi-period Portfolio Optimization*, PhD thesis, University of St. Gallen.

Steinbach, M. (2001). "Markowitz Revisited: Mean-variance Models in Financial Portfolio Analysis," *SIAM Review*, 43, pp. 31–85.

Szegö, G., ed. (2004). *Risk Measures for the 21st Century*, Wiley, New York.

Wallace, S.W. and Ziemba, W.T., eds (2005). *Applications of Stochastic Programming*, MPS-SIAM Series on Optimization, Philadelphia.

Vasicek, O. (1977). "An Equilibrium Characterization of the Term Structure," *Journal of Financial Economics*, 5, pp. 177–88.

CHAPTER 16

Liquidity Risk and Classical Option Pricing Theory

Robert A. Jarrow[1]

T he purpose of this chapter is to review the recent derivatives security research involving liquidity risk and to summarize its implications for practical risk management. The literature supports three general conclusions. The first is that the classical option price is "on average" true, even given liquidity risk. Second, it is well known that although the classical (theoretical) option hedge cannot be applied as theory prescribes, its discrete approximations often provide reasonable approximations. These discrete approximations are also consistent with upward-sloping demand curves. And, third, risk management measures, like VaR, are biased low due to the exclusion of liquidity risk.

INTRODUCTION

This chapter studies liquidity risk and its relation to classical option pricing theory for practical risk management applications. Classical option pricing theory is formulated under two simplifying assumptions. One assumption is that markets are frictionless and the second assumption is that markets are competitive. A frictionless market is one where there are no transactions costs, no bid/ask spreads, no taxes, and no restrictions on trades or trading strategies. For example, one can trade infinitesimal amounts of a security, continuously, for as long or as short a time interval as one wishes. A competitive market is one where the available stock price quote is good for any sized purchase or sale; alternatively stated, there is no quantity impact on the price received/paid for a trade. Both assumptions are idealizations and not satisfied in reality. Both assumptions are necessary for classical option pricing theory; for example, the Black–Scholes option pricing model. The question arises: how does classical option pricing theory change when these two simplifying assumptions are relaxed? The purpose of this chapter is to answer this question, by summarizing my research that relaxes these two assumptions, see Jarrow (1992 and 1994); Çetin et al. (2004); Çetin et al. (forthcoming); and Jarrow and Protter (2005a and forthcoming). The relaxation of these two assumptions is called liquidity risk.

Alternatively stated, liquidity risk is that increased volatility that arises when trading or hedging securities due to the size of the transaction itself. When markets are calm and the transaction size is small, liquidity risk is small. In contrast, when markets are experiencing a crisis or the transaction size is significant, liquidity risk is large. This quantity impact on price can be due to asymmetric information (see Kyle 1985; Glosten and Milgrom 1985) or an imbalance in demand/inventory (see Grossman and Miller 1988). It implies that demand curves for securities are upward sloping and not horizontal, as in classical option pricing theory. But, classical option pricing theory has been successfully used in risk management for over 20 years (see Jarrow 1999). In light of this success, is there any reason to modify classical option pricing theory? The answer is yes! Although successfully employed in some asset classes that trade in liquid markets (for example, equity, foreign currencies and interest rates), it works less well in others (for example, fixed-income securities and commercial loans). Understanding the changes to the classical theory due to the relaxation of this structure will enable more accurate pricing and hedging of derivative securities and more precise risk management.

Based on my research, there are three broad conclusions that one can draw with respect to liquidity risk and classical option pricing theory. The first is that the classical option price is "on average" true, even given liquidity risk. It is "on average" because the classical price lies between the buying and selling prices of an option in a world with liquidity risk. In some sense, the classical option price is the mid-market price. Second, it is well known that although the classical (theoretical) hedge[2] cannot be applied as theory prescribes, its discrete approximations often provide reasonable approximations (see Jarrow and Turnbull 2000). These discrete approximations can, in fact, be viewed as ad-hoc adjustments for liquidity risk. Their usage is consistent with upward-sloping demand curves. And, third, risk management measures like VaR do need to be adjusted to reflect liquidity risk. The classical VaR computations are biased low due to the exclusion of liquidity risk, significantly underestimating the risk of a portfolio. Fortunately, simple adjustments for liquidity risk to risk measures like VaR are available. The rest of the chapter justifies, documents and explains the reasons for these three conclusions.

THE BASIC MODEL

To study liquidity risk in option pricing theory, we need to consider two assets: a default-free or risk-less money market account and an underlying security, called a stock. The money market account earns continuously compounded interest at the default free spot rate, denoted r_t at time t.

The account starts with a dollar invested at time 0, $B(0) = 1$, and grows to $B(T) = e^{\int_0^T r_s ds}$ at time T. For simplicity, we assume that there is no liquidity risk associated with investments in the money market account. In contrast, the stock has liquidity risk. This can be captured via a supply curve for the stock that depends on the size of a trade. Let $S(t, x)$ be the stock price paid/received per share at time t for a trade of size x^3. If $x > 0$ then the stock is purchased. If $x < 0$, the stock is sold. The zero-th trade $x = 0$ is special. It represents the marginal trade (an infinitesimal purchase or sale). On this supply curve, therefore, the price $S(t, 0)$ corresponds to the stock price in the classical theory.

We assume that the supply curve is upward sloping; that is, as x increases, $S(t, x)$ increases. The larger the purchase order, the higher the average price paid per share. An upward-sloping supply curve for shares is consistent with asymmetric information in stock markets (see Kyle 1985; Glosten and Milgrom 1985). Indeed, the market responds to potential informed trading by selling at higher prices and buying at lower ones. An upward-sloping supply curve is graphed in Exhibit 16.1 at time 0. The time 0 supply curve is shown on the left of the diagram.

EXHIBIT 16.1   Stochastic Supply Curve S(t,x)

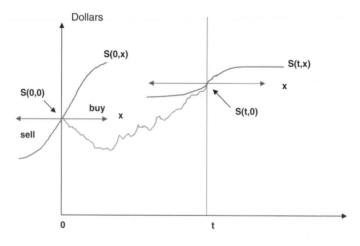

Although most practitioners will accept an upward-sloping supply curve as self-evident, there has been some debate on this issue in the academic literature, called the price pressure hypothesis (see Scholes 1972; Shleifer 1986; Harris and Gruel 1986). The evidence supports the price pressure hypothesis. A recent empirical validation for an upward-sloping supply curve can be found in Çetin et al. (forthcoming).

One of their tests is reproduced here for emphasis in Exhibit 16.2 on page 364. Using the TAQ database, Çetin et al. chose five well-known companies trading on the NYSE with varying degrees of liquidity: General Electric (GE), International Business Machines (IBM), Federal Express

(FDX), Reebok (RBK), and Barnes & Noble (BKS). The time period covered was a four-year period with 1,011 trading days, from January 3, 1995, to December 31, 1998. The left side of Exhibit 16.2 gives the implications of an upward supply curve when both time and information are fixed. The price inequalities indicate the ordering of transaction prices, given different size trades. For example, sales should transact at lower prices than do purchases, and small buys should have lower prices than do large buys. To approximate this set of inequalities, they look at a sequence of transactions keeping the change in time small (one day). Despite the noise introduced by a small change in time (and information), the hypothesized inequalities are validated in all cases. This exhibit supports the upward-sloping supply curve formulation.

The supply curve is also stochastic. It fluctuates randomly through time, its shape changing, although always remaining upward sloping. When markets are calm, the curve will be more horizontal. When markets are hectic, the curve will be more upward tilted. A possible evolution for the supply curve is given in Exhibit 16.1. The supply curve at time t represents a more liquid market than at time 0 because it's less upward sloping. As depicted, the marginal stock price's evolution is graphed as well between time 0 and time t. This evolution is what is normally modeled in the classical theory. For example, in the Black–Scholes model, $S(t, 0)$ follows a geometric Brownian motion. The difference here is that when studying liquidity risk, the entire supply curve and its stochastic fluctuations across time need to be modeled.

There is an important implicit assumption in this model formulation that needs to be highlighted. In the evolution of the supply curve (as illustrated in Exhibit 16.1), the impact of the trade size on the price process is temporary. That is, the future evolution of the price process for $t > 0$ does not depend on the trade size executed at time 0. This is a reasonable hypothesis. The alternative is that the price process for $t > 0$ depends explicitly on the trade size executed at time 0. This happens, for example, when there are large traders whose transactions permanently change the dynamics of the stock price process. In this situation, market manipulation is possible, and option pricing theory changes dramatically (see Bank and Baum 2004; Cvitanic and Ma 1996; and Jarrow 1992 and 1994). Market manipulation manifests a breakdown of financial markets, and this extreme form of liquidity risk is not discussed further herein, but left to the cited references. Suffice it to say that the three conclusions mentioned in the introduction with respect to liquidity risk fail in these extreme market conditions.

Given trading in the stock and a money market account, we also need to briefly discuss the meaning of a portfolio's "value." The word "value" is in quotation marks because when prices depend on trade sizes, there is no unique value for a portfolio. To see this, consider a portfolio consisting of n shares of the stock and m shares of the money market account at time 0. The value of the portfolio is uniquely determined by the time 0 stock

EXHIBIT 16.2 Summary of order flow and transaction prices. Recorded below are the relationships between consecutive transaction prices as a function of order flow. The first two rows impose no constraints on the magnitude of the transaction. The next four rows have small (large) trades defined as those less than or equal to (greater than) 10 lots

Trade Type and Hypothesis			Company Ticker				
First Trade (x1)	Second Trade (x2)	Transaction Hypothesis	GE	IBM	FDX	BKS	RBK
Sell	Buy	S(t1, x1) ≤ S(t2, x2)	100.00%	100.00%	100.00%	100.00%	100.00%
Buy	Sell	S(t1, x1) ≥ S(t2, x2)	100–00%	100–00%	100–00%	100–00%	100–00%
Small Buy	Large Buy	S(t1, x1) ≤ S(t2, x2)	98–77%	98–58%	98.46%	98–58%	99–05%
Small Sell	Large Sell	S(t1, x1) ≥ S(t2, x2)	98–10%	97–99%	98–61%	98.43%	98–95%
Large Buy	Small Buy	S(t1, x1) ≥ S(t2, x2)	93–60%	90.28%	80–59%	80–53%	83.88%
Large Sell	Small Sell	S(t1, x1) ≤ S(t2, x2)	90.33%	87.33%	78.87%	78.67%	81.89%

Source: Çetin et al. (forthcoming, Table 2).

price, but which stock price should be selected from the supply curve? Some economically meaningful choices are apparent. For example, the value of the portfolio if liquidated at time 0 is:

$$liquidation\ value:\ nS(0, -n) + mB(0). \qquad (16.1)$$

Note that in the stock price, the price for selling n shares is used. Another choice is the marked-to-market value, defined by using the price from the marginal trade (zero trade size); that is,

$$marked\text{-}to\text{-}market\ value:\ nS(0, 0) + mB(0). \qquad (16.2)$$

The marked-to-market value represents the portfolio's value held in place, and it also corresponds to the value of the portfolio in the classical model. Given that the supply curve is upward sloping, we have that $S(0, -n) < S(0, 0)$. This implies that the liquidation value is strictly less then the marked-to-market value of the portfolio.

ARBITRAGE PRICING THEORY

To obtain a theory of arbitrage pricing, analogous to the classical case, one needs to impose more structure on the supply curve. In particular, it is very important for the theory to understand the shape of the supply curve near the zero-th trade size ($x = 0$). Unfortunately, due to the discreteness of shares traded in actual markets (units), the shape of the supply curve near zero can never be observed, and it is an abstraction. Nonetheless, to proceed, we need to assume a particular structure and investigate its implications. If the implications are counter-intuitive, other alternative structures can be subsequently imposed. Continuing, the simpler the structure the better. In their initial model, Çetin et al. (2004) assume that the supply curve is continuous (and twice differentiable) at the origin, so that standard calculus-type methods can be applied. This is the structure we will discuss below (see also Exhibit 16.1).

In the classical theory of option pricing, the logical steps in the development of the theory are as follows: step one, the notion of an arbitrage opportunity is defined; step two, a characterization of an arbitrage-free market is obtained in terms of an equivalent martingale measure (alternatively called a risk neutral measure); step three, a complete market is defined; step four, in a complete market, the equivalent martingale measure is used to price an option; and step five, the option's delta (or hedge ratio) is determined from the option's price formula. In our structure with liquidity risk, we will follow these same five steps.

Step 1 Definition Arbitrage

As in the classical theory, an arbitrage opportunity is defined to be the portfolio that starts with zero value (investment), the portfolio has no intermediate cash flows (or if so, they are all non-negative), and the portfolio is liquidated at some future date T with a non-negative value with a probability of one, and a strictly positive value with positive probability. This is the proverbial "free lunch." The only change in the liquidity risk model from the classical definition is that instead of using the marked-to-market value of the portfolio at time T, one needs to use the liquidation value (16.1). The liquidation value implies that all liquidity costs of entering and selling a position are accounted for.

Step 2 Characterization Result

Çetin et al. (2004) show that to guarantee a market is arbitrage free, one only needs to consider the classical case, and examine the properties of the marginal stock price process $S(t, 0)$. In particular, they prove the following result:

Theorem 1 – If there exists an equivalent probability Q such that $S(t, 0)/B(t)$ is a martingale, then the market is arbitrage free.

The intuition for the theorem is straightforward. If there are no arbitrage opportunities when trading with zero liquidity impact (at the zero-th trade), then trading with liquidity can create no arbitrage opportunities that otherwise did not exist. Indeed, the trade size impact on the price always works against the trader, decreasing returns, and decreasing any potential payoffs.

This theorem is an important insight. It implies that all the classical stock price processes can still be employed in the analysis of liquidity risk, but they now represent the zeroth point on the supply curve's evolution. For example, an extended Black–Scholes economy is given by the supply curve:

$$S(t, x) = S(t, 0)e^{\alpha x} \tag{16.3}$$

where $\alpha > 0$ is a constant and $S(t, 0)$ is a geometric Brownian motion. That is,

$$dS(t, 0) = \mu S(t, 0)\, dt + \sigma S(t, 0)dW_t \tag{16.4}$$

where $\mu, \sigma > 0$ are constants and W_t is a standard Brownian motion. The supply curve in (16.3) depends on the trade size x in an exponential manner. Indeed, as x increases, the purchase price increases by the proportion $e^{\alpha x}$. This simple supply curve, as a first approximation, appears to be consistent with the data (see Çetin et al. forthcoming). A typical value of α lies in the set [.00005, .00015]; that is, between 0.5 and 1.5 bps per transaction is a typical quantity impact on the price (see Çetin, et al. forthcoming; Exhibit 16.2).

Since we know that a geometric Brownian motion process in the classical case admits no arbitrage, this theorem tells us that the supply curve extension admits no arbitrage as well. We will return to this example numerous times in the subsequent section to illustrate the relevant insights.

Step 3 Definition Market Completeness

As in the classical case, a complete market is defined to be a market where (dynamic) trading in the stock and money market account can reproduce the payoff to any derivative security at some future date. The same definition applies with supply curves, although in attempting to reproduce the payoff to a derivative security, the actual trade size-determined price must be used. Otherwise, the definition is identical.

Unfortunately, one can show that in the presence of a supply curve, if the market was complete in the classical case (for the marginal price process $S(t, 0)$), it will not be complete with liquidity costs. The reason is that part of the portfolio's value evaporates in the attempt to replicate the option. But, recall that in the classical case, the completeness result for the price process requires that the replicating strategy often involves continuous trading of infinitesimal quantities of a stock in an erratic fashion.[4] Of course, in practice, following such a replicating strategy is impossible. And, only approximating trading strategies can be employed that involve trading at discrete time intervals (see Jarrow and Turnbull (2000) for a more detailed explanation). Thus, in the classical model, the best we can really hope for (in practice) is an approximately complete market. That is, a market that can approximately reproduce the payoff to any derivative security at some future date.

It turns out that under the supply curve formulation, Çetin et al. (2004) prove the following theorem:

Theorem 2 – Given the existence of an equivalent martingale measure (as in Theorem 1), if it is unique, then the market is approximately complete.

In the classical case, if the equivalent martingale measure is unique, then the market is complete. Here, almost the same result holds when applied to the marginal stock price process $S(t, 0)$. The difference is that one only gets an approximately complete market. The result follows because there always exist trading strategies, involving quick trading of small quantities, that incur very little price impact costs (since one is trading nearly zero shares at all times). By reducing the size of each trade, but accumulating the same aggregate quantity by trading more quickly, one can get arbitrarily close to the no liquidity cost case.

Again, the importance of this theorem for applications is that all of the classical stock price process results can still be employed in the analysis of liquidity risk. Indeed, if the classical stock price process is consistent with a complete market, then it will imply an approximately complete market, given liquidity costs. For example, returning to the extended

Black–Scholes economy presented above in (16.3), since we know in the classical case that it implies a complete market, this theorem tells us that the supply curve extension implies an approximately complete market as well.

Step 4 Pricing Options

Just as in the classical case, one can show that in an approximately complete market, the value of an option is its discounted expected payoff, using the martingale measure in taking the expectation. The martingale measure adjusts those statistical (or actual) probabilities to account for risk (see Jarrow and Turnbull (2000) for proof of these statements). For concreteness, let C_T represent the payoff to an option at time T. For example, if the option is a European call with strike price K and maturity T, then $C_T = \max[S(T, 0) - K, 0]$. In the payoff of this European call, the marginal stock price is used (at the zero-th trade size). The reason is that (as explained in step three) the replicating trading strategy avoids (nearly) all liquidity costs. This is reflected in the option's payoff by setting the trade size $x = 0$. For more discussion on this point, see Çetin et al. (2004).

Given this payoff, the price of the option at time 0 is given by:

$$C_0 = E(C_T e^{-\int_0^T r_s ds}) \tag{16.5}$$

where $E(\cdot)$ represents expectation under the martingale measure. This is the standard formula used to price options in the classical case.

Continuing our European call option with strike price K and maturity T example, let us assume that the stock price supply curve evolves according to the extended Black–Scholes economy as in (16.3) above, and that the spot rate of interest is a constant; that is, $r_t = r$ for all t. Then, the pricing formula becomes:

$$C_0 = E(\max[S(T, 0) - K, 0]e^{-rT})$$
$$= S(0, 0)N(h(0)) \, Ke^{-rT} N(h(0) - \sigma\sqrt{T}) \tag{16.6}$$

where $\sigma > 0$ is the stock's volatility, $N(\cdot)$ is the standard cumulative normal distribution function, and:

$$h(t) \equiv \frac{\log S(t, 0) - \log K + r(T - t)}{\sigma\sqrt{T - t}} + \frac{\sigma}{2}\sqrt{T - t}.$$

This is the standard Black–Scholes formula, but in a world with liquidity risk!

Step 5 Replication

In the classical case, the replicating portfolio can often be obtained from the valuation formula by taking its first partial derivative with respect to the underlying stock's time 0 price. For example, with respect to the classical Black–Scholes formula in (16.6) above, the hedge ratio is the option's delta and it is given by:

$$\Delta_t = \frac{\delta C_t}{\delta S(t,0)} = N(h(t)) \tag{16.7}$$

for an arbitrary time t.

This represents the number of shares of the stock to hold at time t to replicate the payoff to the European call option with strike price K and maturity T. The holdings in the stock must be changed continuously in time according to (16.7), buying and selling infinitesimal shares of the stock to maintain this hedge ratio.

In the situation with an upward-sloping supply curve, this procedure for determining the replicating portfolio is almost the case as well. The difference is that the classical replicating strategy will often be too erratic, and a smoothing of the replicating strategy will need to be employed to reduce price impact costs. The exact smoothing procedure is detailed in Çetin et al. (2004). Consequently, the classical hedge (appropriately smoothed) provides an approximate replicating strategy for the option. For the Black–Scholes extended economy that we have been discussing, the smoothed hedge ratio for any time t is given by:

$$\Delta_t = 1_{(\frac{1}{n}, T - \frac{1}{n})}(t)n \int_{(t - \frac{1}{n})^+}^{t} N(h(u))du, \quad \text{if } 0 \leq t \leq T - \frac{1}{n} \tag{16.8}$$

$$\Delta_t = (nT\Delta_{(T - \frac{1}{n})} - n\Delta_{(T - \frac{1}{n})}t), \quad \text{if } T - \frac{1}{n} \leq t \leq T.$$

where $1_{[\frac{1}{n}, T - \frac{1}{n})}(t)$ is an indicator function for the time set $[\frac{1}{n}, T - \frac{1}{n})$ and n is the step size in the approximating procedure. As evidenced in this expression, the smoothing procedure is accomplished by taking an integral (an averaging operation). The approximation improves as $n \to \infty$.

In summary, as just documented, the classical approach almost applies. But, there is a potential problem with the smoothed trading strategy. Just as in the classical case, it usually involves continuous trading of infinitesimal quantities of the stock's shares, which is impossible in practice. And, just as in the classical case, to make the hedging theory consistent with practice we need to restrict ourselves to more realistic trading strategies. This is the subject of the next section.

FEASIBLE REPLICATING STRATEGIES

The implication of Çetin et al. (2004) is that the classical option price must hold in the extended supply curve model. Taken further, this implies that option markets should exhibit no quantity impact on prices, no bid/ask spreads, even if the underlying stock price curve does. This is a counter-intuitive implication of the model, directly due to the ability to trade continuously in time in infinitesimal quantities. Just as in the classical model, if one removes continuous trading strategies, and only admits discrete trading, then this implication changes.

Çetin et al. (forthcoming) explore this refinement. They reexamine the upward-sloping supply curve model considering only discrete trading strategies. As one might expect, the situation becomes analogous to a market with transaction costs. Fixed (or proportionate) transaction costs, due to their existence, preclude the existence of continuous trading strategies, otherwise transaction costs would become infinite in any finite time (see Barles and Soner (1998); Cvitanic and Karatzas (1996); Cvitanic et al. (1999), Jouini and Kallal (1995), Soner et al. (1995); and Jarrow and Protter (forthcoming)). Hence, many of the insights from the transaction cost literature can now be directly applied to Çetin et al.'s market.

In such a market, one cannot exactly or even approximately replicate an option. The market is incomplete. This is due to the fact that transaction costs evaporate value from a portfolio. Consequently, one seeks to determine the cheapest buying price and the largest selling price for an option. If the optimal super- or sub-replicating strategy can be determined, then one gets a relationship between the buying and selling prices, and the classical price:

$$C_0^{sell} \leq C_0^{classical} \leq C_0^{buy}. \tag{16.9}$$

The classical price lies between the buying and selling prices obtainable by super- and sub-replication. In this sense, the classical option price is the "average" of the buying and selling prices. This statement provides the justification for the first conclusion contained in the introduction.

To get a sense for the percentage magnitudes of the liquidity cost band around the classical price, Exhibit 16.3 contains some results from Çetin et al. (forthcoming), where they document the liquidity costs associated with the extended Black–Scholes model given in expression 16.3 above. As a percentage of the option's price, liquidity costs usually are less than 100 bps. This observation serves as the justification for the second conclusion drawn in the introduction. The third conclusion is justified in the next section.

Unfortunately, the optimal strategy for buying (or selling) is often difficult to obtain, because it involves solving a complex dynamic programming problem. For this reason, practical replicating strategies often need to be used instead. For example, the standard Black–Scholes delta

EXHIBIT 16.3 Summary of the optimal trading strategy for 10 options, each on 100 shares. Option prices in the third and fourth columns are reported for an individual option on 100 shares with the other entries representing quantities for an imbalance of 10 options. For emphasis, unlike option prices, the liquidity cost is not linear in the number of options (or shares) under consideration and is not re-scaled as a consequence. For at-the-options, the strike price equals the initial stock price recorded in Exhibit 16.2. The stock price is then increased (decreased) by $5 for in-the-money (out-of-the-money) options

Option characteristics		Individual option	Costs associated with replicating portfolio for 10 options			
Company name	Option moneyness	Option price with $a = 0$	Liquidity cost (at $t = 0$)	Liquidity cost (after $t = 0$)	Total liquidity cost	Percentage impact
GE	In	548.91	19.31	5.77	25.08	0.46
	At	177.94	9.59	10.06	19.65	1.10
	Out	46.94	0.86	0.82	1.68	0.36
IBM	In	730.56	8.61	3.46	12.07	0.17
	At	362.91	4.81	4.46	9.27	0.26
	Out	229.90	2.44	2.29	4.73	0.21
FDX	In	562.42	15.70	4.96	20.66	0.37
	At	188.42	8.46	8.09	16.55	0.88
	Out	56.07	0.92	0.87	1.79	0.32
BKS	In	517.87	23.39	4.52	27.91	0.54
	At	133.50	11.07	10.18	21.25	1.59
	Out	12.25	0.12	0.11	0.23	0.19
RBK	In	513.40	20.02	3.67	23.69	0.46
	At	129.33	9.16	8.44	17.60	1.36
	Out	8.36	0.0	0.0	0.1	0.1

Source: Çetin et al. (forthcoming, Table 3).

hedge, implemented once a day (instead of continuously in time), is one such possibility. Çetin et al. (2005) show that this strategy provides a reasonable approximation to the option's optimal buying or selling strategy. As such, these practical hedging strategies used by the industry can be viewed as adjustments to the classical model for handling liquidity risk.

RISK MANAGEMENT MEASURES

The classical risk measures, like VaR, do not explicitly incorporate liquidity risk into the calculation. Given the liquidity risk model introduced above, a simple and robust adjustment for liquidity risk is now readily available as detailed in Jarrow and Protter (2005a).

As discussed in the section on arbitrage pricing theory above, trading continuously and in infinitesimal amounts enables one to avoid all liquidity costs. In actual markets, this corresponds to slow and deliberate selling of the portfolio's assets. But, when computing risk measures for risk management, one needs to be conservative. The worst case scenario is a crisis situation, where one has to liquidate assets immediately. The idea is that if the market is declining quickly, then one does not have the luxury to sell assets slowly (continuously) in "small" quantities until the entire position is liquidated. In this crisis situation, the supply curve formulation provides the relevant value to be used, the liquidation value of the portfolio from (16.1) above.

The liquidation value of a portfolio can be determined by estimating each stock's supply curve's stochastic process, and knowing the size of each stock position. Supply curve estimation is not a difficult exercise – see Çetin et al. (forthcoming). For example, in the extended Black–Scholes model of (16.3) above, a simple time series regression can be employed. Given time series observations of transaction prices and trade sizes $(S(\tau_i, x_{\tau_i}), \tau_i)_{i=1}^{I}$, it can be shown that the regression equation is:

$$\ln\left(\frac{S(\tau_{i+1}, x_{\tau_{i+1}})}{S(\tau_i, x_{\tau_i})}\right) = \alpha[x_{\tau_{i+1}} - x_{\tau_i}] + \mu[\tau_{i+1} - \tau_i] + \sigma\varepsilon_{\tau_{i+1}, \tau_i}.$$

The error $\varepsilon_{\tau_{i+1}, \tau_i}$ equals $\varepsilon\sqrt{\tau_{i+1} - \tau_i}$ with ε being distributed $N(0, 1)$.[5] Then, in computing VaR one can explicitly include the liquidity discount parameter α to determine the portfolio value for immediate liquidation.

The bias in the classical VaR computation can be easily understood. The classical VaR computation uses the marked-to-market value of the portfolio given in (16.2). In contrast, the VaR computation, including liquidity risk, should use the liquidation value given in (16.1). As noted earlier, the liquidation value in (16.1) is always less than the marked-to-market value in (16.2). This implies that the classical VaR computation will be biased low, indicating less risk in the portfolio than actually exists. This liquidity risk adjustment to VaR based on the portfolio's liquidation value, rather than its marked-to-market value, yields the basis for the third conclusion stated in the introduction.

To illustrate these computations, let us again consider the extended Black–Scholes economy of (16.3). Let us consider a portfolio of N stocks $i = 1, \ldots, N$ with shareholdings denoted by n_i in the i-th stock. We denote the i-th stock price by:

$$S_i(t, x) = Si(t, 0)e^{\alpha_i x}. \tag{16.10}$$

The marked-to-market value of the portfolio at time T is:

$$\sum_{i=1}^{N} n_i S_i(T, 0).$$

The time T liquidation value is:

$$\sum_{i=1}^{N} n_i S_i(T, -n_i) = \sum_{i=1}^{N} n_i S_i(T, 0)e^{-\alpha_i n_i}.$$

When computing VaR either analytically or via a simulation, the adjustment to the realization of $S_i(T, 0)$ is given by the term $e^{-\alpha_i n_i}$. This is an easy computation.

CONCLUSION

This chapter reviews the recent literature on liquidity risk for its practical use in risk management. The literature supports three general conclusions. The first is that the classical option price is "on average" true, even given liquidity risk. Second, it is well known that although the classical (theoretical) option hedge cannot be applied as theory prescribes, its discrete approximations often provide reasonable approximations (see Jarrow and Turnbull 2000). These discrete approximations are also consistent with upward-sloping demand curves. And, third, risk management measures like value-at-risk (VaR) are biased low due to the exclusion of liquidity risk. Fortunately, simple adjustments for liquidity risk to risk measures like VaR are readily available.

NOTES

[1] Johnson Graduate School of Management, Cornell University, Ithaca, NY, 14 853 and Kamakura Corporation, email: raj15@cornell.edu.

[2] This implies trading both continuously in time and in continuous increments of shares.

[3] All technical details regarding the model structure (smoothness conditions, integrability conditions, and so on) are delegated to the references.

[4] By "erratic" I mean similar to the path mapped out by a Brownian motion.

[5] This is the regression equation used to obtain the typical values for α reported earlier.

BIBLIOGRAPHY

Bank, P. and D. Baum (2004). "Hedging and Portfolio Optimization in Illiquid Financial Markets with a Large Trader," *Mathematical Finance*, 14, pp. 1–18.

Barles, G. and H. Soner (1998). "Option Pricing with Transaction Costs and a Nonlinear Black–Scholes Equation," *Finance and Stochastics*, 2, pp. 369–97.

Çetin, U. (2003) *Default and Liquidity Risk Modeling*, PhD thesis, Cornell University.

Çetin, U., R. Jarrow, and P. Protter (2004) "Liquidity Risk and Arbitrage Pricing Theory," *Finance and Stochastics*, 8, pp. 311–41.

Çetin, U., R. Jarrow, P. Protter, and M. Warachka (forthcoming) "Pricing Options in an Extended Black Scholes Economy with Illiquidity: Theory and Empirical Evidence," *The Review of Financial Studies*.

Cvitanic, J. and I. Karatzas (1996). "Hedging and Portfolio Optimization under Transaction Costs: A Martingale Approach," *Mathematical Finance*, 6, pp. 133–65.

Cvitanic, J and J. Ma (1996). "Hedging Options for a Large Investor and Forward-backward SDEs," *Annals of Applied Probability*, 6, pp. 370–98.

Cvitanic, J., H. Pham, and N. Touze (1999). "A Closed-form Solution to the Problem of Super-replication under Transaction Costs," *Finance and Stochastics*, 3, pp. 35–54.

Glosten, L. and P. Milgrom (1985) "Bid, Ask and Transaction Prices in a Specialist Market with Heterogeneously Informed Traders," *Journal of Financial Economics*, 14 (March), pp. 71–100.

Grossman, S. and M. Miller (1988). "Liquidity and Market Structure," *Journal of Finance*, 43 (3), pp. 617–37.

Harris, L. and E. Gruel (1986). "Price and Volume Effects Associated with Changes in the S&P 500 List: New Evidence for the Existence of Price Pressure," *Journal of Finance*, 41 (4), pp. 617–37.

Jarrow, R. (1992). "Market Manipulation, Bubbles, Corners and Short Squeezes," *Journal of Financial and Quantitative Analysis*, September, pp. 311–36.

Jarrow, R. (1994). "Derivative Security Markets, Market Manipulation and Option Pricing," *Journal of Financial and Quantitative Analysis*, 29 (2), pp. 241–61.

Jarrow, R. (1999). "In Honor of the Nobel Laureates Robert C. Merton and Myron S. Scholes: A Partial Differential Equation that Changed the World," *The Journal of Economic Perspectives*, 13 (4), pp. 229–48.

Jarrow, R. and P. Protter (2005a). "Liquidity Risk and Risk Measure Computation," *The Review of Futures Markets*, Summer 2005, pp. 27–39.

Jarrow, R. and P. Protter (forthcoming). "Liquidity Risk and Option Pricing Theory," *Handbook of Financial Engineering*, eds, J. Birge and V. Linetsky, Elsevier Publishers, Amsterdam, The Netherlands.

Jarrow, R. and S. Turnbull (2000). *Derivative Securities*, Southwestern Publishing Co., Cincinnati, Ohio.

Jouini, E. and H. Kallal (1995). ''Martingales and Arbitrage in Securities Markets with Transaction Costs,'' *Journal of Economic Theory*, 66 (1), pp. 178–97.

Kyle, A. (1985). ''Continuous Auctions and Insider Trading,'' *Econometrica*, 53, pp. 1315–35.

Scholes, M. (1972). ''The Market for Securities: Substitution vs Price Pressures and the Effects on Information Share Prices,'' *Journal of Business*, 45, pp. 179–211.

Shleifer, A. (1986). ''Do Demand Curves for Stocks Slope Down?'' *Journal of Finance*, (July), pp. 579–89.

Soner, H.M., S. Shreve, and J. Cvitanic (1995). ''There is no Nontrivial Hedging Portfolio for Option Pricing with Transaction Costs,'' *Annals of Applied Probability*, 5, pp. 327–55.

Part 5

Conclusion

View from the Mountaintop

Leonard Matz and Peter Neu

The single biggest mistake made by liquidity risk managers is focusing intently on day-to-day funding, especially funding costs, while at the same time limiting the scope of the liquidity risk contingency planning for a potential funding crisis. The scope of this thinking is too narrow in the sense that risk managers always need to consider prospective funding scenarios covering a range of normal, near-normal, and abnormal environments. But, far more significantly, the scope of this thinking is too narrow because it ignores far too many of the actions related to planning that should be considered in normal funding conditions.

As we have seen in prior chapters, best practice liquidity risk management involves the bank's strategic plans, balance sheet structure, funding tactics, internal transfer pricing, risk measurement and forecasting capabilities, limits and risk exposure monitoring, and a comprehensive CFP setting out potential responses for a future funding disruption.

MOVING TOWARD BEST PRACTICE

In the opening paragraphs of Chapter 1, we described liquidity risk management as "evolving." While true, that assessment is incomplete. Liquidity risk management practices are certainly progressing, but by no means along linear or curvilinear paths. Instead, the "state of the art" for liquidity risk measurement and management tends to progress in spurts. Specifically, it advances in spurts that coincide with or immediately follow disruptions. Liquidity risk tends to attract intense interest during and immediately following stressed financial conditions, but relatively little interest during benign periods. Major events such as the Asian crisis in 1997, the Russian default on short-term debt in 1998, the downfall of the hedge fund Long-term Capital Management (LTCM) in 1998, and the World Trade Center attack in 2001 all resulted in increased management attention to liquidity risk. While none of these events precipitated major funding problems for major North American and European banks, every one of them highlighted possible impacts of liquidity risk and underscored the necessity for banks to reevaluate their preparedness.

Profound changes have altered bank liquidity risk measurement and management in the past decade. Most retrospective, static, one-dimensional tools have been relegated to the dust bin. And we've finally managed to drive a stake into the heart of the loan-to-deposit ratio. Prospective, scenario-based measurement tools, together with robust contingency funding plans, are now accepted best practices. Better internal pricing incentives, more rigorous stress testing, and improved collateral management are at the cutting edge.

The chapters in this book have shown that – although many "state-of-the-art" practices for liquidity risk measurement are relatively new, they are already very much accepted by leading banks, the BIS and a few national bank regulatory bodies. These "state-of-the-art" concepts refer to:

- Prospective liquidity gap analysis incorporating both expected contractual and forecast behaviorally adjusted liquidation cash flows.
- Scenario analysis spanning a range of normal, near-normal and abnormal (stress) environments, including general and bank-specific stress scenarios, with behavioral adjustments tailored to each scenario.
- A well-constructed liquidity policy with designated risk measurement, monitoring and management responsibilities, limits, and reporting requirements.
- A robust contingency funding plan with triggers, identified potential remedial actions and a crisis management team.
- A risk management system, incorporating limits, that focuses on the three key risk management tools: forecast cash flow coverage by time period, sufficiency of unencumbered liquidity reserves and appropriate diversification.
- Well-designed liquidity risk reporting that provides sufficient detail to risk managers, fully informs senior managers and directors of key risk exposures without overwhelming them, and gives early warning of potential risk exposure increases.
- A liquidity transfer pricing that fairly rewards liquidity suppliers and charges liquidity consumers.
- Coordination of organizational strategic planning, credit risk management, interest rate risk management and earnings management with liquidity risk policies, procedures, strategies and tactics.
- Internal controls including separation of duties between liquidity risk management and liquidity risk controlling functions.

Each of these key tasks has been discussed and explained in the various chapters of this book. Through these processes, management controls the risk profile within acceptable strategic limits and maintains a degree of readiness for the ultimate test – a liquidity crisis.

Best Practice Definitely Does Not Equate to Uniform Practice

Although we believe that common conceptual standards to treat liquidity risk have evolved in the market, we also feel that each bank must implement these concepts in a different way. This refers first of all to the cash flow modeling and the behavioral adjustments of assets and liability classes, but also to the depth and the level of sophistication (for example, number of scenarios, length of the maturity ladder, and so on). Depending, for example, on the customer structure or the market access, the same asset or liability will potentially generate rather different liquidation cash flows. Examples are security positions that can or cannot easily be liquidated in a repurchase agreement, depending on the available counterparty limits in the market for a specific bank. Other examples refer to indeterminate maturity deposits that might exhibit a quite different stability in different markets and for different banks; for example, think of demand deposits of a typical saving bank and those of an Internet bank.

The conclusion of this is a call by practitioners for the recognition of internal models for liquidity risk by regulators. We believe that the more a liquidity analysis becomes realistic and, therefore, useful for senior management, the more it will rely on bank-specific assumptions for cash flow modeling, given the very specific positioning of each bank in the market (for wholesale funding) and the specific customer and product structure.

A FEW WORDS ABOUT COSTS AND BENEFITS

Does the shareholder benefit from liquidity risk management? After everything else is said and done, this is the most fundamental question.

Unfortunately, it is a very difficult question to answer. Start with the table shown in Exhibit 17.1 on page 380. Within the largest 100 US banks, the quintile with the largest holdings of unencumbered securities is less profitable than the quintile with the smallest holdings. The difference is modest using return on equity as a measure of profitability. (Research shows similar results for prior years.) At first glance, these data provide modest support for the premise that more prudent liquidity risk management creates shareholder value.

Before we draw any conclusions from the data in Exhibit 17.1, a few other factors must be considered.

- First, the data only cover normal operating conditions for banks. No large US bank has failed since 1991. (An $8.8 billion and a $2.3 billion bank are the two largest US failures in the past five years.) In normal times, liquidity crises may affect less than one- or two-*tenths*

EXHIBIT 17.1 Relationship between liquid assets and earnings

Top 100 US banks by 12/05 asset size				
Unencumbered securities as a percent of total assets	**ROE**		**ROA**	
	12/05	**12/04**	**12/05**	**12/04**
Quintile with highest holdings	18%	17%	1.5	1.5
Quintile with lowest holdings	13%	19%	1.2	2.0

of 1% of all banks each year. At the same time, large-scale systemic problems such as flights to quality, credit crunches and recessions are relatively infrequent and often mild. For the United States, the only serious systemic problem in recent years, the 1998 capital markets turmoil, didn't last long enough to materially impact on annual figures.

- Second, it is inappropriate to equate the banks with the most prudent liquidity risk management to the banks with the largest holdings of unencumbered securities. Banks with above-average off-balance sheet commitments, below-average levels of sticky liabilities or liability concentrations may need to hold more unencumbered liquid assets because they have above-average liquidity risk.

Consider a different question. Do shareholders value conservative liquidity risk management? An arbitrary selection of data is displayed in Exhibit 17.2. No apparent relationship is evident. But here again, we have the same two flaws discussed above for the liquid assets to earnings relationship.

One more question is necessary to define the full scope of this problem. Are banks that hold higher levels of liquid assets less likely to fail? Probably not. US banks that failed in the period Q1 2000–Q2 2005 held, on average, unencumbered securities equal to 9.7% of total assets about four

EXHIBIT 17.2 Relationship between liquid assets and PE ratios

Bank name	BHC PE January 2006	Lead bank unencumbered securities as a percent of total assets, September 2005
National City	8.53	0.15%
Keybank	13.51	1.09%
Wells Fargo Bank	13.98	1.64%
Regions Bank	16.25	3.91%
SunTrust	13.13	5.01%
Bank of America	10.65	10.59%
Wachovia	12.55	11.29%

or five months before they failed.[1] That is roughly equal to the average holdings of unencumbered securities for all US banks during that period.

None of the data discussed above are probative for the simple reason the holdings of unencumbered securities are probably a very poor indication of strong or weak liquidity risk management. The size of worst case exposures tends to be at least an order of magnitude bigger than typical holdings of unencumbered reserves.

Empirical observations support the suggestion that bank success and shareholder rewards are not necessarily reaped by the banks with the best risk management. Many banks that have been merged out of existence had excellent liquidity risk management. Many acquirers of banks have had no better than average risk management. Because a high stock price gives buyers the currency to buy while a low stock price makes the targets look attractive, banks with lower overheads seem to have an advantage while banks with less contingent risk don't seem to be rewarded.

Why may shareholders not value best practice liquidity risk management? Perhaps it is because shareholders are less aware of a given bank's liquidity or contingent risk. They have considerably less information than management. Perhaps shareholders, whether wisely or foolishly, give more weight to current earnings than to long-term risks. However, another possibility should be considered. Shareholders can diversify their risk exposure.

In the end, the best we can say is that both flawed data and anecdotal evidence lend some support to the premise that liquidity management does not *directly* add shareholder value. But this doesn't mean that shareholders receive zero benefit from "best practice" liquidity risk management.

Good liquidity risk management benefits shareholders in many indirect ways. One of the leading experts in this field summed this up by saying: "The appropriate and efficient management of liquidity is essential to an organization to ensure confidence of the financial markets in order to pursue its identified business strategy through organic, acquisition and growth targets."[2]

A sense of balance is essential. A bank that spends serious money to prepare for a risk with a one-in-a-thousand chance of occurrence may regret that expense. At the other extreme, if your bank is the one in a thousand, you may regret not spending more for sleep-well liquidity, contingency plans and other precautions. A middle course seems wisest.

LOOKING FORWARD

From our perspective the next evolutionary steps that we will see for liquidity risk are improvements in quantifying risk exposures, reporting standards, management information systems and integrated stress testing. Each of these is discussed below:

Quantifying Risk Exposures

Senior managers and directors often underestimate essential points.

- First, like all forecasts, liquidity risk projections are inherently imprecise. This is true for cash flow forecasts, as well as projections for the sufficiency of liquidity reserves.
- Second, actions taken to avoid or reduce risk can actually increase the very risk exposures they are intended to reduce unless decision-makers understand the errors in, and limitations of, measured risk quantities.

Improved Forecasts for Behavior-driven Cash Flows

Looking forward, we see encouraging progress in methods for estimating cash flows tied to counterparty options, bank options and new business. The focus is clearly on the following three cash flow groups:

- treatment of non-maturing assets and liabilities
- drawdowns on committed credit lines
- drawdowns on backup lines, in particular to SPVs with downgrade triggers.

Multiple suggestions for improving each of these are covered in earlier chapters.

Reporting Standards

As we have seen in the previous chapters of this book, there is no single figure that reflects liquidity risk in a bank. Furthermore, liquidity risk is conceptually different from other risk categories in the respect that a bank cannot hold capital against it. In most cases a liquidity risk analysis is very much assumption driven. To understand whether the liquidity profile of a bank is appropriate or not requires a certain understanding of all products in a bank, the balance sheet structure, and capital markets funding opportunities. In many cases liquidity risk can only be described qualitatively. This makes senior management reporting a challenging task.

With liquidity risk becoming increasingly important as a risk category in banks, senior management will also become increasingly more familiar with the various concepts. Additionally, banks will work on improving and simplifying the liquidity risk reports and develop standards; for example, like the cash capital concept.

Management Information Systems

A further key point to note is the complexity in setting up an appropriate management information system. Given the efforts and investment that banks have undertaken to build a Basel II-compliant credit data warehouse, it is understandable that most banks are reluctant to extend these data warehouses to cover the entire balance sheet. Being able to perform a gap analysis in different scenarios, currencies and regions on a daily basis requires high data quality and integrity.

In general, banks have two choices, either building a management information system specifically for liquidity risk with no reference to the general ledger, or leveraging the available data model for the general ledger. The former choice implies huge reconciliation exercises, the latter the usage of a system that has been constructed for a monthly reporting of accounting figures for a daily liquidity risk analysis.

With the Basel II data warehouses and models being in place and functioning, there will be further resources available for building a liquidity management data warehouse.

Better Integrated Stress Tests

Two developments are driving improvements in deterministic stress testing. One is the growing awareness of the correlations between cash flows. The relationship, for example, between changes in interest rates and the cash flows from the exercise of call options has been well understood for decades. What's changing is a better understanding of less obvious correlations, such as changes in drawdowns under committed facilities and the economic cycle.

Another development is the impact of Basel II requirements – especially Basel II requirements for credit risk. Take a look at the table in Exhibit 17.3 on page 386.

Notice the explicit and implicit overlap between credit risk, rate risk and liquidity risk scenarios in Exhibit 17.3. Over time, it seems likely that credit risk managers, rate risk managers and liquidity risk mangers will save time and money by sharing research underlying assumptions and by standardizing at least a few scenario parameters.

Furthermore, each bank needs to understand and decide which stress scenarios and which (and how many) limits are most appropriate for the liquidity risks in its business model, and which management actions need to be taken, if the gap profile looks inappropriate under one scenario.

Frequently, liquidity risk is the last stage of a banking crisis, which started with, for example:

- problems in the loan book
- large losses due to market risk
- large operational losses.

In the end, these problems typically result in a loss of confidence in the market, loss in reputation, and finally in a downgrade.

Credit quality problems, or, to be more precise, the perception of high credit risk, is the most common trigger of a bank-specific liquidity crisis. A change in a bank's level of credit risk often precedes or signals a subsequent change in the level of liquidity risk. A bank that assumes more credit risk, through asset concentrations, asset growth or new business

EXHIBIT 17.3 Scenario analysis recommended by BIS

Proposed Basel II capital requirements for credit risk	Principles for the management and supervision of interest rate risk	Sound practices for managing liquidity in banking organizations
Market risk events	Changes in relationships between market rates	External, market risk events
Changes in the bank's rating		Internal, bank-specific events
Adverse economic conditions and unexpected events	Abrupt changes in the general level of rates	Note 1
Range or economic conditions likely to occur over a business cycle		Note 1
Economic or industry downturns		Note 1
Liquidity conditions	Changes in the liquidity of key financial markets	Note 1 Note 2
Mild recessions		Note 1
Hypothetical or historical scenarios that reflect worst case losses (for equities)		Note 1
	Changes in the slope and shape of the yield curve	Stressful events in the market place as part of day-to-day management
	Changes in the volatility of key market rates	
	Key business assumptions and parameters breakdown/worst case	Note 1 Note 2

Note 1: The corresponding credit or rate risk scenario can easily be construed to comprise an element in a bank external liquidity risk scenario.
Note 2: The corresponding credit or rate risk scenario can easily be construed to comprise an element in a bank external liquidity risk scenario.

lines, may be increasing its liquidity risk in either of two ways. First, credit-sensitive funds providers may worry that the bank's increased credit exposure could lead to credit problems and insufficient profits. In other words, the mere possibility that a business change may lead to future losses can affect confidence. Second, if the assumption of more credit risk actually does lead to higher losses, counterparties are even more likely to lose confidence. Worsening credit problems can impair the bank's ability to meet its own obligations. Wholesale funds providers and rating agencies consider the level of past-due loans, non-performing loans, provisions to the allowance for loan and lease losses, and loan charge-offs for indications of potential liquidity problems. If credit risk is higher than average, a premium rate may be necessary to access funds providers or attract depositors. If credit risk appears to be both high and worsening, funding may not be available at any price. Depositor confidence, ratings and funds availability obviously can be significantly affected by credit risk.

Banks are, of course, very much aware of such scenarios and take appropriate actions. The danger is that they do not recognize the likelihood of such events in time. Currently, stress analyses for credit, market and operational risk are mostly done without considering the impact on the funding situation. On the other side, stress analyses – for example, downgrade scenarios – are done without referring to the likelihood of trigger events arising from other risk categories.

In our view, a modeling of liquidity risk stress scenarios integrated into a comprehensive enterprise-wide stress analysis will be required in future in order to clearly highlight the interdependencies between risk categories.

Correlations Between Risks

Certainly, the fact, just discussed, that liquidity problems are triggered by other risks identifies one set of correlations between risks. But there are more. Consider the following examples:

- Interest rate risk – in the form of price or market risk – can affect liquidity management. For example, plans to sell investments or loans as part of a bank's contingency funding plan can be significantly influenced by changes in prevailing rates. If prevailing rates are high when the sale is needed, it may be very expensive to sell those assets and the price may depress earnings and capital. Similarly, if market conditions are stressed, it may be very hard to find a willing buyer. The same two potential problems affect bank borrowings as well. In high-rate environments, borrowings are more expensive. In stressed markets, less-than-top-rated borrowers may find it hard to borrow.
- Market liquidity can affect the management of interest rate risk (IRR). This is particularly relevant for banks that rely on instruments to alter their rate risk exposure. During periods known as "flights to quality" or simply when markets are distressed and the volume of trades falls, it can be harder to sell securities quickly without discounting the price.
- The use of derivative contracts to reduce interest rate or credit risk exposure can tie up marketable securities as collateral.
- Interest rate and credit quality-related options risk can also have a material effect on liquidity, especially on liquidity in the normal course of business. For example, when prevailing rates are low, loan prepayments and investment calls accelerate cash flows. On the other hand, cash flow projections may prove too high if prevailing rates rise.

- Reputation risk is closely intertwined with liquidity risk. A bank's reputation for operating in a safe and sound manner is essential to attracting funds at a reasonable cost, as well as for retaining funds during crises. Negative public opinion, whatever the cause, may prompt depositors, other funds providers and investors to seek greater compensation, such as higher rates or collateral, for maintaining deposit balances with a bank, or conducting any other business with it. If negative public opinion continues, withdrawals of funding could become debilitating. Reputation risk is clearly more of an issue for banks that depend on unsecured, uninsured funding and for banks that sell or securitize loans.
- Credit risk can impact the bank's ability to raise funds from new securitizations. Liquidity from the sale or securitization of loans depends on the bank's perceived credit skills. If the bank is seen to have credit problems – whether or not losses have occurred – loan buyers will be more reluctant to accept paper originated by the bank. Even in the absence of a legal requirement to buy back non-performing loans, the bank's ability to sell loans in the future may depend on maintaining buyer expectations that the bank will support its outstanding securities. Thus, the bank may face an implied obligation to consume some liquidity by buying back distressed paper in order to preserve the ability to use this liquidity source.
- Draws under some types of off-balance sheet commitments, such as stand-by letters of credit and performance guarantees, are correlated with the counterparty's credit risk.
- Bank commitments to provide liquidity support for special-purpose entities or special-purpose vehicles in asset-backed security (ABS) structures may have to be replaced with cash in the event of a deterioration in the bank's credit quality.
- Liquidity requirements must be seen as proportionate to credit risk exposures. If the whole bank incurs more credit risk, it requires more liquidity. Even though diversification offsets some credit risk, to the extent that the cumulative, net level of credit risk is higher, more liquidity is needed. Liquidity managers can never ignore the close relationship between credit risk and liquidity requirements.

CONCLUSION

Controlling liquidity risk requires both the integration and the customization of many tools. We can describe the tools. We can identify the advantages and disadvantages. We can share best practice ideas developed by industry leaders.

It is up to the risk managers in each bank to take all that information, integrated with bank strategies and risk management practices, and customize the application to fit the bank's situation. Each bank's liquidity need scenarios and available sources are likely to be at least partially unique. Each bank's balance sheet mix, each bank's dependence upon borrowed money and prevailing market conditions at the current time are the primary, but by no means the only, distinguishing features. A sound basis for evaluating and managing liquidity risk requires understanding the bank, its customer mix, the nature of its assets and liabilities, and its economic and competitive environment.

It is important to remember that the quality of liquidity risk management does not determine whether or not an institution will be hit with a liquidity crisis. Rather, it determines how an institution will fare in the event of a liquidity crisis. Best practice liquidity risk management can be thought of as insurance. "It's not insurance against a bad quarter of earnings, or two bad quarters of earnings, which is what we do in the interest rate-risk management area, or even in the credit area. It's really a question of whether you [survive] that 1-in-500 event."[3]

But best practice liquidity risk management is more than just insurance purchased to protect against catastrophe. In Chapter 6, we observed that the best contingency plans are simply well thought out extensions of normal funding and balance sheet management activities. That observation is not just true of contingency plans. It applies to all aspects of liquidity risk management. Whether it contributes to a higher rating and lower cost of funds, more efficient risk management, or a better relationship with the bank's regulators, best practice liquidity risk management should be an integrated element facilitating many other beneficial activities.

NOTES

[1] These data come from the next to last quarterly report filed by each failed bank. In theory the data can be from a date between 180 days to 90 days prior to failure. In reality, a bank that failed in the month after a quarterly report due date is unlikely to have filed the report due for that quarter. So it is safe to guess that this data is as of a date between 180 and 120 days prior to failure.

[2] Richard Pattinson, "Preparing for the Worst: Establishing a Liquidity Contingency Plan," Senior Group Treasury, Barclays Bank, GARP, London, 7 June 2005.

[3] Al de Molina, Treasurer, quoted by Todd Davenport in "B of A Puts Faith, Future in Liquidity", *American Banker*, Friday, April 4, 2003, www.americanbanker.com/search.html.

Index